Yemen

WORLD BIBLIOGRAPHICAL SERIES

General Editors:
Robert G. Neville (Executive Editor)
John J. Horton
Robert A. Myers
Hans H. Wellisch
Ian Wallace
Ralph Lee Woodward, Jr.

John J. Horton is Deputy Librarian of the University of Bradford and was formerly Chairman of its Academic Board of Studies in Social Sciences. He has maintained a longstanding interest in the discipline of area studies and its associated bibliographical problems, with special reference to European Studies. In particular he has published in the field of Icelandic and of Yugoslav studies, including the two relevant volumes in the World Bibliographical Series.

Robert A. Myers is Associate Professor of Anthropology in the Division of Social Sciences and Director of Study Abroad Programs at Alfred University, Alfred, New York. He has studied post-colonial island nations of the Caribbean and has spent two years in Nigeria on a Fulbright Lectureship. His interests include international public health, historical anthropology and developing societies. In addition to *Amerindians of the Lesser Antilles: a bibliography* (1981), *A Resource Guide to Dominica, 1493-1986* (1987) and numerous articles, he has compiled the World Bibliographical Series volumes on *Dominica* (1987), *Nigeria* (1989) and *Ghana* (1991).

Ian Wallace is Professor of German at the University of Bath. A graduate of Oxford in French and German, he also studied in Tübingen, Heidelberg and Lausanne before taking teaching posts at universities in the USA, Scotland and England. He specializes in contemporary German affairs, especially literature and culture, on which he has published numerous articles and books. In 1979 he founded the journal *GDR Monitor*, which he continues to edit under its new title *German Monitor*.

Hans H. Wellisch is Professor emeritus at the College of Library and Information Services, University of Maryland. He was President of the American Society of Indexers and was a member of the International Federation for Documentation. He is the author of numerous articles and several books on indexing and abstracting, and has published *The Conversion of Scripts and Indexing and Abstracting: an International Bibliography*, and *Indexing from A to Z*. He also contributes frequently to *Journal of the American Society for Information Science*, *The Indexer* and other professional journals.

Ralph Lee Woodward, Jr. is Professor of History at Tulane University, New Orleans. He is the author of *Central America, a Nation Divided*, 2nd ed. (1985), as well as several monographs and more than seventy scholarly articles on modern Latin America. He has also compiled volumes in the World Bibliographical Series on *Belize* (1980), *El Salvador* (1988), *Guatemala* (Rev. Ed.) (1992) and *Nicaragua* (Rev. Ed.) (1994). Dr. Woodward edited the Central American section of the *Research Guide to Central America and the Caribbean* (1985) and is currently associate editor of Scribner's *Encyclopedia of Latin American History*.

VOLUME 50

Yemen

Revised Edition

Paul Auchterlonie

Compiler

CLIO PRESS

OXFORD, ENGLAND · SANTA BARBARA, CALIFORNIA

DENVER, COLORADO

British Library Cataloguing in Publication Data

Auchterlonie, Paul
Yemen. Rev. ed. – (World bibliographical series; v. 50)
1. Yemen – Bibliography
I. Title
016.9'533

ISBN 1–85109–255–2

ABC-CLIO Ltd.,
Old Clarendon Ironworks,
35A Great Clarendon Street,
Oxford OX2 6AT, England.

ABC-CLIO Inc.,
130 Cremona Drive,
Santa Barbara,
CA 93117, USA.

Designed by Bernard Crossland.
Typeset by Columns Design Ltd., Reading, England.
Printed and bound in Great Britain by Bookcraft (Bath) Ltd., Midsomer Norton.

THE WORLD BIBLIOGRAPHICAL SERIES

This series, which is principally designed for the English speaker, will eventually cover every country (and some of the world's principal regions and cities), each in a separate volume comprising annotated entries on works dealing with its history, geography, economy and politics; and with its people, their culture, customs, religion and social organization. Attention will also be paid to current living conditions – housing, education, newspapers, clothing, etc. – that are all too often ignored in standard bibliographies; and to those particular aspects relevant to individual countries. Each volume seeks to achieve, by use of careful selectivity and critical assessment of the literature, an expression of the country and an appreciation of its nature and national aspirations, to guide the reader towards an understanding of its importance. The keynote of the series is to provide, in a uniform format, an interpretation of each country that will express its culture, its place in the world, and the qualities and background that make it unique. The views expressed in individual volumes, however, are not necessarily those of the publisher.

VOLUMES IN THE SERIES

1 *Yugoslavia*, Rev. Ed., John J. Horton
2 *Lebanon*, Rev. Ed., C. H. Bleaney
3 *Lesotho*, Rev. Ed., Deborah Johnston
4 *Zimbabwe*, Rev. Ed., Deborah Potts
5 *Saudi Arabia*, Rev. Ed., Frank A. Clements
6 *Russia/USSR*, Second Ed., Lesley Pitman
7 *South Africa*, Rev. Ed., Geoffrey V. Davis
8 *Malawi*, Rev. Ed., Samuel Decalo
9 *Guatemala*, Rev. Ed., Ralph Lee Woodward, Jr.
10 *Pakistan*, David Taylor
11 *Uganda*, Rev. Ed., Balam Nyeko
12 *Malaysia*, Ian Brown and Rajeswary Ampalavanar
13 *France*, Rev. Ed., Frances Chambers
14 *Panama*, Eleanor DeSelms Langstaff
15 *Hungary*, Thomas Kabdebo
16 *USA*, Sheila R. Herstein and Naomi Robbins
17 *Greece*, Richard Clogg and Mary Jo Clogg
18 *New Zealand*, R. F. Grover
19 *Algeria*, Rev. Ed., Richard I. Lawless
20 *Sri Lanka*, Vijaya Samaraweera
21 *Belize*, Second Ed., Peggy Wright and Brian E. Coutts
23 *Luxembourg*, Rev. Ed., Jul Christophory and Emile Thoma
24 *Swaziland*, Rev. Ed., Balam Nyeko
25 *Kenya*, Rev. Ed., Dalvan Coger
26 *India*, Rev. Ed., Ian Derbyshire
27 *Turkey*, Merel Güçlü
28 *Cyprus*, Rev. Ed., P. M. Kitromilides and M. L. Evriviades
29 *Oman*, Rev. Ed., Frank A. Clements
30 *Italy*, Lucio Sponza and Diego Zancani
31 *Finland*, Rev. Ed., J. E. O. Screen
32 *Poland*, Rev. Ed., George Sanford and Adriana Gozdecka-Sanford
33 *Tunisia*, Allan M. Findlay, Anne M. Findlay and Richard I. Lawless
34 *Scotland*, Eric G. Grant
35 *China*, New Ed., Charles W. Hayford
36 *Qatar*, P. T. H. Unwin

37 *Iceland*, Rev. Ed., Francis R. McBride
38 *Nepal*, John Whelpton
39 *Haiti*, Rev. Ed., Frances Chambers
40 *Sudan*, Rev. Ed., M. W. Daly
41 *Vatican City State*, Michael J. Walsh
42 *Iraq*, Second Ed., C. H. Bleaney
43 *United Arab Emirates*, Frank A. Clements
44 *Nicaragua*, Rev. Ed., Ralph Lee Woodward, Jr.
45 *Jamaica*, Rev. Ed., K. E. Ingram
46 *Australia*, Second Ed., I. Kepars
47 *Morocco*, Rev. Ed., Anne M. Findlay and Allan M. Findlay
48 *Mexico*, Rev. Ed., George Philip
49 *Bahrain*, P. T. H. Unwin
50 *Yemen*, Rev. Ed., Paul Auchterlonie
51 *Zambia*, Anne M. Bliss and J. A. Rigg
52 *Puerto Rico*, Elena E. Cevallos
53 *Namibia*, Rev. Ed., Stanley Schoeman and Elna Schoeman
54 *Tanzania*, Rev. Ed., Colin Darch
55 *Jordan*, Ian J. Seccombe
56 *Kuwait*, Rev. Ed., Frank A. Clements
57 *Brazil*, Rev. Ed., John Dickenson
58 *Israel*, Second Ed., C. H. Bleaney
59 *Romania*, Andrea Deletant and Dennis Deletant
60 *Spain*, Second Ed., Graham Shields
61 *Atlantic Ocean*, H. G. R. King
62 *Canada*, Ernest Ingles
63 *Cameroon*, Mark W. DeLancey and Peter J. Schraeder
64 *Malta*, John Richard Thackrah
65 *Thailand*, Michael Watts
66 *Austria*, Denys Salt with the assistance of Arthur Farrand Radley
67 *Norway*, Leland B. Sather
68 *Czechoslovakia*, David Short
69 *Irish Republic*, Michael Owen Shannon
70 *Pacific Basin and Oceania*, Gerald W. Fry and Rufino Mauricio
71 *Portugal*, P. T. H. Unwin
72 *West Germany*, Donald S. Detwiler and Ilse E. Detwiler
73 *Syria*, Ian J. Seccombe
74 *Trinidad and Tobago*, Frances Chambers
75 *Cuba*, Jean Stubbs, Lila Haines and Meic F. Haines
76 *Barbados*, Robert B. Potter and Graham M. S. Dann
77 *East Germany*, Ian Wallace
78 *Mozambique*, Colin Darch
79 *Libya*, Richard I. Lawless
80 *Sweden*, Leland B. Sather and Alan Swanson
81 *Iran*, Reza Navabpour
82 *Dominica*, Robert A. Myers
83 *Denmark*, Kenneth E. Miller
84 *Paraguay*, R. Andrew Nickson
85 *Indian Ocean*, Julia J. Gotthold with the assistance of Donald W. Gotthold
86 *Egypt*, Ragai N. Makar
87 *Gibraltar*, Graham J. Shields
88 *The Netherlands*, Peter King and Michael Wintle
89 *Bolivia*, Gertrude M. Yeager
90 *Papua New Guinea*, Fraiser McConnell
91 *The Gambia*, David P. Gamble
92 *Somalia*, Mark W. DeLancey, Sheila L. Elliott, December Green, Kenneth J. Menkhaus, Mohammad Haji Moqtar, Peter J. Schraeder
93 *Brunei*, Sylvia C. Engelen Krausse and Gerald H. Krausse
94 *Albania*, Rev. Ed., Antonia Young
95 *Singapore*, Stella R. Quah and Jon S. T. Quah
96 *Guyana*, Frances Chambers
97 *Chile*, Harold Blakemore
98 *El Salvador*, Ralph Lee Woodward, Jr.
99 *The Arctic*, H. G. R. King
100 *Nigeria*, Robert A. Myers
101 *Ecuador*, David Corkhill
102 *Uruguay*, Henry Finch with the assistance of Alicia Casas de Barrán
103 *Japan*, Frank Joseph Shulman
104 *Belgium*, R. C. Riley
105 *Macau*, Richard Louis Edmonds
106 *Philippines*, Jim Richardson
107 *Bulgaria*, Richard J. Crampton
108 *The Bahamas*, Paul G. Boultbee
109 *Peru*, John Robert Fisher
110 *Venezuela*, D. A. G. Waddell

111 *Dominican Republic*, Kai Schoenhals
112 *Colombia*, Robert H. Davis
113 *Taiwan*, Wei-chin Lee
114 *Switzerland*, Heinz K. Meier and Regula A. Meier
115 *Hong Kong*, Ian Scott
116 *Bhutan*, Ramesh C. Dogra
117 *Suriname*, Rosemarijn Hoefte
118 *Djibouti*, Peter J. Schraeder
119 *Grenada*, Kai Schoenhals
120 *Monaco*, Grace L. Hudson
121 *Guinea-Bissau*, Rosemary Galli
122 *Wales*, Gwilym Huws and D. Hywel E. Roberts
123 *Cape Verde*, Caroline S. Shaw
124 *Ghana*, Robert A. Myers
125 *Greenland*, Kenneth E. Miller
126 *Costa Rica*, Charles L. Stansifer
127 *Siberia*, David N. Collins
128 *Tibet*, John Pinfold
129 *Northern Ireland*, Michael Owen Shannon
130 *Argentina*, Alan Biggins
131 *Côte d'Ivoire*, Morna Daniels
132 *Burma*, Patricia M. Herbert
133 *Laos*, Helen Cordell
134 *Montserrat*, Riva Berleant-Schiller
135 *Afghanistan*, Schuyler Jones
136 *Equatorial Guinea*, Randall Fegley
137 *Turks and Caicos Islands*, Paul G. Boultbee
138 *Virgin Islands*, Verna Penn Moll
139 *Honduras*, Pamela F. Howard-Reguindin
140 *Mauritius*, Pramila Ramgulam Bennett
141 *Mauritania*, Simonetta Calderini, Delia Cortese, James L. A. Webb, Jr.
142 *Timor*, Ian Rowland
143 *St. Vincent and the Grenadines*, Robert B. Potter
144 *Texas*, James Marten
145 *Burundi*, Morna Daniels
146 *Hawai'i*, Nancy J. Morris and Love Dean
147 *Vietnam*, David Marr and Kristine Alilunas-Rodgers
148 *Sierra Leone*, Margaret Binns and Tony Binns
149 *Gabon*, David Gardinier
150 *Botswana*, John A. Wiseman
151 *Angola*, Richard Black
152 *Central African Republic*, Pierre Kalck
153 *Seychelles*, George Bennett, with the collaboration of Pramila Ramgulam Bennett
154 *Rwanda*, Randall Fegley
155 *Berlin*, Ian Wallace
156 *Mongolia*, Judith Nordby
157 *Liberia*, D. Elwood Dunn
158 *Maldives*, Christopher H. B. Reynolds
159 *Liechtenstein*, Regula A. Meier
160 *England*, Alan Day
161 *The Baltic States*, Inese A. Smith and Marita V. Grunts
162 *Congo*, Randall Fegley
163 *Armenia*, Vrej Nersessian
164 *Niger*, Lynda F. Zamponi
165 *Madagascar*, Hilary Bradt
166 *Senegal*, Roy Dilley and Jerry Eades
167 *Andorra*, Barry Taylor
168 *Netherlands Antilles and Aruba*, Kai Schoenhals
169 *Burkina Faso*, Samuel Decalo
170 *Indonesia*, Sylvia C. Engelen Krausse and Gerald H. Krausse
171 *The Antarctic*, Janice Meadows, William Mills and H. G. R. King
172 *São Tomé and Príncipe*, Caroline S. Shaw
173 *Fiji*, G. E. Gorman and J. J. Mills
174 *St. Kitts-Nevis*, Verna Penn Moll
175 *Martinique*, Janet Crane
176 *Zaire*, Dawn Bastian Williams, Robert W. Lesh and Andrea L. Stamm
177 *Chad*, George Joffé and Valérie Day-Viaud
178 *Togo*, Samuel Decalo
179 *Ethiopia*, Stuart Munro-Hay and Richard Pankhurst
180 *Punjab*, Darshan Singh Tatla and Ian Talbot
181 *Eritrea*, Randall Fegley
182 *Antigua and Barbuda*, Riva Berleant-Schiller and Susan Lowes with Milton Benjamin
183 *Alaska*, Marvin W. Falk
184 *The Falkland Islands*, Alan Day
185 *St Lucia*, Janet Henshall Momsen

186 *Slovenia*, Cathie Carmichael
187 *Cayman Islands*, Paul G. Boultbee
188 *San Marino*, Adrian Edwards and Chris Michaelides
189 *London*, Heather Creaton
190 *Western Sahara*, Anthony G. Pazzanita
191 *Guinea*, Margaret Binns
192 *Benin*, J. S. Eades and Chris Allen
193 *Madrid*, Graham Shields
194 *Tasmania*, I. Kepars
195 *Prague*, Susie Lunt
196 *Samoa*, H. G. A. Hughes
197 *St. Helena, Ascension and Tristan da Cunha*, Alan Day
198 *Budapest*, Mátyás Sárközi
199 *Lisbon*, John Laidlar
200 *Cambodia*, Helen Jarvis
201 *Vienna*, C. M. Peniston-Bird
202 *Corsica*, Grace L. Hudson
203 *Amsterdam*, André van Os
204 *Korea*, J. E. Hoare

Contents

Contents

Preface and Acknowledgements

The first edition of this bibliography, compiled by Rex Smith and published in 1984, reflected the state of scholarship on Yemen at the time – strong on the older-established subjects of history, travel and exploration, archaeology and cartography, and relatively weak in most other areas, with the exception of politics, economics, law and social conditions. The situation has changed significantly over the past fifteen years, however, with the establishment of American and French research centres in Ṣanʿāʾ and the growth in development projects funded by both national and international agencies. This has led to an efflorescence of work on Yemen, and on North Yemen in particular, with individuals based in the research centres working on history, anthropology and sociology, the development teams publishing studies in the social sciences, especially geography, agriculture and irrigation, social welfare and labour studies, and Yemeni students producing American-based doctoral research in a wide variety of areas. In addition, archaeological digs and surveys have been undertaken recently by British, American, Canadian, Italian, French and Soviet/Russian teams, all of which have greatly increased our understanding of the ancient history and culture of South Arabia. There are still significant gaps in our knowledge of Yemen – the fields of education and culture, literature and the arts, libraries and archives, sport and leisure, public administration and even religion are still poorly represented in this new edition, but the situation in general is much healthier than it was when Professor Smith was compiling his work.

In order to reflect the best of recent scholarship, I have included books and articles in French, German and Italian, when I have felt them to be genuine contributions to our knowledge of Yemen. I have also included, apart from the most significant items in the first edition, some older items omitted there, particularly in the fields of travel and the ancient culture of the Yemen. On the other hand, specialized research reports, especially those by the government of Yemen and by commercial firms, have usually been excluded, on the grounds that they are difficult to find in libraries to which the general public has access.

The question of transliteration from Arabic vexes everyone working in the field of Middle Eastern studies. Apart from a few place-names reasonably well known in English – Aden, Hodeida, Hadramawt, Mocha and Marib – I have tried to render all geographical terms in Library of Congress transliteration, although I have often simplified matters by omitting the definite article, e.g. Mukallā and Shiḥr for al-Mukallā and al-Shiḥr. All personal names have been similarly transliterated according to Library of Congress norms, except for President Nasser.

It is a pleasure to acknowledge the help of numerous librarians whose efforts have enabled me to track down material not available in the University of Exeter Library: in Oxford, Colin Wakefield of the Bodleian Library, Martyn Minty of the Oriental Institute Library, and Diane Ring of the Middle East Centre Library; in Cambridge, Dr Geoffrey Roper of the Islamic Bibliography Unit of the University Library; in Durham, John Lumsden of the University Library; in London, Peter Colvin of the Library of the School of Oriental and African Studies; and in Exeter, the entire staff of the Documentation Unit, Centre for Arab Gulf Studies. Thanks are also due to Julia Goddard, my editor at Clio Press, and, above all, to my wife, who has given me constant help and encouragement throughout this bibliographical project.

Introduction

Until recently, the concept of a single, unified Yemen was a state of mind rather than a political reality. This has not always been so, and South Arabia has alternated between one state, usually ruled from the highlands of North Yemen, and a fragmented form of political control, with numerous competing forces and spheres of influence. Much of this is due to the region's geography, which has always played a major role in historical development. The present Republic of Yemen is located in the south-west corner of the Arabian Peninsula, bounded on two sides by the Red Sea and the Gulf of Aden, and on the landward side by frontiers with Saudi Arabia to the north and Oman to the east – borders which are still not completely demarcated. The Republic also possesses various small groups of islands in the Red Sea, and the much larger island of Socotra in the Gulf of Aden, which is closer to the continent of Africa than it is to the coast of Arabia.

The westernmost part of Yemen is the coastal strip bordering the Red Sea; known as the Tihāmah, it is hot, sandy, dry and was formerly badly affected by malaria. Inland are the central highlands, where relatively abundant rainfall has allowed settled communities to practise agriculture for thousands of years. In former North Yemen, the mountains rise to a maximum of 12,000 feet and many towns and villages until very recently were accessible only on foot or by pack-animal. Wheeled transport and a road network are phenomena of the post-independence period. The capital Ṣanʿāʾ lies at about 7,000 feet and as one travels eastwards rainfall declines and the mountains become less dominant. In the former South Yemen, agriculture is concentrated in the zone between Aden and the former border, around Mukallā, and in the Wādī Ḥaḍramawt, which is home to some of Yemen's most spectacular cities, such as Shibām and Tarīm. However, much of former South Yemen, particularly the eastern half, is extremely arid and barely inhabited, although the non-Arabic-speaking

Mahris live on the borders with Oman. Socotra's population also speaks a modern South Arabian language quite distinct from Arabic. Yemen covers a total area of 536,869 square kilometres (207,286 square miles), which is about the same size as France, and has a population of 14,587,807 as recorded by the census of December 1994.

Yemen's recorded history stretches far back in time. Recent research suggests that humans reached the Arabian Peninsula as early as two million years ago, and Pleistocene (glacial era) sites have recently been discovered in southern Yemen. Prior to these discoveries, the earliest sites to be excavated in Yemen dated from the Bronze Age (between 2700 and 2000 BC) and these show evidence of widespread trading, agricultural settlements, and pottery and flint-knapping. However, it was the spread of writing from the north, and the development of both extensive irrigation and the frankincense trade which transformed Yemen from a backwater to a minor if significant player on the stage of Middle Eastern civilizations. While nowhere near as splendid as the great cultures of ancient Egypt and Mesopotamia, the pre-Islamic South Arabian kingdoms were complex societies of considerable wealth, which left behind numerous monuments and thousands of inscriptions on stone.

There is disagreement among scholars as to the precise chronology of the kingdoms, but it is generally accepted that they arose between the 8th and the 5th century BC. The most important of the kingdoms and the longest lasting was the Kingdom of Saba, with its capital in Marib. At times, its rule seems to have covered most of what is now present-day Yemen. To the north, in the pre-Christian period, the kingdom of Maʿin developed into a short-lived trading empire, while to the east, around the Wādī Bayḥān, the kingdom of Qataban dominated, at roughly the same time. The fourth kingdom, that of the Hadramawt, was based at Shabwah in the desert to the east of Marib, and was decisively defeated by the Kingdom of Saba and Himyar and disappears from view in the 3rd century AD. All these peoples used distinct Semitic dialects, which collectively form Ancient (or Epigraphic) South Arabian. Both Greeks and Romans were familiar with the Yemen, with the Romans even mounting a military expedition under Aelius Gallus which penetrated deep into the mountains around 26 BC. However, the politics of Yemen became confused after the 4th century AD, and the decline in the economy, symbolized by the collapse of the Marib dam, led both to invasions from Ethiopia and, later, Persia in the 5th and 6th centuries. In the same period there were politically significant Christian and Jewish communities, and while the former disappeared over the course of time, the Jewish community played a substantial role in Yemeni society and economy, until emigrating almost en masse in 1948-49.

The Muslims found a somewhat chaotic situation when their envoys arrived in 632 AD, but they quickly established formal control over the country. It is difficult to assess how quickly Islamicization progressed in such mountainous and difficult terrain, but certainly large numbers of Yemenis participated in the Islamic wars of conquest. The Umayyads (661-750) and the ʿAbbāsids (750-1258) sent governors to Ṣanʿāʾ, but various small states broke away from central control and flourished for limited periods. These includes the Ziyādids in Zabīd (818-1018), the Yuʿfurids in Ṣanʿāʾ and Janad (847-997), the Najāḥids in Zabīd (1022-1158), the Ismāʿīlī Ṣulayḥids in Ṣanʿāʾ and Dhū Jiblah (1047-1138), the Zurayʿids of Aden, also Ismāʿīlīs (1080-1175), the Hamdānids of Ṣanʿāʾ (1099-1174), and the Mahdīds of Zabīd (1159-73). The most important event of the early medieval period was the arrival of al-Hādī ilā al-Ḥaqq in Yemen in 897; he won over many of the northern tribes to his form of Shīʿism, known as Zaydism. This strain of heterodox Islam has played a major role in the affairs of North Yemen ever since, with successive Imams exercising both political and spiritual power. The territory they have controlled has shrunk and expanded according to circumstances, but the Imam has always been a major player on the stage of Yemeni politics. Even now, with the Imamate abolished, Zaydī tribes still figure heavily in Yemeni politics and dominate the Yemeni army, although the majority of Yemenis (including the whole of Hadramawt) are Sunnī Muslims of the Shāfiʿī school. Equally important in the short term, was the arrival in Yemen of Saladin's brother, Tūrānshāh, in 1173, leading a large Ayyūbid army from Egypt. The Ayyūbids dominated large tracts of Yemen, which their successors, the Rasūlids (1229-1454) built on and increased. They ushered in a golden age of political stability and wealth, as Yemenis grew rich on the spice trade, and developed a brilliant culture, full of distinguished writers and scientists, with the sultans themselves playing a major literary role. The Rasūlids were keen patrons of the arts as well as literature and left numerous buildings and artefacts behind. They were succeeded by the Ṭāhirids (1454-1517), who continued the traditions of their predecessors, but to a less conspicuous and successful degree. They were shaken by the arrival of the Portuguese on the southern coast in the early 16th century and the Ottomans who arrived via the Red Sea in 1517. The Ottomans failed to maintain a solid grip over the whole of Yemen, however, engaging in continuous warfare with the Zaydīs in the north of the country, and they finally withdrew in 1635. The Imams consolidated their hold on the northern part of the country until the 19th century, when the Ottomans re-invaded, capturing Ṣanʿāʾ in 1871, and remaining in control of North Yemen until the dissolution of their empire in 1919. This period also saw the entry of European powers on the stage. The Portuguese of the 16th century, were followed by British, French and Dutch traders in textiles and coffee in the 17th and 18th centuries, and the famous scientific expedition led by Carsten Niebuhr, who reached Hodeida in 1762. The areas south of Ṣanʿāʾ were outside the control of the Imams for much of the period after the Ottoman departure in 1635, and the Imams were in no position to dispute the capture of Aden by the British in 1839. The British had originally been looking for a coaling station on the 'overland' route to India, but the opening of the Suez Canal in 1869 increased Aden's importance enormously, and prompted by threats from the Turks in the north, the British signed treaties with many of the tribal leaders in the Hadramawt and Laḥij shortly afterwards. The delimiting of a frontier beween North and South Yemen was undertaken during the early years of the 20th century by representatives of the Ottoman and British forces, and remained in place until unification in 1990. European penetration during this period was still limited, with many parts of the Hadramawt remaining unvisited until the 1930s, but the scientific study of inscriptions was begun in the 19th century by a variety of travellers, while the British began to collect and classify the flora and fauna of Aden and Socotra around the same time.

The First World War brought about the departure of the Turks from the North, whereupon, after an abortive attempt by the Idrīsī ruler of ʿAsīr to take control of the Tihāmah, Imam Yaḥyā (d. 1948) closed Yemen to foreign influences. Political opposition did develop despite his efforts, however, although his successor Imam Aḥmad (d. 1962) pursued a similar policy. When Aḥmad died, a civil war broke out between republican forces led by ʿAbd Allāh al-Sallāl and royalist (Imamate) forces, with the Egyptians playing a very large part in the fighting. Nasser's defeat by Israel in 1967, as well as the emergence of a more moderate republican leader in ʿAbd al-Raḥmān al-Iryānī led to a limited reconciliation between royalists and republicans, the ending of the civil war, and the full emergence of the new country of the Yemen Arab Republic in 1970.

Meanwhile, the southern part of Yemen had also been undergoing major changes. The British system of indirect rule by treaty, begun in the 19th century and continued up to the 1930s by administrators such as Harold Ingrams, was changed when the governance of Aden was transferred from the Government of India to the Colonial Office in

1937, and the Aden Protectorate (comprising all the British-administered territory outside Aden and its immediate hinterland) was divided into the Eastern and Western Aden Protectorates with a resident British adviser based in Mukallā. The Second World War and the independence of India in 1947 hastened further changes, with limited local elections taking place in 1949 and political organizations and trade unions appearing in the 1950s. The building of a refinery in Aden in 1952 and the dramatic increase in service personnel after the British Defence White Paper of 1957 created an economic boom, and led to the immigration of thousands of North Yemenis to work in Aden (a trend which had begun in the 19th century). The British tried to integrate the protectorates with Aden and the creation of the Federation of South Arabia in 1959 led to increasing opposition within Aden and, after the civil war broke out in North Yemen, to an outright liberation struggle. The incoming Labour government in 1964 reviewed Britain's defence policy and realigned Aden's role as a military base, and consequently decided to grant the Federation independence in 1968. Increasing violence brought independence forward to 1967, the year which saw the creation of the People's Republic of Southern Yemen (which became the People's Democratic Republic of Yemen in 1970.)

Independence brought dramatic changes to both North and South Yemen. In the north, the opening up of the country to outside forces led to a mass exodus of workers to Saudi Arabia, and, to a lesser extent, the Gulf States. The remittances sent home by the migrant labour force were used by many to buy land, set up small firms, especially in construction, and to form cooperatives, which in turn built roads, and brought running water and electricity to many towns and villages which previously had been almost completely isolated. The government participated relatively little in the economy in the 1970s, but played a progressively stronger role in the 1980s, involving itself in many activities which it had previously ignored. The 1970s and 1980s also saw the arrival of many foreign experts, who worked with varying degrees of success on collaborative projects in agriculture, forestry, irrigation, health care, education, administration, transport, and in many other areas. Socially, tribalism continued to be the dominant form of social organization in both North and South Yemen. The complexity of social stratification with the *sayyids* and *sharīfs* (descendants of the Prophet) at the top and the *akhdām* at the bottom proved fairly resistant to change, and continued to attract the interest of numerous anthropologists, while cultural activities such as music, dance and literature flourished, often with state support. Conditions for women improved to some extent, but they continued to play little part in public life. Politically, the period saw a relatively stable country, pursuing a foreign policy of relative even-handedness, although relations with South Yemen were often strained. President ʿAbd al-Raḥmān al-Iryānī was sent into exile in 1974, to be replaced by Colonel Ibrāhīm al-Ḥamdī, who suspended the constitution, launched a 'corrective movement' and was assassinated in 1977. His successor, Aḥmad al-Ghashmī, also a colonel, lasted only a year, until he, too, was murdered, whereupon ʿAlī ʿAbd Allāh Ṣāliḥ, took over as President, and after a difficult few years, stabilized the country. Ex-presidents al-Sallāl and al-Iryānī returned in 1981, and limited democracy was introduced in 1982. The 1970 constitution was restored in full in 1988, while oil exports began the previous year. This generally positive picture, combined with major and negative changes in South Yemen, led to a meeting between the presidents of both North and South Yemen in late 1989, and a decision to unify both states in 1990.

South Yemen, meanwhile, had taken an entirely different direction. The avowedly Marxist leadership introduced a command economy, nationalizing businesses and concentrating most economic activities in the hands of the state. The 1970 constitution endorsed socialism (although Islam was tolerated), protected, indeed promoted the rights of women, and vested all political power in the party (the National Liberation Front, which became the Yemeni Socialist Party in 1978). Close relations were established with the Soviet Union, Cuba, East Germany, China and other socialist states, and the government, in keeping with its 'revolutionary' stance, aided a rebellion in the neighbouring state of Oman and provided sanctuary to various extreme groups. Although many areas of life, such as education, health care and communications improved, South Yemen remained a desperately poor country with the economy kept alive by Soviet aid, and, to a lesser extent, remittances. The long tradition of emigration from Hadramawt to India, Indonesia and Malaysia, and East Africa died hard, and even in the 1970s a substantial proportion of the South Yemeni labour force worked abroad. Politically dominated by the Party, the country was rocked on several occasions by major periods of bloodshed between rival factions, notably in 1978 when the Party Chairman, Sālim Rubayʿ ʿAlī, was executed, thereby consolidating power in the hands of ʿAbd al-Fattāḥ Ismāʿīl, and again in 1986 when ʿAlī Nāṣir Muḥammad (who had succeeded Ismāʿīl as President in 1980) was forced into exile, to be succeeded by ʿAlī Sālim al-Bayḍ. The disintegration of South Yemen's major sponsor, the Soviet Union, and the continuing underperformance of the economy led the South Yemeni leadership to seek unity talks with North Yemen, and the new Republic of Yemen was proclaimed on 22 May 1990, with ʿAlī ʿAbd Allāh Ṣāliḥ as President and ʿAlī Sālim al-Bayḍ as Vice-President.

The new republic had hardly been created when it was shaken by a crisis from which it has yet fully to recover. Its lack of support for Saudi Arabia and the Coalition forces in the Gulf War of 1990-91 led Saudi Arabia and the Gulf States to withdraw Yemeni workers' preferential status, and in the space of a few months, at least 800,000 return migrants poured over the border. It proved extremely difficult to integrate most of the migrants, many of whom ended up marginalized in large squatter camps near Hodeida and Aden, as did the 60,000 or so refugees from the civil war in Somalia. Economically, this reverse exodus shook the new union, which also suffered from political problems. The springing up of new political parties, periodicals and newspapers, the freeing of political prisoners, and the introduction of universal suffrage disguised to a large extent the failure of many of the integration measures introduced in 1990. Although the North outnumbered the South by a ratio of at least five to one in terms of population, northerners resented having to find so many posts for southerners, whom they considered secular and un-Islamic. The armies of both former states refused to unify, and there were numerous attacks and murders of prominent polticians, particularly those belonging to the southern Yemeni Socialist Party. Strikes and riots in 1992 forced a postponement of the scheduled elections, which eventually took place in April 1993. In what was generally considered a fair poll, the General People's Congress (northern) won 40 per cent of the vote, the Yemeni Socialist Party (southern) won 20 per cent and *al-Iṣlāḥ* party (representing northern tribal leaders, Islamic reform and reportedly financed from Saudi Arabia) won 20 per cent. However, relations between President Ṣāliḥ and Vice-President al-Bayḍ worsened considerably after the elections, with al-Bayḍ withdrawing to Aden and boycotting goverment functions. The situation, exacerbated by several armed clashes, degenerated into outright civil war in 1994, which resulted in victory for the northern forces. Al-Bayḍ went into exile, the government clamped down on the Yemeni Socialist Party and its members, and introduced strict austerity measures under pressure from the World Bank and the International Monetary Fund. Tension also continued between the General People's Congress and *al-Iṣlāḥ* party, and in further elections held in April 1997, President Ṣāliḥ's General People's Congress scored a massive victory, winning 60 per cent of the seats, with *al-Iṣlāḥ* party winning around 20 per cent. This left the South almost completely unrepresented, since the Yemeni Socialist

Party had boycotted the elections. On the positive side, however, foreign relations have improved slowly, the oil continues to flow, tourism is regarded as a major growth industry, and the government has introduced measures to eliminate the budget deficit by 1998. While the prospects for the Republic of Yemen are by no means rosy, this unique region, with its complex social structure, highly individual style of architecture, great natural beauty, and a cultural tradition stretching back several thousand years is still one of the most attractive and interesting countries in the whole Arab world.

Paul Auchterlonie
December 1997

The Country and Its People

1 **The Middle East.**
Edited by Michael Adams. New York; Oxford, England: Facts on File, 1988. 865p. maps. (Handbooks to the Modern World).

This useful reference work is divided into six sections: 'Basic information'; 'General background'; 'The countries of the Middle East'; 'Political affairs'; 'Economic affairs'; and 'Social affairs'. The first section, compiled by Howard Bowen-Jones, offers background information such as basic statistics on the economy and biographies of prominent personalities for each country in the Middle East; the Yemen Arab Republic is covered on pages 163-70 and the People's Democratic Republic of Yemen on pages 171-9. Part three, 'The countries of the Middle East', allows a specialist to survey the history and recent political developments in each country and in this chapter R. L. Bidwell deals with the Yemen Arab Republic on pages 522-32, while J. E. Peterson covers the People's Democratic Republic of Yemen on pages 533-44.

2 **Arabian and Islamic studies: articles presented to R. B. Serjeant on the occasion of his retirement from the Sir Thomas Adams's Chair of Arabic Studies at the University of Cambridge.**
Edited by R. L. Bidwell, G. R. Smith. London: Longman, 1983. 282p. bibliog.

Thirteen of the twenty-three articles in this collection deal with Yemen. They are: 'Women in Saba' (A. F. L. Beeston); 'Biblical and old South Arabian institutions: some parallels' (Jacques Ryckmans); 'A document concerning the sale of Ghayl al-Barmakī and al-Ghayl al-Aswad by al-Mahdī 'Abbās, Imam of the Yemen' (Ḥusayn ibn ʿAbdullāh al-ʿAmrī); 'The mosque of al-Janad' (Paolo Costa); 'The apostasy of ʿAlī b. al-Faḍl' (C. L. Geddes); 'The painted dome of the Ashrafiyyah in Taʿizz, Yemen' (Ronald Lewcock); 'Feminism and feminist movements in the Middle East, a preliminary exploration: . . . People's Democratic Republic of Yemen' (Leila Ahmed); 'Some notes on the history of Socotra' (C. F. Beckingham); 'Some remarks on the ritual significance of the bull in pre-Islamic South Arabia' (Walter Dostal); 'Anglo-Ottoman confrontation in the Yemen: the first Mocha incident, 1817-22' (Caesar E.

Farah); 'The system of enumeration in the South Arabian languages (T. M. Johnstone); and 'Notes on some ordinances, decrees and laws of the Kathīrī sultanate, 1942-64' (Abdullah M. A. Maktari). The volume concludes with a bibliography by J. D. Pearson of the writings of Professor Serjeant up to 1982, the majority of which deal with Yemen and its culture. A supplementary bibliography of Serjeant's works from 1983 to 1994 with details of earlier items omitted by Pearson was published by Ronald E. Kon in *New Arabian Studies*, vol. 3 (1996), p. 69-78.

3 **La Péninsule arabique d'aujourd'hui.** (The Arabian Peninsula today.)
Edited by Paul Bonnenfant. Paris: Éditions du Centre National de la Recherche Scientifique, 1982. 2 vols.

A valuable collection of articles, all of which are in French. Volume one deals with general issues affecting the countries of the Arabian Peninsula, and both Yemens feature prominently in many articles, particularly those by Michel Chatelus, 'De la rente pétrolière au développement économique: perspectives et contradictions de l'évolution économique dans la péninsule' (From oil income to economic development: prospects for and inconsistencies in the economic growth of the Peninsula) and by Philippe Fargues, 'Présentation démographique des pays de la péninsule Arabique' (Demographic survey of the countries of the Arabian Peninsula). The second volume contains articles on specific countries in the Peninsula and devotes over 250 pages to both Yemens. Relevant articles cover topics such as tribal society, Islam and political culture, cultural life, domestic architecture, emigration, demography and infrastructure, state formation and chronological surveys of both Yemens.

4 **Yemen: 3000 years of art and civilisation.**
Edited by Werner Daum. Innsbruck, Austria: Pinguin-Verlag; Frankfurt am Main, Germany: Umschau-Verlag, 1988. 483p.

This collective work was commissioned to accompany a major exhibition on Yemen held at the Staatliches Museum für Völkerkunde in Munich from April 1987 to April 1988. It contains forty-seven articles of varying length, covering a variety of topics of which the most important are archaeology and ancient history (twelve articles), medieval history (eight articles) and art and architecture (four articles). Among unusual subjects dealt with are 'Traditional beekeeping in North Yemen' (Jan Karpowicz), 'Medicine and the herbal in medieval Yemen' (Daniel Martin Varisco), 'Yemen and Ethiopia: ancient cultural links between two neighbouring countries on the Red Sea' (Walter Raunig), and 'Slaves and mamelukes in the history of Yemen' (Ḥusayn ibn ʿAbdallāh al-ʿAmrī). A simultaneous German version was also published as, *Jemen: 3000 Jahre Kunst und Kultur des Glücklichen Arabien.*

5 **Socotra: island of tranquillity.**
D. B. Doe, with contributions from R. B. Serjeant, A. Radcliffe-Smith, K. M. Guichard. London: Immel Publishing, 1992. 237p. maps. bibliog.

An excellent survey of the island of Socotra, which had been administered by South Yemen since the arrival of the British in Aden in 1839. The bulk of the book is taken up with a description of the many archaeological sites on the island, based on the findings of the expedition of 1967; this repeats to some extent the information given in Doe's *Socotra, an archaeological reconnaissance in 1967* (see item no. 230), but there are, in addition, new sections on entomology, botany, history, geography and ethnography. The work also contains brief descriptions of the island of ʿAbd al-Kūrī, about fifty miles west of Socotra, and of the Kuria Muria Islands, which lie off the coast of Dhofar.

6 **Western Arabia and the Red Sea.**
Great Britain. Admiralty. Naval Intelligence Division. London: HM Stationery Office, 1946. 659p. 48 maps. bibliog. (Geographical Handbook Series, BR 527).

The purpose of this series was, according to the preface, 'to provide, for the use of Commanding Officers, information in a comprehensive and convenient form about countries which they may be called upon to visit, not only in war but in peace-time'. In fact, the handbooks provide in many cases the most complete information on the geography, history, ethnography and administration available at the time and are often an invaluable record of life before postwar modernization altered living patterns irrevocably. This volume deals with Saudi Arabia and the two Yemens, and contains in addition to the subjects mentioned above information on public health, economics, agriculture, communications and trade, as well as particularly useful maps and photographs.

7 **An account of the British settlement of Aden in Arabia.**
F. M. Hunter. London: Cass, 1968. 232p. 2 maps.

A reprint of the edition published in London by Trubner in 1877. It consists of a detailed report drawn up at the request of the Director-General of Statistics to the Government of India, which was responsible for administering Aden at the time. The book as a whole gives a valuable picture of life in Aden and its hinterland in the mid-19th century, particularly regarding economic and social conditions. There are separate chapters on: geography; ethnography; agriculture; trade, commerce and industry; the British administrative system; and relations with the tribes of the interior.

8 **A survey of social and economic conditions in the Aden Protectorate.**
Doreen Ingrams. Asmara, Eritrea: Printed by the Government Printer, British Administration, Eritrea, 1949. 169p. map. bibliog.

A very thorough survey of life in the Aden Protectorate, beyond the confines of the Colony of Aden. The author had spent almost ten years in the Eastern Arab Protectorate, and was able to use her own observations, allied to those of British government officials, to provide an unparalleled picture of the conditions of life among the tribes of Hadramawt. Subjects dealt with include: geography; population; social and class structure; education; health; agriculture and irrigation; industries and crafts; communications and transport; trade, currency and finance; and nutrition.

9 **Yémen avec les montagnards de la Mer Rouge.** (Yemen along with the mountain people of the Red Sea.)
Simon Jargy. Paris: Hachette Réalités, 1978. 152p.

A general historical survey of both Yemens followed by chapters on architecture, landscape, and social practices such as marriage, circumcision and *qāt* parties. The whole work is richly illustrated by the photographs of Alain Saint-Hilaire.

10 **Yemen: present and past.**
Edited by Bengt Knutsson, Viking Mattsson, Magnus Persson. Lund, Sweden: Lund University Press, 1994. 116p. (Lund Middle Eastern and North African Studies, no. 1).

A collection of nine short articles on Yemen mainly by Scandinavian scholars. Many subjects are discussed: tribalism and democracy; *qāt*; the architecture of Ṣanʿāʾ; and the historiography of the Ottomans in Yemeni sources, but, by and large, the articles are too short to penetrate beyond the surface. Perhaps the most interesting contributions are those on two medieval Yemeni scholars: 'Nashwān ibn Saʿīd al-Ḥimyarī and his lexicon Shams al-ʿUlūm, the sun of the sciences', by Mikael Persenius; and 'Al-Hamdānī, the Linnaeus of al-Yaman – an Arabic philosopher and scholar a thousand years ago', by Christopher Toll.

11 **Alt-arabische Träume: Pilgerreise in eine andere Welt und eine andere Zeit.** (Ancient Arabian dreams: a pilgrim's journey into another world and another time.)
Fritz Kortler. Wörgl, Austria: Perlinger Verlag, 1984. 2nd ed. 208p.

This book consists mainly of wonderful colour photographs of the Yemen Arab Republic, linked by a brief travel narrative. The images include views of Ibb, Taʿizz, Zabīd and Ṣaʿdah and their inhabitants.

12 **Democratic Yemen today.**
Farouk M. Luqman. Printed in Bombay, India, 1970. 206p. map.

A general introduction to the People's Democratic Republic of Yemen, with chapters on: geography; history; the economy; agriculture; the port of Aden; government; development; geology; archaeology; and flora and fauna.

13 **Yemen 1970.**
Farouk M. Luqman. Aden, Yemen Republic: the author, 1970. 150p.

A stable companion to the preceding volume, with similar chapters on history, geography, and various facets of government such as education, public works, public health and the defence forces.

14 **The Arabs.**
Peter Mansfield. London: Penguin Books, 1992. 3rd ed. 557p.

Each of the three editions of this popular work begins with a general history of the Arab world, which is followed by a country-by-country survey. The third edition contains a chapter on 'The Republic of Yemen: a belated marriage' (p. 372-83), which concentrates on the political and economic history of the two Yemens from 1962 up to the union in 1990. The second edition (Harmondsworth, England: Penguin Books, 1978. 576p.) contains two separate chapters: 'The People's Democratic Republic of Yemen: the first Marxist Arab state?' (p. 389-93), and 'The Yemen Arab Republic: the awakened recluse' (p. 394-9).

15 **Arabia Felix: the Yemen and its people.**
Pascal Maréchaux. London: Thames & Hudson, 1979. 81p. map.

The first of a series of photographic albums on the Yemen Arab Republic and its inhabitants. Other similar publications by the author are: *Arabian moons: passages in time through Yemen,* photographs by Maria Maréchaux and Pascal Maréchaux, text by Dominique Champault (Singapore: Concept Media, 1987. 168p.); *Villages d'Arabie Heureuse* (Villages of Arabia Felix), photographs and text by Pascal Maréchaux (Paris: Éditions du Chêne, 1979. 81p.); and *Yémen* (Yemen), photographs by Maria Maréchaux and Pascal Maréchaux, text by Dominique Champault (Paris: Phébus, 1993. 237p.). The photographs cover a variety of subjects, but Maréchaux specializes in capturing human activities like nursing a baby or bringing in the harvest.

16 **Yémen: l'état face à la démocratie.** (Yemen: the state faces democracy.)
Edited by Franck Mermier. *Monde Arabe Maghreb Machrek,* no. 155 (1997), p. 6-86.

Over half of this special issue of the leading French academic journal on the contemporary Middle East is devoted to recent events in Yemen, and together the articles represent the fullest survey of the country since the civil war of 1994. On the political front, Franck Mermier looks at tensions between secular and Islamist currents in Yemen, paying particular attention to education, the cult of saints, and welfare organizations. In the economic field, Renaud Detalle explores the economic reforms undertaken by the new government, Mohamed A. Al-Saqqaf discusses the emergence of Islamic banking since 1991, and Muḥammad ʿAbd al-Wahid al-Maytami analyses the fall in the value of the Yemeni riyal and the divergence between the official and the grey market. On other subjects, Eric Mercier describes, through reports in the press, the uncontrolled urban development in Aden, while Marc Lavergne examines relations between Yemen and Eritrea through their disputes over maritime boundaries in the Red Sea.

17 **Middle East and North Africa.**
London: Europa Publications, 1948- . annual.

One of the leading reference works on the Middle East. Each issue covers the physical geography, recent history and current economic performance of every Middle Eastern country. In addition, appendices list the most recent statistical information, a full directory of ministers, political organizations and diplomatic representation, as well as names and addresses in the fields of the press and publishing, banking, trade and industry, transport and many other fields. The volume for 1997 deals with Yemen on pages 1060-1104.

18 **Middle East Contemporary Survey.**
New York: Holmes & Meier (vols. 1-7); Boulder, Colorado: Westview Press (vol. 8-), 1977- . annual.

The most thorough annual survey of events in the Middle East. Compiled by staff at the Moshe Dayan Center for Middle Eastern and African Studies, the Shiloah Institute, Tel Aviv University (Israel), the research for this reputable and reliable publication is based on an exhaustive survey of the Middle Eastern press. Each volume is divided into two sections: the first contains a series of essays on broad regional issues and on the overall relations of the region with other parts of the world (with a strong emphasis on the Arab–Israeli question), while the second section deals with individual countries. In the 1994 issue (published in 1996), Joseph Kostiner surveyed events in Yemen on pages 702-24, concentrating on the civil war of 1994.

19 **Middle East Review: the Economic and Business Report.**
Saffron Walden, England: World of Information (1981-93); London: Kogan Page & Walden (1993/94-), 1981- . annual.

In a format similar to a very condensed version of *Middle East and North Africa* (q.v.), this annual publication gives a brief account of each Middle Eastern country's internal and external politics, and its economic performance and prospects. A few basic facts about each country are given, but there are no statistical tables. The volume for 1996 deals with Yemen on pages 149-52. It was first published as the *Middle East Annual Review* (Saffron Walden, England: World of Information 1974-80. annual).

20 **The Cambridge encyclopedia of the Middle East and North Africa.**
Edited by Trevor Mostyn, advisory editor Albert Hourani. Cambridge, England: Cambridge University Press, 1988. 504p. 36 maps.

This encyclopaedia is arranged thematically, rather than alphabetically, which has enabled the editors to maintain considerable consistency. The work contains six sections: lands and peoples; history; societies and economies; culture (including religion, literature and the arts); the countries; and inter-state relations. Professor Fred Halliday provides the entries on North Yemen and South Yemen (p. 453-60), which contain a historical summary of each country from 1962 to the mid-1980s.

21 **The Yemens: country studies.**
Edited by Richard F. Nyrop. Washington, DC: American University, 1986. 2nd ed. 376p. bibliog. (Foreign Area Study Series).

A volume in a very useful American series which covers most countries of the world, this work replaces *Area handbook for the Yemens* (by Richard F. Nyrop (et al.). Washington, DC: American University, 1977. 240p. maps. bibliog.). The new edition begins with historical summaries of both Yemens up to 1967, followed by analyses of the contemporary situation in both North and South Yemen. These chapters deal with subjects like social life, the economy, contemporary government and politics, foreign relations and national security. Although based on a synthesis of the works of other scholars, this is a useful compendium of basic facts for the general reader.

22 **Contemporary Yemen: politics and historical background.**
Edited by B. R. Pridham. London: Croom Helm, 1984. 276p.

A selection of the papers presented to the historically significant symposium organized by the Centre for Arab Gulf Studies, University of Exeter, in July 1983, where, for the first time, academics from both North and South Yemen participated officially in a formal conference along with Western scholars. The papers, along with the selection published in 1985 (see item no. 23), cover a very wide range of topics. This volume contains two historical articles, 'Towards a sociology of the islamisation of Yemen' (D. Thomas Gochenour); and 'Memduh Pasha and Aziz Bey: Ottoman experience in Yemen' (Jon Mandaville); and a number of important contributions on contemporary Yemeni political structures, foreign policy, and the judicial system.

23 **Economy, society and culture in contemporary Yemen.**
Edited by B. R. Pridham. London: Croom Helm, 1985. 257p.

The second selection of papers from the 1983 conference held at the Centre for Arab Gulf Studies, University of Exeter, focuses mainly on the social sciences, and covers topics such as development planning, land usage, agriculture, fiscal policy, the banking sector, consumers and the weekly market, emigration and remittances, health care, education, tourism, cultural policy and the conservation of the architectural heritage. The two volumes together represent the most significant overview of the culture and society of both Yemens for the 1970s and early 1980s.

24 **Yemen: Land am 'Tor der Tränen'.** (Yemen: land at the gate of tears.)
Heinz Rudolf von Rohr, Gottfried Rohner. Kreuzlingen, Switzerland: Verlag Welsermühl; Neptun Verlag, 1979. 287p.

A very well-produced general volume on the Yemen Arab Republic. Full of excellent colour photographs, this is more than a coffee-table book, with its statistical tables, diagrams for climatology and precise information about the agricultural year, population distribution and export performance. Although the economic data are now no longer current, this book will still be of interest to geographers, economists and serious travellers who can read German.

25 **Les Yémen et leurs populations.** (The Yemens and their peoples.)
Alain Rouaud. Brussels: Éditions Complexe, 1979. 240p. (Pays et Populations).

Rouaud's interesting general book covering both Yemens concentrates on history and sociology. Among the subjects tackled are women and the family, leisure activities, tribes and castes; religion; and the Yemeni diaspora. The author concludes with chapters on recent developments in North and South Yemen, and forecasts that unity will be achieved when both Yemens have thrown off the shackles of their protecting powers.

26 **Encyclopedia of the modern Middle East.**
Edited by Reeva S. Simon, Philip Mattar, Richard W. Bulliet. New York: Macmillan Reference; Simon & Schuster, 1996. 4 vols.

An encyclopaedia of people, places, parties, movements, events, treaties, but few concepts, this work contains numerous articles and references to Yemen and South Arabia since the beginning of the 19th century until the civil war of 1994. Some of the articles are a little cursory, but the index is excellent, and the contributors (among whom are the specialists on contemporary Yemen, Robert D. Burrowes and Manfred W. Wenner [qq.v.]) are well chosen. The style of the work contrasts with the thematically arranged, *Oxford encyclopedia of the modern Islamic world,* edited by John L. Esposito (New York; Oxford: Oxford University Press, 1995. 4 vols), which offers detailed expositions of topics such as class and tribe, but little on Yemen, apart from one main article, which focuses on the organization of the Zaydī state.

27 **South Yemen: a Marxist republic in Arabia.**
Robert W. Stookey. Boulder, Colorado: Westview Press; London: Croom Helm, 1982. 124p. map. (Profiles/Nations of the Contemporary Middle East).

A textbook designed for the general reader, this work contains chapters on the geography, history, politics, economics, and international relations of South Yemen. Its main interest derives from the author's familiarity with both historical and contemporary events in the People's Democratic Republic, and the information he gives regarding such important, but often little-discussed current matters such as the constitution, income distribution and regional relations. On the other hand, the author does not neglect the historical background, and gives succinct accounts of the medieval period, Britain's occupation of Aden (1839-1967), her relations with the tribes of the interior, and her transformation of Aden into the world's second busiest port in 1958. The work concludes with a knowledgeable 'Suggested further reading'. A work in the same series has also been published on North Yemen by Manfred W. Wenner (see item no. 30).

28 **Le Yémen: passé et présent de l'unité.** (Yemen: its unity in the past and present.)
Edited by Michel Tuchscherer. *Revue du Monde Musulman et de la Méditerranée,* no. 67 (1993). 186p.

The whole issue of this important French journal is devoted to considerations of the essential unity of Yemen. Articles in English look at the unity of Yemeni dance (Najwa Adra), at tribalism and identity (Paul Dresch), at the ability of Muḥammad ibn ʿAlī al-Shawkānī (d. 1834) to bridge the jurisprudential gap between Yemen's two main Muslim sects (Bernard Haykel), and at the unification achieved under the Rasūlid ruler al-Malik al-Muẓaffar (Daniel Martin Varisco). Articles in French study, among other topics, the bases of Zaydī power (Nahida Coussonet and François Blukacz), economic unity (Blandine Destremau), a unified labour market (Muḥammad ʿAbd al-Wahid al-Maytami), and regional music and national identity (Jean Lambert).

29 **Welcome to Aden: a comprehensive guidebook.**
Nairobi: Guides and Handbooks of Africa Publishing Company, 1963. 2nd ed. 268p.

A fascinating introduction to Aden designed to familiarize the newcomer with life in the British colony. The information provided ranges from the mundane and everyday (What do you do if the street light outside your house is not working? Where is the best place to go swimming?), to the more long-term and general (the organization of Middle East Command in Aden; port and export statistics; history of Aden; population figures; Muslim beliefs and Adeni customs). The book provides both a panorama of life in Aden from the British point of view, and an interesting sidelight on colonial psychology. The first edition was published in 1961.

30 **The Yemen Arab Republic: development and change in an ancient land.**

Manfred W. Wenner. Boulder, Colorado: Westview Press, 1991. 194p. bibliog. (Profiles/Nations of the Contemporary Middle East.)

As in Stookey's work on South Yemen (see item no. 27), this is a textbook designed for the general reader. It contains chapters on people and culture (dealing with population, religion, social stratification, the human landscape, and domestic arts); economic problems and prospects (covering agriculture, industry, landholding, water, labour problems, development planning and trade); history before the Republic (i.e. up to 1970); and the Republic (which looks at issues like domestic politics, tribalism, law and administration, and the current economic situation). The unification of both Yemens achieved in May 1990 is touched upon, but not analysed in any detail, and the Gulf War of 1990-91 and its repercussions on Yemen are not dealt with at all.

31 **Who's who in the Arab world, 1995-96.**

Beirut: Publitec; Munich, Germany: K. G. Saur, 1995. 12th ed. 978p.

Published since 1966, each edition of this biographical directory has contained a country-by-country survey of the Arab world. Yemen is covered on pages 855-62 of this edition, and the information given is similar to, but much briefer than, the annual *Middle East and North Africa* (see item no. 17). The members of the Yemen government are listed, followed by addresses for foreign embassies and consulates, banks, trade organizations, higher education establishments, and radio, television and newspaper corporations.

32 **The Middle East: a political dictionary.**

Lawrence Ziring. Santa Barbara, California: ABC-Clio, 1992. 401p.

A thematically arranged encyclopaedia with seven sections, ranging from 'Political geography and geopolitics', and 'Islam', through 'Israelis and Palestinians', to 'Diplomacy', and 'Conflict'. The entries on Yemen (both North and South) can be traced through the index and cross-references, but this system is not foolproof, and it is quite possible to miss references to Yemen embedded in other articles. The information is also not as up-to-date as the single-volume *Dictionary of the Middle East*, by Dilip Hiro (Basingstoke, England: Macmillan, 1996. 367p.), which uses a straightforward alphabetical approach plus index. It, too, suffers from inadequate indexing, but is easier to use, and is as reliable as Ziring. Despite its title, Hiro's work deals only with the modern Middle East, basically since the Second World War.

Geography and Geology

General

33 **The Middle East: a geographical study.**
Peter Beaumont, Gerald H. Blake, J. Malcolm Wagstaff. London: David Fulton, 1988. 2nd ed. 623p. maps. bibliog.

An important general textbook, which covers the following topics in depth: geology, soils and geomorphology; climate and water resources; landscape evolution; rural land use; population; towns and cities; economic development; industry, trade and finance; petroleum; and the political map. Both the Yemens figure prominently in several chapters (notably population, economic development, and industry, trade and finance), but not in the case-studies of individual countries, which comprise the second half of the book.

34 **Arabische Republik Jemen: Wirtschaftsgeographie eines Entwicklungslandes.** (The Yemen Arab Republic: the economic geography of a developing country.)
H. Dequin. Riyadh: Published by the author, 1976. 252p. map. bibliog.

Dequin has produced the only general geographical study of either Yemen available in a Western language. His analysis deals with physical geography (climate, hydrology, soils); the infrastructure (transport, education, health services and nutrition); economic geography (industry, mining, finance, trade); agriculture; and development policy. The last two sections are the most detailed as the author is able here to make use of his experiences as an agricultural aid worker in North Yemen from 1960 to 1965. The author sees the main objectives of economic planning to be: growing crops for import substitution; earning foreign currency from industrial crops; prioritizing private investment; creating social programmes to protect employees; reducing unemployment; and balancing urban and rural growth by regional planning. There are summaries of the text in English, French, Spanish and Arabic, and fifty-two statistical tables.

35 **Wirtschafts- und sozialgeographische Untersuchungen in der Wâdî Mawr Region (Arabische Republik Jemen).** (Studies in the social and economic geography of the Wādī Mawr region, Yemen Arab Republic.)
Hermann A. Escher. Wiesbaden, Germany: Reichert, 1976. 220p. 5 maps. bibliog. (Beihefte zum Tübinger Atlas des Vorderen Orients, Reihe B, no. 23).

This study is based on fieldwork conducted by a small team of Yemeni, Swiss and American geographers in 1973 and 1974. After two introductory chapters on the methodology of the study and the physical characteristics of the Wādī Mawr region, the author turns to the local system of agriculture. Here the study concentrates on the crops grown, how the growing season is financed, and how the fields are irrigated. Further research centres on the village markets, who attends them and who controls them. The fourth chapter studies the transportation patterns within the region, and the work concludes with a discussion of the externally funded irrigation project planned for the region.

36 **Entwicklungsimpulse durch Verkehrserschliessung: wirtschafts- und sozialgeographische Auswirkungen des jungen Infrastrukturausbaus in der Arabischen Republik Jemen.** (Stimuli for growth through the development of a traffic network: economic and social-geographical effects of the construction of the new infrastructure of the Yemen Arab Republic.)
Hans Gebhardt. Wiesbaden, Germany: Reichert, 1987. 185p. maps. bibliog. (Jemen-Studien, Band 6).

The author shows how the network of asphalt highways, built up over the previous fifteen years, has altered the 'location values of settlements', with a concentration of economic activities along the new roads. The new markets are often independent of tribal affiliations, and reflect the economic boom in consumer goods, caused by the inflow of workers' remittances. However, they are also unstable in comparison with the older weekly markets, and the author is uncertain as 'to what extent the recent developing attempts, road markets and new towns can become permanent components in a system of central places'.

37 **Towns, road-markets, and economic geographical development in the Yemen Arab Republic.**
Hans Gebhardt. In: *Petites villes et villes moyennes dans le monde arabe.* (Small and medium-sized towns in the Arab world.) Tours, France: URBAMA, Université de Tours, 1986, p. 209-29.

A briefer version of the monograph listed above, in which the author shows how the network of new roads in North Yemen has altered the economic and spatial structure of the country. On the one hand, old regional centres are losing their former importance due to the lack of effective road connections, while new road-orientated markets and settlements have developed at the crossings of important long-distance roads. The author sees the road markets and new towns as 'representing a transitional phenomena [*sic*] on the way from an agrarian tribal society to a market economy with a new central-place system'.

38 **Middle East patterns: place, peoples, and politics.**
Colbert C. Held. Boulder, Colorado: Westview Press, 1989. 442p. bibliog.

A geographical textbook of the Middle East designed for the American undergraduate, this work emphasizes cultural and political patterns as well as the physical features of the region. Topics covered include climate, hydrology, soils and vegetation, mineral and hydrocarbon resources, industry, transport, urbanization, and geopolitics. The work includes a survey of the main geographical features of each Middle Eastern country, including both Yemens (p. 316-26).

39 **Die Al Maḥwīt Provinz/Jemen: das natürliche Entwicklungspotential einer randtropischen Gebirgsregion: eine ökologische Landklassifizierung auf der Grundlage einer physiographischen Bodenkartierung.** (The Al Maḥwīt province/Yemen: the natural potential for development of a mountain region on the edge of the tropics: an ecological land-classification on the basis of a physiographical soil mapping.)
Dietmar Schorlemer. Giessen, Germany: Selbstverlag des Geographischen Instituts der Justus-Liebig-Universität Giessen, 1990. 156p. maps. bibliog. (Giessener Geographische Schriften, Heft 65).

A very thorough study of the interaction between climate, soil and land use in al-Maḥwīt Province, situated to the northwest of Ṣanʿāʾ. The author find that the pattern of land use reflects the climatic circumstances very closely, and that constraints of soil types and water supply limit the amount of new types of cultivation that could be introduced. He suggests that instead of concentrating on irrigated farming, re-afforestation should be undertaken, and pasture land and meadows in mountain areas should be introduced; this would, in his opinion, prevent the loss of valuable soil resources, create a new tree stock and minimize social disruption.

40 **Studies on the Tihamah: the report of the Tihamah Expedition 1982 and related papers.**
Edited by Francine Stone. London: Longman, 1985. 148p.

This volume of collected papers grew out of an independent research project which, in early 1982, surveyed the wildlife, archaeology, architecture, music and ethnography of the coastal plain of North Yemen. The picture it presents of a little-studied region of Yemen is a fascinating, but incomplete one, since the history of the region is merely sketched in, the agriculture and transport patterns touched on in passing, and the complex tribal structure of the province not investigated at all.

41 **Böden als Nutzungspotenzial im System der semiariden Tropen: Untersuchungen zur Bewertung von Bodeneigenschaften und Bodenwasserhaushalt am Beispiel des Beckens von Aṭ Ṭūr (Nordjemen).** (Soil potential in the semi-arid tropical system: evaluation studies of soil properties and soil water balance in the basin of Aṭ Ṭūr – Yemen Arab Republic.)
Rudolf Straub. Wiesbaden, Germany: Reichert, 1986. 275p. maps. bibliog. (Jemen-Studien, Band 4).

A technical study of the physical and chemical characteristics of the soils in the Al-Ṭūr Basin. The author analyses numerous profile strips and combines the results with a study of the mechanisms of the soil moisture regime in the region. His basic conclusions are that the soil has a high nutrient factor, that it has been subject to extensive changes through human interference and that the most important limiting factor to its use is the water supply. In an important appendix, numerous soil profiles are described in detail.

42 **Beiträge zur physikalischen Geographie und Landschaftsgliederung des südlichen Jemen (ehemals VDRJ).** (Contributions to the physical geography and landscape division of southern Yemen – formerly PDRY.)
Gerd Villwock. Wiesbaden, Germany: Reichert, 1991. 205p. maps. bibliog. (Jemen-Studien, Band 10).

One of the few geographical studies of South Yemen, this work concentrates on analysing the various components of the landscape, on evaluating the landscape divisions for their agricultural potential, and on estimating the amount of landscape change caused by human interference. The landscape has been divided into forty-two natural regions, of which only four per cent show natural conditions suitable to arable crop production. The author recommends improved mapping and detailed investigations of land-use projects.

43 **Bodenerosion im Terrassenfeldbau: Kulturlandzerstörung durch Landnutzungswandel im Ḥarāz-Gebirge/Nordjemen.** (Soil erosion in terrace construction: the destruction of ancient lands through a change in land use in the Ḥarāz Mountains, North Yemen.)
Horst Vogel. Wiesbaden, Germany: Reichert, 1988. 137p. maps. bibliog. (Jemen-Studien, Band 8).

The author combines an analysis of climate, soil structure, water provision and general geological conditions in this study of recent soil erosion in the Ḥarāz Mountains, which lie between Ṣanʿāʾ and the coast. He concentrates on natural factors to the virtual exclusion of the human element and makes numerous suggestions for preserving the traditional terrace cultivation by improved water run-off and terrace construction.

44 **Geographie im Jemen: Bedeutungswandel einer Wissenschaft für ein Entwicklungsland.** (Geography in Yemen: the changing significance of a science for a developing country.)
Matthias Weiter. Wiesbaden, Germany: Reichert, 1988. 157p. (Jemen-Studien, Band 9).

This interesting work examines the teaching of geography in Yemeni universities and schools and how Yemeni geographers can best interact with their foreign counterparts working on development projects in the Yemen Arab Republic. After a conceptual introduction, and a survey of both Western travellers to Yemen and medieval Yemeni geographers, the author focuses on three joint development projects: one between Swiss experts and the Survey Authority on mapping; one between German experts and the University of Ṣanʿāʾ on development planning; and one between the German Agency for Technical Cooperation and the Ministry of Municipalities on urbanization in the smaller cities of Nọrth Yemen. The effectiveness of these collaborative ventures is assessed, and recommendations for the training of Yemeni geographers at both school and university level put forward.

Urban geography

45 **Building and resettlement, 9 years later: a case-study of the contractor built reconstruction in Yemen, following the 1982 Dhamar earthquake.**
Sultan Barakat. York, England: Institute of Advanced Architectural Studies, University of York, 1993. 60p. bibliog.

According to the author, the aim of the book was to investigate how people affected by a disaster, and subsequently by a massive programme of rehabilitation, responded to extreme and unfamiliar circumstances after nine years. It was designed to test the hypothesis that 'the assumed efficiency of centralised project-based reconstruction tends to deny the importance of the culturally sensitive approach to reconstruction, built on the direct involvement of the local people'. The study contains a description of the earthquake in Dhamār and its consequences; lists the different emergency and reconstruction policy decisions and approaches adopted by the Yemeni government; discusses the author's fieldwork findings, focusing on factors which might have affected the local population's acceptance of the new housing settlements; and offers a number of recommendations, concerning methods of post-disaster intervention, and general reconstruction policies and their management.

46 **Zabîd: anti-développement et potentialités.** (Zabīd: anti-development and opportunities.)
Paul Bonnenfant. *Peuples Méditerranéens/Mediterranean Peoples,* nos. 72-73 (1995), p. 219-42.

A wide-ranging survey of the chief town of the Tihāmah, on the western coastal plain of North Yemen. The author looks briefly at the decrease in the historical importance of Zabīd as a religious centre, before moving on to the corresponding decline of its economy as traditional industries such as dyeing, weaving and pottery have been challenged by cheaper imported materials, and the agricultural base has been weakened by changes in irrigation, marketing and contractual arrangements. After a survey of the government and cooperative organizations created to further Zabīd's development, the author concludes with a look into the future, which he sees as paradoxically positive, since the relative decline in the city's fortunes has prevented the excesses of urban growth and has thus preserved many of the city's ancient monuments.

47 **Ṣanʿāʾ.**
Paolo M. Costa. In: *The Islamic city: selected papers from the Colloquium held at the Middle East Centre, Faculty of Oriental Studies, Cambridge, United Kingdom, from 19 to 23 July 1976.* Edited by R. B. Serjeant. Paris: UNESCO, 1980, p. 151-65.

After a historical survey of the various building phases through which Ṣanʿāʾ has passed since medieval times, the author concentrates on the period after 1962. He describes how 'the first stage of the pseudo-modernization of Ṣanʿāʾ [in the early 1960s] has disrupted the very neat and almost ideal layout of the town of the nineteenth century'. He goes on to show how collaboration between outside experts and the Yemeni government has begun to safeguard the artistic heritage of Ṣanʿāʾ, although he concludes by identifying eight sites where urgent action is required to prevent unsightly redevelopment.

48 **Der Markt von Ṣanʿāʾ.** (The market in Ṣanʿāʾ.)
Walter Dostal. Vienna: Verlag der Österreichischen Akademie der Wissenschaften, 1979. 121p. bibliog. (Veröffentlichungen der Arabischen Kommission, Band 1).

After a historical survey of the Ṣanʿāʾ market, the author moves on to analyse the results of the fieldwork he conducted in 1974, when he questioned 238 people who were active in the market. He investigates the family relationship of the shop and stall owners, the social classes involved, and he pays particular attention to the artisans and the tools they produce or sell. He concludes his study by examining the relationship between the market and its rural hinterland, and the characteristics which make Ṣanʿāʾ market unique in North Yemen.

49 **Development and urban metamorphosis: proceedings of Seminar eight in the series Architectural Transformations in the Islamic world, held in Sana'a, Yemen Arab Republic, May 25-30, 1983.**
Edited by Ahmet Evin. Singapore: Concept Media, 1983. 2 vols. (The Aga Khan Award for Architecture).

A most important collection of papers on urban geography, which deals with conservation, housing, the construction industry, earthquake protection, the co-operative movement and energy issues in the Yemen Arab Republic. Not only is architectural development in Ṣanʿāʾ fully covered, but individual papers also deal with the port cities of Hodeida and Mocha, and with nine separate highland towns. The comments of the discussants at the conference add interesting alternative views from those presenting the papers, while both volumes are well illustrated with black-and-white photographs.

50 **Sanaa hors les murs: une ville arabe contemporaine.** (Ṣanʿāʾ beyond the walls: a contemporary Arab city.)
Edited by Gilbert Grandguillaume, Franck Mermier, Jean-François Troin. Tours, France: URBAMA, Université de Tours; Ṣanʿāʾ: Centre Français d'Études Yéménites, 1995. 247p. (Collection Villes du Monde Arabe, no. 1).

After an introduction by Gilbert Grandguillaume to this collection of seven separate articles, Jean-François Troin looks at how Ṣanʿāʾ has coped with an increase in its population from 80,000 to 800,000 between 1970 and 1990. In other articles, Franck Mermier shows how the administration of Ṣanʿāʾ is divided between a formal centralizing state sector and an informal coalition of tribal groups and residents associations, Renaud Detalle compares the local elections of 1988 with those of 1993, while Jean Lambert studies social change and the institution of the afternoon *qāt* party. Jean-Charles Depaule describes how the inhabitants use the public space of Ṣanʿāʾ; Jean-Luc Arnaud considers the new private arcḥitecture of the city; and Nafissa Al-Weshali concludes the volume with a brief examination of the commercial centre of Ṣanʿāʾ and its markets.

51 **Saving Sanaʿa.**
Bahman Kia, Vivian Craddock Williams. *Geographical Magazine,* vol. 61, no. 5 (1989), p. 32-6.

A popular, illustrated article which describes UNESCO's Campaign for the Preservation of the Old City of Ṣanʿāʾ. It shows that modern technology is not always appropriate for ancient cities, and how it is essential to involve local planners in international projects.

52 **City of Ṣanʿāʾ.**
Edited by James Kirkman. London: World of Islam Festival Publishing Company, 1976. 83p. bibliog.

Designed to accompany the exhibition held at the Museum of Mankind in 1976 as part of the World of Islam Festival, this well-illustrated work is the result of collaboration between members of the British Museum staff and the University of Cambridge Middle East Centre. It covers important features of Ṣanʿānī society such as the house, the public baths, the mosque and the market from geographical, social and architectural points of view.

53 **Beiträge zur Stadtgeographie von Sana'a.** (Contributions to the urban geography of Ṣanʿāʾ.)
Horst Kopp, Eugen Wirth. Wiesbaden, Germany: Reichert, 1990. 97p. 4 maps. bibliog. (Beihefte zum Tübinger Atlas des Vorderen Orients, Reihe B, no. 95).

The authors put forward the theory that Ṣanʿāʾ assumed its unique architectural form during the second Ottoman occupation (1872-1918), as it was only during this period that the population of the city commanded the financial resources necessary for the rebuilding programme undertaken. The recent urban redevelopment is also studied, and contrasted with earlier division of space along tribal lines. Finally, the authors consider the role of the market and its relationship to the central business district of the city. The work is enhanced by black-and-white aerial photographs of Ṣanʿāʾ and its principal buildings.

54 **Die Erhaltung des Altstadtmarktes von Sanaa.** (The preservation of the old city market of Ṣanʿāʾ.)
Werner Lingenau. Wiesbaden, Germany: Reichert, 1993. 138p. 7 maps. bibliog. (Jemen-Studien, Band 12).

This work by an architect and town planner considers the best way to conserve the market in Ṣanʿāʾ. The author asserts that the revolution in 1962 and the subsequent rapid modernization led to an identity crisis among Yemenis, and, a clash between traditional self-governing guilds and the central government. The creation of a new central-government-controlled trading area in the Old City Market has soured relations between the traders and the city authorities, and the author looks at ways in which the two parties can work together most effectively, while preserving the historic buildings to the advantage of all.

55 **Sanaa: parcours d'une cité d'Arabie.** (Ṣanʿāʾ: journey through an Arabian city.)
Edited by Pascal Maréchaux. Paris: Institut du Monde Arabe, 1987. 127p.

Designed to accompany an exhibition held in Paris in 1987, this collective work looks at town planning, the market area, architecture, spatial divisions, and social life in the city. Compiled by several French experts on the Yemen, the book manages very effectively to give a flavour of what life is like in a traditional Arab city. There are numerous black-and-white photographs and an accompanying Arabic text.

56 **Ṣaʿda: Bauten und Bewohner in einer traditionellen islamischen Stadt.** (Ṣaʿdah: buildings and inhabitants in a traditional Islamic city.)
Elke Niewöhner-Eberhard. Wiesbaden, Germany: Reichert, 1985. 304p. map. (Beihefte zum Tübinger Atlas des Vorderen Orients, Reihe B, no. 64).

An important study of the largest town in the north of the Yemen Republic. After a detailed description of the domestic housing styles, the author goes on to survey the inhabitants and to classify them by profession, nationality, religion, length of stay in Ṣaʿdah, and social class. She goes on to conduct a detailed survey of each of the twelve quarters of Ṣaʿdah, then analyses the market, the mosques, the city walls and all the other public buildings, such as the baths, the warehouses and the schools. This is one of the most comprehensive descriptions we have for any Yemeni city apart from Ṣanʿāʾ, based on fieldwork stretching over a nine-year period.

57 **L'urbanisation du Yémen du Nord.** (The urbanization of North Yemen.)
Jean-Marc Prost-Tournier. *Maghreb Machrek*, vol. 81 (1978), p. 63-72.

A brief description of the major towns of North Yemen, concentrating on their modern development. More than half the article is devoted to Ṣanʿāʾ – its ancient quarters, the density of its population, and its style of architecture. The author goes into more detail on the Yemeni capital in his earlier article 'Sana'a: présentation de la capitale du Yémen' (Ṣanʿāʾ: a profile of the capital of Yemen), *Revue de Géographie de Lyon*, vol. 1, no. 4 (1975), p. 361-81.

58 **The Middle Eastern city: ancient traditions confront a modern world.**

Edited by Abdulaziz Y. Saqqaf. New York: Paragon House, 1987. 392p.

Three presentations in these conference proceedings deal with Ṣanʿāʾ. Ali Oshaish in 'Old Sanaʿa as an existing model for the Islamic city' argues that 'the old city of Sanaʿa is known to be one of the few Islamic cities that remained untouched and intact from the urban and architectural standpoints' and goes on to discuss the physical layout and urban plan of the medieval quarters of the city. In 'Sanaʿa Al-Qadeema: the challenges of modernization', Fritz Piepenburg surveys the damage wrought by rapid modernization, and analyses the efforts made by both foreign and Yemeni agencies to preserve the city's artistic heritage. 'Sanaʿa: a profile of a changing city' (Abdulaziz Y. Saqqaf) examines the interaction between old and new Ṣanʿāʾ and stresses the need to study the urbanization process in the whole city rather than any single part of it.

59 **Ṣanʿāʾ: an Arabian Islamic city.**

Edited by R. B. Serjeant, Ronald Lewcock. London: World of Islam Festival Trust, 1983. 631p. 9 maps. bibliog.

One of the most exhaustive studies of any Middle Eastern city, this lavishly illustrated work exemplifies the best in collaboration between Yemeni and Western scholars. It deals with most aspects of life in the city prior to the revolution of 1962, beginning with five chapters on the history of Ṣanʿāʾ from pre-Islamic times up to the eve of the modern city, to which section can be added 'Western accounts of Ṣanʿāʾ, 1510-1962' by R. L. Bidwell. Administrative and legal concerns dominate the next section, which is followed by chapters on the historical architecture of the market, the mint, the mosques, the public baths and the domestic architecture of the city (the longest chapter in the book). Social concerns are not neglected either, with chapters on the Jews of Ṣanʿāʾ, the Hindu traders there, the organization of the Yemeni mosque, and Ṣanʿānī dress, food and children's games. This is one of the most significant contributions to our knowledge on Yemen, based, as it is, on much fundamental pioneering research.

60 **Tribe, Hijrah and Madīnah in North-West Yemen.**

Shelagh Weir. In: *Middle Eastern cities in comparative perspective/Points de vue sur les villes du Maghreb et du Machrek: Franco-British symposium, London, 10-14 May, 1984.* Edited by Kenneth Brown (et al.). London: Ithaca Press, 1986, p. 225-39.

This paper describes a small settlement in the northern Yemeni highlands called by the author the Madīnah of al-Jabal. The settlement is known locally as a *Madīnah* (town) since it possesses a large market and mosque and as a *Ḥijrah* (protected settlement), since the most important families of the religious élite are under the protection of the local tribe. The paper traces the history of the tribal relationships and structures, and outlines the main geographical and political features, which have contributed to the rise of the Madīnah of al-Jabal as an important tribal market town.

61 **Les forces économiques et sociales de l'aménagement de Sana'a: transformations de la Médina et croissance périphérique d'une ville d'aspect médiéval.** (The economic and social factors affecting the development of Ṣan'ā': changes in the Medina and suburban growth in a medieval city.)

Eugen Wirth. In: *Politiques urbaines dans le monde arabe: table ronde C. N. R. S. tenue à Lyon du 17 au 20 novembre, 1982.* (Urban policies in the Arab world: C. N. R. S. round table held in Lyon from 17 to 20 November 1982.) Edited by F. Métral. Lyon, France: Maison de l'Orient, 1984, p. 451-9.

The author explains how feverish activity in the construction industry has led since 1969 to important economic changes in the city of Ṣan'ā'. Several major companies have moved out of the old city (the Medina) to the suburbs and the many of the warehouses *(samsarah)* in the inner city are crumbling. The water table in Ṣan'ā' has also been reduced, with the result that many wells which formerly supported small agricultural communities in the north of the city have now dried up. There appears to be a marked absence of urban planning or zoning by the city authorities.

Geology

62 **Seismicity of Yemen.**

N. N. Ambraseys, C. P. Melville. *Nature,* vol. 303, no. 5915 (May 1983), p. 321-3.

Using historical Arabic sources, the authors have been able to show that there has been 'a fairly continuous occurrence of medium magnitude, damaging shocks over the past 12 centuries, including a destructive event in 1941 that in many respects resembled the recent earthquake of December 1982'.

63 **Geology of the Arabian Peninsula: Eastern Aden Protectorate and part of Dhufar.**

Z. R. Beydoun. Washington, DC: US Government Printing Office, 1966. 49p. map. bibliog. (United States Geological Survey, Professional Paper, 560-H).

This account is divided into four parts: the first outlines previous geological investigations; the second discusses the geography of the area; the third describes the stratigraphy; and the fourth discusses the structure. A similar survey for the Western Aden Protectorate was carried out by Greenwood and Bleackley (see item no. 66).

64 **The Middle East: regional geology and petroleum resources.**
Z. R. Beydoun. Beaconsfield, England: Scientific Press, 1988. 292p. maps.

The first section of this textbook describes the stratigraphy and geological structure of the Middle East – including Yemen – in periodic order. The second part of the book looks at petroleum geology and offers a brief overview of the hydrocarbon finds made in both Yemens by the mid-1980s.

65 **The evolution of the volcanoes of Aden and Little Aden, South Arabia.**
K. G. Cox (et al.). *The Quarterly Journal of the Geological Society of London,* vol. 124, no. 4 (1969), p. 382-408.

A general survey of six central-vent volcanoes situated along the coast of southern Arabia, describing in detail the stratigraphy and lava flow from three volcanoes. The authors pursue further researches on the topic, including the introduction of a comparative dimension, in 'The peralkaline volcanoes of Aden and Little Aden, South Arabia', *Journal of Petrology*, vol. 11, no. 3 (1970), p. 433-61.

66 **Geology of the Arabian Peninsula: Aden Protectorate.**
J. E. G. W. Greenwood, D. Bleackley. Washington, DC: Government Printing Office, 1967. 96p. maps. bibliog. (United States Geological Survey, Professional Paper, 560-C).

As in the work on the Eastern Aden Protectorate by Beydoun (see item no. 63), this survey is divided into four parts. Part one discusses previous geological surveys, while Part two describes the general geographical features of the Western Aden Protectorate. The bulk of the work is devoted to a description of the stratigraphy and the geological structure of the region, with an interesting excursus on the mineral and hydro-geological resources of Aden and its hinterland.

67 **Geological and archaeological reconnaissance in the Yemen Arab Republic, 1985.**
William C. Overstreet, Maurice J. Grolier, Michael R. Toplyn. Washington, DC: American Foundation for the Study of Man, 1988. 505p. maps. bibliog. (The Wādī Al-Jubah Archaeological Project, no. 4).

The Wādī Al-Jubah Project (see item no. 257) was conceived in 1981 and is one of the most detailed archaeological investigations undertaken in Yemen in recent years. The Wādī itself lies near Marib and is rich in archaeological sites, with evidence of human habitation from Palaeolithic to modern times. This volume of the project is devoted to a geological analysis of the area and includes: 'Chemical and mineralogical investigations of silts'; 'Microbiological study of sediments'; 'Reconnaissance geology of the Al-Jubah Quadrangle'; 'Geomorphology of the Al-Jubah Quadrangle'; and 'Mineral resources of the Al-Jubah Quadrangle', as well as contributions about plant resources, gastropod remains, artefacts, and irrigation and landscape analysis.

Maps, atlases, gazetteers and historical geography

68 **Al-Yaman and the Hadramawt: translations from medieval Arabic geographers and analysis.**
Walter Bascom Bevens. PhD dissertation, University of Arizona, 1988. 185p. (Available from University Microfilms International, Ann Arbor, Michigan, order no. 8814209).

After an overview of Arabic geographical literature, and an introduction to the life and works of the seven Arab geographers studied, the author translates the passages relating to Yemen and South Arabia found in the works of Ibn Rustah (fl. 909-13), al-Ḥasan ibn Aḥmad al-Hamdānī (d. c. 945), Ibn Ḥawqal (d. c. 988), Ibn al-Faqīh al-Hamadhānī (fl. 903), Zakarīyā ibn Muḥammad al-Qazwīnī (d. 1283), Ibn Faḍl Allah al-ʿUmarī (d. 1349) and al-Qalqashandī (d. 1418). The main themes found in the geographers' works are physical geography (climate, landforms); economic geography (mines and mining, agriculture, wildlife, markets, trade routes, harbours); and historical geography (ancient monuments, fabled cities).

69 **The Cambridge Atlas of the Middle East & North Africa.**
Gerald Blake, John Dewdney, Jonathan Mitchell. Cambridge, England: Cambridge University Press, 1987. 124p. 58 maps. bibliog.

This is not a conventional atlas in the sense of defining where physical features are situated, but a topical atlas where each map deals with a particular subject and is accompanied by a page of text. The themes dealt with are: physical environment (vegetation, water, landscape); culture (historical developments, religions, literacy); demography; economy (agriculture, fishing, oil, minerals, tourism, trade); communications; and special topics. All the maps except the special topics give information on both Yemens.

70 **An historical atlas of Islam.**
Edited by William C. Brice, under the patronage of the Encyclopaedia of Islam. Leiden, The Netherlands: Brill, 1981. 71p. 51 maps.

This work covers the Middle East and India from the rise of Islam in the 7th century until the present day. Spain, Indonesia and China are included during the period of Muslim rule or expansion in their territories. The maps are neither particularly detailed nor comprehensive, and the only three examples which deal principally with the Arabian Peninsula show the area in Classical times, on the eve of Islam and the medieval pilgrim routes. Ṣanʿāʾ is shown on four maps and Mukallā on two.

71 **Handbook of Yemen.**
Compiled by K. Cornwallis, D. G. Hogarth. Neuchâtel, Switzerland: Archive International Group, 1988. 161p. (Military Handbooks of Arabia, 1913-1917, no. 2).

A facsimile reprint of the edition produced for the Arab Bureau, Cairo, and published by the Government Press, Cairo, in 1917. It provides details of districts and towns in North Yemen, often relying on the accounts of earlier travellers, plus descriptions of twelve routes between major settlements in the country. Additional chapters give information on physical geography, agriculture and industry, tribal organization, politics and leading personalities. The work was partially continued by *Gazetteer of Arabia*, by Sheila A. Scoville (see item no. 79).

72 **Historical atlas of the Middle East.**
G. S. P. Freeman-Grenville. New York: Simon & Schuster, 1993. 144p. 113 maps.

This atlas concentrates on the Middle East – there are few maps of India and none of Indonesia or Malaysia – from the earliest settlements to the Iraqi invasion of Kuwait in 1990. The maps are simply drawn in no more than two colours, but cover the ground more thoroughly than Brice (see item no. 70). Medieval Yemen is not particularly well served, except for trade maps (maps 68 and 69), but there are useful maps of European travellers to the Middle East (map 87) and the expansion of Saudi Arabia in the 20th century (map 88). The index is very misleading, with many individual towns being listed only on their first occurrence in the atlas, and some cities like Hodeida appear on several maps but are entirely absent from the index.

73 **Skizze der Geschichte und Geographie Arabiens von den ältesten Zeiten bis zum Propheten Muḥammad.** (A sketch of the history and geography of Arabia from the earliest times to the time of the Prophet Muḥammad.)
Eduard Glaser. Hildesheim, Germany: Olms, 1976. 575p.

A reprint of the edition published in Berlin in 1890, only the second volume of this work was ever published. In it, the author attempts to identify all the names used by classical authors and by biblical sources for the places and physical features of Arabia. His sources for this study are Arab geographers, travel literature, archaeological reports and the pioneering work of Aloys Sprenger, *Die alte Geographie Arabiens als Grundlage der Entwicklungsgeschichte des Semitismus* (The ancient geography of Arabia as a basis for determining the early history of the Semitic peoples) (Amsterdam, The Netherlands: Meridian Publishing, 1966. 343p. map. Reprint of edition published in Berne, Switzerland, 1875). Many places in Yemen feature in both works, but it is easier to track them down in Sprenger since Glaser's book has no index.

74 **Yemen Arab Republic: YAR 500 (K465.)**
Great Britain, Directorate of Overseas Surveys. London: HM Stationery Office, 1978. Scale: 1:500,000. 1 sheet.

A general topographical map, based on the more detailed but less accurate eight sheets of *The Yemen Arab Republic and surrounding areas* (London: HM Stationery Office, 1974. Scale: 1:250,000), produced by the British Ministry of Defence. The naming is based on the field collection of names by the Survey Department of the Yemen Arab Republic and other sources, and is a great improvement on the 1974 sheets. The map itself uses Universal Transverse Mercator grids in 10 km squares, and has sufficient contours (mainly at 500 m intervals) to show general landforms. Similar maps were produced on different scales by the Ministry of Defence for Aden, and the Eastern and Western Aden Protectorates, from the late 1950s to the mid-1960s, and have still to be superseded.

75 **Yemen Arab Republic: YAR 50.**

Great Britain, Ministry of Overseas Development. London: HM Stationery Office, 1979- . Scale: 1:50,000.

This series was produced for the Survey Department, Ministry of Public Works, Yemen Arab Republic. Each sheet covers an area of approximately 27 km by 27 km, and the Universal Transverse Mercator grid is shown at 1000 m intervals. Although the name collection has been restricted to places accessible by motor vehicle, the names of settlements are comprehensively and accurately recorded, but geographical features are less consistently shown, while the road-building programme of the 1980s has rendered obsolete many of the data on the road transport system.

76 **Geologic map of the Yemen Arab Republic (San^ca.)**

Maurice J. Grolier, William C. Overstreet. Reston, Virginia: US Geological Survey, 1978. Scale: 1:500,000. 1 sheet. (United States Geological Survey, Miscellaneous Investigations Series Map, 1-1143-B).

Based on Landsat imagery and 'miscellaneous source maps of the Yemen Arab Republic', this map shows the geological units as identified by the US Geological Survey and the Arabian American Oil Company (ARAMCO). Rock formations, anticlines and synclines, volcanoes, oil wells and mineral deposits are all clearly identified. A map showing geographical features was produced by the same team and publisher and issued in the same series as 1-1143-A.

77 **The maps of Carsten Niebuhr 200 years after.**

I. W. J. Hopkins. *Cartographic Journal,* vol. 4, no. 2 (1967), p. 115-18.

After an account of the expedition to Yemen in 1762-63, the author looks at Niebuhr's two general maps of Yemen. Both show latitude and relief, as well as streams and wadi beds, and both are quite rich in details of settlement along the route of the expedition, though less so outside the itinerary. Niebuhr also produced large-scale maps for certain localities in Yemen, such as Bayt al-Faqīh, as well as individual towns, such as Ṣanʿāʾ, Taʿizz and Laḥij. Although these may be inaccurate and not particularly well drawn, they are unique for their period. For Niebuhr's own account of his travels, see *Travels through Arabia . . .* (item no. 114).

78 **Economic coordinates of localities from Islamic sources.**

E. S. Kennedy, M. H. Kennedy. Frankfurt am Main, Germany: Institut für Geschichte der Arabisch-Islamischen Wissenschaften an der Johann-Wolfgang-Goethe-Universität, 1987. 723p. (Veröffentlichungen des Instituts für Geschichte des Arabisch-Islamischen Wissenschaften, Reihe A, Band 2).

This list of place-names in medieval Islamic times has been compiled from seventy-four sources, most of which are astronomical handbooks, or books of mathematical geography. Each place is identified by the latitude and longitude assigned to it by each geographer, and among the towns of Yemen to feature in the list are Ṣanʿāʾ, Taʿizz, Zabīd, Aden and Shibām while Hadramawt is treated as a region in its own right. There are also tables by astronomer and by latitude and longitude.

79 **Gazetteer of Arabia: a geographical and tribal history of the Arabian Peninsula. vol. 1: A–E; vol. 2: F–H.**

Sheila A. Scoville. Graz, Austria: Akademische Druck- u. Verlagsanstalt, 1979-85. 2 vols.

Designed as a revision and updating of the *Military Handbooks of Arabia, 1913-1917* series (see item no. 71), this work has progressed only to volume two. For most entries, the compiler has been able to confirm the form of the name from the relevant gazetteer published by the United States Board on Geographic Names (see items 82, 83), add the form of the name as found in Arabic script sources, and supply the geographical coordinates. Other information of a geographical, economic or social nature has been taken from the earlier gazetteers, from modern geographical works, and from the reports of consulting engineering and petroleum companies like ARAMCO. This is a fruitful and important source of information for geographers and historians.

80 **Arabia in early maps: a bibliography of maps covering the Peninsula of Arabia printed in Western Europe from the invention of printing to the year 1751.**

G. R. Tibbetts. Santa Maria la Bruna, Italy: Falcon Press; Cambridge, England: Oleander Press, 1978. 175p.

A list of several hundred maps of the Arabian Peninsula, both those published separately, and those found within atlases and works of travel. The bibliography begins in 1477 with the first edition of Ptolemy's Geography to be printed with maps, and ends in 1751, when D'Anville's map of Asia showed the Western world its ignorance of inland Arabia, which led in turn to the famous Danish expedition of 1761-67 led by Carsten Niebuhr (q.v.). Each map is thoroughly described bibliographically as well as cartographically, and twenty-two of them are illustrated (in colour, where appropriate).

81 **Tübinger Atlas des Vorderen Orients.** (Tübinger Atlas of the Near East.)

Edited by the Sonderforschungsbereich 19 of the University of Tübingen. Wiesbaden, Germany: Reichert, 1977-94. 3 vols. 295 sheets.

The largest project ever mounted in Middle Eastern cartography, this atlas contains 378 separate maps on 295 sheets plus a *Register zu den Karten/General Index* in three volumes, compiled by Beate Siewert-Mayer and others. Four maps deal with Yemen specifically (land use in al-Qāsim, and maps of Radāʿ, Ṣaʿdah and Ṣanʿāʾ), while several others cover the whole of the Arabian Peninsula, dealing with subjects like geomorphology, vegetation, hydrology and history. Yemen also features in the fifty-six general maps of the Middle East, which deal with a wide variety of topics, ranging from air temperature to traffic density.

82 **People's Democratic Republic of Yemen: official standard names gazetteer.**

Prepared by the United States Board on Geographic Names. Washington, DC: US Board on Geographic Names, 1976. 204p. map.

This gazetteer contains standard and variant names of population settlements, physical features and administrative divisions, together with precise locational references using latitude and longitude.

83 **Yemen Arab Republic: official standard names gazetteer.**
Prepared by the United States Board on Geographic Names.
Washington, DC: US Board on Geographic Names, 1976. 124p. map.

As with the *People's Democratic Republic of Yemen: official standard names gazetteer* (see item no. 82), this is the most comprehensive work available on population settlements, physical features and administrative divisions for North Yemen.

84 **A contribution to the geography and cartography of North-West Yemen (based on the results of the exploration of Eduard Glaser, undertaken in the years 1882-1884.)**
Josef Werdecker. *Bulletin de la Société Royale de Géographie d'Égypte,* vol. 20 (1939), p. 1-160.

In this book-length article, Werdecker uses the information contained in the manuscript copy of Glaser's *Geographische Forschungen in Yemen* (Geographical explorations in Yemen) to create a map of the area extending northwards of Ṣanʿāʾ as far as Ṣaʿdah. In addition to the map, the author also supplies a detailed description of Glaser's journeys, a biography of the explorer, one of the fullest ever surveys of previous travellers to Yemen and a complete (if still partially inaccurate) list of all the places which appear on the map together with their geographical coordinates.

85 **Gazetteer of historical North-West Yemen in the Islamic period to 1650.**
Robert T. O. Wilson. Hildesheim, Germany: Olms, 1989. 374p.

This gazetteer provides some 900 entries on place-names mentioned in Yemeni Arabic texts and pre-Islamic inscriptions in an area extending approximately 100 km north and west of Ṣanʿāʾ. The information has been derived from the various geographical texts and several extensive field trips. Entries are listed in transcription in Arabic alphabetical order with a standard grid reference, current administrative area, date when first mentioned and notes and references. The introduction, in five chapters, examines the physical geography of the area covered, the works of al-Ḥasan ibn Aḥmad al-Hamdānī (d. c. 945) and his geographical method, the use of Yemeni historical texts as geographical sources, and the development of the modern cartography of Yemen since the 18th century.

86 **Beiträge zur historischen Geographie des vorislamischen Südarabien.** (Contributions to the historical geography of pre-Islamic South Arabia.)
Hermann von Wissmann, Maria Höfner. *Abhandlungen der Geistes- und Sozialwissenschaftlichen Klasse, Akademie der Wissenschaften und der Literatur zu Mainz,* no. 4 (1952), p. 221-385.

A detailed updating, taking account of the work of modern travellers and scholars, of the work of Glaser and Sprenger (see item no. 73). Hundreds of toponyms mentioned in classical and medieval sources are identified and placed on the accompanying folded map.

87 **A new map of Southern Arabia.**

Hermann von Wissmann. *Geographical Journal,* vol. 124 (1958), p. 163-7.

Based on Wissmann's journeys with Dan van der Meulen (see items 175, 177) between 1931 and 1939, with additional information up to 1951, this article is designed to introduce Wissmann's map of *Southern Arabia* (see below). R. B. Serjeant contributes an appendix on 'The problem of the place names', where he deals with the divergence of the local dialect from classical Arabic, and provides a list of technical topographical terms prevalent in Hadramawt.

88 **Southern Arabia.**

Compiled by Hermann von Wissmann, rendering and partial correction of the place-names prepared by R. B. Serjeant. London: Royal Geographical Society, 1958. Scale: 1:500,000. 2 sheets.

This map covers the area from Shuqrā᾿ and Bayḥān in the west to Shiḥr and Hadramawt in the east. Geographical features as well as settlements are shown.

Archäologische Berichte aus dem Yemen. (Archaeological reports from Yemen.)

See item no. 227.

The Middle Eastern city and Islamic urbanism.

See item no. 923.

Travel Guides

89 **Hadramaut: Geschichte und Gegenwart einer südarabischen Landschaft.** (Hadramawt: the history and present state of a South Arabian landscape.)
Karl-Heinz Bochow, Lothar Stein. Munich, Germany: Verlag Ludwig Simon, 1986. 191p.

One of the few travel guides to South Yemen, this book is short on practical information (flights, internal communications, hotels) and strong on atmosphere and photographs.

90 **Voyage en Arabie Heureuse: le Yémen.** (Journey in Arabia Felix: the Yemen.)
Jalel Bouagga. Paris: Peuples du Monde et Itinérances, 1988. 304p. (Domaine Maghreb Proche-Orient).

A detailed guide to North Yemen by a Tunisian ethnologist who has spent many years in the country. There are numerous illustrations and architectural line-drawings, plus knowledgeable introductions to Yemeni society, architecture and history, and a final section on hotels, transport and travel agencies.

91 **Discovery guide to Yemen.**
Chris Bradley. London: Immel Publishing, 1995. 366p. maps.

A very detailed and up-to-date guide by someone who has clearly travelled over the whole of the united country. There are numerous diagrams illustrating the major towns, information about hotels and restaurants (although not much at budget prices) and some historical and archaeological background. The guide is well illustrated, but the pictures are not allowed to swamp the text.

92 **Yemen.**
Edited by Joachim Chwaszcza. Singapore: APA Publications, 1992. 2nd ed. 331p. (Insight Guides).

A very good guide compiled by a team of specialists including Werner Daum, Fritz Piepenburg, Joke Buringa and Werner Lingenau. This well-illustrated guide to both the northern and southern parts of the Yemen Republic contains informative chapters on the history of Yemen, the importance of Islam, social customs and dress, and 'travel tips'.

93 **Yémen.** (The Yemen.)
Claudie Fayein. Paris: Seuil, 1975. 188p. (Petite Planète, no. 49).

The author, a French doctor and long-time resident of North Yemen, here mingles personal reminiscences and intimate knowledge of the country with a guide to both the Yemen Arab Republic and the People's Democratic Republic of Yemen. There are numerous interesting insights into the relationship between the two states and many other matters interspersed in the text.

94 **Yémen.** (Yemen.)
Emmanuel Giroud. Paris: Arthaud, 1996. 260p. maps. (Guides Arthaud/Grands Voyages).

A serious and scholarly guide to both North and South Yemen for French-speaking travellers. The substantial introduction covers economic affairs, society, and culture and the arts as well as history, and the touristic excursions are well described. The sections on practical information deal with health problems, transport within Yemen, and accommodation, and are reasonably up to date.

95 **Yemen: a Lonely Planet travel survival kit.**
Pertti Hämäläinen. Hawthorn, Victoria, Australia: Lonely Planet Publications, 1996. 3rd ed. 240p. maps.

This is one of the best guides for the independent traveller, and one of only two (the other is by Chris Bradley (see item no. 91)) to incorporate the changes resulting from unification (and the civil war of 1994) which have affected the whole country, and South Yemen in particular. There are precise directions for sight-seeing, back-packing and finding the recommended hotels.

96 **Yemen: invitation to a voyage in Arabia Felix.**
Jacques Hébert. Ottowa, Canada: Azal Publications, 1989. 140p.

A description of the peregrinations of a professional travel writer around North Yemen. There are excellent colour photographs, some historical background and considerable local colour. The book is also available in French (*Yémen: invitation au voyage en Arabie Heureuse*), and German (*Jemen: Einladung zu einer Reise nach Arabia Felix*).

97 **Jemen: Nord-Jemen, Süd-Jemen, Djibouti.** (Yemen: North Yemen, South Yemen, Djibouti.)
Gerhard Heck, Manfred Wöbcke. Hattorf, Germany: Schettler Publikationen, 1985. 265p. maps.

A good guide, full of useful information, geared to the needs of German tourists.

98 **Yemen rediscovered.**
Michael Jenner. London; New York: Longman, 1983. 160p.

Produced in conjunction with the Yemen Tourist Company, this is a lavishly illustrated, armchair tour of both Yemens, which includes three brief chapters on history, one on exploration and one on travelling in Yemen.

99 **New traveller's guide to Yemen.**
Fritz Piepenburg. Ṣanʿāʾ: Yemen Tourist Company, 1987. 146p.

This replaces the *Traveller's guide to Yemen* produced in 1983. It begins with an overview of Yemeni customs, moves on to history and architecture, before reaching the central section on 'Major sightseeing tours in Yemen', which offers itineraries in and around the centres of Ṣanʿāʾ, Taʿizz, Hodeida, Marib, Ṣaʿdah, Aden, and Mukallā and the Hadramawt. The guide concludes with a rather scanty section on useful practical information on both North and South Yemen.

100 **Yemen.**
Peter Wald, translated from the German by Sebastian Wormell. London: Pallas Guides, 1996. 332p.

Translated from the sixth German edition (*Der Jemen.* Cologne, Germany: DuMont Verlag, 1992. 355p.), this is a very thorough cultural guide to the archaeological, historical, architectural and artistic riches of the two Yemens. Very well illustrated with photographs, drawings and maps, the work's main weaknesses are the limited nature of the practical information about hotels and internal communications, and the fact that the text has not been updated to take account of recent political and social developments. For the archaeologist and historian, however, this is an indispensable vade-mecum.

Travellers' Accounts and Exploration

General

101 **Travellers in Arabia.**

R. L. Bidwell. London: Hamlyn, 1976. 224p.

Devotes a chapter to Niebuhr's (q.v.) expedition of 1762-77 which explored Yemen from a scientific point of view, and one to 'Travellers in South-West Arabia', which deals with both North and South Yemen and Socotra. Bidwell's survey is by no means comprehensive, but he has an eye for the telling phrase and is familiar with the country over which these travellers ventured, which lends his judgements considerable authority.

102 **Far Arabia: explorers of the myth.**

Peter Brent. London: Weidenfeld and Nicolson, 1977. 239p. map.

A much more detailed survey than Bidwell's (see above), and one which focuses on the more colourful travellers in Arabia. A chapter is devoted to Niebuhr, and several pages to the Bents, von Wrede and Philby (all qq.v.) among visitors to South Arabia, but there is no mention of Glaser, Halévy or the Ingrams, and only a few lines about Freya Stark (qq.v.).

103 **Le Yémen dans les écrits des voyageurs d'Hérodote à l'anthropologie moderne.** (Yemen in the writings of travellers from Herodotus to modern anthropology.)

Radhi Daghfous. *Cahiers de Tunisie,* vols. 27-28, nos. 145-148 (1988-89), p. 43-82.

A survey of travel writing on Yemen, set in the context of the country's historical development. The author begins with the Greek geographers, passes on to medieval Muslim geographers and travellers such as Muḥammad ibn ʿAbd Allāh Ibn Baṭṭūṭah (d. 1368 or 1377) (q.v.), and finishes with the major European contributions up to and including the archaeological expeditions of the 1980s. This article is useful as a starting point for further research both for its extensive time-span and its inclusion of many modern non-English-speaking travellers and explorers.

104 **Jemen – zwischen Reisebeschreibung und Feldforschung: ein Beitrag zum Begriff der Erfahrung in der Ethnologie.** (Yemen – between travel narrative and field study: a contribution to the concept of experience in ethnology.)
Tawfiq Dawani. Berlin: Baalbek Verlag, 1987. 156p. (Studien zum Modernen Islamischen Orient, Band 4).

The author, a Palestinian Christian Arab, investigates how the ethnographer can combine personal experience with the objective analysis of his subject. After a conceptual introduction dealing with ideas such as 'participatory observation', the author compares the experiences of five German travellers to Yemen in the eighteenth and nineteenth centuries (Niebuhr, Ulrich-Jaspar Seetzen, von Wrede, Siegfried Langer and Hermann von Burchardt), with his own fieldwork in the Yemen Arab Republic village of Riṣābah.

105 **Aden in history: an account of Aden as recorded by visitors in the past.**
D. B. Doe. Aden, Yemen Republic: Government Printer, 1965. 26p.

Beginning with Ibn al-Mujāwir (d. 1291), the author recounts the early descriptions of the fortifications, the water tanks and the buildings of Aden. Among authors he discusses are well-known visitors such as Albuquerque, Varthema, Haines and Wellsted (qq.v.) as well as less famous ones such as John Jourdain and de Merville.

106 **The penetration of Arabia: a record of the development of Western knowledge concerning the Arabian Peninsula.**
David George Hogarth. London: Alston Rivers, 1905. 358p.

Based on wide reading in the major European languages, Hogarth's book was an excellent summary of the state of the explorer's art at the turn of the century. He describes with a critical eye the journeys of not only the well-known travellers to Yemen and the Hadramawt such as Niebuhr and Wellsted (qq.v.), but also those like J. B. Haines, Charles Cruttenden and Paul Émile Botta, who may not have been great explorers, but whose writings have added to the sum of our knowledge of South-West Arabia. There are good illustrations to the text, but the work does suffer overall from a lack of maps. This is remedied to some extent in *The unveiling of Arabia: the story of Arabian travel and discovery* (R. H. Kiernan. London: Harrap, 1937. 360p. maps), which has reasonable maps and which updates Hogarth's book in the chapter on 'Twentieth century explorers' (but without mentioning the Ingrams [q.v.]).

107 **À la découverte de l'Arabie: cinq siècles de science et d'aventure.** (On the tracks of Arabia: five centuries of science and adventure.)
Jacqueline Pirenne. Paris: Le Livre Contemporain, 1958. 328p. maps.

A good account of Arabian exploration, which covers the major figures until 1870, although some later 19th-century travellers in Yemen such as Glaser and Halévy (qq.v.) are mentioned in passing.

Early and medieval Islamic period (7th-18th centuries)

108 **The commentaries.**

Afonso d'Albuquerque, translated from the Portuguese by Walter de Gray Birch. New York: Burt Franklin, 1970. 4 vols. (Hakluyt Society, first series, vols. 53, 55, 62, 69).

A reprint of the edition published by the Hakluyt Society in London in 1880-84. Afonso d'Albuquerque was one of the greatest Portuguese admirals, who, en route to Goa in 1507, sent Tristão da Cunha to Socotra. His visit there and his encounter with the 'native Christians' is described in the first volume of Albuquerque's memoirs, collected after his death in 1515 by his son Pero. The attack of the Portuguese fleet on Aden, and its subsequent exploration of the Red Sea coast as far as Yanbuʿ (in present-day Saudi Arabia) in 1513 is recounted in considerable detail in volume four, where Aden is said to contain 'very beautiful houses, very lofty, all made of stone and mortar'.

109 **Between Islam and Christendom: travellers, facts and legends in the Middle Ages and the Renaissance.**

C. F. Beckingham. London: Variorum Reprints, 1983. 326p.

A collection of twenty-five articles which Beckingham published between 1949 and 1981. While quite a number touch on travel in Yemen and South Arabia, the most important are, firstly, 'Some early travels in Arabia', which describes real and supposed Arabian travellers in the sixteenth century, such as the fictitious Arnold von Harff and John Cabot and the genuine Pero da Covilha, Alvaro de Castro, the Jesuits Páez and Montserrat (see also item no. 110) and Antonio de Almeida and, secondly, the two-part 'Dutch travellers in Arabia in the seventeenth century', which translates three extracts from the journal of Pieter van den Broeke, describing his visits to Aden, Shiḥr, Socotra, Taʿizz, Ṣanʿāʾ and Mokha in the years 1614, 1616 and 1620 and charts the decline of the Dutch trade with Yemen in the 1620s, until the Dutch East India Company abandoned its efforts to establish a permanent factory in Arabia in 1629.

110 **A journey by two Jesuits from Dhufar to Ṣanʿāʾ in 1590.**

C. F. Beckingham, R. B. Serjeant. *Geographical Journal,* 115 (1950), p. 194-207.

A translation of chapters 15 to 21 of Pedro Páez's *Historia de Ethiopia*, which narrates the journey of Páez and his fellow Jesuit, Antonio de Montserrat, from Dhofar through the Wādī Ḥaḍramawt to Marib and Ṣanʿāʾ as prisoners of the Arabs. At the time the authors wrote their article, Helfritz (q.v.) was the only other European who claimed to have reached Ṣanʿāʾ by this route. Páez was a shrewd observer and his narrative is of considerable historical interest, much enhanced by the excellent critical commentary.

111 **Arabia Felix: the Danish expedition of 1761-1767.**
Thorkild Hansen, translated from the Danish by James and Kathleen McFarlane. London: Collins, 1964. 381p. map. bibliog.

A detailed account of the ill-fated Danish scientific expedition to Yemen to collect specimens of plants and animals as well as Islamic manuscripts. Only Carsten Niebuhr (q.v.) survived and the tale of misfortunes and disasters as well as considerable fortitude is well told. The section when the expedition reached its goal of Yemen, their explorations there, and the dissensions among the team and the deaths of most of them, appear on pages 212-303.

112 **The travels of Ibn Battuta, A. D. 1325-1345.**
Muḥammad ibn ʿAbd Allāh Ibn Baṭṭūṭah (d. 1368 or 1377). Translated by H. A. R. Gibb, C. F. Beckingham. Cambridge, England; London: Hakluyt Society, 1958-94. 4 vols. (Hakluyt Society, second series, vols. 110, 117, 141, 178).

The Muslim world's most famous traveller whose twenty years of travel took him from his home in Morocco to China, India, Ceylon, the Maldives, South-East Asia, Central Asia, Iran, Afghanistan, the Middle East, North Africa, Sardinia, Spain and East and West Africa. On his third journey around 1331 (found in volume two of the translation), he visited Yemen and South Arabia, and found that the women of Zabīd were 'virtuous and generous in character' and possessed 'exceeding beauty', that Aden was 'an exceedingly hot place and is the port of the merchants of India', and that the city of Ẓafārī, to which he returned after an excursion to East Africa had 'one of the dirtiest, most stinking and fly-ridden of bazaars'. His historical and ethnographic observations, although laced with fantastic stories, are valuable raw material for the historian and geographer, as well as being a very entertaining read.

113 **Arab navigation in the Indian Ocean before the coming of the Portuguese, being a translation of Kitāb al-Fawā'id fī uṣūl al-baḥr wa'l-qawā'id.**
Aḥmad ibn Mājid al-Najdī (fl 1460-90), translated by G. R. Tibbetts. London: Royal Asiatic Society, 1981. 614p. maps. (Oriental Translation Fund, new series, vol. 42).

Ibn Mājid was one of the greatest Arab navigators of the Middle Ages, and an author of numerous works in both prose and verse. The *Fawā'id* is his most extensive work and deals with the principles of navigation, including lunar mansions, and the sea-routes of the Indian Ocean. There are numerous references in it to Aden, Socotra and Shiḥr, rather fewer to Mukallā, Hodeida and Mocha, and the book as a whole is a summation of the knowledge of medieval Arab seafarers. The translator provides a wealth of biographical and topographical notes. Previously, he had summarized the information given by Ibn Mājid and his near contemporary Sulaymān al-Mahrī (d. before 1553) regarding navigation and commerce in the Red Sea, Gulf of Aden and Persian Gulf in two articles, 'Arab navigation in the Red Sea', *Geographical Journal,* vol. 127 (1961) p. 322-34; and 'Arabia in the fifteenth-century navigational texts', *Arabian Studies,* vol. 1 (1974), p. 86-101.

114 **Travels through Arabia and other countries in the East.**
Carsten Niebuhr, translated from the German by Robert Heron.
Beirut: Librairie du Liban, [c. 1968]. 2 vols.

A facsimile reprint of the edition published in Edinburgh, in 1792, this is Niebuhr's own account of the ill-fated expedition to Yemen of 1761-67. The expedition visited numerous towns in North Yemen such as Ṣanʿāʾ, Taʿizz, Bayt al-Faqīh and Mocha, and these are described in sections eight to fifteen of volume one, including the author's audience with the Imam. Volume two contains all the information that the expedition could discover about Yemen, Hadramawt and Oman, including the disposition of the Imam's military forces, 'on the religion and character of the Arabs', 'on the language and science of the Arabians', and on the agriculture, tribal society and natural history of the region. For more information on the expedition, the reader should consult Thorkild Hansen (see item no. 111) and the books by Stig Rasmussen (see items 115, 166).

115 **Den Arabiske Rejse, 1761-1767: en dansk ekspedition set i vitenskabshistorisk perspectiv.** (The Arabian journey, 1761-67: a Danish expedition set in its scientific and historical perspective.)
Edited by Stig Rasmussen. Copenhagen: Munksgaard, 1990. 413p.

The ultimate word on the Danish expedition to Yemen of 1761-67, this book contains a series of articles describing and evaluating the scientific results of Niebuhr (q.v.) and his companions. It covers numerous fields: botany; zoology; geography; cartography; bibliography; and philology, and the text is much enhanced by more than 150 excellent illustrations, which include facsimiles of Niebuhr's maps, and beautiful reproductions of the engravings of flowers and sea creatures collected by Petrus Forskål (q.v.), and published after his death by Niebuhr in 1776.

116 **Carsten Niebuhr und die Arabische Reise, 1761-1767: Ausstellungen der Königlichen Bibliothek Kopenhagen, Landesbibliothek Kiel, November 1986-Februar 1987.** (Carsten Niebuhr and the Arabian journey, 1761-67: exhibition of the Royal Library, Copenhagen held at the Landesbibliothek, Kiel, November 1986 to February 1987.)
Compiled by Stig Rasmussen. Heide in Holstein, Germany: Boyens, 1986. 132p.

The exhibition contains seventy-nine exhibits, mainly books and specimens, but also includes personal objects belonging to Niebuhr himself, such as his tea caddy. The introduction sets the expedition in its scientific context, describes the vicissitudes which befell its members, and attempts to evaluate its significance.

117 **Ibn al-Mujāwir on Dhofar and Socotra.**
G. R. Smith. *Proceedings of the Seminar on Arabian Studies,* vol. 15 (1985), p. 79-91.

Ibn al-Mujāwir (d. 1291) was a businessman, who travelled widely in the western and southern parts of the Arabian Peninsula and beyond, and whose endless fascination with people and their social customs is recorded in his *Tārīkh al-mustabṣir.* Professor Smith has translated and annotated various extracts from this work, all of which are important contributions to our knowledge of medieval Arab society in South Arabia. This article deals with Hadramawt as well as Dhofar and Socotra, and further contributions in the same vein are: 'Ibn al-Mujāwir's 7th/13th-century Arabia: the wondrous and the humorous' (in: *A miscellany of Middle Eastern articles: in memoriam Thomas Muir Johnstone, 1924-83.* Edited by A. K. Irvine, R. B. Serjeant, G. R. Smith. London: Longman, 1988, p. 111-24); 'Some anthropological passages from Ibn al-Mujāwir's guide to Arabia and their proposed interpretations' (in: *Studies in Oriental culture and history: Festschrift for Walter Dostal.* Edited by André Gingrich (et al.). Frankfurt am Main, Germany: Peter Lang, 1993, p. 160-71); and 'Magic, jinn and the supernatural in medieval Yemen: examples from Ibn al-Muğāwir's 7th/13th century guide' (*Quaderni di studi arabi,* vol. 13 (1995), p. 7-18). Other essays, listed in Professor Smith's collected articles on Yemen (see item no. 363), deal with Ibn al-Mujāwir's name, life, travels and style.

118 **The travels of Ludovico de Varthema in Egypt, Syria, Arabia Deserta and Arabia Felix, in Persia, India, and Ethiopia, A.D. 1503 to 1508.**

Ludovico de Varthema, translated from the Italian by John Winter Jones, edited by George Percy Badger. New York: Burt Franklin, [1970]. 321p. map. (Hakluyt Society, first series, vol. 32).

A reprint of the edition published by the Hakluyt Society in 1864. Little is known about Varthema beyond the fact that his father was a physician and came from Bologna. He was the first European to visit Yemen, landing at Aden, and being immediately arrested and detained in the Sultan's prison. He tried to gain his liberty by pretending to be mad ('truly, I have never found myself so wearied or so exhausted as during the first three days that I feigned madness'), but was eventually released through the intervention of one of the Sultan's wives. He then visited Laḥij, Ṣanʿāʾ, Taʿizz, Zabīd and Dhamār, describing the latter three as 'very large cities' before leaving for Ethiopia via Aden, which he called 'the strongest city that ever was seen on level ground'.

19th and early 20th centuries (1800-1919)

119 **Relation d'un voyage à Mareb (Saba) dans l'Arabie Méridionale entrepris en 1843.** (Narrative of a journey to Marib in South Arabia, undertaken in 1843.)

Thomas Joseph Arnaud. *Journal Asiatique,* 4e série, vol. 5 (1845), p. 208-45, 309-435.

In 1843 Arnaud accompanied a Turkish delegation from Jedda to Ṣanʿāʾ. Once there, he decided to visit Marib and, after five days' march, he became the first European to set foot in the ancient capital. He also visited the chief of the ʿAbīdah tribe, who put him under his protection, which enabled him to visit the ruins of Maḥram Bilqīs and Ṣirwāḥ (al-Kharībah) during his return to Ṣanʿāʾ. His manuscript copies of fifty-six

Travellers' Accounts and Exploration. 19th and early 20th centuries (1800-1919)

Sabaean inscriptions formed the first collection of importance from the region and laid the foundations for the study of South Arabian epigraphy. In 1847, Arnaud together with another Frenchman, Vaissière, explored the Tihāmah from their base in Hodeida and wrote an important article about the lowest social class in Yemen, the *Akhdām,* whom they compared to the lowest stratum of the Hindu castes: 'Les Akhdam de l'Yémen, leur origine probable, leurs moeurs' (The *akhdām* of Yemen: their probable origin and their customs) (*Journal Asiatique,* 4e série, vol. 15 (1850), p. 376-87).

120 **Southern Arabia.**

Theodore Bent, Mrs. Theodore Bent. Reading, England: Garnet, 1994. 455p. 3 maps.

A reprint of the edition published in London in 1900 with the addition of a useful introduction by R. L. Bidwell, this is a most important early account of travels around the Red Sea and South Arabia in the years 1893-94. The authors' first journey into the interior of Hadramawt took them from Mukallā to Shibām, where they were received by the Sultan, and back to the coast at Shiḥr, while their second, in 1897, took in the island of Socotra and the Faḍlī country inland of Shuqrā' on the mainland. Their observations encompass language (they include a word-list of Mahri, Socotri, and South Arabian Arabic), topography, ethnography, local politics and natural history and their book includes the first photographs of the Hadramawt and its inhabitants.

121 **Arabia Infelix, or the Turks in Yamen.**

G. Wyman Bury. London: Macmillan, 1915. 213p.

The value of this book lies not so much in the description of the Hodeida to Ṣanʿāʾ road and Ṣanʿāʾ itself (Bury does not seem to have ventured to other towns), but his knowledge of conditions in Ottoman Yemen. There are estimates of population and trade, assessments of agricultural production, and some rather generalized observations on the nature of Turkish rule, and Yemeni social customs and the character of the people.

122 **The land of Uz.**

Abdullah Mansûr (G. Wyman Bury). London: Macmillan, 1911. 354p. map.

The author participated in the Boundary Commission which explored and demarcated the frontier between Aden and its Protectorate and Ottoman Yemen in 1902-3. In this book, he describes his experiences with the Commission, and his subsequent journeys among tribes outside the sway of British rule such as the ʿAwlaqīs, Bayḥān and Dathīnah. His interest as a sportsman in the fauna of the country is very evident, but he also discusses the physical landscape and agricultural production.

123 **Narrative of a journey from Mokhá to Sanʿá by the Ṭaríḳ-esh-Shám, or Northern route, in July and August, 1836.**

Charles Cruttenden. *Journal of the Royal Geographical Society,* vol. 8 (1838), p. 267-89.

The author, one of the crew of the *Palinurus* like Haines and Wellsted (qq.v.), had previously tried to reach Ṣanʿāʾ from Aden. His second attempt at visiting the Imam's capital from Mocha via Taʿizz and Dhamār was frustrated by 'the intestine feuds of the Bedawí sheïkhs'. His third attempt, dressed in native costume and accompanied by the *Palinurus'* surgeon, Dr Hulton, was successful and the couple travelled via Zabīd and Bayt al-Faqīh to Ṣanʿāʾ without too much trouble. The author was interested in all aspects of Yemeni life, which he often compared to his experiences in Socotra, and provides us with interesting descriptions of various varieties of coffee, of the character of the Imam ('much addicted to drinking spirits'), and the various groups inhabiting Ṣanʿāʾ. The author's expressed desire to visit Marib excited the Imam's suspicions, and, after having been confined to quarters, the couple were permitted to leave for Mocha, which they reached fourteen days later.

124 **Eduard Glaser – Forschungen im Yemen: eine quellenkritische Untersuchung in ethnologischer Sicht.** (Eduard Glaser – explorations in Yemen: a critical study of the sources from an ethnological point of view.)
Walter Dostal. Vienna: Verlag der Österreichischen Akademie der Wissenschaften, 1990. 246p. (Veröffentlichungen der Arabischen Kommission, no. 4).

Using Glaser's unpublished diaries as well as the printed texts of his expeditions, Dostal examines the Austrian scholar's journeys to Arḥab (1884) and Marib (1888) (see below) from a social-anthropological viewpoint. After tracing Glaser's life and setting his journeys in the context of contemporary political and social relations in Yemen, particularly regarding the position of the stranger, Dostal analyses Glaser's dealing with the tribesmen he met during his travels. Two particular issues, matrilineal succession and customary law, are dealt with in separate appendices. The author commented on actual extracts from Glaser's diaries in *Ethnographica Jemenica: Auszüge aus den Tagebüchern Eduard Glasers mit einem Kommentar versehen* (Ethnographica Yemenica: extracts from the diaries of Eduard Glaser with commentary) (Vienna: Verlag der Österreichischen Akademie der Wissenschaften, 1993. 276p. [Veröffentlichungen der Arabischen Kommission, no. 5]).

125 **Eduard Glasers Reise nach Mârib.** (Eduard Glaser's expedition to Marib.)
Eduard Glaser, edited by David Heinrich Müller, N. Rhodokanakis. Vienna: Hölder, 1913. 215p. maps.

This work was edited after Glaser's death from his notebooks by his academic arch-enemy David Heinrich Müller. The work describes Glaser's expedition in 1888 to collect South Arabian inscriptions from the ancient site of Marib to the east of Ṣanʿāʾ in North Yemen, and, apart from archaeological information, contains valuable data on the climate and the ethnography of the region. There are numerous appendices about previous travellers, tribal relations, the famous Marib dam, and much else.

126 **My journey through Arḥab and Ḥāshid.**
Eduard Glaser, translated by David Warburton, introduction by Daniel Martin Varisco. Westbury, New York: American Institute for Yemeni Studies, 1993. 31p. (Yemen Translation Series, no. 1).

This short work is a translation of an article in German in *Petermanns Mitteilungen* (vol. 30, 1884, p. 204-13), which describes Glaser's visit to the central highlands north of Ṣanʿāʾ in 1884. One of the most valuable aspects of the article according to the author of the introduction is 'the light it sheds on the disputes between the two rival tribal confederations of Ḥāshid and Bakīl, and how both of these tribes interacted with the Ottomans', while another 'valuable contribution' is the 'description of Yemeni dialect and customs'. The article concludes with a full bibliography of works by and about Glaser and a detailed topographical index.

127 **Travels in Yemen: an account of Joseph Halévy's journey to Najrān in the year 1870 written in Ṣanʿānī Arabic by his guide Hayyim Habshush.**

Edited by S. D. Goitein. Jerusalem: Hebrew University Press, 1941. 102p. (English text) and 138p. (Arabic text in Hebrew characters).

Joseph Halévy visited Najrān on the borders on North Yemen in 1870 and from there went to Marib and Ṣanʿāʾ. He left two descriptions of his journey (see item no. 130), but neither is complete. His supposed guide, the Ṣanʿānī Jew, Ḥayyīm Ḥabshūsh, wrote down his memories of the expedition in the 1890s after he had accompanied Eduard Glaser (q.v.) on several of his journeys through Yemen in search of inscriptions. The editor here provides an edition of the text, and a full annotated synopsis in English, along with a glossary of vernacular words. The narrative itself concentrates on four themes: tribal society, with its raids, battles and intense rivalry; archaeological and epigraphic finds; historical anecdotes about Yemen; and, above all, information about Yemeni Jews.

128 **Immagine dello Yemen.** (A picture of Yemen.)

Hayyim Habšūš (Ḥayyīm Ḥabshūsh), translated by Gabriella Moscato Steindler. Naples, Italy: Istituto Orientale di Napoli, 1976. 167p.

The first full translation into a Western language of Ḥabshūsh's description of Joseph Halévy's travels in 1870. In it, there are discussions of customary law among the bedouin, political events of the time, and the condition of Yemeni Jewry, as well as a straightforward travel narrative. In the introduction, the translator goes into the question of the authenticity of Ḥabshūsh's story, and effectively demolishes Philby's (q.v.) claim that Ḥabshūsh was not Halévy's guide and companion. A recent translation in French has appeared by Samia Naïm-Sanbar, entitled *Yémen* (Arles, France: Actes Sud, 1995. 200p.).

129 **Memoir to accompany a chart of the South coast of Arabia from the entrance of the Red Sea to Misenát, in 50 43′ 25″ E.**

S. B. Haines. *Journal of the Royal Geographical Society*, vol. 9 (1839), p. 125-56.

The record of a survey carried out by the Royal Navy vessel *Palinurus* off the coast of South Arabia. Haines was naturally interested in the nature of the coast, safe anchorages, and any sources of fresh water, but he also acquired information about the political situation of any inhabited areas. Aden, mentioned by earlier travellers like Varthema (q.v.) as a strongly fortified port, was described as 'a ruined village of 600 persons' of whom '250 are Jews, 50 Banians, and the rest Arabs'. A second article, 'Memoir of the South and East coasts of Arabia' (*Journal of the Royal Geographical Society*, vol. 15 (1845), p. 104-60) continued the voyage east of Hadramawt into Dhofar, but included a description of Socotra and general remarks about wind, weather and navigation along the whole of the south coast. The voyage was also undertaken by Wellsted who published his account in *Travels in Arabia* (see item no. 144).

130 **Rapport sur une mission archéologique dans le Yémen.** (Report on an archaeological mission to Yemen.)
Joseph Halévy. *Journal Asiatique,* 6e série, vol. 19 (1872), p. 5-98, 129-266.

The purpose of this article was to publish the epigraphic finds Halévy made during his journey of 1870, and the second part of the article reproduces all of the 686 inscriptions he discovered. The journey the author made from Ṣanʿāʾ to Najrān (where he was mistaken for a Christian and kept prisoner for eight days), and then on to Ṣirwāḥ (al-Kharībah), and eventually, Marib, is also described, but Halévy gives few details, preferring to dwell on the difficulties he faced in his quest for inscriptions. The author's other article on the subject is much more detailed regarding the journey itself, but stops at Najrān on the borders with North Yemen and does not continue the narrative southwards: 'Voyage au Nedjran' (Journey to Najrān) (*Bulletin de la Société de Géographie,* 6e série, vol. 6 [1873], p. 5-31, 249-73, 581-606; vol. 13 [1877], p. 466-79).

131 **A journey through the Yemen and some general remarks upon that country.**
Walter B. Harris. London: Darf, 1985. 385p. map.

A facsimile reprint of the edition published in Edinburgh in 1893. The interest in Harris's narrative lies in the fact that his journey took place during an uprising against Ottoman rule in North Yemen and his observations on the Turks in Ṣanʿāʾ and his interview with the Turkish governor are useful additions to our knowledge of conditions during this period. He was not a traveller in the class of Glaser (q.v.), however, and he has little new to say on Yemeni Arab society, or the country of the Western Aden Protectorate through which he passed, while his historical introduction is for the most part based on other people's works.

132 **A journey in Hadramaut.**
Leo Hirsch. *Geographical Journal,* 3 (1894), p. 196-205.

A rather dry account of a circular journey made by the author in 1893 from Mukallā to Shibām and Tarīm. He offers a summary of tribal relations in the Wādī Ḥaḍramawt and of agricultural and mineral production in the region (including an attempt to sink a shaft for coal near Wādī Rayyān). For a full version of his travels, the reader should consult the original German edition (see below).

133 **Reise in Süd-Arabien, Mahra-Land und Hadramut.** (Journey in South Arabia, the Mahra region and Ḥaḍramawt.)
Leo Hirsch. Frankfurt-am-Main, Germany: Institute for the History of Arabic-Islamic Sciences at the Johann-Wolfgang-Goethe University, 1995. 331p. map.

A facsimile of the edition published in 1897 by Brill in Leiden, The Netherlands. Leo Hirsch was an archaeologist and South Arabian specialist, who became the first European to explore fully the Wādī Ḥaḍramawt. He received a cordial reception from the Quʿaytī shaykhs, and was able to visit Shibām at length. However, his excursions to Tarīm and Say'ūn were less successful, and he was able to spend only a few hours at the former. Tarīm, with its great market square, is described as the most metropolitan of the towns in the Wādī, while Say'ūn had the largest gardens and Shibām was the most populous and possessed of large palm groves.

Travellers' Accounts and Exploration. 19th and early 20th centuries (1800-1919)

134 **Die Expedition nach Süd-Arabien.** (The expedition to South Arabia.) Count Carlo von Landberg. Munich, Germany: Seitz und Schauer, 1899. 91p.

One of the most famous quarrels in the annals of Arabian exploration was between the Swede Landberg and the Austrian David Heinrich Müller. In 1898 they had intended to travel together into the interior of Ḥaḍramawt, but the expedition reached only Wādī Mayfaʿah, a few dozen miles inland from the coast at Balḥāf, before Landberg was obliged to return to Aden, having been accused of trying to murder his companion. This short work represents more of an apologia for Landberg's actions than a genuine travel narrative, but is an entertaining read, nonetheless, and a salutary lesson for all would-be explorers. For a more balanced account of the expedition, see the article by Eric Macro 'The Austrian Imperial Academy's expeditions to South Arabia' (item no. 135).

135 **The Austrian Imperial Academy's expeditions to South Arabia, 1897-1900: C. de Landberg, D. H. Müller and G. W. Bury.** Eric Macro. *New Arabian Studies,* vol. 1 (1993), p. 54-82.

The author has long had an interest in the Arabian activities of G. Wyman Bury (q.v.), and in this article he chronicles Bury's activities as a member of the seven separate expeditions mounted by the Austrian Imperial Academy of Sciences (Kaiserliche Akademie der Wissenschaften) between 1897 and 1900. The other members were the Austrians David Heinrich Müller (q.v.), Franz Kossmat, Stefan Paulay and Simony, plus the Swede, Landberg (q.v.). The various expeditions visited Socotra (twice), Wādī Mayfaʿah (where Landberg had his famous quarrel with Müller), Niṣāb (twice), Bayḥān and, finally, in 1900, made an ill-fated attempt to reach Marib, which had to be abandoned as cholera struck the party at Aḥwar. This is an interesting piece based on considerable archival research, which sheds light on the South Arabian activities of one of the lesser Great Powers.

136 **Robert Finlay's journey in Yemen – 1823.** Eric Macro. *Proceedings of the Seminar for Arabian Studies,* vol. 14 (1984), p. 67-76.

Robert Finlay, an official of the Bombay Government and assistant surgeon to the Mocha Residency, set off from the British factory at Mocha on 4 August 1823 and seventeen days later arrived in Ṣanʿāʾ. His brief was to attend the Imam's brother, who was 'extremely fond of spirituous liquors', and he spent a month and a half in the capital, looking after his patient, and seeing the sights. His manuscript report, of which this is a summary, discusses the commerce of Yemen (only the Jews were allowed to mint coins), the constitution (prosecutions which might involve the death penalty were heard by a tribunal of judges, with the Imam as president), the people, the food, the Imam, and the city itself (the best mosques were built by the Turks, and he counted eight with tall minarets). The greater part of the text of Finlay's journal was published in 1990 by P. J. L. Frankl, 'Robert Finlay's description of Ṣanʿāʾ in 1238-1239/1823' (*British Society for Middle Eastern Studies Bulletin,* vol. 17, no. 1 [1990], p. 16-32).

137 **Reise nach Südarabien und geographische Forschungen im und über den südwestlichsten Theil Arabiens.** (Journey to Arabia and geographical researches in and about the most south-westerly part of Arabia.)
Heinrich von Maltzan. Brunswick, Germany: Friedrich Vieweg, 1873. 422p. map.

Von Maltzan is best known to us as the publisher of Adolph von Wrede's diary (see item no. 146). However, he was, if not a great traveller, then certainly someone who was particularly interested in Arabian exploration. His book tells of his journey from Cairo to Aden, via Yanbuʿ, Jeddah, Suakin and Massawa. While in Aden, he spent three months questioning over one hundred Arabs from the interior over the conditions in the regions from which they came. As a result, he built up a dossier of geographical information (which he admits is of variable value) over the country between Aden and Ibb in the southern region of North Yemen. He himself gives us a vivid description of the buildings and inhabitants of Aden (particularly the Jews and the *akhdām* or lowest social class), and the book includes a map of South Arabian exploration showing the inland route von Maltzan used to travel between Aden and Shuqrā'.

138 **El Yèmen: tre anni nell'Arabia felice: escursioni fatte dal settembre 1877 al marzo 1880.** (The Yemen: three years in Arabia Felix: journeys made between September 1877 and March 1880.)
Renzo Manzoni. Rome: Botta, 1884. 446p. 2 maps.

One of the fullest descriptions of life in Ṣanʿāʾ and Turkish-occupied North Yemen, by the grandson of the famous Italian novelist Alessandro Manzoni. The author was interested in most aspects of Arab life: social customs; religious traditions; tribal divisions; architecture (the volume contains a detailed map of Ṣanʿāʾ, as well as numerous engravings); geography and agriculture, and – in contradistinction to many contemporary travellers – the Arabic language. A modern edition of the book, including nearly half the text and covering the author's first year in Yemen, has been published as: *El Yèmen: un viaggio a Sanaʿa, 1877-1878* (The Yemen: a journey to Ṣanʿāʾ, 1877-78) (Turin, Italy: EDT, 1991. 274p.).

139 **Account of an excursion into the interior of Southern Arabia.**
S. B. Miles, M. W. Munzinger. *Journal of the Royal Geographical Society,* vol. 41 (1871), p. 210-45.

A report of a journey in 1870 from Bi'r ʿAlī near Balḥāf on the coast into the interior, visiting Naqab al-Ḥajar, Ḥawṭah and Ḥabbān, and returning to Aden along the coast. Miles was particularly interested in the tribes he encountered along the route, such as the 'Awlaqī and Faḍlī, and any traces of ancient inscriptions. He also remarked on the agriculture, trade and education of the inhabitants ('There is but one Fakih, or learned man, in Hota; and there are no schools, but a few boys receive a little instruction during the month of Ramzan'). Munzinger was a geologist and contributes a long section at the end on rock-formations and watersheds.

Travellers' Accounts and Exploration. 19th and early 20th centuries (1800-1919)

140 **Notes of a journey in Yemen.**

Charles Millingen. *Journal of the Royal Geographical Society,* vol. 44 (1874), p. 118-26.

The author performed a circular journey from Hodeida to Bājil, Mifḥāq and Ṣanʿāʾ, and back via Kawkabān, al-Ṭawīlah and al-Maḥwīt. The most interesting aspects of his information are the descriptions of fruit, cereals and other plants he found growing along the route ('The plain of Shibām is very fertile, cereals, clover, beans, and mustard being the chief products') and of the Turkish presence in the country (the author travelled shortly after Ottoman troops had re-entered Ṣanʿāʾ in 1872).

141 **Halévy in Yemen.**

H. St. J. Philby. *Geographical Journal,* vol. 102 (1943), p. 116-24.

An attempt to disentangle the varying accounts of the journey in the Yemen undertaken by Joseph Halévy and his Jewish guide, Ḥayyīm Ḥabshūsh (qq.v.). Philby is inclined to believe Halévy's drier and less detailed account, compared to Ḥabshūsh's more florid rendering and 'my conclusion from the evidence before us, is that, while Ḥabshūsh certainly travelled, perhaps more than once, over most of the ground covered by Halévy and copied inscriptions in the same and other localities, he did not do so in Halévy's company'. For the opposite view, see Gabriella Moscati Steindler's introduction to Ḥayyīm Ḥabshūsh's text (item no. 128).

142 **A modern pilgrim in Mecca and a siege in Sanaa.**

A. J. B. Wavell. London: Constable, 1913. 349p. map.

A narrative of Wavell's adventures in Turkish-occupied Yemen in 1910-11, where his attempts to defy the government's prohibitions on travel caused his arrest and expulsion. The interest of his story lies in the descriptions of an Arab uprising and the measures adopted by the Turkish army for suppressing it, but the author's sneering tone and his self-satisfied sense of moral superiority (and his inability to speak either Turkish or Arabic) make for tedious interludes, best exemplified by his correspondence with the Foreign Office on his return, where he demanded that the British Government take up his case for compensation with the Sublime Porte.

143 **Narrative of a journey from the Tower of Bá-'l-ḥaff on the Southern Coast of Arabia to the ruins of Naḳab al Hajar, in April, 1835.**

J. R. Wellsted. *Journal of the Royal Geographical Society,* vol. 7 (1837), p. 20-34.

A description of a journey in Western Ḥaḍramawt, about forty miles inland from Balḥāf on the coast to the ruins of what Wellsted took to be a pre-Islamic temple, where he discovered (and published in this article) the first Himyarite inscription. Along the way, he discusses the agricultural pursuits he observed, ranging from date palms and the arak tree to the 'fields ploughed with furrows, which for neatness and regularity would not shame an English peasant'.

144 **Travels in Arabia.**

J. R. Wellsted, introduction by Fred Scholz. Graz, Austria: Akademische Druck- und Verlagsanstalt, 1978. 2 vols. maps.

A reprint of the edition published in London in 1838. Wellsted was a naval lieutenant, whose ostensible reason for his travels in Oman and along the south coast of Arabia was to investigate suitable sites for establishing coaling stations. He sailed along the coast of Ḥaḍramawt in 1834 in the *Palinurus,* and in the second volume of his book (p. 381-456) reports on Aden, Shuqrā', Mukallā, Shiḥr and Socotra in considerable detail, particularly their form of government, their commerce and their landscape. Much of the information in the book can also be found in the two articles by S. B. Haines (see item no. 129).

145 **An account of an excursion in Hadramaut.**

Adolph von Wrede. *Journal of the Royal Geographical Society,* vol. 14 (1844), p. 107-12.

This brief account of the author's journey in the interior of Ḥaḍramawt in 1843 consists mainly of descriptions of the landscape and the climate, including the intense heat of the foothills, which abated as he reached the deep ravines of the Wādī Dūʿan. The author also recounts his experiments with disappearing plumb-line and cord (one of the factors which led to his being disbelieved) and his imprisonment after he stumbled upon a huge crowd celebrating the feast day of Shaykh Saʿīd ibn ʿĪsā. A much fuller version of the author's two-month long journey appeared in German in 1870 (see below).

146 **Reise in Hadhramaut, Beled Beny ʿIssà und Beled el Hadschar.**

(Journey in Ḥaḍramawt, Balad Bani ʿIsa and Balad al-Hajar.)

Adolph von Wrede, edited by Heinrich von Maltzan. Amsterdam, The Netherlands; Meridian, 1967. 375p. map.

A reprint of the edition published in Brunswick, Germany, in 1870. This is a full published version of von Wrede's diary which describes a journey he undertook in 1843 from Aden to Mukallā and then into the interior of Ḥaḍramawt, where he travelled up the Wādī Dūʿan, reaching al-Khuraybah and pushing on towards Shabwah and the Wādī ʿAmd, before returning to the coast. His detailed descriptions of the country established for the first time the general contours of the inland landscape (as well as giving much information on climate and tribal customs), and although his exploits, first recorded in the *Journal of the Royal Geographical Society* (see above), were doubted, this edition, with its geographical and historical notes and additional data and information, proved the veracity of his claims.

Modern travellers (1919-)

147 **Hawks of the Hadhramaut.**
P. S. Allfree. London: Robert Hale, 1967. 192p.

A vivid description of the author's life in the Eastern Aden Protectorate as an Assistant Adviser to the British Adviser. He visited many of the inland towns such as Tarīm, Thamūd and Ṣanāw, and had intimate contact with a wide variety of tribesmen as well as the local shaykhs and rulers, as he sought to keep order among the many warring factions.

148 **À travers l'Arabie inconnue: des villes mortes du Royaume de Saba aux palais des seigneurs des sables.** (Across unknown Arabia: from the dead cities of the Kingdom of Sheba to the palaces of the lords of the sands.)
François Balsan. Paris: Amiot Dumont, 1954. 191p.

A description of a journey undertaken by the author and his wife by jeep from Aden to Bayḥān on the border with North Yemen, to find the famous salt-mines of King Solomon.

149 **Inquiétant Yémen.** (Disquieting Yemen.)
François Balsan. Paris: La Palatine, 1961. 234p.

The author recounts the difficulties he faced in trying to travel in North Yemen during the last years of the reign of Imam Aḥmad. Much of the five-month period was spent trying to get out of the port cities of Hodeida and Mocha, before he finally succeeding in reaching Taʿizz in the south-west of the country. The author does have an unfortunate tendency to dwell on his own predicament, rather than observe the manners and customs of the regions through which he travelled.

150 **The Kingdom of Melchior: adventure in South West Arabia.**
The Master of Belhaven (Alexander Hamilton). London: John Murray, 1949. 212p.

An entertaining account of the author's travels through the Western Aden Protectorate, firstly with a platoon of Aden Levies in the 1930s, where his task was to maintain peace on the border with North Yemen and secondly, as a Political Officer when, among other things he accompanied Sir Bernard Reilly on a mission to the Imam at Ṣanʿāʾ. The book contains a good deal of information about political relations, topography, archaeology and the tribal situation, particularly in the regions around Bayḥān and Shabwah. The author's story is continued by *The uneven road* (see below).

151 **The uneven road.**
The Master of Belhaven (Alexander Hamilton). London: John Murray, 335p. 2 maps.

A sequel to *The Kingdom of Melchior* (see above), which goes backwards to the author's childhood and forwards to his experiences in Italy during the Second World War, but is mostly concerned with his life in Aden and the Protectorate in the 1930s.

To some extent it covers the same ground as the previous book (there is, for example, another account of the author's visit to the Imam at Ṣanʿāʾ), but there is considerable added detail on tribes in the Quṭaybī, Faḍlī and Ṣubayḥi territories.

152 **Behind the veil of Arabia.**
Jørgen Bisch, translated from the Danish by Reginald Spink. London: Allen & Unwin, 1962. 148p.

In a semi-serious quest to establish whether slavery still existed in the Arabian Peninsula, the author undertook a journey from Mukallā to Shibām and Say'ūn in the Ḥaḍramawt, and then on to Saudi Arabia. His camera brought him untold problems as did his lack of Arabic, but his photographs are impressive, and his adventures entertaining, if not very informative.

153 **Island of the dragons' blood.**
Douglas Botting. London: Hodder and Stoughton, 1958. 251p.

The first general book about Socotra, the result of the Oxford University Exploration Club's expedition to the island in 1956. The team consisted of an archaeologist (P. L. Shinnie), a biologist, two medical undergraduates and two others and they spent two months in Socotra, surveying remains, collecting plants for the British Museum, and taking a wide selection of blood samples. The descriptions of life on the island are general rather than scientific, but the author was well aware of what has been written about the island by previous visitors, and his observations are careful as well as colourful.

154 **Socotra: 'Island of Bliss'.**
P. C. Boxhall. *Geographical Journal*, vol. 132, part 2 (June 1966), p. 213-25.

An account of a joint Royal Air Force/Army expedition, which explored Socotra between December 1964 and February 1965, to prepare the way for a general survey and mapping project. The author describes the flora and fauna, the customs of the bedouin of the interior, and the architectural and archaeological remains found by the expedition.

155 **Yémen 62-69: de la révolution 'sauvage' à la trêve des guerriers.**
(The Yemen, 1962-69: from the 'savage' revolution to the warriors' truce.)
Claude Deffarge, Gordian Troeller. Paris: Robert Laffont, 1969. 303p. map. (L'Histoire que Nous Vivons).

The authors undertook three journeys during the civil war of 1962-70 in North Yemen: the first in 1962 in Republican territory took them from Aden to Ṣanʿāʾ via Taʿizz; the second from Saudi Arabia enabled them to investigate the Royalist army's stronghold in the north in 1963; and the third, again from Aden to Ṣanʿāʾ via Ibb and Taʿizz, enabled them to visit the Republican capital under siege. The book contains some interesting interviews but no deep analysis of the political, military or religious situation. The map on the end-papers, showing the routes of European travellers in North Yemen from Ludovico de Varthema (q.v.) to Eric Rouleau, is very useful.

156 **Yemen.**

Laurence Deonna, translated from the French by Corinne Borel. Washington, DC: Three Continents Press, 1991. 199p.

An updated version of the original published in French in 1982, this is the work of a seasoned observer of the Middle East. Her most significant observations on North Yemeni society deal with the position of women, education and the economy, and the text is illustrated by good colour and black-and-white photographs.

157 **Meine Jahre in Arabien, 1955-1988: aus den Tagebuchaufzeichnungen eines landwirtschaftlichen Entwicklungshelfers.** (My years in Arabia, 1955-88: from the diary of an agricultural development assistant.)

H. Dequin. Hamburg, Germany: Westerhorn, 1988. 332p.

The author spent the period from June 1960 to February 1965 working as an agricultural development officer in the Yemen Arab Republic, mainly in the region of Taʿizz in the south of the country. This book mainly consists of extracts from his diary with the addition of some historical background. The author was present during the early part of the civil war, and makes some interesting observations about Imam Aḥmad and the Republican opposition, as well as about the projects on which he worked, and the many Yemenis he met.

158 **Au pays de la Reine de Saba.** (In the land of the Queen of Sheba.)

Maurice Déribéré, Paulette Déribéré. Paris: Éditions France-Empire, 1977. 350p. maps.

An archaeological adventure, which took the authors from Ṣanʿāʾ to Marib, Ṣirwāḥ, Timnaʿ and Shabwah, where they describe the ruins, and discuss previous archaeologists like Wendell Phillips and Albert Jamme (qq.v.). They also crossed the Red Sea to Ethiopia, which they describe briefly, and they conclude their travelogue-cum-potted ancient history with short chapters on the Queen of Sheba in Western and Islamic art and on the Jews of Yemen.

159 **The riddle of Arabia.**

Ladislas Farago. London: Robert Hale, 1939. 287p

The author attempted to visit North Yemen in 1937, but got no further than the port of Hodeida. His observations on the country and Imam Aḥmad are second-hand, but he did meet Germans and Italians as he waited for an entrance visa, and his comments on the activities of those countries in the region are not without value. He also explored the area around Aden, Mukallā and Laḥij both before and after his abortive attempts to reach Ṣanʿāʾ, and comments caustically on the activities of Philby (q.v.) and the repercussions in the Ḥaḍramawt.

160 **A French doctor in the Yemen.**

Claudie Fayein, translated from the French by Douglas McKee. London: Robert Hale, 1957. 288p.

The author spent eighteen months in North Yemen in the early 1950s as a doctor in Ṣanʿāʾ. Her descriptions of the poverty and lack of medical facilities are very moving as are her encounters with her patients, who were mostly women, but also included the merchant class and princes of the royal blood. She also visited Marib, Dhamār and several other areas to the south of Ṣanʿāʾ.

161 **A visit to the Idrisi territory in ʿAsir and Yemen.**
Rosita Forbes (Mrs. McGrath). *Geographical Journal,* 62 (1923), p. 271-8.

An interesting account of a visit to ʿAsīr, at that time an independent principality, and the neighbouring coastal territory of North Yemen. Comparisons are made between the two regions as regards religious tolerance, law and order, social customs, and prices and values.

162 **Landscape with Arabs: travels in Aden and South Arabia.**
Donald Foster. Brighton, England: Clifton Books, 1969. 216p.

The author, who was a political officer in Aden and the Protectorate from 1952 to 1966, conducts the reader on an intelligent and knowledgeable tour of Aden and its hinterland as far as Tarīm and Say'ūn. His remarks on the tribes, British administration and the British colony are shrewd and laced with somewhat bitter humour, but never devoid of interest.

163 **Les exilés du Yémen heureux.** (The exiles of Arabia Felix.)
Dawoud Hamami. Paris: L'Harmattan, 1994. 197p. map.

Much of this book concerns the author's life in France, Switzerland and Israel, where he heard much from his grandmother about Jewish life in North Yemen. However, the last quarter traces his journey to Ṣanʿāʾ and Ṣaʿdah in search of his Jewish inheritance. He finds a Jewish shoemaker in Ṣaʿdah, is nearly arrested as an Israeli spy, and is finally taken to see his great-uncle who still lives in the village of Nadhīr in the north-west of the country, which his grandparents had left many years before.

164 **Motoring with Mohammed: journeys to Yemen and the Red Sea.**
Eric Hansen. London: Hamish Hamilton; Boston, Massachusetts: Houghton Mifflin, 1991. 240p.

The entertaining tale of an American whose sailing-boat was wrecked off the North Yemeni coast on ʿUqbān Island, and his adventures among Eritreans, Yemenis, Austrians and his fellow countrymen as he travelled round Yemen from Taʿizz to Zabīd and from Hodeida to Ṣanʿāʾ, trying to find a way out of the country. Paperback versions were published in London by Sphere in 1992 and Abacus in 1993.

165 **Land without shade.**
Hans Helfritz, translated from the German by Kenneth Kirkness. London: Hurst & Blackett, 1937. 287p. maps.

A journey from Mukallā to Hodeida via Shibām and Ṣanʿāʾ, which included a three-week spell in prison and an interview with the Imam Yaḥyā. The author recounts the same adventures in *The Yemen: a secret journey* (London: Allen & Unwin, 1958. 180p. map).

166 **Excursion in the Hajr Province of Hadramaut.**
Doreen Ingrams. *Geographical Journal,* vol. 98, no. 3, (1941), p. 121-34.

A circular journey by donkey from Mukallā to Sidārah in the interior and back again. The author's colloquial style belies a keen interest in the geography and archaeology of the region she visited, which she describes vividly.

167 **The exploration of the Aden Protectorate.**
Harold Ingrams. *Geographical Review,* vol. 28, no. 4 (1938), p. 638-51.

After a somewhat cursory review of travellers to the region before the First World War, the author describes in more detail the recent investigations by British explorers and administrators into the Wādī Ḥaḍramawt, Bayḥān and Socotra, including those by British women like Freya Stark and Gertrude Caton Thompson (qq.v.).

168 **From Cana (Husn Ghorab) to Sabbatha (Shabwa): the South Arabian incense road.**
Harold Ingrams. *Journal of the Royal Asiatic Society* (Oct. 1945), p. 169-85.

One of Ingrams's most interesting journeys from Mukallā on the coast to Shabwah in the interior. The author, who was well versed in the classics, contrasts what Pliny, Ptolemy and the author of the *Periplus of the Erythraean Sea* (see item no. 299) described as the ancience incense road with what he and his companions found along the route, and with what British travellers and archaeologists such as Gertrude Caton Thompson and Freya Stark (qq.v.) had discovered. His conclusion is that the ancient kingdom of Saba and present-day Ḥaḍramawt each had the same social structure, and each was unable to sustain its economy by agriculture alone. The temples of Saba were financed by the incense trade, while the palaces of Say'ūn and Tarīm are paid for by the remittances from Ḥaḍramī émigrés in Java and Singapore.

169 **Hadramaut: a journey through the Seiʿar country and through Wādī Maseila.**
Harold Ingrams. *Geographical Journal,* vol. 88 (1936), p. 524-51. map follows p. 591.

The author describes a journey made in the autumn of 1934 through Wādī Dūʿan to Shibām, on to Tarīm, and back along Wādī Masaylah to the coast at Sayḥūt. Much of the narrative deals with the changing landscape and the various groups of bedouin encountered en route.

170 **The Hadramaut: present and future.**
Harold Ingrams. *Geographical Journal,* vol. 102 (1943), p. 289-302.

The author, a political officer in Ḥaḍramawt, discusses the changes brought to the region by the recent construction of motor roads and air strips, and the signing of a major peace treaty among the tribes. He goes on to describe a journey from Shiḥr to Tarīm and on to Ḥiṣn al-ʿAbr on the Saudi border, plus visits to Say'ūn and ʿAzzān. As befits his profession, much of the discussion centres on his relations with the local tribal leaders.

171 **Freya Stark: a biography.**
Molly Izzard. London: Hodder & Stoughton, 1993. 342p.

A frank biography of one of the most famous of British travellers to South Arabia and elsewhere in the Middle East. The author attempts to understand Freya Stark's motivations behind her journeys as well as exploring episodes of her experiences in Ḥaḍramawt such as her well-publicized quarrel with Gertrude Caton Thompson (q.v.), her meetings with Harold and Doreen Ingrams, and her relations with Philby (qq.v.).

172 **The sultans came to tea.**
June Knox-Mawer. London: John Murray, 1961. 218p.

The entertaining memoir of the young wife of the Chief Magistrate in Aden in the late 1950s. Many of the anecdotes deal with the author's relations with the many Adenis she met, both male and female, but there are also descriptions of journeys to Laḥij and Mukayris in the Western Aden Protectorate.

173 **The barren rocks of Aden.**
James Lunt. London: Herbert Jenkins, 1966. 196p. maps.

The author spent two and a half years, from 1961 to 1964, as Commander of the Army of the Federation of South Arabia. Most of his time, on his own admission, 'was spent among the tribes who inhabit the tortuous mountain valleys which lie between the coast and the Yemen' and he recounts many adventures in the country around Dhala (al-Ḍāliᶜ), Mukayris and Bayḥān. He also visited the Eastern Arab Protectorate, including the desert areas around Thamūd.

174 **Yemen: travels in dictionary land.**
Tim Mackintosh-Smith, with etchings by Martin Yeoman. London: John Murray, 1997. 280p. bibliog.

An entertaining trip through modern Yemen, by an author who lived in the country for thirteen years and whose passion for all things Yemeni shines through every page. There are many memorable encounters, made all the more lively by the author's deep knowledge of Yemeni history and literature and the splendid etchings of Martin Yeoman.

175 **Aden to the Hadhramaut: a journey in South Arabia.**
Dan van der Meulen. London: John Murray, 1947. 254p.

Van der Meulen had worked both in Saudi Arabia as the Dutch chargé d'affaires and in the Dutch East Indies, where he was particularly interested in the conditions of the many Ḥaḍramī immigrants. This book describes his travels through the Ḥaḍramawt on the eve of the Second World War with several companions, including Hermann von Wissmann and his wife. His route took him by lorry to just above Shuqrā' and from there the party travelled by camel to Niṣāb, Shibām, Say'ūn and Tarīm, northwards into the mountains, and then back to the coast at Shiḥr and Mukallā. Van der Meulen is a shrewd observer, and it is interesting to compare his views of the tribesmen with those of British administrators and travellers like Harold Ingrams and Freya Stark (qq.v.).

176 **Faces in Shem.**

Dan van der Meulen. London: John Murray, 1961. 194p.

More a series of autobiographical sketches than a full-blown travel narrative, this book has an even more jaundiced view of British administration in the Ḥaḍramawt and of Harold Ingrams in particular than *Aden to the Hadhramaut* (see above). The section on South Arabia comes at the end of the book, and is preceded by episodes from the author's life in Saudi Arabia and North Yemen, including an interview with Imam Yaḥyā in 1931.

177 **Hadramaut: some of its mysteries unveiled.**

Dan van der Meulen, Hermann von Wissmann. Leiden, The Netherlands: Brill, 1964. 248p. map. (Publications of the De Goeje Fund, 9).

A reprint of the 1932 edition, this describes a journey made in 1931 from Mukallā up the Wādī Ḥajar to the Wādī Ḥaḍramawt and its towns of Shibām, Say'ūn and Tarīm and back to the coast via Wādī Dūʿan. The author's brief was to try to extend Dutch influence over the Ḥaḍramawt, particularly by using his knowledge of the many Ḥaḍramī families who had emigrated to Indonesia. In this he was not particularly successful, but between the descriptions of landscape, tribal customs, folk medicine and agriculture, there is much discussion of a political nature, which sheds an interesting light on British administrative methods.

178 **Quest for Sheba.**

Norman Stone Pearn, Vernon Barlow. London: Nicholson and Watson, 1937. 258p.

The chronicle of Norman Pearn's obsession with the figure of the Queen of Sheba, and his journey in South Arabia in search of her kingdom, as recounted by Vernon Barlow. Pearn set off from Mukallā and passed up the Wādī Dūʿan to Shibām in the Wādī Ḥaḍramawt, where he met several of the more important men of the region, as well as Philby. In contradistinction to Ingrams and Freya Stark (qq.v.), he was not interested in the intricacies of tribal enmities, and his descriptions of people and the landscape have a certain freshness as well as naïvety.

179 **Sheba's daughters: being a record of travel in Southern Arabia.**

H. St. J. Philby. London: Methuen, 1939. 485p. map.

A lengthy account by one of Arabia's best-known travellers of his one journey to the Yemens. This took place in 1936, when Philby left Najrān on the Saudi–Yemeni border and travelled to Shabwah in the Ḥaḍramawt by motor car. His purpose was to record the archaeological remains and ancient inscriptions of the site, but as his journey was unauthorized, it occasioned some conflict with the British authorities and his remarks on the Aden administration are not complimentary. Nevertheless, he was able to proceed from Shabwah to Shiḥr and Mukallā, and then back to Najrān via Shibām and Tarīm, skirting Marib and the Jawf in North Yemen, and many of his observations of places and people are interesting and entertaining. The inscriptions are reproduced at the end of the volume, with comments by A. F. L. Beeston.

180 **Arabian peak and desert: travels in Al-Yaman.**
Ameen Rihani. London: Constable, 1930. 280p.

The author, a Lebanese Christian who had emigrated to the United States when he was twelve, undertook several journeys to the Arabian Peninsula in the 1920s and 1930s. His trip to Yemen was made via Aden, and he took twelve days to reach Ṣanʿāʾ at an average of three miles an hour. He was particularly interested in the Zaydī sect of Islam, which predominates in North Yemen, in how the Imam ruled his people, and in the general economic state of the country. He also observed the changes in habits and customs, as he left Ṣanʿāʾ to travel through the highlands to Hodeida on the coast.

181 **Around the coasts of Arabia.**
Ameen Rihani. London: Constable, 1930. 364p.

Another narrative of the author's travels in Arabia, this book takes in visits to Hodeida (then under the rule of the Idrīsīs of ʿAsīr), the Hijaz, Kuwait, Bahrain, and Aden and Laḥij. In Hodeida, Rihani paid great attention to the religious activities in the city and witnessed a special ceremony for the founder of the Mīrghanīyah, one of the local *ṣūfī* orders, which he described eloquently. In Aden, Rihani also made the acquaintance of a holy man, but most of this chapter is given over to a discussion of the relations between Britain and the tribes of the Western Protectorate and their rulers, such as Sultan ʿAbd al-Karīm al-Faḍlī of Laḥij.

182 **Freya Stark in Southern Arabia.**
Malise Ruthven. Reading, England: Garnet Publishing, 1995. 120p. map. (The St. Antony's College Middle East Archives).

A study and selection of Freya Stark's (q.v.) black-and-white photographs of Aden and the Ḥaḍramawt made between 1935 and 1940 with the addition of material from her albums relating to her visit to North Yemen in 1976. Her interest was as much in people as in architecture, and the collection as a whole gives an interesting insight into life in the colonial protectorate.

183 **Je reviens du Yémen et t'en rapporte des nouvelles vraies.** (I have returned from Yemen and brought you some true news.)
Alain Saint-Hilaire. Paris: Éditions de la Pensée Moderne, 1975. 190p.

The author spent nine months in North Yemen in 1974, and in this book he describes how the country was finally coming to terms with the civil war of 1962-70. As he travelled through the country, he paid particular attention to the economy, agriculture, the situation among the tribes, and the endemic violence.

184 **In the high Yemen.**
Hugh Scott. London: John Murray, 1947. 2nd ed. 260p. bibliog.

The author formed part of the British Museum (Natural History) Expedition to South-West Arabia in 1937-38. They travelled from Aden through Laḥij and Dhala (al-Ḍāliʿ) into North Yemen, where the party visited Taʿizz, Ṣanʿāʾ and the country round about, and left via Hodeida. The author, an entomologist, has a great interest in the history, geography and architecture of the region, which he describes with a very sharp eye and illustrates with some excellent black-and-white photographs. The final section of the book offers the reader a summary history of Yemen from the earliest times till the present day, and is interesting for its analysis of the political aims of the Imam (whom the party met in Ṣanʿāʾ). The scientific results of the expedition were published in the *British Museum (Natural History) Expedition to South-West Arabia, 1937-8* (London: British Museum, 1941-57) (see item no. 199).

185 **Tribes and tribulations: a journey in Republican Yemen.**
Peter Somerville-Large. London: Robert Hale, 1967. 187p.

The author was friendly with several Yemenis studying at Trinity College, Dublin, and accepted their invitation to visit North Yemen in 1963, just four months after the civil war had broken out. His descriptions of the chaos caused by the Egyptian army, of his friends' relations with the new Republican government of President al-Sallāl and of his encounters with numerous foreigners are vivid, as are his experiences as a prisoner of pro-Royalist tribesmen somewhere along the Ṣanʿāʾ–Taʿizz road. The author was eventually deported to Aden by the Egyptian authorities after four event-filled months in Ṣanʿāʾ, Taʿizz and Dhamār.

186 **The coast of incense: autobiography, 1933-1939.**
Freya Stark. London: John Murray, 1953. 287p.

In this third volume of autobiography, the author follows her normal method of alternating letters written at the time with her reflections from the present. The book itself covers her period in South Arabia, and the letters are revealing both of the minutiae of every day in Ḥaḍramawt, and of her feelings at the time. Her anger and indignation when she heard that Helfritz (q.v.) was likely to reach Shabwah before her as she lay seriously ill of a fever (p. 87-9) are particularly dramatic, as is her delight when she believes that she is going to acquire a full manuscript copy of al-Ḥasan ibn Aḥmad al-Hamdānī's (d. c. 945) *al-Iklīl* (p. 202).

187 **East is West.**
Freya Stark. London: John Murray, 1945. 218p.

The first quarter of this account of the author's experiences during the Second World War deals with her time in Aden in 1940. At the time, the colony feared imminent invasion from the Italian forces stationed in Somalia and Eritrea, and Freya Stark was able to help in the destruction of two submarines by translating Italian operational naval orders captured by British destroyers. When the threat of an invasion had receded, she travelled to Egypt, and thence to Palestine, Jordan, Syria and Iraq, putting her knowledge of Arabic and the Arabs at the disposal of the British forces there.

188 **Seen in the Hadhramaut.**
Freya Stark. London: John Murray, 1938. 199p.

Basically, this book is a collection of the author's wonderful black-and-white photographs taking during her journeys through Ḥaḍramawt in 1937-38. The subjects are mainly tribesmen and buildings, and cover Shibām, Tarīm, ʿAzzān, Ḥurayḍah, and many other places in the Wādī Dūʿan and Wādī Ḥaḍramawt. The introduction surveys British rule in the Protectorate, and issues a baleful warning against the 'Western expert', whom the author maintains 'comes for what he can take away . . . and does not know the harm he does'. She is very concerned to prevent 'the disappearance of something as perfect in its remoteness and antiquity as the life of these long-forgotten towns of South Arabia', since there 'romance is ready to take you by the handʿ (p. xx-xxi). The full narrative of the journey can be found in *A winter in Arabia* (see item no. 190).

189 **The southern gates of Arabia: a journey in the Hadhramaut.**
Freya Stark. London: John Murray, 1936. 328p. 2 maps.

The story of the author's journey from Mukallā to Tarīm in 1935 is told vividly and with many references to historical and geographical sources. Freya Stark was particularly interested in the ancient frankincense road, and spent much time visiting archaeological sites as well as striking up acquaintances with as many Ḥaḍramīs as possible. Near the end of her journey, she was delighted to receive a certificate from a Kathīrī sayyid stating that she was 'the first woman to travel from England to Hadhramaut alone – and is mistress of endurance and fortitude in travel and in the suffering of terrors and danger'.

190 **A winter in Arabia.**
Freya Stark. London: John Murray, 1940. 265p. map.

The diary of Freya Stark's stay at Ḥurayḍah in the Wādī Dūʿan, where an archaeological dig led by Gertrude Caton Thompson, was taking place to try to establish whether there were any links between the Sabaean culture of South Arabia and the Zimbabwe ruins in southern Africa (the scientific results of the expedition were published as *The tombs and moon temples of Hureidha* [see item no. 220]). Relations between the two were not cordial, with Freya Stark never referring to her erstwhile friend by name, but merely as 'the archaeologist'. Freya eventually left by herself and the latter half of the book narrates her three-week journey by camel caravan from Ḥurayḍah to ʿAzzān and on to the coast at Balḥāf. This was to be her last independent voyage of exploration and her last direct contribution in the field of geographical science and discovery.

191 **A new journey in southern Arabia.**
Wilfred Thesiger. *Geographical Journal,* vol. 108 (1946), p. 129-45. map following p. 288.

The author actually made two journeys between October 1945 and February 1946, one from Salālah to Mughsin (both in Oman) and the other from Salālah to Tarīm in Wādī Ḥaḍramawt. These journeys were undertaken on behalf of the Middle East Anti-Locust Mission to investigate locust breeding, seasonal rainfall and local vegetation. The author supplies considerable data on the flora and fauna of the regions visited and about the the tribes he encountered en route.

192 **The highway of the kings: Arabia – from South to North.**
Barbara Toy. London: John Murray, 1968. 188p.

A somewhat more superficial account of travel in Ḥaḍramawt and beyond than Freya Stark's (see items 186, 188, 189), but also rather less self-obsessed. The first attempt to drive from Mukallā to North Arabia ended in failure near Wādī Jardān. The second attempt was more successful and the party reached Ḥiṣn al-ʿAbr, and on to North Yemen, where they became entangled in the civil war raging there, but passed through safely to emerge in Saudi Arabia at Najrān.

193 **Le Yémen: pays de la Reine de Saba.** (Yemen: the country of the Queen of Sheba.)

Reinhold Wepf. Berne: Kümmerly & Frey, 1967. 104p.

Wepf worked for five months for the Red Cross during the Yemeni civil war of the early 1960s, and in this well-illustrated account he describes his life as a doctor under immensely difficult conditions. He is clearly a shrewd observer of life, and sympathetic towards his patients, which gives his book a warmth and interest beyond the purely medical narrative. The book concludes with chapters on the civilizations of Yemen by Walter Dostal, and on the geography of the country by Hermann von Wissmann.

Flora and Fauna

194 **Biology of the Arabian Peninsula: a bibliographic study from 1557-1978.**

Mohammed Ataur-Rahim. Riyadh: Biological Society of Saudi Arabia, University of Riyadh, 1979. 180p. (Saudi Biological Society Publications, no. 3).

The author spent three years researching this work, which lists over 1,400 books and articles on zoology in the Arabian Peninsula, and 450 on botany. Most of the references are to articles in scientific journals, but travel and geographical literature have not been ignored and the names of Philby (q.v.) and Bertram Thomas crop up many times. The whole gamut of biological sciences is encompassed from protozoa up to mammals and includes birds, fish and molluscs as well as range management and animal production, while no area of botany is negelected. Geographically, the coverage extends from the Gulf of ʿAqabah in the North to the Gulf of Aden in the South and there are a great many references to Yemen, Aden and Ḥaḍramawt. This is an admirable work; the only drawbacks are a lack of author and place indexes, and the fact that it does not include any publications issued after 1978.

195 **The freshwater fishes of the Arabian Peninsula.**

Keith Edward Banister, Margaret Anne Clarke. In: *The scientific results of the Oman Flora and Fauna Survey, 1975.* Oman: Ministry of Information and Culture, 1977, p. 111-54. (A *Journal of Oman Studies* Special Report).

The authors discuss nine species of freshwater fish, of which the greatest concentration is found in the Yemen and Ḥaḍramawt. There are specimens of most of the species in the British Museum (Natural History), collected by travellers like Philby (q.v.) or colonial officers serving in Aden and the Protectorates, and the authors are able to give very full physical details of each fish recorded. Their catalogue is updated by an important article in volume five (1983) of *Fauna of Saudi Arabia* (see item no. 216).

196 **Birds of ʿAsir and parts of Hijaz and Northern Yaman collected by H. St. J. Philby on his 1936 journey.**
G. L. Bates. *Ibis,* 14th series, vol. 1 (1937), p. 786-830.

A list of the birds collected by Philby in his journey from Najrān to Shabwah recounted in *Sheba's daughters* (see item no. 179). It fills in several gaps in the list for Yemen found in W. L. Sclater's articles in *Ibis* (see item no. 214), and describes in total 166 birds, giving full zoological name, size, and place where sited. Several birds had not been recorded in Arabia before.

197 **On birds from Hadhramaut.**
G. L. Bates. *Ibis,* 14th series, vol. 2 (1938), p. 437-62.

Details of ninety-eight birds collected during two journeys by M. T. Boscawen in 1932 and 1933, and by Harold Ingrams during a trip in 1936-37. The area covered includes the Wādī Ḥaḍramawt as far as Tarīm, and the Wādī Ḍahr up to within sight of Shabwah as well as the coastal regions around Mukallā and Shiḥr. The form of entry for each bird is as described in item no. 196.

198 **Flora of Aden.**
Ethelbert Blatter. Calcutta, India: Superintendent of Government Printing, 1914-16. 418p. maps

Published as part of the *Records of the Botanical Survey of India* (vol. 7, nos. 1-3 [1914-16], p. 1-418), this is a massive work and still of considerable interest. After surveying the history of botanical exploration in Aden and surrounding districts, the author goes on to discuss climate, hydrology and the physical features of the landscape, before listing all the plants in systematic order. Each plant is fully described, botanical references are noted, and the plant's distribution is listed. For the plants of North Yemen and the Ḥaḍramawt, as well as the history of the botanical exploration of the rest of Arabia, the reader can consult the author's subsequent survey, *Flora Arabica* (Calcutta, India: Superintendent of Government Printing, 1919-33), which was published as volume 8 (in five parts) of the *Records of the Botanical Survey of India.*

199 **British Museum (Natural History) Expedition to South-West Arabia, 1937-1938.**
British Museum (Natural History). London: British Museum, 1941-57. 504p.

The records of this expedition were published in thirty-three separate parts over a number of years, and include well-illustrated chapters on Coleoptera, Trichoptera, Arachnida, Diptera, Hemiptera, Lepidoptera, Hymenoptera, Isoptera, Crustacea, freshwater Mollusca, freshwater fish, and reptiles and amphibians. Specimens were collected from seventy-one stations from Aden in the south, northwards through the Western Aden Protectorate (Laḥij, Dhala/al-Ḍāliʿ), and on into North Yemen (Ibb, Yarīm, Dhamār, Ṣanʿāʾ, Hodeida). For a narrative version of the expedition see *In the high Yemen* by Hugh Scott (item no. 184).

200 **The wildlife of Saudi Arabia and its neighbours.**
Introduction by W. Büttiker. London: Stacey International, 1990. 2nd ed. 96p.

This beautifully illustrated book for the general reader contains chapters on: mammals; birds; reptiles and amphibians; insects and arachnids; and marine life. Among the creatures shown are the puff adder, the tufted guineafowl, the bean-blue butterfly and the white-tailed mongoose, all four of which are inhabitants of Yemen.

201 **Repertory of drugs and medicinal plants of Yemen.**
Jacques Fleurentin, Jean-Marie Pelt. *Journal of Ethnopharmacology*, vol. 6 (1982), p. 85-108.

The authors worked for two and a half years at the Franco-Yemeni hospital in Taʿizz in North Yemen, and conducted research both on medicinal plants and on traditional kinds of medicine practised in Yemen (including magical healing). In this article, they identify 130 medicinal plants which are presented in a single table with both the scientific and the vernacular names, the geographical and ecological distribution, the medicinal use of the plant within Yemen, and the plants' pharmacological properties. The authors published a supplement to this article as 'Additional information for a repertory of drugs and medicinal plants of Yemen', in *Journal of Ethnopharmacology*, vol. 8 (1983), p. 237-43, and in conjunction with Guy Mazars, they examined the social conditions under which these drugs were administered in 'Cultural background of medicinal plants of Yemen' (*Journal of Ethnopharmacology*, vol. 7 [1983], p. 183-203) and 'Additional information on the cultural background of drugs and medicinal plants of Yemen' (*Journal of Ethnopharmacology*, vol. 8 [1983], p. 335-44).

202 **The natural history of Sokotra and Abd-el-Kuri: being the report of the Conjoint Expedition to these islands in 1898-9.**
Edited by Henry O. Forbes. Liverpool, England: Free Public Museums, 1903. 598p. map.

A beautifully illustrated report on the conjoint expedition undertaken by representatives of the British and Liverpool Museums in 1898-99. Subjects recorded included mammals, birds, reptiles, spiders, insects, flora and geological formations, and for each species the Latin name is given, followed by size, where sited, and a description (which varies in depth according to the rarity of the subject).

203 **Fishes of the Red Sea and southern Arabia. vol. 1: Branchiostomidae to Polynemidae.**
H. W. Fowler. Jerusalem: Weizmann Science Press of Israel. 240p.

A classified list, illustrated by pen-and-ink drawings, of the Red Sea and Arabian Sea fish identified by the author. Each species is identified by its Latin name, followed by references to the scientific literature, locality where found, and a full description. The vernacular name is added where known, but the Arabic and Persian forms are poorly transcribed. Further volumes dealing with Percida, freshwater fishes, and Dactyl-opterida to Lophida were planned but never published.

204 **The mammals of Arabia.**
David L. Harrison. London: Benn, 1964-72. 3 vols.

The standard work in its field. The animals are listed in systematic order and each species is described with reference to its typology and nomenclature, its external and cranial characteristics and its distribution within the Arabian Peninsula. The entries conclude with general remarks, often based on the writings of travellers and zoologists. Distribution maps are given for each species, so that it is possible to tell easily which animals occur in Yemen and South Arabia.

205 **The plants in Pehr Forsskål's 'Flora Aegyptiaco-Arabica' collected on the Royal Danish Expedition to Egypt and the Yemen, 1761-63.**
F. Nigel Hepper, I. Friis. Kew, England: Royal Botanic Gardens in association with the Botanical Museum, Copenhagen, 1994. 400p. bibliog.

Forskål was the botanist who accompanied the Danish Expedition to Yemen. He lost his life there, but his specimens and notes were taken back to Copenhagen, where the only survivor of the expedition, Carsten Niebuhr (q.v.), had them published posthumously in 1775 as *Flora Aegyptiaco-Arabica.* This work is a comprehensive guide to the general botanical work of Forskål, to the botanical names published in his book and to the specimens present in the Herbarium Forsskålii in Copenhagen, which contains about 1750 sheets. Each entry lists the Latin name, the vernacular name if known, site where found, the Herbarium reference, references to the plant in other publications, and any other details considered useful.

206 **An introduction to the vegetation of Yemen: ecological basis, floristic composition, human influence.**
A. Al-Hubaishi, K. Müller-Hohenstein. Eschborn, Germany: Deutsche Gesellschaft für Technische Zusammenarbeit, 1984. 209p. (English text) and 65p. (Arabic text). bibliog.

After a general introduction which sets North Yemen in its continental context, the six natural regions of the country are studied from the points of view of climate, zonal plant formations, riverine plant formations and human influence. There is an important illustrated section which shows different environments, ranging from the mangrove swamps near al-Luḥayyah to the sand dunes of the desert near Marib, as well as photographs of around 120 different plants and a distribution chart.

207 **The mosquitoes of the Yemen.**
Kenneth L. Knight. *Proceedings of the Entomological Society of Washington,* vol. 55 (1953), p. 212-34. bibliog.

Twenty-seven kinds of mosquitoes were gathered from thirty-five sites in North Yemen. Between them they represented all the different topographical features of North Yemen (coastal plain, foothills, highland plateau), except the easternmost regions bordering the desert. Prior to this expedition, the author, who formed part of a United States Medical Research Unit, notes that only five kinds of mosquitoes had been recorded in North Yemen. Most of the specimens are described in considerable detail, and the article includes a full-page line-drawing.

208 **Arabia: sand, sea and sky.**
Michael McKinnon. London: BBC Books, 1990. 224p.

A well-illustrated general survey of the ecology and natural history of the whole Arabian Peninsula, which was written during the production of the television series of the same name. The book attempts to link geological formation, geography and climatic change with the evolution and behaviour of Arabian wildlife, and although many of the examples are specific to Saudi Arabia, there are numerous references to southern Arabia, and North Yemen in particular.

209 **The birds of Arabia.**
R. Meinertzhagen. Edinburgh, Scotland: Oliver & Boyd, 1954. 624p.

The first and largest monograph of the birds of the Arabia Peninsula. After a long introduction, dealing with geology, geography, and climate; desert coloration; distribution and migration; and systematics and nomenclature, the author provides a systematic list by family of all birds sighted in the Peninsula. For each bird, there is given (where possible) the Latin name, where first described, the description, the distribution, the habits, and allied forms. Nineteen birds are illustrated by coloured plates, and a further fifty by figures in the text. There are also thirty-five maps show the distribution of particular species.

210 **On the birds of southern Arabia.**
W. R. Ogilvie-Grant, with field notes by A. Blayney Percival.
Novitates Zoologicae, vol. 7 (1900), p. 243-73.

The first in a series of articles on Arabian ornithology produced by the author over the following fourteen years, this paper describes the results of an expedition which sought specimens in the area around Laḥij and further north, as well as incorporating the earlier work of J. W. Yerbury, H. E. Barnes and R. M. Hawker, all of which had been published in the journal *Ibis* between 1886 and 1898. In all, 193 species are noted, often in rather cursory fashion, with no more details than Latin name, references in the literature, where sited and brief description. For full bibliographical details of Ogilvie-Grant's other articles, see Ataur-Rahim (item no. 194).

211 **L'ittionimia nei paesi arabi dei Mari Rossi, Arabico e del Golfo Persico (o Arabico) = Fish names in the Arab countries of the Red and Arabian seas and the Arabian Gulf = L'ichtyonimie dans les pays arabes de la Mer Rouge, de l'Océan Indien et du Golfe Arabique.**
Giovanni Oman. Naples, Italy: Istituto Universitario Orientale, 1992. 194p. bibliog.

An illustrated list – there are 343 illustrations in all – of all the fish and marine creatures found off the coast of the Arabian Peninsula, including North and South Yemen. The Latin name is given, followed by the equivalents in English, French and Arabic, with any Arabic dialect variations noted by the author. There is a multilingual set of indexes, but the introduction is in Italian only.

212 **Some mammals of Yemen and their ectoparasites.**
Colin Campbell Sanborn, Harry Hoogstraal. *Fieldiana Zoology,* vol. 34 (1953), p. 229-52.

A report by members of the United States Medical Research Unit about parasite-bearing mammals found in North Yemen, particularly the area around Hodeida and Taʿizz. Since the party were advised not to bring firearms with them, mostly the smaller mammals such as mice, rats, bats and shrews were collected and examined, but the party did also trap a hyena, two gazelles, two foxes and several hares. Each mammal is fully described zoologically, but, surprisingly, sometimes only cursory data are offered on some of the parasites. This volume of *Fieldiana Zoology* contains two more reports by members of the Unit: 'Amphibians and reptiles of Yemen', by Karl P. Schmidt (p. 253-61), and 'Some mites of Yemen', by Charles D. Radford (p. 295-313).

213 **The birds of Yemen, southwestern Arabia, with an account of his journey thither by the collector G. W. Bury.**
W. L. Sclater. *Ibis,* 10th series, vol. 5 (1917), p. 129-86.

G. Wyman Bury visited Hodeida, Manākhah and Ṣanʿāʾ in North Yemen in 1912-13 and sent back more than 400 skins representing a hundred or so species to the British Museum. This article lists all the birds recorded by Bury in systematic order, with full Latin name, site where found, and any peculiarities. Quotations from Bury's travel notes are incorporated into the descriptions where appropriate. The article is updated in part by the 1937 article by G. L. Bates (see item no. 196).

214 **Biological diversity assessment of the Republic of Yemen.**
Daniel Martin Varisco, James Perran Ross, Anthony Milroy, edited by Michael R. W. Rands. Cambridge, England: International Council for Bird Preservation, 1992. 129p. bibliog. (ICBP Study Report, no. 52).

The results of a survey conducted during 1989, the purpose of which was to 'describe the state of Yemen's natural flora and fauna, identify the unique and endangered species and habitats, and develop a strategy for conservation of the country's biological resources within its overall development policy'. The main conclusion was that 'biological diversity is being drastically reduced by the rapid degredation of the environment'. The authors concentrate on North Yemen, and the Tihāmah in particular, and discuss the ecosystem, enivironmental policy, environmental awareness and training, and the impact of development on biological resources. Their recommendations emphasize the dangers of short-term development policies and the inability of local institutions to carry out conservation initiatives without external assistance and funding. Among the numerous appendices are lists of North Yemen's flora and fauna, and a case-study of the Jabal Buraʿ in the Tihāmah.

215 **Studies in the flora of Arabia: III: a biographical index of plant collectors in the Arabian Peninsula (including Socotra.)**
G. E. Wickens. *Notes from the Royal Botanic Gardens, Edinburgh,* vol. 40, no. 2 (1982), p. 301-30.

A fascinating guide to British, Arab, French, German, Dutch, Italian and American botanists (over 300 in all) who collected plants anywhere in the Arabian Peninsula. Many of the collectors specialized in the Yemens, from Petrus Forskål in the 18th century through the German geographers such as Rathjens and von Wissman to contemporary Yemenis like Ali Saleh Balaidi. In the previous issue of the *Notes from the Royal Botanic Gardens, Edinburgh* (vol. 40, no. 1 [1982], p. 43-61), A. G. Miller, I. C. Hedge and R. A. King have prepared a useful botanical bibliography, which partially updates the work of Ataur-Rahim (see item no. 194), 'Studies in the flora of Arabia: I: a botanical bibliography of the Arabian peninsula'.

216 **Fauna of Saudi Arabia.**
Edited by W. Wittmer, W. Büttiker, F. Krupp, V. Mahnert. Basle, Switzerland: Pro Entomologia; Riyadh: National Commission for Wildlife Conservation and Development, 1979- . annual.

The most important scientific work on the biology of Saudi Arabia, this periodical also contains numerous articles from volume five (1983) onwards which deal with the whole of the Arabian Peninsula, and some from volume six (1984) onwards which deals specifically with Yemen. Among articles with material relevant to Yemen are: freshwater fishes, and Lepidoptera (vol. 5); Coleoptera, Lepidoptera, and Odonata (vol. 6); terrestrial isopods, amphibians, and Carnivora (vol. 7 and vol. 15); Crustacea, and geckoes (vol. 8); Hymenoptera, and snakes (vol. 9); Coleoptera, Diptera and lizards (vol. 10); Odonata, Apionidae, and mammals (vol. 11); insects, arachnids, and molluscs (vol. 12); scorpions (vol. 14); and mites (vol. 15). All of the articles are thoroughly researched with full bibliographies, and many are of considerable length, particularly J. Gasparetti's catalogue of 'Snakes of Arabia' in volume nine, which runs to almost 300 pages, and the article by J. Gasparetti and others, 'Turtles of Arabia' in volume thirteen, which is almost 200 pages long.

217 **On the mammals of Aden.**
J. W. Yerbury, Oldfield Thomas. *Proceedings of the Zoological Society of London* (1895), p. 542-55.

The first serious attempt to classify mammals in any part of South Arabia. Yerbury collected thirty-two specimens in Aden, Shaykh ʿUthmān and Laḥij, ranging from bats, gerbils and mice to porcupines, foxes and hares.

A new journey in southern Arabia.
See item no. 191.

Prehistory and Archaeology

218 **Archaeological discoveries in South Arabia.**
Richard LeBaron Bowen, Frank P. Albright. Baltimore, Maryland: The Johns Hopkins Press, 1958. 315p. maps. bibliog. (Publications of the American Foundation for the Study of Man, vol. 2).

This volume deals with South Arabian material uncovered in Wādī Bayḥān (Western Aden Protectorate) and Marib (North Yemen) by expeditions funded by the American Foundation for the Study of Man between 1950 and 1952. The principal excavations in Wādī Bayḥān revealed the site of Timnaʿ, the ancient capital of the kingdom of Qataban, and the associated field system and irrigation canals. Inscriptions and bronze sculptures were also discovered. In Marib, the team excavated the oval temple enclosure known as Maḥram Bilqīs or the ʿAwwām Temple, and the linked mausoleum and tomb complex.

219 **Fouilles de Shabwa: rapports préliminaires.** (Excavations at Shawbah: preliminary reports.)
Edited by Jean-François Breton. Paris: Geuthner, 1992. 431p.

Originally issued a a special volume of the journal *Syria* (vol. 68, nos. 1-4 [1991]), this collected work contains sixteen contributions mainly in French, which summarize the results of fifteen years' work excavating the capital of Ancient Ḥaḍramawt. Five authors deal mainly with the Royal Palace in Shabwah, while the others look at the architecture of the site in general, at its altars and tombs, at the beads, seals and coinage found there, and at the irrigation system which served the city.

220 **The tombs and moon temple of Hureidha (Hadhramaut.)**
G. Caton Thompson. London: Society of Antiquaries, 1944. 191p. 80 plates. bibliog. (Reports of the Research Committee of the Society of Antiquaries, no. 13).

The results of the first systematic excavations in the Ḥaḍramawt, conducted under difficult conditions in 1937-38 by Gertrude Caton Thompson, Elinor Gardiner and

Freya Stark (for a different perspective on the expedition see *A winter in Arabia* by Freya Stark [item no. 190]). The party conducted detailed excavations at Ḥurayḍah in Wādī ʿAmd, and, although there were no spectacular discoveries or rich finds, it was possible to establish that the ancient inhabitants lived 'on the fruits of diligent, if sparse, agriculture and the products of their flocks', and that there were significant contacts with Hellenistic, and, possibly, Sasanian culture.

221 **Zabid Project pottery manual 1995: pre-Islamic and Islamic ceramics from the Zabid area, North Yemen.**
Christopher Ciuk, E. J. Keall. Oxford, England: Tempus Reparatum, 1996. 119p. map. bibliog. (British Archaeological Reports, International Series, no. 655).

The Royal Ontario Museum began excavations in Zabīd in the winter of 1981-82 and continued up to and including 1995. Given the continuity of their work, the authors have been able in this volume to provide the most detailed descriptions of pottery found in any site in either North or South Yemen. Using techniques of ceramic analysis developed by scholars at the University of Warsaw and their own developing knowledge of local typology, they have succeeded in distinguishing ten different periods of manufacture ranging from prehistory (before 1500 BC) to the modern (1950 to the present). Each find is given a provenance, a period, a reference to a comparable find elsewhere in Yemen (if available) and is illustrated by a line-drawing (sometimes coloured in).

222 **An ancient South Arabian necropolis: objects from the second campaign (1951) in the Timnaʿ cemetery.**
Ray L. Cleveland. Baltimore, Maryland: The Johns Hopkins Press, 1965. 188p. (Publications of the American Foundation for the Study of Man, vol. 4).

A descriptive catalogue of objects from Timnaʿ in Wādī Bayḥān (Western Aden Protectorate), uncovered during the 1951 campaign mounted by the American Foundation for the Study of Man. The objects are arranged by type, rather than by burial groups or by stratum, and range from statuettes of the human figure, to bronze objects, beads and stone housings for memorial objects. The largest single group described is the array of bases designed to hold upright polished plaques, although only about twenty or so plaques were recovered compared to some 180 bases. Almost all of the objects in the catalogue are illustrated by black-and-white photographs.

223 **The pre-Islamic antiquities at the Yemen National Museum.**
Paolo M. Costa. Rome: L'Erma di Bretschneider, 1978. 52p. map. (Studia Archaeologica, no. 19).

The catalogue of and guide to the 121 exhibits in the Yemen National Museum in Ṣanʿāʾ. It is divided into four sections: on religious objects; sculptures; architectural decoration; and inscriptions. Most of the objects are illustrated by photographs, and the catalogue contains a useful introduction to the history of archaeological exploration in Yemen, and to the problems of South Arabian chronology.

224 **The Bronze Age culture of Hawlān aṭ-Ṭiyāl and al-Ḥadā (Republic of Yemen): a first general report.**
Edited by Alessandro de Maigret. Rome: IsMEO, 1990. 2 vols. (50p. English text and 74p. Arabic text. maps. 45 figs. 52 plates) (Reports and Memoirs, Istituto Italiano per il Medio ed Estremo Oriente, Centro Studi e Scavi Archeologici, vol. 24).

In 1981, the Italian Archaeological Mission in Yemen discovered a promising site to the east of Ṣanʿāʾ on the road to Ṣirwāḥ and Marib and conducted field research there and on three other sites nearby until 1985. The site turned out to date from the 3rd-2nd millennium BC, a period hitherto unattested in South Arabian archaeology. The first volume of this report contains a comprehensive survey of all the ecological and environmental observations made by the team, and a study of all the material it collected, while volume two consists of drawings, photographs and a portfolio of maps.

225 **The excavations of the Temple of Nakraḥ at Barāqish (Yemen).**
Alessandro de Maigret. *Proceedings of the Seminar for Arabian Studies,* vol. 21 (1991), p. 159-72.

Barāqish was the second largest city of the Kingdom of Maʿin and was captured by the Roman general Aelius Gallus in 24 BC. It was destroyed shortly afterwards, re-occupied during the Islamic period, and definitively abandoned in the seventeenth century. This report of the preliminary excavations by the Italian Archaeological Mission in 1989-90 describes the findings from both the Islamic and the Minaean periods, but concentrates on the ancient hypostyle temple of Nakraḥ. It is called by the author 'without doubt the most spectacular [temple] of all those discovered so far [in South Arabia]'.

226 **The Sabaean archaeological complex in the Wādī Yalā (Eastern Hawlān aṭ-Ṭiyāl, Yemen Arab Republic): a preliminary report.**
Edited by Alessandro de Maigret. Rome: IsMEO, 1988. 59p. (English text) and 83p. (Arabic text). maps. 36 figs. 56 plates. (Reports and Memoirs, Istituto Italiano per il Medio ed Estremo Oriente, Centro Studi e Scavi Archeologici, vol. 21).

Research by the Italian Archaeological Mission in North Yemen began in 1980, with the purpose of discovering 'the cultural and historical premises that determined the sudden appearance of great state complexes in the southern corner of the Arabian Peninsula during the first half of the first millennium B.C.'. In 1985, the Mission transferred its attention to the previously unknown area of Wādī Dhanah, and discovered 'an entire, hitherto unexplored city, complete with its own external economic system and its own ritual/cultic features'. This volume presents the initial findings in both English and Arabic, with numerous illustrations, photographs and maps.

227 **Archäologische Berichte aus dem Yemen.** (Archaeological reports from Yemen).
Deutsches Archäologisches Institut Ṣanʿāʾ. Mainz am Rhein, Germany: Verlag Philipp von Zabern, 1982- .

Eight volumes have so far been published of this survey of the activities of the German Archaeological Institute in Ṣanʿāʾ, which has been operating since 1978. Some of the research is devoted to Islamic archaeology, such as the Great Mosque of Ṣanʿāʾ, but most of it concentrates on pre-Islamic sites, in particular the excavations at Marib, and there are several chapters on the discoveries there, including inscriptions, masonry, and aquatic sediments. The whole of the second volume is devoted to a study of the geomorphology of the site by Ueli Brunner – *Die Erforschung der antiken Oase vom Marib mit Hilfe geomorphologischer Untersuchungsmethoden* (Researching the ancient oasis of Marib with the help of geomorphological methods of inquiry).

228 **Monuments of South Arabia.**
D. B. Doe. Santa Maria la Bruna, Italy: Falcon Press; Cambridge, England: Oleander Press, 1983. 284p. bibliog.

A very detailed survey of every pre-Islamic archaeological site in both North and South Yemens and Oman from Najrān in the east to Musandam in the west. Many of these sites had been personally visited by the author during his tenure of office as Director of Antiquities and Archaeological Adviser in Aden and his views of early historical developments in the region carry considerable weight. The book begins with a geographical survey of the region, moves on to the prehistoric period, when he describes monuments by type (tombs, standing stones, walled sites, etc.), passes on to a discussion of the cultures of southern Arabia during the time of the kingdoms of Qataban and Saba, and finishes with an analysis of the great towns and temples of the pre-Islamic period.

229 **Pottery sites near Aden.**
D. B. Doe. *Journal of the Royal Asiatic Society* (Oct. 1963), p. 150-62.

An extension of the article by Lane and Serjeant (see item no. 242), which goes further in identifying some of the sites, particularly in the region above Zinjibār, and around Laḥij.

230 **Socotra: an archaeological reconnaissance in 1967.**
D. B. Doe. Miami, Florida: Field Research Projects, 1970. 156p. bibliog.

An extensive historical, geographical and archaeological survey of Socotra, ʿAbd al-Kūrī and the Kuria Muria islands, which records all significant buildings, including cave-dwellings and ruins. There are photographs of every site, as well as reproductions of any inscriptions or graffiti found. The author covers the same ground in his later publication, *Socotra, island of tranquillity* (see item no. 5).

231 **An archaeological journey to Yemen, March–May 1947.**
Ahmed Fakhry. Cairo: Government Press, 1951-52. 3 vols. map. bibliog.

The author, a trained archaeologist, was able to visit Ṣirwāḥ, Marib, Raghwān and the Jawf areas of North Yemen in 1947. He made a thorough study of all the ruins visible, relating his survey to the information given in earlier travel accounts, from Thomas Joseph Arnaud in 1843 to Muḥammad Tawfīq in 1944-45. He also took his camera with him and volume three comprises ninety-two photographs, mainly of archaeological sites, but also shots of 'land and people in Yemen'. One of Fakhry's principal objects in visiting North Yemen was to study inscriptions, and volume one records everything he was permitted to copy, although many of the texts had previously been published in critical editions. Volume two, on the other hand, contains a translation and interpretation (in French) by Gonzague Ryckmans of all the previously unpublished inscriptions, and is an important contribution to South Arabian epigraphy.

232 **The Dhamār plain, Yemen: a preliminary study of the archaeological landscape.**
McGuire Gibson, T. J. Wilkinson. *Proceedings of the Seminar for Arabian Studies,* vol. 25 (1995), p. 159-81.

An investigation of the relatively neglected area of Central Yemen, emphasizing 'the relationship between archaeological sites and the development of the anthropogenic landscape comprising suites of terraces, dams and field systems'. The team from the Oriental Institute, Chicago, selected a number of small areas, which were examined for between one and four days, in order to provide representative samples of the region's diversity. The team's conclusions were that before the rise of the kingdom of Himyar, the region was 'rather densely populated', and that 'the shift of political power that took place with the emergence of Himyar may have been accompanied by developments in the economy and agricultural technology that enabled the growing Himyarite population to adapt to the moist highlands of the Yemeni core'. Further information was published in 1997 under the name of T. J. Wilkinson (see item no. 260).

233 **Archaeology in the Aden Protectorates.**
G. Lankester Harding. London: HM Stationery Office, 1964. 61p. 61 plates.

The first survey by an archaeologist of all the sites open to inspection in both the Western and Eastern Aden Protectorates (some sites, notably Shabwah and Ḥajar al-Nab were considered too dangerous to visit). Most of the sites had been visited before, either by travellers or administrators, but the author was able to add six new sites in his survey which he conducted in 1960-61. For each site, the author records the location and condition, and describes any remains of buildings, inscriptions, pottery or other artefacts. All these are illustrated by black-and-white photographs or drawings.

234 **Archaeological research into the Islamic period in Yemen: preliminary notes on the French expedition, 1993.**
Claire Hardy-Guilbert, Axelle Rougeulle. *Proceedings of the Seminar for Arabian Studies,* vol. 25 (1995), p. 29-44.

The authors note that the Islamic period is very badly documented archaeologically in Yemen, with the exact chronology of Yemeni pottery still inadequately known. This article attempts to rectify the situation in part, by listing the ceramic finds from three sites near Aden and three sites from the Tihāmah, including Mocha (which, interestingly, yielded only sherds of Far Eastern or European imports, mainly from the 16th to the 19th centuries). The authors are able to identify many of the pottery finds as from the Islamic period, but, due to the paucity of material, do not draw any general conclusions from their findings.

235 **Sabaean inscriptions from Maḥram Bilqîs (Mârib).**
A. Jamme. Baltimore, Maryland: The Johns Hopkins Press, 1962. 477p. map. bibliog. (Publications of the American Foundation for the Study of Man, vol. 2).

Part one of this book contains the 300 or so inscriptions gathered by the author in Marib in 1951-52, as part of the archaeological team excavating the site. Each inscription comes with a full translation and detailed notes on textual and grammatical points. In Part two, the author attempts to establish a chronology for some of the dynasties which ruled Saba and Raydan.

236 **A map of Southern Yemeni rock art with notes on some of the subjects depicted.**
Michael Jung. *Proceedings of the Seminar for Arabian Studies,* vol. 24 (1994), p. 135-56.

A list of thirty-four sites in Southern Yemen where rock art is to be found, along with precise descriptions of the subjects depicted. The gazetteer is followed by a synthesis of the nature of the art, a good bibliography, and three plates.

237 **The religious monuments of ancient Southern Arabia: a preliminary typological classification.**
Michael Jung. *Annali dell'Istituto Universitario Orientale di Napoli,* vol. 48 (1988), p. 177-218. bibliog.

A wide-ranging survey of the archaeological literature on South Arabia, based, in the main, on the researches of the French, German, Italian, and UNESCO missions. The author divides the religious monuments into three kinds: rock sanctuaries (the oldest sites, with few human additions); sanctuaries with a rectangular grand plan (the author distinguishes seven varieties); and sanctuaries with a non-rectangular plan (two varieties). All these varieties are illustrated by line-drawings and photographs (where available). The author goes on to consider the chronology of early South Arabian history, discussing the theories of Jamme and Beeston (qq.v.), before moving on to the links between South Arabian constructions and those elsewhere proposed by numerous archaeologists and epigraphers.

238 **Research on rock art in North Yemen.**

Michael Jung. Naples, Italy: Istituto Universitario Orientale, 1991. 59p. maps. 14 plates. (Supplemento no. 66 agli *Annali*, vol. 51, no. 1 [1991]).

A complementary study to the one published by the author in 1994 for South Yemen (see item no. 236), this monographs lists the sixty-three sites at which rock art can be found in North Yemen. The catalogue is followed by a discussion of the chronology of the art, the oldest of which goes back to the Neolithic period, and by an illustrated analysis of the motifs employed by the artists.

239 **The dynamics of Zabīd and its hinterland: the survey of a town on the Tihāmah plain of North Yemen.**

E. J. Keall. *World Archaeology,* vol. 14, no. 3 (1983), p. 378-91.

A report of the early site reconnaissance of Zabīd by the Canadian Archaeological Mission designed 'to locate sites to establish a ceramic typology and to examine standing architectural remains'. The Mission was unable to undertake excavations, but succeeded in establishing working hypotheses regarding settlement patterns and the classification of pottery. The finds of the Mission are set in historical context particularly regarding trading links, both inland and overseas through Mocha.

240 **A few facts about Zabīd.**

E. J. Keall. *Proceedings of the Seminar for Arabian Studies,* vol. 19 (1989), p. 61-9.

A report on the excavations undertaken in Zabīd by the Canadian Archaeological Mission in 1988. While previous expeditions between 1981 and 1983 had concentrated on recording architectural features and documenting historical traditions connected with standing monuments (see above), this report looked at the pottery recovered from sites in Zabīd, at brick-lined septic pits, and at the history of the Citadel. Reports of the 1982 and 1983 seasons are published as 'Zabīd and its hinterland: 1982 report' (*Proceedings of the Seminar for Arabian Studies,* vol. 13 [1983], p. 53-69) and 'A preliminary report on the architecture of Zabīd' (*Proceedings of the Seminar for Arabian Studies,* vol. 14 [1984], p. 51-65), while later work includes 'Drastic changes in 16th century Zabīd' (*Proceedings of the Seminar for Arabian Studies,* vol. 21 [1991)] p. 79-96), 'Smokers' pipes and the fine pottery tradition of Ḥays' (*Proceedings of the Seminar for Arabian Studies,* vol. 22 [1992], p. 29-46), another article on pipes for tobacco,'One man's Mede is another man's Persian: one man's coconut is another man's grenade' (*Muqarnas,* vol. 10 [1993], p. 275-85) all by E. J. Keall. In addition Ingrid Hehmeyer wrote 'Physical evidence of engineered water systems in mediaeval Zabīd' (*Proceedings of the Seminar for Arabian Studies,* vol. 25 [1995], p. 45-54).

241 **A survey of the Islamic sites near Aden and in the Abyan district of Yemen.**

Geoffrey King, Cristina Tonghini. London: School of Oriental and African Studies, University of London, 1996. 95p. bibliog.

The first part of this survey establishes the historical geography of the region, its mapping, and the progress of archaeological research in the area, before moving on to a field survey and report on eight different sites. Part two describes the glass and pottery finds of the survey, and the volume concludes with a full range of photographs and maps.

242 **Pottery and glass fragments from the Aden littoral, with historical notes.**
Arthur Lane, R. B. Serjeant. *Journal of the Royal Asiatic Society* (Oct. 1948), p. 108-31.

A two-part article devoted to pottery and glass finds at three sites near Aden, two inland and one on the coast, at Zinjibār, 35 miles west of Aden. Much of the pottery found in Zinjibār is of Far Eastern origin, and Serjeant contributes a learned disquisition on references to Chinese porcelain in South Arabian historical sources, and on the importation of glass from both the Far East and Venice. Lane, on the other hand, classifies the finds, and attempts to identify their origin and dating.

243 **Monuments of Socotra.**
Vitalij V. Naumkin, Alexander V. Sedov. In: *Athens, Aden, Arikamedu: essays on the interrelations between India, Arabia and the Eastern Mediterranean.* Edited by Marie-Françoise Boussac, Jean-François Salles. New Delhi: Manohar; Centre des Sciences Humaines, 1995, p. 193-250.

Building on the data supplied by P. L. Shinnie and D. B. Doe (see items 230, 253), a joint Russian–Yemeni expedition carried out excavations and archaeological investigations on Socotra in 1983-85, 1987 and 1989. The earliest evidence found of human habitation on the island were the remains of a flint workshop near Rakuf, plus a small cemetery with specific dolmen-shaped grave structures, dating from the second half of the first millennium BC. The authors discuss data from several other pre-Islamic cemeteries, before moving on to the remains of the Mahrī colonization from South Arabia in the 15th-16th centuries and the brief Portuguese conquest at the beginning of the 16th century.

244 **Qataban and Sheba: exploring ancient kingdoms on the biblical spice routes of Arabia.**
Wendell Phillips. London: Gollancz, 1955. 335p.

An entertaining account of the trials and tribulations of archaeological excavation in South Arabia. The author accompanied the expeditions mounted by the American Foundation for the Study of Man to Bayḥān in the Western Aden Protectorate and Marib in North Yemen in 1950-51, and conducted many of the negotiations on their behalf. The scientific results of the excavations were published by Gus W. Van Beek, A. Jamme, Frank P. Albright and William LeBaron Bowen (see items 218, 235, 255).

245 **Ce que trois campagnes de fouilles nous ont déjà appris sur Shabwa, capitale du Hadramout antique.** (What three seasons of excavations have already taught us about Shabwah, the ancient capital of Ḥaḍramawt.)
Jacqueline Pirenne. *Raydan: Journal of Ancient Yemeni Antiquities and Epigraphy,* vol. 1 (1978), p. 125-42.

The results of a French expedition to Shabwah in 1975-77, which excavated two large structures near the North Gate.

246 **Corpus des inscriptions et antiquités sud-arabes.** (Corpus of South Arabian inscriptions and antiquities.)
Jacqueline Pirenne (et al.). Louvain, Belgium: Peeters, 1977-86. 4 vols in 6 vols.

A very important collective work, which catalogues several hundred inscriptions and objects recovered in South Arabia by particular expeditions (volume 1, sections 1 and 2), and thus continues the work undertaken in part four of the *Corpus Inscriptionum Semiticarum* (Paris: Imprimerie Nationale), three volumes of which appeared between 1889 and 1927; the publication also lists the objects displayed in Aden Museum (volume 2, sections 1 and 2). The detailed descriptions are complemented by two separate volumes, one a most thorough *Bibliographie générale systématique* (General classified bibliography) by Christian Robin, which lists several thousand books and articles in Western languages on all aspects of ancient South Arabia (language, epigraphy, archaeology, religion, history, travel and exploration, and flora and fauna), the other the *Tables* (Indexes) to the whole work, compiled by C. Fauvéaud-Brassaud.

247 **Les témoins écrits de la région de Shabwa et l'histoire.** (The written evidence of the Shabwah region and history.)
Jacqueline Pirenne. Paris: Geuthner, 1990. 161p. 83 plates. (Bibliothèque Archéologique et Historique/Institut Français d'Archéologie du Proche-Orient, vol. 134).

The author was the director of the French Archaeological Mission in Yemen, most of whose results were published in the journal *Raydan* (see item no. 918). In this book, she presents a study of the inscriptions found at Shabwah, along with the inscriptions and graffiti from the surrounding area, in order to place the excavations in their historical context. Numerous other issues in South Arabian prehistory are also dealt with, including chronological problems, Ethiopian immigration and the nature of the kingdom of Ḥaḍramawt.

248 **Sabaica: Bericht über die archäologischen Ergebnisse seiner zweiten, dritten und vierten Reisen nach Südarabien: Teil 1 – Der Reisebericht; Teil 2 – Die unlokalisierte Funde.** (Sabaica: report on the archaeological results of his second, third and fourth journeys to South Arabia: Part 1 – The travel narrative; Part 2 – The unlocalized finds.)
Carl Rathjens. Hamburg, Germany: Ludwig Appel, 1953-55. 2 vols. (Mitteilungen aus dem Museum für Völkerkunde in Hamburg, Band 24).

A comprehensive report on journeys undertaken in 1931, 1934 and 1937-38 to ʿAmrān, Shibām, Kawkabān, Ṣanʿāʾ and elsewhere in North Yemen in search of archaeological remains. These are described in great detail, both in volume one, where there are numerous sketches of inscriptions and rock carvings, and especially in volume two, which provides more than 500 photographs of statuettes, reliefs, ceramics and other objects. Rathjens also describes his first journey of 1927-28, which he undertook in the company of Hermann von Wissman in the region of Ḥajjah and Ḥāz, to the north and west of Ṣanʿāʾ.

249 **The pre-Islamic South Arabian bronze horse in the Dumbarton Oaks collection.**
Jacques Ryckmans. *Dumbarton Oaks Papers,* vol. 29 (1975), p. 280-307.

A study of one of the most important pre-Islamic artefacts ever discovered. The evidence for dating and reconstruction is re-examined by Margaret Lyttleton in 'The South Arabian bronze horse at Dumbarton Oaks' (*Proceedings of the Seminar for Arabian Studies,* vol. 21 [1991], p. 147-57).

250 **Archaeology along the spice route of Yemen.**
James A. Sauer, Jeffrey A. Blakely (et al.). In: *Araby the Blest: studies in Arabian archaeology.* Edited by D. T. Potts. Copenhagen: Carsten Niebuhr Institute of Near Eastern Studies, University of Copenhagen; Museum Tusculanum Press, 1988, p. 91-115. maps. bibliog.

After an overview of the first expeditions to Yemen sponsored by the American Foundation for the Study of Man in 1950-52 (see items 218, 222, 235, 255), the authors describe and evaluate the second expedition, the Wādī al-Jubah Archaeological Project (see item no. 257), which has been excavating sites since 1982 in a previously unexcavated valley in the Marib region. The aim is 'to discover sites of all periods, place them in chronological sequence, and discern human use of the area from the evidence of early man to modern times'. While there is archaeological evidence from the Neolithic period (5th to 4th millennia BC), the majority of the finds have come from the pre-Islamic period, in the first millennium BC, showing 'an almost symbiotic relationship between trade and agriculture along the spice routes between Qataban and Sheba'.

251 **Bi'r Ḥamad: a pre-Islamic settlement in the western Wādī Ḥaḍramawt.**
Alexander V. Sedov. *Arabian Archaeology and Epigraphy,* vol. 6, no. 2 (1995), p. 103-15.

The first in a series of articles discussing various sites investigated by the joint Russian–Yemeni Archaeological Expedition to southern Yemen between 1983 and 1994 and published under the overall title of 'Notes on an archaeological map of the Ḥaḍramawt'. Each site is described in detail, sketch maps of the monuments provided, and the artefacts catalogued. The second article, 'Al-Guraf in the Wâdî ʿIdim', was published in *Arabian Archaeology and Epigraphy,* vol. 7, no. 1 (1996), p. 52-62 (with A. as-Saqqaf), and the third, 'Monuments of the Wādī al-ʿAyn', in vol. 7, no. 2 (1996), p. 253-78.

252 **Temples of Ancient Ḥaḍramawt.**
Alexander V. Sedov, Ahmad Bâtâyiʿ. *Proceedings of the Seminar for Arabian Studies,* vol. 24 (1994), p. 183-90.

Basing themselves on work conducted by the Russian–Yemeni joint expedition, particularly in the oasis of Raybān (Wādī Duʿan), the authors describe the religious buildings dedicated to different gods in the Ḥaḍramawt pantheon. Nearly all of them date from the second half of the first millennium BC, or later, and are similar in style, i.e. rectangular in layout with a hypostyle hall. The authors discuss the internal decoration of the temples and speculate on the rituals involved. The article includes photographs of the existing buildings, and reconstructions of the supposed originals.

253 **Socotra.**
P. L. Shinnie. *Antiquity,* vol. 134 (1960), p. 100-10.

The author participated in the 1956 Oxford University expedition to the island of Socotra, a general account of which was written by Douglas Botting (see item no. 153). This article describes the archaeological remains found by the expedition, namely some forts, and a mosque. The earliest traces of human occupation were from the late Middle Ages.

254 **Arabian archaeology and epigraphy: special issue on the Tihāmah.**
Edited by Francine Stone. Copenhagen, Munksgaard, 1995, p. 209-85. map.

This special issue (vol. 6, no. 4) of *Arabian Archaeology and Epigraphy* contains seven articles on the archaeology of the Tihāmah, the coastal plain of North Yemen, which stretches from the Bab al-Mandab in the south to present-day Saudi city of Jīzān in the north. In the first article, Lionel Casson gives a useful summary of the Greek and Latin sources on the Tihāmah from Herodotus to Ptolemy, and in the second, Christian Robin draws together all the strands of epigraphic evidence from South Arabian inscriptions, 'giving the most coherent picture to date of the Tihama tribes'. A. F. L. Beeston, to whose memory the volume is dedicated, assesses, in a posthumous contribution, how much influence Saba exerted over the coastal plain, then Barbara Davidde analyses a newly discovered horde of imitation Athenian tetradrachms. Articles by two Yemeni archaeologists follow, both translated from the Arabic, and both on the city of al-Sawā, the ancient capital of the province of al-Maʿāfir in the southern Tihāmah. Finally, Robert T. O. Wilson looks at the Arabic sources for the pre- and early Islamic history of the Tihāmah, particularly al-Ḥasan ibn Aḥmad al-Hamdānī (d. c. 945) and Ibn al-Mujāwir (d. 1291).

255 **Hajar Bin Humeid: investigations at a pre-Islamic site in South Arabia.**
Gus W. Van Beek. Baltimore, Maryland: The Johns Hopkins Press, 1969. 419p. (Publications of the American Foundation for the Study of Man, vol. 5).

A very full description of the pottery unearthed at Ḥajar ibn Ḥumayd in Wādī Bayḥān by the expeditions mounted by the American Foundation for the Study of Man in 1950 and 1951. The stratigraphy, chronology, and typology of both the pottery and the other finds from the mound – such as beads, stone and metal objects – are fully discussed. There is a chapter on inscriptions by A. Jamme and the whole work is illustrated by numerous line-drawings, diagrams, and photographs.

256 **Archaeological observations around Marib, 1976.**
Rosalind Wade. *Proceedings of the Seminar for Arabian Studies,* vol. 9 (1979), p. 114-23.

Using aerial photographs and an on-the-ground survey, the author, along with Christian Robin, studied the hydrology of the ancient Marib dam, showing that the north and south sluices were linked by an earth-banked dam, and that the whole south canal system had now disappeared. Further related work on the dam by J. E. Dayton can be found in 'A discussion of the hydrology of Marib' (*Proceedings of the Seminar for Arabian Studies,* vol. 9 [1979], p. 124-9) and 'Marib revisited' (*Proceedings of the Seminar for Arabian Studies,* vol. 11 [1981], p. 7-26).

257 **The Wadi al-Jubah Archaeological Project.**
Washington, DC: American Foundation for the Study of Man, 1984-96. 5 vols.

One of the most extensive explorations of any South Arabian site, the Wādī al-Jubah project has been investigating, since 1982, a twelve-mile-long valley in the west of the Republic of Yemen, about twenty miles south of Marib. The volumes published by the Project include: *Site reconnaissance in North Yemen, 1982,* by Michael R. Toplyn (volume 1); *Site reconnaissance in North Yemen, 1983,* by Jeffrey A. Blakely, James A. Sauer, Michael R. Toplyn (volume 2); *Site reconnaissance in the Yemen Arabic Republic, 1984: the stratigraphic probe at Hajar ar-Rayhani,* by William D. Glanzman, Abdu O. Ghaleb (volume 3); *Geological and archaeological reconnaissance in the Yemen Arab Republic,* by William C. Overstreet, Maurice J. Grolier, Michael R. Toplyn (volume 4 [see item no. 67]); and *Environmental research in support of archaeological investigations in the Yemen Arab Republic, 1982-1987,* by William C. Overstreet, Robert Brinkmann, Jeffrey A. Blakely (volume 5). A general evaluation of the Project is given by James A. Sauer and Jeffrey A. Blakely in a separately published article (see item no. 250).

258 **Pleistocene sites in southern Yemen.**
Norman M. Whalen, Kevin E. Schatte. *Arabian Archaeology and Epigraphy,* vol. 8, no. 1 (1997), p. 1-10.

The authors continue the work of the Russian archaeological team under K. Amirkhanov in investigating the earliest sites of human occupation in South Arabia. In the autumn of 1992, they discovered thirty-seven sites to the north-west of Aden, with sixteen having a pebble-tool industry (Mode 1) and twenty-seven a bifacial industry (Mode 2). Precise dating for the Yemeni sites is not yet possible, but evidence points to the arrival of humans in Arabia rather earlier than had previously been supposed.

259 **Islamic archaeology in Aden and the Hadhramaut.**
Donald S. Whitcomb. In: *Araby the Blest: studies in Arabian archaeology.* Edited by D. T. Potts. Copenhagen: Carsten Niebuhr Institute of Ancient Near Eastern Studies, University of Copenhagen; Museum Tusculanum Press, 1988, p. 176-263. maps. bibliog.

Using ceramic finds and historical sources, the author studies, in a most stimulating way, 'the cultural ties binding coastal settlements and agricultural highlands'. Archaeologically, he is able to distinguish three periods in the Islamic history of South Arabia: from the 9th to the 12th centuries, when the pottery shows distinct ʿAbbāsid influence; from 1150 to 1500, when the Rasūlid dynasty (1229-1454) brought Mamlūk trade to the region, and the disruptions and changes of the 16th century to the 19th, where the archaeological remains of Aden are overshadowed by the complexity of finds from the Ḥaḍramawt and its ports.

260 **The archaeology of the Yemen High Plains: a preliminary chronology.**
T. J. Wilkinson, C. Edens, McGuire Gibson. *Arabian Archaeology and Epigraphy,* vol. 8, no. 1 (1997), p. 99-142.

The authors, from the Oriental Institute in Chicago, undertook a detailed survey of a sample area northeast of Dhamār, an area of considerable rainfall and agricultural activity. Their preliminary findings were published in 1995 under the name of McGuire Gibson (see item no. 232), and this report gives more details of the ceramics, lithics and buildings dating from several periods which the team found. Although there were few artefacts which fitted in easily to the aceramic pre-Bronze Age Holocene cultures, later evidence suggested that settlements began suddenly in the area, probably in the third millennium BC, with some sites being as much as five to six hectares in size and being characterized by some degree of social complexity. The article concludes with an illustrated description of the Dhamār Survey finds.

261 **Zur Archäologie und antiken Geographie von Südarabien: Ḥaḍramaut, Qatabân und das ʿAden-Gebiet in der Antike.** (On the archaeology and ancient geography of South Arabia: Ḥaḍramawt, Qataban and the Aden region in ancient times.)
Hermann von Wissmann. Istanbul, Turkey: Nederlands Historisch-Archaeologisch Instituut in het Nabije Oosten, 1968. 119p.

A survey of archaeological research in South Yemen, comparing the discoveries of Doe, Harding and Bowen (qq.v.) with epigraphic information and data from the ancient geographers such as Ptolemy. The work is extremely scholarly, but somewhat episodic, and the length of each chapter varies considerably, from one paragraph on al-Ḍāliʿ (Dhala) to 25 pages on the highlands of ancient Madhay, depending mainly on the number of inscriptions available.

Eduard Glasers Reise nach Mârib. (Eduard Glaser's expedition to Marib.)

See item no. 125.

Rapport sur une mission archéologique dans le Yémen. (Report on an archaeological mission to Yemen.)

See item no. 130.

History

General

262 **The new Islamic dynasties: a chronological and genealogical manual.**
Clifford Edmund Bosworth. Edinburgh, Scotland: Edinburgh University Press, 1996. 389p. bibliogs.

A thoroughly revised and reworked version of the author's *The Islamic dynasties: a chronological and genealogical handbook* (1967), this is an invaluable guide for the historian, giving the names of the rulers of every Muslim dynasty, along with their dates and their honorific title (if any). The first chapter deals with the dynasties who ruled Yemen from the Fertile Crescent, such as the Umayyads (661-750) and the ʿAbbāsids (750-1258), while chapter seven deals with the Arabian Peninsula and includes all local Yemeni dynasties, i.e. the Zaydī Imams (897-1962), the Ziyādids of Zabīd (818-1018), the Yuʿfurids of Ṣanʿāʾ and Janad (847-997), the Najāḥids of Zabīd (1022-1158), the Ṣulayḥids of Ṣanʿāʾ and Dhū Jiblah (1047-1138), the Zurayʿids of Aden (1080-1175), the Hamdānids of Ṣanʿāʾ (1099-1174), the Mahdids of Zabīd (1159-73), the Rasūlids of Taʿizz (1229-1454), and the Ṭāhirids of al-Miqrānah (1454-1517). Chapter twelve lists the rulers of the Ottoman Empire, which twice conquered and administered parts of North Yemen. There are brief historical notes on each dynasty as well as useful bibliographical references.

263 **Historical dictionary of Yemen.**
Robert D. Burrowes. Lanham, Maryland; London: Scarecrow Press, 1995. 507p. map. bibliog. (Asian Historical Dictionaries, no. 17).

A very useful publication, compiled by an expert in the contemporary politics of Yemen. It contains a descriptive essay, a chronology, a bibliography (p. 433-507), and almost a thousand entries on people, places, dynasties, organizations and themes in Yemeni history. The emphasis is clearly on the modern period in the history of both Yemens – the articles on the important medieval dynasties of the Rasūlids and the

Ṣulayḥids are together shorter than the article on the Supreme Yemeni Council, while the descriptive essay devotes less than a page to the pre-Islamic history of the country. Having said that, the entries on modern Yemen (and its two predecessors) – personalities, politics, administration and economic situation – are full and extremely informative.

264 **L'Arabie du Sud: histoire et civilisation.** (South Arabia: history and civilization.) Vol. 1: **Le peuple yéménite et ses racines.** (The people of Yemen and their roots.); Vol. 2: **La société yéménite de l'Hégire aux idéologies modernes.** (Yemeni society from the rise of Islam up to modern ideologies.)
Edited by Joseph Chelhod. Paris: Maisonneuve et Larose, 1984. 2 vols. (Islam d'Hier et d'Aujourd'hui, vols. 21-22).

A composite volume containing mainly articles in French, and covering the pre-Islamic, medieval and modern history of Yemen, as well as religion in Yemen since the rise of Islam (three articles) and physical and cultural anthropology (four articles). There are noteworthy contributions on the history of the Jews in Yemen (Yosef Tobi), the history of Islamic religious thought in Yemen (Etienne Renaud) and on emigration from Yemen (Alain Rouaud); and two articles by A. F. L. Beeston, 'The religions of pre-Islamic Arabia', and 'Judaism and Christianity in pre-Islamic Yemen', which are masterly summaries of what epigraphic material can tell us on these topics. The third volume on culture and institutions is mainly by Joseph Chelhod (q.v.).

265 **The Encyclopaedia of Islam.**
Leiden, The Netherlands: Brill, 1960-. New edition.

The single most indispensable source of information on all aspects of the history, geography, language, literature and culture of all Middle Eastern countries from the rise of Islam until this century, along with the history and culture of the whole of the pre-Islamic Arabian peninsula. There are numerous references to places, dynasties and individuals in the history of Yemen in the eight volumes (up to the letter S) published so far, and individual articles are cited where appropriate throughout this bibliography. The work is being continued at the rate of around four fascicules a year, and should be completed at some time during the first decade of the 21st century, at which point the original edition, published in four volumes plus supplement between 1908 and 1938, will be wholly superseded.

266 **Studies in Oriental culture and history: Festschrift for Walter Dostal.**
Edited by André Gingrich (et al.). Frankfurt am Main, Germany: Peter Lang, 1993. 287p.

Ten of the seventeen papers in this volume dedicated to the Austrian anthropologist and sociologist Walter Dostal deal with South Arabia. Three contributions deal with early South Arabian history and archaeology: Walter W. Müller looks at the concept of 'Heilige Hochzeit' (Holy Wedding), Hannes Galter investigates the occurrences of Saba in Assyrian royal inscriptions, while Jacques Ryckmans deciphers two rare examples of South Arabian epigraphy. In the medieval field, G. R. Smith elucidates Ibn al-Mujāwir's (d. 1291) interest in social relations, Ḥusayn ibn ʿAbdallāh al-ʿAmrī gives us an overview of the history of North Yemen between 1620 and 1918, Franck

Mermier uses 19th-century chronicles to explore the concept of 'pouvoir citadin', or people's power in Ṣanʿāʾ, Klaus Kreiser looks at the Ottoman bureaucracy in early 20th-century Yemen through the eyes of ʿAlī Emīrī, and André Gingrich examines how the relationship of major tribal groups to the central state authority has varied over time in North Yemen. There are also two anthropological studies: 'Zinā, some forms of marriage and allied topics in western Arabia' by R. B. Serjeant, and 'The plateau-and-valley complex in Ḥaḍramawt: Bā Tays case study' by Mikhail Rodionov.

267 **Arabian studies in honour of Mahmoud Ghul: symposium at Yarmouk University, December 8-11, 1984.**
Edited by Moawiyah M. Ibrahim. Wiesbaden, Germany; Harrassowitz, 1989. 177p. (English text) and 160p. (Arabic text). (Yarmouk University Publications, Institute of Archaeology and Anthropology Series, vol. 2).

This volume is the outcome of a conference held in memory of Mahmoud Ghul, Professor of Arabic at Yarmouk University, Jordan. It contains numerous important contributions both in English and Arabic on Yemen among which are: 'Mạhra and Arabs in South Arabia: a study in inter-ethnical relations', by Walter Dostal, which surveys how Arabs travellers and historians like Ibn al-Mujāwir (d. 1291) and al-Ḥasan ibn Aḥmad al-Hamdānī (d. c. 945) viewed the non-Arabic-speaking Mahrī tribe; 'A confrontation of the main hagiographic accounts of the Najrān persecution', by Jacques Ryckmans, which investigates the textual evidence for the martyrs of Najrān, with particular reference to the work of Irfan Shahid (see *The martyrs of Najrân,* item no. 307), who himself contributes a refutation, 'Further reflections on the sources for the Martyrs of Najrān'; and 'Dawlah, tribal shaykhs, the Manṣab of the Waliyyah Saʿīdah, *qasāmah,* in the Faḍlī Sultanate, South Arabian Federation', by R. B. Serjeant, who looks, with his customary erudition, at historical and legal issues in the Faḍlī Sultanate, particularly regarding the sanctuary of Saʿīdah ibn ʿUmar.

268 **A history of Arabia Felix or Yemen.**
R. L. Playfair. Farnborough, England: Gregg International, 1970. 193p. map.

A facsimile of the original edition published in Bombay, India, in 1859 (another facsimile was also published in 1970 by Philo Press of Amsterdam, The Netherlands), which has been included more as an example of 19th-century scholarship than as a major contribution to contemporary knowledge. Playfair attempts to survey the history of North Yemen plus Aden and Laḥij from the beginning of the Christian era up to 1856. He relies very heavily on travellers like Niebuhr (q.v.) (whom he consistently misquotes as Neibuhr) and orientalists like Caussin de Percival in providing the basic data for Yemeni history, and the end-result is of variable quality. Nevertheless, his work has been influential on many subsequent writers and cannot be entirely dismissed.

269 **Ḥāshid wa-Bakīl.**
G. Rentz. In: *The Encyclopaedia of Islam,* new edition. Leiden, The Netherlands: Brill, 1971, vol. 3, p. 259-60.

A summary of the historical role played by the two major tribal confederations of North Yemen, but the article is too short to do justice to its subject. Rather more useful is the article by J. Schleifer, 'Ḥāshid and Bakīl' in *The Encyclopaedia of Islam,* old edition, Leiden, The Netherlands: Brill, 1927, vol. 1, p. 285-6, which, basing itself on the work of al-Ḥasan ibn Aḥmad al-Hamdānī (d. c. 945) amd Eduard Glaser (q.v.), goes into much more detail about the clans making up the confederations and their geographical disposition.

270 **Historians and historiography of Ḥaḍramawt.**
R. B. Serjeant. *Bulletin of the School of Oriental and African Studies,* vol. 25 (1962), p. 239-61.

A very detailed survey of historical sources, mostly still in manuscript, for the Islamic period of Ḥaḍramī history. The author has discovered little relating to the first few centuries of Islamic rule, but references to Ḥaḍramawt become more extensive from the 13th century onwards, both in historical chronicles as well as books of *ansāb,* or genealogies of prominent families. The author also studies the sources available for the history of the struggle for supremacy in Ḥaḍramawt between the Kathīrī and Yāfiʿī tribes in the 19th century as well as the ʿAlawī-Irshādī dsipute between rival groups of Ḥaḍramī emigrants in Indonesia. The article concludes with an analysis of the works of living historians, with many of whom he was personally acquainted. For further bibliographical analyses of South Arabian historical sources, see the author's two-part article, 'Materials for South Arabian history', in the *Bulletin of the School of Oriental and African Studies,* vol. 13 (1950), p. 281-307 and p. 581-601.

271 **The interplay between tribal affinities and religious (Zaydī) authority in the Yemen.**
R. B. Serjeant. *Al-Abḥāth,* vol. 30 (1982), p. 11-50.

A complex, but very interesting article, which examines the relationship between the tribes of Yemen and central state power, mainly manifested in the Zaydī Imams of Ṣanʿāʾ. The author examines, firstly, the attitude of the Prophet to tribal power, and in particular how the great Southern confederacy of Hamdān eventually came to adhere to Islam. He follows this with an analysis of certain tribal concepts such as *mawaddah* (love and, thereby, loyalty) and *hijrah* (inviolable enclave), and how these relate to Zaydī authority from the time of the first ruler, al-Hādī ilā al-Ḥaqq (d. 911) up to and including the Imam Muḥammad al-Badr and the civil war of 1962-70.

272 **Society and trade in South Arabia.**
R. B. Serjeant, edited by G. R. Smith. Aldershot, England: Variorum, 1996. unpaged.

Eighteen articles, published between 1958 and 1995, by one of the leading historians and scholars of South Arabia. The topics dealt with include Yemeni trading families, customary law as a source of history, the Zaydī tribes of North Yemen, the coastal population of Socotra, and society, particularly Islamic society, in South Arabia. Individual articles are quoted where relevant in this bibliography, but the book as a whole makes a valuable contribution to our knowledge of South Arabia, as does its companion volume listed below.

273 **Studies in Arabian history and civilisation.**
R. B. Serjeant. London: Variorum Reprints, 1981. unpaged.

A collection of another thirteen articles, first published between 1948 amd 1978, by one of the leading figures in South Arabian studies. The topics range from pre-Islamic prophets, through the import of Chinese pottery to South Arabia, to medieval travel and contemporary social stratification. As in the collection above, some individual articles have been quoted in this bibliography in the appropriate chapters.

274 **Yemen: the politics of the Yemen Arab Republic.**
Robert W. Stookey. Boulder, Colorado: Westview Press, 1978. 322p. maps. bibliog. (Westview Special Studies on the Middle East).

Despite its title, this is a general history from the earliest times to the present day. Having said this, the initial chapter on 'The ancient states' offers no more than a cursory summary of early Yemeni history, but the same cannot be said of the Islamic period, where the political history of each dynasty from the conquest to the civil war is fully delineated, with an ample use of quotations from original Arabic sources. Social history is touched upon, but economic matters are rather neglected (there is no mention of the Dutch, coffee, trade, commerce or Mocha in the index, for example). Nevertheless, this is one of the few modern surveys of Yemen to link the past to the present in an interesting and scholarly manner.

Pre-Islamic period (pre-7th century AD)

275 **Problemi storici della regione di al-Ḥadā' nel periodo preislamico e nuove iscrizioni.** (Historical problems in the gion of al-Ḥadā' in the pre-Islamic period and new inscriptions.)
Alessandra Avanzini. In: *Studi yemeniti* (Yemeni studies). Edited by Pelio Fronzaroli. Florence, Italy: Istituto de Linguistica e di Lingue Orientali, Università di Firenze, 1985, p. 53-115. (Quaderni di Semitistica, 14).

Avanzini's article is divided into three parts. Parts two and three deal with a description and a translation of new epigraphic texts from an area south of Ṣanʿāʾ, but part one is of a more general nature and discusses the proposition that the confederations of Saba and Himyar were hostile to each other and were culturally independent. She also tackles the question of royal chronology and to what extent civilization was confined to the valley systems, often taking issue with other scholars in the field, notably A. F. L. Beeston and Christian Robin.

276 **L'unification du Yémen antique: la lutte entre Saba', Himyar et le Hadramawt du Ier au IIIème siècle de l'ère chrétienne.** (The unification of ancient Yemen: the struggle between Saba, Himyar and the Ḥaḍramawt from the first to the third centuries AD.)
Muḥammad 'Abd al-Qādir Bāfaqīh. Paris: Geuthner, 1990. 469p. maps. bibliog. (Bibliothèque de Raydan, vol. 1).

Bāfaqīh distinguishes three periods in ancient South Arabian history: the high, the low and the intermediate, and in this book, he examines how the intermediate period developed and what were the major events which occurred during it. Among particular questions investigated are: the hypothesis that a central authority existed in the

Kingdom of Saba; the relationships between the political institutions of the two kingdoms of Saba and Himyar; and the role played by forces outside the kingdoms, such as the bedouin, the tribes, and the inhabitants of the Tihāmah.

277 **Epigraphic South Arabian calendars and dating.**

A. F. L. Beeston. London: Luzac, 1956. 47p.

The author lists eleven month names found in epigraphic texts from the 4th to the 6th centuries AD, and attempts to place approximately in which order seven of the months occurred during the year (the place of four of the months could not be determined). With the help of an Arabic poem on the seasons and a medieval Yemeni treatise on agriculture, both of which listed the Himyarite months, the author was able to continue his researches, which he published as 'New light on the Himyarite calendar' (*Arabian Studies,* vol. 1 [1974], p. 1-6). In this article, he was able to place all the months in their correct order, assign them their Western equivalents, and ascertain in which month the Himyarite year began (May), thus enabling epigraphers to determine many dates much more accurately.

278 **Ḥaḍramawt.**

A. F. L. Beeston. In: *The Encyclopaedia of Islam,* new edition. Leiden, The Netherlands: Brill, 1971, vol. 3, p. 51-3.

A summary of our historical knowledge concerning pre-Islamic South Arabia, based on inscriptions, sources in Greek and Latin, and the one major excavation at Ḥurāyḍah by G. Caton-Thompson (see item no. 220). The author singles out Shabwah as of particular importance, since it was the principal entrepôt for the frankincense trade and a major cultic centre, but also mentions Libnah and Ḥiṣn al-Ghurāb. He also tackles the origin of the name of the region (derived from the root *drm*), the language of the ancient Ḥaḍramīs, and the forms of religion found there. Some additional information on ancient Ḥaḍramawt is given by the author in the article 'Ḥaḍramawt' published on pages 336-7 of fascicules 5-6 of the Supplement to *The Encyclopaedia of Islam,* new edition (Leiden, The Netherlands: Brill, 1982), which also contains a history of Ḥaḍramawt in Islamic times by G. R. Smith (see item no. 357).

279 **The Himyarite problem.**

A. F. L. Beeston. *Proceedings of the Seminar for Arabian Studies,* vol. 5 (1975), p. 1-7. map.

The author confronts the issue raised by the *Periplus of the Erythraean Sea* (see item no. 299) of the double titulature of the kings of Saba and Himyar. His conclusion is that both kingdoms were mutually antagonistic to each other during the first three centuries of the Christian era, and that the ruler named Charibael in the *Periplus* might have been alluding to his rule of both highland and lowland Sabaic-speaking peoples when he called himself King of Saba and Dhu-Raydan. The author also asserts that the culture of Saba did not penetrate south of the Dhamār, Yarīm, Ẓafār frontier, where no 4th-century inscriptions, ancient temples or irrigation works are to be found. Beeston finally takes issue with von Wissmann over the latter's claim that the Himyarites possessed the port of Qana' and were a good seafaring nation, maintaining that it was the Ḥaḍramīs who were 'the really conspicuous seafarers'.

280 **Ḳatabān.**

A. F. L. Beeston. In: *The Encyclopaedia of Islam,* new edition. Leiden, The Netherlands: Brill, 1978, vol. 4, p. 746-8.

An evaluation of the role that Qataban played in the history of pre-Islamic South Arabia. The author does not take sides in the controversy over whether the history of Qataban began in the 6th or the 4th century BC, but points out that all are agreed that it disappeared from the political and social map in the 4th century AD. From the inscriptions recovered by the American Foundation for the Study of Man expeditions (see items 218, 222, 235, 255), it is possible to determine the religion and language of Qataban, that the state was interested in trade, that it was based principally in the Wādī Bayḥān, and that its original administrative centre might have been Ḥajar ibn Ḥumayd, before Timnaʿ became the capital. The author also tries to distinguish between the role played by the head of the Qatabanian people proper, where the title adopted was king (*malik*), and the head of the confederacy of which Qataban was the leading member (where the title employed was *mkrb,* often vocalized *mukarrib).*

281 **Kingship in ancient South Arabia.**

A. F. L. Beeston. *Journal of the Economic and Social History of the Orient,* vol. 15 (1972), p. 256-68.

The author argues that the peoples of ancient South Arabia were organized not by kinship-based tribes but by *bayt* or agricultural community, and that the word *shaʿb,* often translated as tribe, is not synonymous with a nomadic grouping but with a settled community. The head of a *shaʿb* was a king (*malik*), but the term did not denote supreme or autocratic power, and ultimate authority except in times of war rested in a legislative body of which the king was only a member. The author goes on to debate whether the 'important functionary called the *mkrb'* was a priest-king (he refutes this), and comes to the conclusion that the '*mkrb* was a title used purely formally by the king of a dominant *shaʿb* in a commonwealth of *shaʿb* groups, in circumstances in which he wished to stress his capacity as head of the commonwealth as well as head of his own *shaʿb'*.

282 **Maʿin.**

A. F. L. Beeston. In: *The Encyclopaedia of Islam,* new edition. Leiden, The Netherlands: Brill, 1991, vol. 6, p. 88.

Maʿin is the name of an ancient people of South Arabia, mentioned by the 3rd-century BC Greek geographer Eratosthenes, as one of the four principal peoples of the region (the others being the Sabaeans, the Qatabanians and the Ḥaḍramī). They figure largely in the frankincense trade, and inscriptions in Minaean are found as far afield as the Aegean Sea and the Egyptian Fayyum. Their main area of settlement was at Qarnaw (modern Khirbat Maʿin) in the Jawf area of North Yemen, where they constructed an impressive urban settlement, but it would appear that their trading monopoly was broken up around the beginning of the Christian era, at which point they disappear from the historical record.

283 **Problems of Sabaean chronology.**

A. F. L. Beeston. *Bulletin of the School of Oriental and African Studies,* vol. 16, no. 1 (1954), p. 37-56.

Basing himself on the writings of Procopius, Assyrian texts and epigraphic evidence, the author suggests that the date for the beginning of the Sabaean era is 110 BC. He also supplies a list of the *mkrb*s who ruled Saba until the latter half of the 4th century BC, who were then succeeded by the kings of Saba who ruled until about 30 BC.

284 **Saba'.**

A. F. L. Beeston. In: *The Encyclopaedia of Islam,* new edition. Leiden, The Netherlands: Brill, 1993, vol. 8, p. 663-5.

A summary of our existing knowledge of Sabaean culture. The author describes the Sabaean language, suggests that the controversy over the date of the earliest inscriptions is still not resolved, and gives a brief account of the history of Saba, dividing it into an archaic phase, from the 8th century BC to the beginning of the Christian era, an era of expansion during the first three centuries AD, and the period of decline from the 4th to the 6th centuries AD, when the Sabaean state was under Himyarite dominion. The author also discusses Sabaean religion, rejecting the view of Nielsen (q.v.) that 'all the deities in the pagan pantheon were nothing more than varying manifestations of an astral triad of sun, moon and Venus-star'. For further evidence of the complexities of South Arabian religion, see Giovanni Garbini, 'Il dio sabea Almaqah' (The Sabaean god Almaqah), *Rivista degli Studi Orientali,* vol. 48 (1974), p. 15-22.

285 **Some features of social structure in Saba.**

A. F. L. Beeston. In: *Studies in the history of Arabia.* Vol. 1, *Sources for the history of Arabia.* Riyadh: Riyadh University Press, 1979, part 1, p. 115-23.

The author begins by discussing the concept of tribe as it applies to Sabaean culture. He defines it a grouping of sedentary agricultural people (*sha'b)* 'at a level above that of the clan or village and below that of the nation'. Each tribe had a *hajar* or town as its centre and forum, and society possessed a marked stratification, with the balance between the rural population and the citizens of urban centres varying constantly. Among the ruling classes, women had 'a considerable degree of social and economic independence', and the author uses the epigraphic evidence to explain the structure of marriage and family life. The author explores the topic of woman and marriage in two further articles: 'Temporary marriage in pre-Islamic South Arabia', *Arabian Studies,* vol. 4 (1978), p. 21-5, and 'Women in Saba', in *Arabian and Islamic studies,* edited by R. L. Bidwell and G. R. Smith (London: Longman, 1983, p. 7-13).

286 **Warfare in ancient South Arabia (2nd-3rd centuries AD).**

A. F. L. Beeston. London: Luzac, 1976. 72p. (Qahtan: Studies in Old South Arabian Epigraphy, fasc. 3).

The armies of both Saba and Himyar comprised three main elements: the *khamīs,* or élite fighting force composed of native-born soldiers; the levies, supplied by the highland areas; and the cavalry, who operated in small numbers, and never formed more than ten per cent of an army. To these can be added bedouin mercenaries, who fought for both sides. The weapons employed were lance and dagger for the rank and file, and sword and shield for the nobility; the bow was not a normal weapon of war. The strategic aims in the long war between Saba and Himyar was either the occupation of key towns, or the defeat of the enemy in open battle, normally by executing a pincer movement, and the author draws interesting parallels between South Arabian and Anglo-Saxon warfare.

287 **Roman Arabia.**

G. W. Bowersock. Cambridge, Massachusetts: Harvard University Press, 1983. 224p. maps.

This work includes a description and analysis of the only Roman expedition to Arabia Felix, namely the attempt to annex Marib and to control the Sabaean incense trade by the Roman prefect of Egypt, Aelius Gallus. The expedition took place in about 26 BC, and after establishing a garrison at Athloula (Barāqish in present-day North Yemen, where a unique Graeco-Roman inscription has been discovered), the army marched on Marib, but were defeated by lack of water, and retreated booty-less to Egypt. The author discusses the inscription from Barāqish in an appendix, as well as previous works on the expedition.

288 **Études sud-arabes: recueil offert à Jacques Ryckmans.**

(South Arabian studies: collection offered to Jacques Ryckmans.) Louvain, Belgium: Institut Orientaliste, Université Catholique de Louvain, 1991. 234p. (Publications de l'Institut Orientaliste de Louvain, no. 39).

Jacques Ryckmans is one of the foremost scholars in his field and this volume in his honour contains a bibliography of his works from 1947 to 1990, in addition to twelve individual papers. Several of these deal with the interpretation of individual inscriptions, or groups of inscriptions, and with problems in ancient South Arabian languages, particularly the forms of nomenclature. The work also contains three papers of a more general nature, by Jean-François Breton on a particular type of fortified town found in Yemen, by A. F. L. Beeston on the ritual hunt, while Giovanni Garbini offers some new data on the nature of the succession of the *mukarrib* in South Arabia.

289 **L'Arabie préislamique et son environnement historique et culturel: actes du Colloque de Strasbourg, 24-27 juin, 1987.**

(Pre-Islamic Arabia and its historical and cultural environment: acts of the Strasbourg Colloquium, 24-27 June 1987.)

Edited by T. Fahd. Leiden, The Netherlands: Brill, 1989. 584p.

Many of the thirty-three contributions in this book deal with the relationship between the Greek and Roman worlds and the Arabian Peninsula, and several scholars specifically examine the external relations of South Arabia during the Hellenistic epoch. Lionel Casson studies maritime trade as described by the *Periplus of the Erythraean Sea* (see item no. 299), and concludes that the most important ports were Muza (present-day Mocha) and Kane (modern Bi'r ʿAlī). Jacqueline Pirenne and Ernest Will (in French), Klaus Parlasca (in German) and Paolo Costa (in English) continue the debate about the relations between Greek culture and South Arabia, and discuss the artistic independence of local craftsmen.

290 **Agricultural practices in ancient Radman and Wādī al-Jubah (Yemen.)**

Abdu O. Ghaleb. PhD dissertation, University of Pennsylvania, 1990. 521p. bibliog. (Available from University Microfilms International, Ann Arbor, Michigan, order no. 9101160).

Using archaeological, geomorphological and epigraphic evidence, the author attempts to explain the developments in agriculture from around the fourth millennium BC up to the early centuries of Islam in the Radmān region of North Yemen. His conclusion is that agricultural practices began around 3200 BC and spread gradually over large areas of the highlands and lowlands. Later demographic changes led to an increased demand for food, which caused in turn a transition from dry farming to irrigation agriculture. While the conclusions he draws from his fieldwork are well presented, his excursions into the early history of South Arabia are less convincing, and his unqualified statement that demographic changes and agricultural developments 'led to the creation of a new political system, known as "mukarrib" or "kingship", wherein Saba, Maʿin, Qataban, Ḥaḍramawt and the Himyar states came to the fore as kingdoms', needs to be supported with much more solid evidence.

291 **Frankincense and myrrh: a study of the Arabian incense trade.**

Nigel Groom. London: Longman, 1981. 285p. bibliog.

The author has undertaken very detailed research on the place of frankincense in the ancient Middle East, from its first mention around 1500 BC in inscriptions near Queen Hatshepsut's temple near Thebes in Egypt, through the references in the Bible, to the evidence found in the Greek geographers such as Pliny. The author has also studied the trade routes, both maritime and overland, the cultivation of all the relevant trees in ancient times and today, and the effect that climatic change may have had upon the trade. There are, however, surprisingly few references to Arabic sources in the work, to the wider ritual significance of incense in the Ancient World, and to its supposed medicinal properties; for a discussion of these (and other matters connected with incense), consult the works by Walter W. Müller (item no. 295).

292 **The antiquities of South Arabia: being a translation from the Arabic with linguistic, geographic, and historic notes of the eighth book of Al-Hamdānī's al-Iklīl.**

Al-Ḥasan ibn Aḥmad al-Hamdānī (d. c. 945), translated by Nabih Amin Faris. Westport, Connecticut: Hyperion Press, 1981. 119p.

A facsimile of the edition published in Princeton, New Jersey, in 1938, as volume three in the series Princeton Oriental Texts. The author, who was born in Ṣanʿāʾ in the latter half of the 9th century, was one of the few Muslim historians to write about pre-Islamic civilization, and although much of the information he has set down may be legendary, the importance of his works lies in the fact that 'they record the traditions relating to South Arabia which were current in his time'. Book eight of *al-Iklīl* deals mainly with the public buildings of ancient Yemen, but includes a great many historical data, as well as a chapter on the Himyarite language and its incriptions.

293 **Pre-Islamic Yemen: socio-political organization of the Sabaean cultural area in the 2nd and 3rd centuries AD.**
Andrey Vitalyevich Korotayev. Wiesbaden, Germany: Harrassowitz, 1996. 205p. map. bibliog.

The author looks at the political formation in the Sabaean cultural area, studying firstly the concept of *shaʿb,* described variously as tribe, community or people, and which he divides into three orders, and, secondly, the concept of *bayt,* defined as village or clan community. The author goes on to survey royal power, discussing, among other topics, royal succession, administration, taxation and temples, and clan alliances. Several of the six chapters in this work previously appeared either wholly or partly in article format between 1993 and 1995.

294 **Arabia and the Bible.**
James A. Montgomery. 2nd edition with introduction by G. W. Van Beek. New York: Ktav Publishing House, 1969. 207p.

A reprint of the edition published in Philadelphia by the University of Pennsylvania Press in 1934, with the addition of a 'Prolegomenon' by the archaeologist Van Beek, which corrects several misconceptions by Montgomery – notably his view that the Sabaeans had migrated to Yemen from North Arabia – and offers a useful overview of pre-Islamic cultural history. The work itself is based on a series of lectures, and chapters 6: 'Araby the Blest', 7: 'South Arabia and the Bible', and much of chapter 8: 'Relations of Arabia with the History and Culture of Palestine', deal with the pre-Islamic history of South Arabia. The work is still usable but it should be read with caution, and only in conjunction with more recent scholarship.

295 **Arabian frankincense in antiquity according to Classical sources.**
Walter W. Müller. In: *Studies in the history of Arabia*. Vol. 1, *Sources for the history of Arabia.* Riyadh: Riyadh University Press, 1979, part 1, p. 79-92.

A first-rate survey, which covers not only Greek and Roman references to the frankincense trade in South Arabia, but also considers the place of incense in the spiritual life of the Ancient World. For an even more detailed analysis, which deals not only with trade, and the Classical sources, but also with the cultivation of incense, the archaeological evidence, the use of the plant as a medicine, and the references in classical Arabic sources, see the eminently scholarly article by the same author, *Weihrauch: ein arabisches Produkt und seine Bedeuting in der Antike* (Frankincense: an Arabian product and its significance in the Ancient World (in: *Realencyclopädie von Pauly-Wissowa* (Pauly-Wissowa's Encyclopaedia). Munich, Germany: Alfred Druckenmüller, 1978, Supplementband 15, p. 700-77). For a summary treatment of the subject, which uses Arabic as well as Classical sources, but on the other hand disappointingly fails to take account of recent Western historical and archaeological research, see the article, 'Lubān', by A. Dietrich (in: *The Encyclopaedia of Islam,* new edition. Leiden, The Netherlands: Brill, 1986, p. 786-7).

296 **Marib.**

Walter W. Müller. In: *The Encyclopaedia of Islam,* new edition. Leiden, The Netherlands: Brill, 1991, vol. 6, p. 559-67. 2 maps. bibliog.

A succinct but immensely detailed and knowledgeable account of the most famous city in South Arabia, home to a very extensive network of irrigation canals, sluices and dams, as well as important temples like Maḥram Bilqīs. The author makes full use of travel narratives, inscriptions, the writings of later Arab geographers and historians, and, most importantly, archaeological evidence, including the recent excavations by the Deutsches Archäologisches Institut (German Archaeological Institute) in Ṣanʿāʾ, to build up a comprehensive picture of the city. He continues the history of Marib into Islamic times, when it gradually lost its importance, until its population was dispersed during the civil war of 1962-70. The village itself has fewer than 300 inhabitants today.

297 **A history of the Jews of Arabia from ancient times to their eclipse under Islam.**

Gordon Darnell Newby. Columbia, South Carolina: University of South Carolina Press, 1988. 177p. map.

Much of the book concerns the Jews of the Hijaz and their relations with the Prophet Muḥammad, but chapter four, 'The southern Jewish kingdoms', focuses on the conflict between Christians and Jews in Najrān and Himyar in the 6th century AD, and on the rise of the Jewish kingdom of Yūsuf Ashʿar Dhū Nuwās, and its subsequent destruction by the Abyssinians. For material on the same conflict, presented from the Christian standpoint, see Irfan Shahid (item no. 307).

298 **Handbuch der altarabischen Altertumskunde.** (Handbook of Ancient Arabian archaeology.)

Edited by Detlef Nielsen. Copenhagen: Busch, 1927. 272p.

In its day, this was the standard survey of ancient South Arabian culture (despite its title, the work does not deal with any other areas of the Arabian peninsula), but now several of its contributions have been superseded by more recent research. This is particularly true of, 'Geschichte Südarabiens im Umriss' (A historical sketch of South Arabia), by Fritz Hommel, whose chronology has been displaced by the work of A. F. L. Beeston, Jacqueline Pirenne, and Jacques Ryckmans (qq.v.). and, 'Das öffentliche Leben in den alten Südarabischen Staaten' (Public life in the ancient South Arabian states), by N. Rhodokanakis, whose theories about the role of the *mukarrib* have now been discredited. On the other hand, the contribution of Adolf Grohmann on archaeology, and the two chapters by the editor (a general overview, and a study of ancient Arabian religion) still retain a certain value, even if their conclusions now require modification.

299 **The Periplus of the Erythraean Sea.**

Translated by G. W. B. Huntingford. London: Hakluyt Society, 1980. 225p. map. bibliog. (Hakluyt Society, second series, no. 151).

The author of this most important geographical text, was probably a Greek, living in Egypt some time between 95 and 130 AD. Of greater importance than his precise identification, is the fact that he is the only writer with personal knowledge of the

Indian Ocean in ancient times whose work has survived, and in this book he describes the places in the Red Sea and Indian Ocean between Egypt and the mouth of the Ganges which he visited by ship, and the trade carried on in the various ports. The translator has tried to identify all the places mentioned by the author, and has added appendices on the products mentioned, the ethnology of the Indian Ocean region, and an indication of the sort of vessels trading there in ancient times. Some commentatators have preferred the translation and notes of Wilfred H. Schoff in: *Periplus of the Erythraean Sea* (New York: Longmans, Green, 1912. 323p.), while another translation, including an edition of the Greek text was made by Lionel Casson and published as *Periplus Maris Erythraei* (Princeton, New Jersey: Princeton University Press, 1989. 320p.).

300 **The background of Islam: being a sketch of Arabian history in pre-Islamic times.**
H. St. J. B. Philby. Alexandria, Egypt: Whitehead Morris, 1947. 152p.

One of the few attempts to write a chronological history of ancient South Arabia, from about 1100 BC to the 6th century AD. Now inevitably overtaken by more recent research, it still has some value as a straightforward narrative, but is perhaps best known as a collector's item, as only 500 copies, all signed by the author, were ever printed.

301 **Recently discovered inscriptions and archaeology as sources for the history of ancient South-Arabian kingdoms.**
Jacqueline Pirenne. In: *Studies in the history of Arabia*. Vol. 1, *Sources for the history of Arabia,* Riyadh: Riyadh University Press, 1979, part 1, p. 45-56.

An interesting paper, which, on the basis of newly discovered inscriptions, shows the sort of questions which archaeologists and epigraphers can now ask, in this case about the historical framework surrounding the struggle between Ethiopians and Himyarites during the 4th-6th centuries AD, about the cultic relevance of raised stones, about the colonization of Ẓafār, the capital of the Himyarites, and about the violent end of the ancient city of Shabwah in the 5th century AD.

302 **Le royaume sud-arabe de Qataban et sa datation d'après l'archéologie et les sources classiques jusqu'au *Périple de la Mer Érythrée.*** (The South Arabian kingdom of Qataban and its dating according to archaeology and Classical sources up to the *Periplus of the Erythraean Sea.*)
Jacqueline Pirenne. Louvain, Belgium: Publications Universitaires; Institut Orientaliste, 1961. 248p. bibliog. (Bibliothèque du Muséon, vol. 47).

The author makes full use of all newly discovered sources such as the finds made during the excavations undertaken by the American Foundation for the Study of Man (see items 218, 222, 235, 255) to check the data offered by Classical authors such as Pliny, Strabo and Eratosthenes, regarding the expedition of Aelius Gallus to Yemen and the decline of Qataban. She concludes her efforts at a new chronology with a study of the *Periplus of the Erythraean Sea* (see item no. 299).

303 **L'Arabie antique de Karib'îl à Mahomet.** (Ancient Arabia from Karib'il to Muḥammad.)
Edited by Christian Robin. Aix-en-Provence, France: Édisud, 1992. 166p. (*Revue du Monde Musulman et de la Méditerranée*, no. 61).

A special issue of a well-known French academic journal, this contains nine contributions by Christian Robin, and single papers by Alessandra Avanzini, Jacques Ryckmans and F. Briquel-Chatonnet. The paper by Ryckmans, dedicated to the memory of Jacqueline Pirenne, looks at the role of palaeography in the dating of inscriptions, and concludes that the South Arabian alphabets were already distinct from the other Semitic alphabets as early as the 13th century BC. Christian Robin also contributes a chapter on the alphabet, as well as two historical surveys, an overview of pre-Islamic religion, and a comparative study of all the ancient languages of Arabia. In perhaps his most interesting paper, he looks at the relationship of the bedouin tribes with the settled civilization of the Yemen, using historical, epigraphic and linguistic criteria. The volume concludes with a study by Alessandra Avanzini of the place of matrilineal succession and the position of women in ancient South Arabia.

304 **Les hautes-terres du Nord-Yémen avant l'Islam.** (The highlands of North Yemen before Islam.)
Christian Robin. Istanbul, Turkey: Nederlands Historisch-Archaeologisch Instituut, 1982. 2 vols.

Based on the author's doctoral thesis at the University of Paris I, this is not a narrative history, but rather a cultural overview of the region of Khawlān Quḍāʿah, or the area around Ṣaʿdah, based on epigraphic evidence. In volume one, the author looks at the archaeological discovery of North Yemen, historical geography, tribal distribution, the spread of different cults, social organization and the role of the *qayl,* and the contribution of al-Ḥasan ibn Aḥmad al-Hamdānī (d. c. 945). In volume two, he considers the various epigraphic sites in North Yemen, and translates and comments upon numerous inscriptions discovered there.

305 **L'institution monarchique en Arabie méridionale avant l'Islam (Maʿin et Saba).** (The institution of the monarchy in pre-Islamic South Arabia.)
Jacques Ryckmans. Louvain, Belgium: Publications Universitaires; Institut Orientaliste, 1951. 368p. bibliog. (Bibliothèque du Muséon, vol. 28).

One of the most influential books in the history of South Arabian studies, this was the first work to study systematically the institutions which governed life in the pre-Islamic South Arabian states of Maʿin and Saba. The author examines the titulature of both the kings and the *mukarrib*, and attempts to devise a chronology for the two kingdoms from the 2nd century BC to the 6th century AD.

306 **L'Arabie et ses mers bordières.** (Arabia and its surrounding seas.) Vol. 1: **Itinéraires et voisinages** (Routes and neighbouring countries.)
Edited by Jean-François Salles. Lyon, France: G. S. Maison de l'Orient, 1988. 199p. maps. bibliogs. (Travaux de la Maison de l'Orient, vol. 16).

Most of the papers in this research seminar deal with the Arabo-Persian Gulf, but two focus on South Arabia, mostly through the medium of the *Periplus of the Erythraean Sea* (see item no. 299): 'La navigation en Mer Erythrée dans l'antiquité' (Navigation in the Erythraean Sea in antiquity), by Jean Rougé, and 'La circumnavigation de l'Arabie dans l'antiquité classique' (The circumnavigation of Arabia in Classical Antiquity), by Jean-François Salles.

307 **The martyrs of Najrân: new documents.**
Irfan Shahid. Brussels: Société des Bollandistes, 1971. 306p. bibliog. (Subsidia Hagiographica, no. 49).

The struggle between Christianity and Judaism in pre-Islamic Arabia came to a climax in the sixth century, which witnessed two persecutions of Christians in Yemen. Little is known about the first persecution, but the second is much better documented, and took place in the city of Najrān on the northern border of Yemen around 520 AD. It led to military intervention by the Christian state of Ethiopia, brought about the downfall of the Himyarite kingdom of South Arabia, and spread the Christian faith across the region, until the Persians in their turn occupied Yemen in 570 AD. This work examines the Greek, Syriac, Arabic and Ethiopic sources for the early history of Najrān, and provides the Syriac text plus English translation of an important letter by Simeon of Bêth-Arshâm. The dating of the second persecution has been contested by François de Blois, who puts it at 523 AD in, 'The date of the "martyrs of Nağrān"' (*Arabian archaeology and epigraphy,* vol. 1, nos. 2/3 [Dec. 1990], p. 110-28), which has called forth a rejoinder by Irfan Shahid, 'On the chronology of the South Arabian martyrdoms' (*Arabian archaeology and epigraphy,* vol. 5, no. 1 [Feb. 1994], p. 66-9).

308 **Al-Hudhud: Festschrift Maria Höfner zum 80. Geburtstag.**
(Al-Hudhud: Festschrift for Maria Höfner's 80th birthday.)
Edited by Roswitha G. Stiegner. Graz, Austria: Karl-Frankens-Universität, 1981. 338p.

Maria Höfner spent her academic life working on South Arabian matters at the universities of Vienna, Tübingen and Graz. This celebratory volume concentrates on linguistic and epigraphic topics, many of which touch on historical matters, but among more general contributions there is a paper in German by A. G. Lundin on the goddesses Ruḍā and al-ʿUzzā, one in French by Christian Robin on mountains in pre-Islamic religion, and a further paper in German by Claus Schedl, which suggests that the passages in the Qur'ān dealing with Solomon and Sheba are a reflection of an ancient Iranian myth about the sun-king and the first man.

309 **Studies in the history of Arabia.** Vol. 1: **Sources for the history of Arabia;** Vol. 2: **Pre-Islamic Arabia.**
Riyadh: Riyadh University Press, 1979-84. 3 parts.

The result of two international conferences held in 1977 and 1979, both volumes contain valuable contributions by many of the best-known scholars of South Arabia, some of which have been cited individually. Among articles not quoted separately, but which contain important data are A. F. L. Beeston on chronology, A. Jamme on Safaitic cairns, Jacques Ryckmans on epigraphy and Christian Robin on social organization in Maʿin.

310 **Christianity among the Arabs in pre-Islamic times.**
J. Spencer Trimingham. London: Longman, 1979. 342p. bibliog.

The penultimate chapter, 'Christianity in South-West Arabia', takes the reader through the story of Najrān, from the shadowy first persecution, to the second persecution by the Himyarite king Dhū Nuwās, who had converted to Judaism, and the subsequent invasion and conquest by Ethiopian forces around 520 AD. The author ascribes the 'failure of Christianity in Yemen', not to the Persian conquest in 570 AD, but 'almost entirely to the dissensions disgracing the Christian world far removed from the highlands of Yemen'. This contrasts with the views of Irfan Shahid (see item no. 307), who sees the Persian invasion as adversely affecting Najrān, and considers in particular that it was 'the rise of Islam and the Muslim conquest of Arabia which finally dealt Christian Nadjran a fatal blow'. This is also the view Shahid expresses in his historical overview, 'Nadjrān' (in: *The Encyclopaedia of Islam*, new edition. Leiden, The Netherlands: Brill, 1993, vol. 7, p. 871-2).

311 **Die Geschichte von Saba.** (The history of Saba.) Vol. 1: **Über die frühe Geschichte Arabiens und das Entstehen des Sabäerreiches.** (On the early history of Arabia and the origins of the Kingdom of Saba.); Vol. 2: **Das Grossreich der Sabäer bis zum seinem Ende im frühen 4. Jh. v. Chr.** (The empire of the Sabaeans up to its end in the early 4th century BC.)
Hermann von Wissmann. Vienna: Österreichische Akademie der Wissenschaften, 1975-82. 2 vols.

Not so much a narrative history, more a collection of short articles using mainly inscriptions, but also the writings of Greek historians and geographers, as well as archaeological evidence to explore many facets of the kingdom of Saba.

Early and medieval Islamic period (7th-18th centuries)

312 **Political history of Yemen at the beginning of the sixteenth century: Abū Makhrama's account of the years 906-927 H (1500-1521 AD) with annotations.**
Al-Ṭayyib ibn ʿAbd Allāh Abū Makhramah (d. 1540), translated by Lein Oebele Schuman. Groningen, The Netherlands: V. R. B. Kleine, 1960. 142p. map. bibliog.

Presented as the author's doctoral dissertation at the University of Amsterdam, this translation of the final chronological section of *Qilādat al-naḥr fī wafayāt aʿyān al-dahr* is one of the few Arabic sources for the history of medieval Yemen to have been translated into a Western language. It is fully annotated and together with *The Portuguese off the South Arabian coast,* by R. B. Serjeant (see item no. 351), gives a full picture of South Arabian society at the time of its first major encounter with European expansionism.

313 **Les débuts de l'imamat zaidite au Yémen.** (The beginnings of the Zaydī Imamate in the Yemen.)
C. van Arendonk, translated from the Dutch by Jacques Ryckmans. Leiden, The Netherlands: Brill, 1960. 375p. bibliog. (Publications de la Fondation de Goeje, no. 18).

A pioneering study of the founder of the Zaydī Imamate in the Yemen, al-Hādī ilā al-Ḥaqq, who died in 911, this study was originally presented (and published) in Dutch as the author's doctoral dissertation at the University of Leiden in 1919. The author used all the Arabic sources available to him at the time, and looks not only at al-Hādī's political career, but also at his role as a theologian and spiritual leader. This is a well-annotated work of considerable scholarship, and remains the primary source for our knowledge of the Imam.

314 **Imams, notables et bédouins du Yémen au XVIIIe siècle ou Quintessence de l'or du règne du Chérif Muḥammad b. Aḥmad.** (Imams, notables and bedouins of Yemen in the 18th century, or Quintessence of gold of the reign of the Sharīf Muḥammad ibn Aḥmad.)
ʿAbd al-Raḥmān ibn Aḥmad al-Bahkalī (d. 1809), translated into French by Michel Tuchscherer. Cairo: Institut Français d'Archéologie Orientale, 1992. 225p. map. bibliog. (Textes Arabes et Études Islamiques, no. 30).

This translation of *Khulāṣat al-asjad fī ayyām al-amīr Muḥammad ibn Aḥmad* was originally presented by the translator as his doctoral thesis at the University of Aix-en-Provence in 1985. It chronicles the activities of Muḥammad ibn Aḥmad Āl Khayrāt who ruled part of the Tihāmah (which straddles the present-day borders of Yemen and Saudi Arabia) between 1730 and 1771. The history is a vivid insight into the perennial tensions and conflict between the social groups inhabiting Yemen: highland tribes, coastal tribes, townsmen and traders, peasants, *ʿulamā'* (religious scholars) and *sayyids* (descendants of the Prophet), and goes beyond the bounds of a mere local history, since the same groups are still active to certain extent today. There is a long introduction which sets the chronicle in its historical context, and a wealth of footnotes.

315 **The early history of the Yemeni port of al-Ḥudaydah.**
John Baldry. *Arabian Studies,* vol. 7 (1985), p. 37-51.

Basing himself on Arabic chronicles, European travel and consular reports, and personal observations, the author traces the history of Hodeida from pre-Islamic days to the end of the 18th century. Its fortunes were dependent very much on external political forces, and the author shows how its early prosperity was badly damaged by an attack by Egyptian forces in 1515, only to revive after the Turkish evacuation of Yemen in 1636. It shared with Mocha in the growth of the coffee trade, but its fortunes took another downturn in the late 18th century when it was subjected to various raids from inland; it finally took over as North Yemen's principal port only after the Turks recovered possession of the Tihāmah in 1849.

316 **Yemen in early Islam: an examination of non-tribal traditions.**
Suliman Bashear. *Arabica,* vol. 36, no. 3 (1989), p. 327-61.

Using early Arabic religious texts (mainly *ḥadīth*, or Islamic traditions), as well as lexicographical and geographical sources, the author suggests that the terms *Yaman* and *Tayman* were 'initially applied to denote the lands of the Arabs outside and to the south of the great powers' spheres of influence in the area'. Further data from biblical and Christian–Gnostic sources link the area with 'the apocalyptic idea of messianic delivrance from the South', with the converse idea that the the North or East was 'a source of evil and error'. At one point, Mecca was called *al-Yamanīyah* (the southern one), although there was a later shift to the idea of *Yaman* being applied only to the extreme south of the Peninsula, while the 'messianic and other religious elements originally inherent on the concept of *Yaman'*, gave way later in the first Islamic century to the term being used 'only in the contexts of tribal strife and political conflicts'.

317 **Yemen and its conquest by the Ayyubids of Egypt (A.D. 1137-1202).**
Michael L. Bates. PhD dissertation, University of Chicago, 1975. 346p. bibliog. (Available from University Microfilms International, Ann Arbor, Michigan, order no. 0292071).

A fine analysis of a crucial period in the history of Yemen. The author has a good command of the Arabic sources, and as well as discussing the historical course of events in Ṣanʿāʾ, Zabīd, Aden and elsewhere, he examines the military and administrative innovations brought in by the Ayyūbids, and their relations with both the Zaydī and the Ismāʿīlī hierarchy and with the tribes of the central highlands. The author concludes that the Ayyūbids' successes against the Ismāʿīlīs in southwestern Yemen and their inability to eliminate Zaydī strongholds in the north changed the balance of power in North Yemen, and enabled the Zaydīs over the course of centuries to become the dominant political force in the country.

318 **The collapse of Ottoman authority in Yemen, 968/1560–976/1568.**
J. R. Blackburn. *Die Welt des Islam,* new series, vol. 19 (1979), p. 119-76.

A scholarly account, based mainly on Ottoman sources, which narrates how Turkish authority in Yemen began to ebb with the appointment of Maḥmūd Pasha as *beylerbeyi* (governor) in 1560. His main interest in the province was 'as a source for personal wealth for self-promotion', and, although he left Yemen to take up the governorship of Egypt in 1565, his influence resulted in the disastrous decision to divide the province of Yemen into two *beylerbeyiliks,* or governorates. This weakened Ottoman power to such an extent that the Imam al-Muṭahhar rebelled in 1567 and by mid-1568 had confined the Turkish forces to an enclave around Zabīd. There they remained until the relief expedition of 1569 led to the Ottoman reconquest of the province. Details of the administrative documents which ordered the division of Yemen into two parts, complete with Ottoman Turkish text and English translation, can be found in J. R. Blackburn's 'Two documents on the division of Ottoman Yemen into two *beglerbegiliks*' (*Turcica,* vol. 27 [1995], p. 223-36).

319 **al-Manṣūr Billāh.**
J. R. Blackburn. In: *The Encyclopaedia of Islam,* new edition. Leiden, The Netherlands: Brill, 1991, vol. 6, p. 436-7.

al-Manṣūr Billāh (d. 1620) was the founder of the Qāsimī dynasty which dominated much of Yemen from the 17th century until the revolution of 1962. He was a productive author (he is credited with forty-one works) as well as a great warrior-imam who defeated the Ottoman Turks on numerous occasions over two decades and kept Zaydī power intact in the central highlands of Yemen.

320 **Cauwa ende comptanten: de Verenigde Oostindische Compagnie in Jemen = Cowha and cash: the Dutch East India Company in Yemen, 1614-1655.**
C. G. Brouwer. Amsterdam, The Netherlands: D'Fluyte Rarob, 1988. 100p.

In the seventeenth century, the Dutch East India Company was the world's largest and most powerful trading enterprise. This booklet in Dutch and English traces the Company's attempt to establish a factory at Mocha, and their turbulent relations with the rulers of Yemen. Based on research into the Company's archives, this is a solid, but very readable contribution to scholarship. For those who can read Arabic, C. G. Brouwer and A. Kaplanian have translated the full texts of many of the relevant Company documents into Arabic in *Early seventeenth-century Yemen: Dutch documents relating to the economic history of Southern Arabia, 1614-1630* (Amsterdam, The Netherlands: D'Fluyte Rarob, 1989. 2nd ed. 320p.).

321 **A fiscal study of the medieval Yemen: notes preparatory to a critical edition of the Mulahhaṣ al-fitan of al-Ḥasan b. ʿAlī al-Šarīf al-Ḥusaynī.**
C. Cahen, R. B. Serjeant. *Arabica,* 4 (1957), p. 23-33.

It is a matter of great regret that the research begun by Cahen and Serjeant in 1957 was left unfinished at the time of the latter's death in 1993 (Cahen had died in 1991). In this joint article, Serjeant describes the physical nature of the rare manuscript *Mulakhkhaṣ al-fitan wa-al-albāb wa-miṣbāḥ al-hudā lil-kuttāb* by al-Ḥasan ibn ʿAlī al-Sharīf al-Ḥusaynī (fl. 1400-1420), and puts it into its historiographical context. In the second part, in French, Claude Cahen discusses the content of the work, in particular its importance as a source for the economic history of Yemen, since it contains taxation registers for several South Arabian ports. The work of Serjeant and Cahen has now been taken up by Professor G. R. Smith of Manchester (q.v.).

322 **Introduction à l'histoire sociale et urbaine de Zabīd.** (Introduction to the social and urban history of Zabīd.)
Joseph Chelhod. *Arabica,* vol. 25 (1978), p. 48-88.

Using the main Arabic histories of Yemen, the author traces the history of Zabīd on the coastal plain of North Yemen from its supposed foundation by Muḥammad ibn Ziyād in the early 9th century, through its development as major centre of Sunnī learning and the construction of most of its major monuments under the Rasūlids (1229-1454), to its slow decline under the early Ottomans. Under the control of the Imams of Ṣanʿāʾ for the following two centuries, Zabīd regained part of its prestige as the seat of the Turkish governor following the third Ottoman occupation of 1849, but suffered again from internal unrest during this century. When the author visited it for the first time in 1969, he considered it to be no more than a large village (*bourg*), interesting only for its imposing historical monuments.

323 **Zabîd under the Rasulids of Yemen, 626-858 AH/1229-1454 AD.**
Barbara Eileen Croken. PhD dissertation, Harvard University, 1990. 268p. (Available from University Microfilms International, Ann Arbor, Michigan, order no. 9113147).

A narrative history of medieval Zabīd and its monuments, using the standard printed histories, biographies, geographies and travel accounts. The author was unable to consult more than a few of the manuscripts which abound in the numerous and extensive private libraries in Zabīd, and had difficulty throughout her stay in Yemen in gaining access to relevant material; as a result, her thesis offers little radically new information, but is an admirable synthesis of existing data.

324 **Une dynastie yéménite autonome: les Yuʿfurides (213-393/828-1002).**
(An independent Yemeni dynasty: the Yuʿfurids, 213-393/828-1002.)
Radhi Daghfous. *Cahiers de Tunisie,* nos. 119-120 (1982), p. 43-121.

A useful article, summarizing the political history of the Yuʿfurids, one of Yemen's least-known dynasties. The author includes the Arabic texts of six important documents as appendices, and the article as a whole can be seen as a chronological continuation of the author's magnum opus listed below, as can his later paper, 'La dynasties des Ziyadides à Zabīd (204-407/819-1016)' (The Ziyādid dynasty in Zabīd, 204-407/819-1016) (*Cahiers de Tunisie,* nos. 162-163 [1992-93], p. 33-69), which looks at the political history of Yemen's first independent dynasty and its relations with the ʿAbbāsids in Baghdad.

325 **Le Yaman islamique des origines jusqu'à l'avènement des dynasties autonomes (Ier-IIIème s./VIIème-IXème s.).**
(Islamic Yemen from its origins until the coming of the independent dynasties, 1st-3rd centuries/7th-9th centuries.)
Radhi Daghfous. Tunis: Université de Tunis, 1995. 2 vols. (Publications de la Faculté des Sciences Humaines et Sociales, série 4, vol. 25).

The most detailed description of the early Islamic history of Yemen available to us in a Western language. The author has combed all the relevant Arabic sources, including those available only in manuscript, to provide a rich documentation of the arrival in Yemen of both the Ethiopians and Persians (525-632 AD), the conversion to Islam of the tribes and their role in the civil war of 632-33, and of the contribution of Yemenis to Arab conquests. He goes on to discuss how Yemen was administered by the early caliphs (up to 660), the Umayyads (661-750), and the early ʿAbbāsids (until 832), and the part Yemen played in the various revolts against the authorities. While the author pays little attention to economic factors, and has not taken the historical dimensions of recent work by ethnographers and anthropologists into account, this is still a major contribution to our knowledge of early Islamic Yemen.

326 **al-Mukallā.**

E. van Donzel. In: *The Encyclopaedia of Islam,* new edition. Leiden, The Netherlands: Brill, 1993, vol. 7, p. 496-7.

A brief article, which shows that the port in South Arabia was not known to the Portuguese, and overlooked by most Arab and European travellers until the 18th century, when it became the object of a struggle between two rival rulers. The situation was finally resolved in 1902 when the Government of India recognized Mukallā as the capital of the Quʿayṭī sultanate, since which time its fortunes have prospered, and it is now the largest town and port of the Ḥaḍramawt.

327 **al-Mukhā.**

E. van Donzel. In: *The Encyclopaedia of Islam,* new edition. Leiden, The Netherlands: Brill, 1993, vol. 7, p. 513-16.

Known to the Greek geographers, Mocha lost importance in early Islamic times and was not mentioned by many of the major geographers. However, the appearance of the Portuguese off Aden and the arrival of the Ottomans in the Red Sea, signalled a revival of the port's fortunes, and in the 17th century it became the centre of the international coffee trade. Unfortunately, the planting of coffee in Réunion, Java and elsewhere contributed to a decline in the town's prosperity, and the description by Sir Home Popham in 1801 portrays a town in decay. Subsequent turmoil in the hinterland exacerbated the situation, and by the mid-19th century, Mocha had been supplanted by Hodeida as the major port for North Yemen.

328 **Al-Hādī Yaḥya b. al-Ḥusayn b. al-Qāsim (245-98/859-911): a biographical introduction and the background and significance of his Imamate.**

A. B. D. R. Eagle. *New Arabian Studies,* vol. 2 (1994), p. 103-22.

Adapted from the author's M. Litt. thesis at the University of Durham (1990), this article uses sources not available to van Arendonk (see item no. 313) to discuss al-Hādī ilā al-Ḥaqq's early career, and, in particular, why he chose the Yemen as the country in which to set up an Zaydī Imamate.

329 **Yemeni fortification and the second Ottoman conquest.**

Caesar E. Farah. *Proceedings of the Seminar for Arabian Studies,* vol. 20 (1990), p. 31-42.

A short but interesting discussion of how the Yemeni forts like Thulā and Kawkabān were used by the Zaydīs to obstruct the attempted Ottoman reconquest of the Yemen under Sinan Pasha in 1569-71. In the end, after repeated failed assaults on the last remaining Zaydī strongholds, Sinān was left with only 1,200 troops (out of an original complement of 8,000), and was compelled to negotiate a truce with an enemy he had underestimated.

330 **Miswar and its human geography: a historical view.**

D. Thomas Gochenour. *Die Welt des Orients,* vol. 13 (1982), p. 79-94.

The author explored the mountainous region of Jabal Miswar (also know as Maswar) in the Western highlands of North Yemen in 1982, and was able to confirm the continuing existence of the names of villages, wadis and mountains mentioned by al-Ḥasan ibn Aḥmad al-Hamdānī (d. c . 945). He also investigated the administrative units which comprise present-day Miswar and found that the current arrangements 'legitimized a naturally recognized border'. He concludes his article with a survey of Miswar's place in history from its first mention in the 8th century, to the height of its importance as the seat of the first Fāṭimid *daʿwah* in Yemen (9th-10th centuries), its subsequent decline under the Ottomans and its present position as a minor administrative centre in the Hajjah province.

331 **The penetration of Zaydī Islam into early medieval Yemen.**
D. Thomas Gochenour. PhD dissertation, Harvard University, 1984. 343p. (Available from University Microfilms International, Ann Arbor, Michigan, order no. 8419446).

A very detailed and important contribution to our knowledge of how Zaydīsm succeeded in establishing itself in the Yemen. The author, who in addition to the standard printed works consulted several previously unstudied manuscripts, contends that Zaydism had already developed a theoretical and philosophical foundation by the time of its introduction into Yemen. Armed with this dogma, the Zaydī immigrants proselytized among the tribes, using tribal concepts such as honour and *hijrah* (emigration and protected space) to win converts. Much of what the author claims may be controversial, but he does treat tribalism, which he calls 'an intimidatingly complex, inconsistent and ambiguous subject', with a degree of seriousness it has not always received from other historians.

332 **A revised bibliography of medieval Yemeni history in the light of recent publications and discoveries.**
D. Thomas Gochenour. *Der Islam,* vol. 63, no. 2 (1986), p. 309-32.

A thorough and scholarly examination of the four main historiographical traditions in Yemen: the nationalist, the Zaydī, the Sunnī and the Ismāʿīlī. The author evaluates the value of the existing histories for the contemporary historian, discussing their completeness, their interrelationships and the accuracy of the printed editions (if any).

333 **Kawkabān.**
A. Grohmann. In: *The Encyclopaedia of Islam,* new edition. Leiden, The Netherlands: Brill, 1978, vol. 4, p. 779-80.

Kawkabān is the name of several places in South Arabia, the most important of which is the provincial capital, north-west of Ṣanʿāʾ. This articles traces its history from the Ottoman period up to the first half of the 20th century, and gives a description of its urban geography and principal buildings.

334 **A Yemenite embassy to Ethiopia, 1647-1649.**
al-Ḥasan ibn Aḥmad al-Ḥaymī (d. 1660), translated into English by E. van Donzel. Stuttgart, Germany: Franz Steiner, 1986. 252p. bibliog. (Äthiopische Forschungen, vol. 21).

In 1642, the Ethiopian king Fasiladas wrote to the Zaydī Imam of the Yemen, al-Mu'ayyad Billāh, in an attempt to open up trading relations through the Ethiopian port of Baylul, which is almost directly opposite Mocha. The Imam replied a year later, and the upshot of the correspondence was the visit of the Yemeni legal scholar al-Ḥaymī to Ethiopia in 1647-49. al-Haymī wrote an account of his visit, *Sīrat al-Ḥabashah,* and, although it is concerned much more with Ethiopia than with Yemen, it is still a valuable insight into the background to the Yemeni politics of the time, particularly foreign policy. The translation and scholarly apparatus are exemplary.

335 **Historical and social aspects of Ṣaʿdah, a Yemeni town.**
Johann Heiss. *Proceedings of the Seminar for Arabian Studies,* vol. 17 (1987), p. 63-80. maps.

Using the works of classical Arab geographers, such as al-Ḥasan ibn Aḥmad al-Hamdānī (d. c. 945), and modern ethnographers like Niewöhner-Eberhard (q.v.), the author traces the origins of the town and its political and economic development during the first few centuries of Islamic rule.

336 **The genesis of Ismaʿili daʿwa activities in the Yemen.**
Shainool Jiwa. *British Society for Middle Eastern Studies Bulletin,* vol. 15, nos. 1-2 (1988), p. 50-63.

A historical study of the first two Ismāʿīlī *dāʿīs*, or missionaries, who arrived in Yemen in 881 and attempted to convert the population to their own brand of heterodox Islam. The author considers why they chose Yemen, how well they fared militarily, and why one of the *dāʿīs,* Ibn al-Faḍl, repudiated his allegiance to the Ismāʿīlī Imam and declared himself independent in 909.

337 **El-Khazreji's history of the Resulí dynasty of Yemen.**
ʿAlī ibn al-Ḥasan al-Khazrajī (d. 1410), translated by J. W. Redhouse. Leiden, The Netherlands: Brill; London: Luzac, 1906-8. 3 vols. (E. J. W. Gibb Memorial Series, nos. 3/1, 3/2. 3/3).

The translation of an important (though, by no means, the most important – see G. R. Smith, items 355 ff.) chronicle of the Rasūlid dynasty (1229-1454) entitled *al-ʿUqūd al-lu'lu'īyah fī akhbār al-dawlah al-rasūlīyah.* The work is based on earlier histories, and contains 'fulsome eulogies' of the Rasūlid dynasty. The first two volumes of the set contains the translation by Redhouse, volume three contains the notes, and volumes four and five the Arabic text.

338 **ʿAdan.**
O. Löfgren. In: *The Encyclopaedia of Islam,* new series. Leiden, The Netherlands: Brill, 1960, vol. 1, p. 180-2.

A historical survey of South Arabia's greatest port, which concentrates on the pre-Islamic and medieval period to the detriment of the development of Aden under the British, and also gives surprisingly little information about the nature and volume of goods traded through Aden.

339 **The founding of the Great Mosque (al-Jāmiʿ al-Kabīr) in Ṣanʿāʾ.**
ʿAbd al-Muḥsin Madʿaj M. al-Madʿaj. *New Arabian Studies,* vol. 1 (1993), p. 175-88.

The author tries to answer the two questions: when was the Great Mosque of Ṣanʿāʾ built and who was its founder. He sifts the claims of different historians and, assembling a wide variety of evidence from historical sources, shows that the mosque was not built during the Prophet's lifetime, but probably in 633 AD, a few months after Muḥammad's death. The builder was most likely the first governor of Ṣanʿāʾ, Aban ibn Saʿīd, who carried out the Prophet's instructions, as they were conveyed to him by Wabr ibn Yuḥannis, who had been appointed the Muslim envoy to the city in April 632.

340 **The Yemen in early Islam, 9/233 – 630-847: a political history.**
ʿAbd al-Muḥsin Madʿaj M. al-Madʿaj. London: Ithaca Press for the Centre for Middle Eastern and Islamic Studies, University of Durham, 1988. 265p. maps. bibliog. (Durham Middle East Monographs, no. 3).

A very detailed description of the early history of Islamic Yemen, based on the works of Arabic chroniclers, supplemented by geographical and numismatic evidence. The author divides his work, which is based on his doctoral thesis at the University of Durham, into three parts: the first deals with the relations between the Prophet and the tribes and confederations of Yemen; the second concerns the participation of the Yemeni tribes in the early Islamic conquests, the role the Yemeni migrants played in major internal crises during the period of the first four caliphs, and the development of resistance to caliphal authority in Yemen itself, while the third part looks at the political history of Yemen between 661 and 847, and the policy of central government towards the country.

341 **Land ownership and land tax in northern Yemen and Najrān: 3rd-4th/9th-10th century.**
Wilferd Madelung. In: *Land tenure and social transformation in the Middle East.* Edited by Tarif Khalidi. Beirut: American University of Beirut, 1984, p. 189-207.

Using anonymous biographies of two early Zaydī imams in Yemen, including that of al-Hādī ilā al-Ḥaqq (d. 911), the author shows how the Zaydī rulers were most anxious to apply the strict letter of Islamic law to all matters of land tenure and land taxation. This was not always possible given the local resistance to the tax collectors, and the sources indicate how the major tribal confederation of Hamdān was able to claim 'far-reaching exemptions and privileges with regard to their *zakāt* [alms]'. The author elaborates on the measures adopted by both imams to deal with resistance and rebellion and makes the telling point, that whereas in most of the areas conquered by Islam, the towns dominated the countryside, in Yemen the countryside dominated the towns.

342 **The origins of the Yemenite Hijra.**
Wilferd Madelung. In: *Arabicus Felix Luminosus Britannicus: essays in honour of A. F. L. Beeston on his eightieth birthday.* Edited by Alan Jones. Reading, England: Ithaca Press for the Board of the Faculty of Oriental Studies, Oxford University, 1991, p. 25-44.

The author refutes the view that the term *hijrah* in its meaning of 'protected enclave in tribal territory' reflects a pre-Islamic Arabian tribal institution, suggesting instead that it was introduced by the Zaydīs for whom *hijrah* had the meaning of emigration from the land of the sinful. Some time after the introduction of the general concept, the term came to denote specific localities where the Zaydīs 'could live in accordance with their own religious law and practice their ritual without outside interference'. On the basis of the early historical sources, the author traces the development of the term in Zaydī Yemen and studies the foundation of the early *hijrahs* in considerable detail.

343 **The historical development of Aden's defences.**
H. T. Norris, F. W. Penney. *Geographical Journal,* vol. 121, no. 1 (1955), p. 11-20.

An excellent survey of the historical geography of Aden, using the works of Arab chroniclers and European travellers. The authors show how the prosperity of medieval Aden led to the building of three lines of fortifications, but that these declined under Ottoman rule, only to be rebuilt by the British soon after their occupation of 1839.

344 **Münzen der Rasuliden nebst einem Abriss der Geschichte dieser jemenischen Dynastie = Coins of the Rasūlids comprising a synopsis of the history of that Yemenite dynasty.**
Heinrich Nützel, translated from the German by Alfred Kinzelbach. Mainz, Germany: Verlag Donata Kinzelbach, 1987. 170p.

Although Nützel's work was originally presented as his doctoral dissertation in 1891, his comprehensive study of Rasūlid coinage (1229-1454) is still unique in the field of Yemeni numismatics and can stand alongside the works of Ramzi J. Bikhazi, 'Coins of al-Yaman, 132-569 A. H.' (*Al-Abḥāth,* vol. 23 [1970], p. 3-127) and G. C. Miles, 'The Ayyubid dynasty of the Yaman and their coinage' (*Numismatic Chronicle,* vol. 9 [1949], p. 62-97), which deal with earlier periods in the history of Yemen. The text of the German original is given, with a rather laboured English translation appearing on the facing page. There has been little attempt by the translator to update the text.

345 **The Ottoman budgets of the Yemen in the sixteenth century.**
Salih Özbaran. In: *The Ottoman response to European expansion: studies on Ottoman–Portuguese relations in the Indian Ocean and Ottoman administration in the Arab lands during the sixteenth century.* Essays by Salih Özbaran. Istanbul, Turkey: Isis Press, 1994, p. 49-60.

The author looks at the budgets for Yemen during the first Ottoman occupation, which have been preserved in the archives in Istanbul. He notes that the administration was based on the *iltizām* (tax farm) rather than the *timar* (land grant), and that the revenues went to pay for the governor, high-ranking officials (there were seventeen in 1561-62), the wages of government officials (mainly soldiers) and miscellaneous payments, such as the purchase of fodder for the army and the repair of fortifications. The author concludes with a translation of the budget for AH 968 (1560-61).

346 **The Ottoman penetration of Yemen: an annotated translation of Özdemür Bey's Fethnâme for the conquest of San'a' in Rajab, 954/August 1547.**
Özdemür Bey, translated from the Turkish by J. R. Blackburn. *Archivum Ottomanicum,* vol. 6 (1980), p. 55-100.

Özdemür Bey was the *serdar* or commander-in-chief of the Ottoman forces at the time of their conquest of Ṣanʿāʾ in 1547, and 'was unquestionably the person most responsible for Ottoman expansion in Yemen and the dominant figure in its first thirty years as a province of the Empire'. This article is a translation from the Ottoman Turkish of the *Fethnâme*, or victory letter, which was sent to Istanbul just ten days after the fall of the Yemeni city. It recounts briefly the details of the Ottoman campaign, but the translator has enriched our knowledge by copious annotations and references to other historical sources in Arabic and Turkish.

347 **Late ancient and early mediaeval Yemen: settlement traditions and innovations.**

Mikhail B. Piotrovsky. In: *The Byzantine and early Islamic Near East.* vol. 2: *Land use and settlement patterns.* Edited by G. R. D. King, Averil Cameron. Princeton, New Jersey: Darwin Press, 1994, p. 213-20.

The author, who was leader of the joint Soviet–Yemeni Historical Expedition between 1983 and 1990, begins this article by showing how, in late antiquity, the main centres of state and culture were transferred from the semi-desert plains (Marib and Shabwah) to the agricultural highlands (Himyar and Ṣanʿāʾ). He goes on to examine the settlement of nomads in and around trade routes and markets in early medieval times, and concludes with the role Yemeni settlers played in the Islamicization of al-Fusṭāṭ in Egypt and Ḥimṣ in Syria. This article is really too short to do justice to an important and complex topic, but the author does at least show the sorts of questions that historians can ask of the existing material.

348 **Shibām.**

Alain Rouaud, Christian Robin. In: *The Encyclopaedia of Islam,* new edition. Leiden, The Netherlands, 1995, vol. 9, p. 425-6.

Shibām is the name of three towns and one mountain in South Arabia. The two most famous are Shibām al-Ḥaḍramawt 'famed for its lofty houses in sun-dried brick, warranting its designation as a UNESCO site of world significance'. Important in early medieval times, it passed under the sway of the Kathīrī sultan in the fifteenth century, and of the Quʿayṭī sultan in 1858. It was one of the trio of important towns in Wādī Ḥaḍramawt (Say'ūn and Tarīm are the other two), owing its importance more to its position on a caravan route than its agricultural resources.The other important settlement named Shibām is Shibām Kawkabān, northwest of Ṣanʿāʾ, which shared the fate of its neighbouring stronghold of Kawkabān (see Clive Smith, item no. 353), while Shibām al-Ghirās is a village and archaeological site northeast of Ṣanʿāʾ.

349 **al-Ḥudayda.**

Lein Oebele Schuman. In: *The Encyclopaedia of Islam,* new edition. Leiden, The Netherlands: Brill, 1971, vol. 3, p. 539-40.

The second city in North Yemen, Hodeida vied with Mocha (see van Donzel, item no. 327) during the late medieval and early modern period as the main port for the export of coffee and other goods, but did not become important until the late 19th century. The construction of modern harbour facilities in the 1960s by engineers from the Soviet Union gave the city a dramatic boost, and it now plays host to much of Yemen's commercial and industrial development.

350 **The ports of Aden and Shiḥr (mediaeval period).**

R. B. Serjeant. In: *Les grandes escales: 10ème colloque international d'histoire maritime.* (The great ports; 10th colloquium of maritime history.) Brussels: Éditions de la Librairie Encyclopédique, 1972-74, vol. 1, p. 207-24.

The author uses evidence from the *Mulakhkhaṣ al-fitan*, an important 15th-century manual, and compares it with other medieval sources, along with his own observations at various small ports in South Arabia and Socotra, to determine the organization of maritime trade in medieval Aden and Shiḥr.

351 **The Portuguese off the South Arabian coast: Ḥaḍramī chronicles, with Yemeni and European accounts of Dutch pirates off Mocha in the seventeenth century.**

R. B. Serjeant. Oxford, England: Clarendon Press, 1963. 233p. 2 maps.

One of Professor Serjeant's most substantial and important contributions to South Arabian studies which yields much new information on European expansion in Asia. The work contains a detailed introduction to the political and commercial background of trading in the Indian Ocean, a translation of the relevant Arabic chronicles detailing Portuguese activities between 1498 and 1577, and a further translation concerning Dutch activities around 1650, with corroborating evidence taken from Dutch archives and European travellers. Various appendices tackle subjects as diverse as Arabic terms for shipping, Portuguese inscriptions from a fort in Muscat and money and coinage in 16th-century South Arabia. A more narrative approach is taken by Joseph Chelhod who, in a posthumous article, traces the activities of the Portuguese off the coast of Yemen between 1502 and 1547, 'Les Portugais aux Yémen d'après les sources arabes' (The Portuguese in Yemen according to Arabic sources) (*Journal Asiatique,* vol. 283, no. 1 [1995], p. 1-18).

352 **Yemeni merchants and trade in Yemen, 13th-16th centuries.**

R. B. Serjeant. In: *Marchands et hommes d'affaires asiatiques dans l'Océan Indien et la Mer de Chine, 13e-20e siècles.* (Asian merchants and businessmen in the Indian Ocean and the China Sea between the 13th and 20th centuries). Edited by Denys Lombard, Jean Aubin. Paris: Éditions de l'École des Hautes Etudes en Sciences Sociales, 1988, p. 61-82.

The author looks at general trading conditions throughout South Arabia in the medieval period. After studying the conditions of the caravan, the social position of merchants in general, and the role of Aden, the author concentrates on the Karīmī merchants, who are recorded as trading in Yemen between the 11th and 15th centuries and the *baniyān,* or Hindu merchants, who were active throughout the medieval period. In the same volume, Serjeant wrote another article 'The Ḥaḍramī network' (p. 147-54), which deals with the great merchant families of the Ḥaḍramawt, many of whom had emigrated to South and South-East Asia in the Middle Ages.

353 **Kawkabān: some of its history.**
Clive Smith. *Arabian Studies,* vol. 6 (1982), p. 35-50.

Kawkabān stands 1,000 feet above the surrounding countryside about 20 miles north-west of Ṣanʿāʾ and has always had a reputation as an impregnable fortress. The author discusses its history from the ninth century AD until the present day, paying particular attention to its role as the seat of the powerful Sharaf al-Dīn family, who dominated the city from the sixteenth century until the second Ottoman conquest in 1872. The author also describes Kawkabān's principal monuments whose whereabouts he pinpoints on the accompanying map.

354 **The Suleihid dynasty in the Yemen.**
Clive Smith. *Asian Affairs,* vol. 68 (new series, vol. 12) (1981), p. 19-28.

One of the few studies of the medieval Ismāʿīlī dynasty, the Ṣulayḥids, who ruled most of Yemen in the name of the Fāṭimid Caliphate from around 1047 to 1138. The author treats his topic in an informal manner, with no annotations, and several excursi regarding visits he himself made to former centres of Ṣulayḥid power. Nonetheless, this is a well-informed piece of writing, which is especially interesting when it deals with al-Mukarram Aḥmad ibn ʿAlī (r. 1067-84), and his more than capable consort al-Sayyidah Arwā, who held supreme authority from 1084 to 1138.

355 **The Ayyūbids and early Rasūlids in the Yemen (567-694/1173-1295.)**
G. R. Smith. London: E. J. W. Gibb Memorial Trust, 1974-78. 2 vols. (E. J. W. Gibb Memorial Series, no. 26).

One of the most important contributions to medieval Yemeni history, this work consists in volume one of an edition of the Arabic text of *al-Simṭ al-ghālī al-thaman fī akhbār al-mulūk min al-ghuzz bi-al-Yaman,* by Muḥammad Ibn Ḥātim (d. after 1303), and in volume two of notes to the text, geographical and tribal indexes, a glossary and four historical chapters. These deal with the author Ibn Ḥātim and his work, with the history of the Ayyūbids prior to their conquest of the Yemen, with the history of Yemen before the coming of the Ayyūbids and, briefly, with the Rasūlids.

356 **The Ayyūbids and Rasūlids: the transfer of power in 7th/13th century Yemen.**
G. R. Smith. *Islamic Culture,* vol. 53 (1969), p. 175-88.

The author's detailed narrative of the changeover in Yemen from Ayyūbid to Rasūlid authority is based on a comparison of the accounts of two Yemeni historians, ʿAlī ibn al-Ḥasan al-Khazrajī (d. 1410) and Muḥammad Ibn Ḥātim (d. after 1303). The author feels that 'al-Khazraji from the start alienates our confidence in his historical assessment by his continual panegyrics of the Rasūlid princes', while Ibn Ḥātim, 'because of his background and position, was able to write history with a degree of accuracy, sincerity and impartiality, all too rare in the historiography of the times'.

357 **Ḥaḍramawt.**

G. R. Smith. In: *The Encyclopaedia of Islam,* new edition. Leiden, The Netherlands: Brill, 1982, fascicules 5-6 of the Supplement, p. 337-9.

After describing the region geographically, the author surveys the history of Ḥaḍramawt from the arrival of Islam up to the sixteeenth century. He also discusses the social organization of the region dividing the people into four classes, the *Mashāyikh* (noble families), *Sayyids* (descendants of the Prophet), *Qabā'il* (tribesmen) and *Masākin* or *Ḍuʿafā'* (the poor). More tribal and geographical detail, albeit outdated, can be found in the article 'Ḥaḍramawt' by J. Schleifer in *The Encyclopaedia of Islam,* old edition (Leiden, The Netherlands: Brill, 1927, vol. 1, p. 207-10), while for ancient Ḥaḍramawt, consult the article by A. F. L. Beeston in the new edition of *The Encyclopaedia of Islam* (item no. 278).

358 **Have you anything to declare? maritime trade and commerce in Ayyubid Aden: practices and taxes.**

G. R. Smith. *Proceedings of the Seminar for Arabian Studies,* vol. 25 (1995), p. 127-40.

Basing himself of the work of Ibn al-Mujāwir (d. 1291), the author explains precisely how trade was conducted in the ports of South Arabia like Aden under the Ayyūbids (1173-1228). He describes the arrangements for examining the cargo and crew, how slave girls are sold, and what taxes were paid and on which goods. He surmises that Ibn al-Mujāwir may well have been a merchant himself, since his observations are 'certainly from the businessman's point of view'. The author continues his researches into the early Rasūlid period, using the anonymous *al-Daftar al-Muẓaffarī* and *Mulakhkhaṣ al-fitan wa-al-albāb wa-miṣbāḥ al-hudā lil-kuttāb* by al-Ḥasan ibn ʿAlī al-Sharīf al-Ḥusaynī (fl. 1440-20), in 'More on the port practices and taxes of mediaeval Yemen' (*New Arabian Studies,* vol. 3 [1996], p. 208-18).

359 **Laḥdj.**

G. R. Smith. In: *The Encyclopaedia of Islam,* new edition. Leiden, The Netherlands: Brill, 1986, vol. 5, p. 601-2.

A short exposé of the history of Laḥij, an important town and district to the north of Aden, whose fortunes it normally shared. In 1839, however, the Sultan of Laḥij ceded Aden to the Government of Bombay, but maintained his own rule inland and actually expanded westwards into the territory of the Ṣubayḥah. Up to independence, the Laḥij sultan remained one of the most important figures in the Western Aden Protectorate.

360 **Rasūlids.**

G. R. Smith. In: *The Encyclopaedia of Islam,* new edition. Leiden, The Netherlands: Brill, 1993, vol. 8, p. 455-7.

A summary of the history of the Rasūlids, one of Yemen's most important Sunnī dynasties, who held power from 1229 to 1454. The author also deals with coins and mints, monuments (particularly at Taʿizz, the capital city), trade and commerce, and literature, although this section is limited to works composed by members of the royal house. The author considers that the period after 1235 'was without doubt the most brilliant in the mediaeval history of the country'.

361 **Ṣanʿāʾ.**

G. R. Smith. In: *The Encyclopaedia of Islam,* new edition. Leiden, The Netherlands: Brill, vol. 9, 1995, p. 1-3.

A summary of the history of the chief town of Yemen and the present capital of the unified Republic, followed by brief information about the buildings of the Old City, especially the mosques, public baths and the market, and the coinage associated with the city. The author lists further sources for study, concluding that 'it is difficult to exaggerate the scholarly importance of R. B. Serjeant and R. Lewcock's work [see item no. 59] for almost any aspect of the history, culture and daily life of the town'.

362 **Say'ūn.**

G. R. Smith. In: *The Encyclopaedia of Islam,* new edition. Leiden, The Netherlands: Brill, 1995, vol. 9, p. 115.

A town in the Wādī Ḥaḍramawt, famed for its fertility and date-growing. It is not a town of great antiquity, appearing for the first time in the fifteenth century, but it acquired importance as the capital of the Kathīrī Sultanate and was a centre of Islamic scholarship, although not as much as the neighbouring town of Tarīm. The spelling Saywūn is also found.

363 **Studies in the medieval history of the Yemen and South Arabia.**

G. R. Smith. Aldershot, England: Variorum, 1997. unpaged.

Twenty previous published articles, the majority of which deal with medieval Yemeni history, with six being devoted to the traveller and businessman, Ibn al-Mujāwir (d. 1291). The papers show the author's mastery of the complex sources for Yemeni history and together add up to one of the best available introductions to the history of the Rasūlids and Ṭāhirid periods (1229-1517).

364 **The Ṭāhirid sultans of the Yemen (858-923/1454-1517) and their historian Ibn al-Daybaʿ.**

G. R. Smith. *Journal of Semitic Studies,* vol. 29, no. 1 (1984), p. 141-54.

The article begins with a brief summary of how the Ṭāhirids took over power in southern Yemen and the Tihāmah, and then moves on to an evaluation of the Arabic sources for the history of the dynasty. While the author looks at sources from all quarters, Sunnī, Zaydī and Ismāʿīlī, he concentrates on the life and works of 'Abd al-Raḥmān ibn ʿAlī Ibn al-Daybāʿ (d. 1537), finishing with two extracts from the chronicler's works in English translation, the first describing the capture of Aden by the Ṭāhirids in 1454 and the second the first use of firearms against the Ṭāhirid army in 1516. A more narrative approach to the Ṭāhirids can be found in the author's 'Some observations on the Ṭāhirids and their activities in and around Ṣanʿāʾ (858-923/1454-1517)' (in: *Studies in history and literature in honour of Nicola A. Ziadeh, on the occasion of his eighty-fifth birthday.* Edited by Iḥsān ʿAbbās, Shereen Khairallah, Ali Z. Shakir. London: Hazar Publishing, 1992, p. 29-36).

365 **The Yemenite settlement of Thaʿbāt: historical, numismatic and epigraphic notes.**

G. R. Smith. *Arabian Studies,* vol. 1 (1972), p. 119-34.

Thaʿbāt is a village just outside the town of Taʿizz in the south of Yemen, which was mentioned with some frequency in the medieval Arab chronicles, particularly under the early Rasūlids, who used it a retreat and embellished it with several attractive and substantial buildings. Several epigraphic inscriptions survive from the early period as do four coins minted in the town in the fourteenth century, all of which are discussed in considerable detail by the author. By the fifteenth century, however, the town had lost its popularity with the ruling family, and gradually returned to the small, quiet village it had once been, and which it remains today.

366 **The rise of the imams of Sanaa.**

A. S. Tritton. Westport, Connecticut: Hyperion Press, 1981. 141p.

A reprint of the edition published in 1925 in Oxford, England, by Oxford University Press. Despite its age, this is one of the few works in Western languages dealing with the first Turkish occupation of the Yemen. Relying mainly on one Arabic source, the author narrates the military struggles between the Zaydī Imams and the Ottoman forces between 1580 and 1629 in strict chronological fashion. A final chapter discusses religious and social life under the Imams, but is too short to offer more than cursory information.

367 **Yemen: its early mediaeval history; also the abridged history of its dynasties, and an account of the Karmathians of Yemen.**

ʿUmārah al-Yamanī (d. 1175), translated by Henry Cassels Kay. Farnborough, England: Gregg International, 1968. 358p.

An edition and annotated translation of one of the most useful chronicles of early Yemen from around 900 AD to the Ayyūbid conquest in the twelfth century, this is a reprint of the edition published in London by Edward Arnold in 1892. The work was composed for an important official of the Fāṭimid government in Egypt who 'was widely noted for his talent as an elegant and ingenious letter-writer' and, as a result, al-Yamanī's history is full of entertaining anecdotes as well as historical information. The translator has appended relevant selections in text and translation from two further works: the history of Yemen taken from the general Islamic history of Ibn Khaldūn (d. 1382) known as *al-ʿIbar,* and a brief account of the Ismāʿīlīs of Yemen by Bahā' al-Din al-Janadī (d. 1332) taken from his *Kitāb al-sulūk fī ṭabāqāt al-ʿulamā' wa-al-mulūk.*

368 **Texts and pretexts: the unity of the Rasūlid state under al-Malik al-Muẓaffar.**

Daniel Martin Varisco. *Revue du Monde Musulman et de la Méditerranée,* no. 67 (1993), p. 13-23.

A sophisticated historical analysis of the reign of one of the most important of all Rasūlid rulers, al-Malik al-Muẓaffar, who was 'the first ruler to unify Yemen in the Islamic period'. His reign ran from 1250 to 1295 and during it Ṣanʿāʾ, Ṣaʿdah, Shiḥr and even Dhofar to the east of Ḥaḍramawt were incorporated into the Rasūlid dominions. The author also looks at high culture, administration, commerce and industry under the Rasūlids and concludes that the opening up of new avenues of trade to Europe combined with the upheaval engendered by the Mongols led to 'the emergence of Yemen as a distinct international player' for the first time in Islamic history.

Modern period (19th-20th centuries)

369 **The Yemen in the 18th and 19th centuries: a political and intellectual history.**
Ḥusayn ibn ʿAbdullāh al-ʿAmrī. London: Ithaca Press for the Centre for Middle Eastern and Islamic Studies, University of Durham, 1985. 225p. bibliog.

A revised version of the author's PhD dissertation at the University of Durham, this is one of the rare Western works to look at the history of North Yemen between the two Ottoman invasions. The author has based the first part of his work, which deals with political events during the reigns of four Zaydī Imams at Ṣanʿāʾ between 1753 and 1835, on manuscript and printed works available mainly in the library of al-Jāmiʿ al-Kabīr (the Great Mosque) in Ṣanʿāʾ. As such, it is a mine of information about little-known events. The second half of the book deals with the life, works and ideas of Muḥammad ibn ʿAlī al-Shawkānī (d. 1834), who was the leading intellectual figure of his time in Yemen, and, again, it is a major contribution to our understanding of Yemeni cultural life of the period.

370 **Al-Yaman and the Turkish occupation, 1849-1914.**
John Baldry. *Arabica,* vol. 23 (1976), p. 156-96. maps.

A long and detailed article about the Ottomans' occupation of North Yemen and ʿAsīr, based mainly on British archives, in particular despatches to the Foreign Office. The Turks' original invasion in 1849 led to the conquest of the coastal regions only, and the Ottomans did not penetrate the highlands successfully until 1871, Ṣanʿāʾ, the Imam's capital, falling to them in 1872. The article then details the long series of revolts, rebellions, and disturbances which characterized Ottoman rule in Yemen, the most serious being the rebellion led by the Imam in 1904-5, when 30,000 out of the 55,000 Turkish troops in Yemen are said to have perished, and the revolt led by Sayyid Muḥammad al-Idrīsī, which began in 1909. This final revolt was the most serious and long-lasting, and was exacerbated by the support the Idrīsīs received from Italy during the Italian–Turkish war of 1911-12, and from the British during the First World War. In 1919, the Ottomans evacuated all their territories in the Arabian Peninsula, but the dispute between the Idrīsīs, the Imam and Saudi Arabia was not finally settled until the Saudi–Yemeni war of 1934, when the modern frontier between the two states was finally defined.

371 **An imperial twilight.**
Sir Gawain Bell. London: Lester Crook, 1989. 267p. maps.

Sir Gawain Bell served Britain as a diplomat for many years in Nigeria, the Sudan and the Middle East, and this book recounts his experiences as a colonial administrator.

On pages 151-70 he tells how, in 1965, he and Sir Ralph Hone (q.v.) were asked to prepare a new constitution for the soon to be independent Federation of South Arabia. He discusses the major differences in religion and social structure between Aden and the rest of the Federation and how the Federal Supreme Council had become 'sadly ineffective', but does not go into any detail either regarding the people he encountered in South Arabia, or how the constitutional report was drafted. The report itself presented in January 1966 proposed a 'United Republic of South Arabia', but 'produced as it was just before the Defence White Paper, which settled the fate of the area, it was still-born'.

372 **The Political Residents of Aden: biographical notes.**
R. L. Bidwell. *Arabian Studies,* vol. 5 (1979), p. 149-59.

The author sketches the careers of twenty-five Political Residents from the first and longest-serving, Captain S. B. Haines, who was appointed in 1839 but dismissed for financial mismanagement in 1854, to the career of the second longest-serving Resident, Sir Bernard Reilly, who was appointed in 1931, became Chief Commissioner in 1932, Governor in 1937 and left the post in 1940. The Residents ranged from the incompetent (e.g., Major-General David Levinge Shaw, who was removed from two posts for sundry military disasters) to the able and effective (e.g., Major-General William Marcus Coghlan, who forestalled the French at Perim Island, and Major-General Sir George John Younghusband, who defeated the Turks at Shaykh 'Uthmān in the First World War).

373 **The Turkish attack on Aden 1915-1918.**
R. L. Bidwell. *Arabian Studies,* vol. 6 (1982), p. 171-94. map.

An entertaining but informative account of one of the least-known fronts of the First World War. Using a wide variety of British sources, the author describes how the Turks advanced from North Yemen as far as Shaykh 'Uthmān in 1915, defeating a British force at Laḥij on the way. The British counter-attacked and recaptured Shaykh 'Uthmān, but were both unwilling and, later, unable to advance much further, and the war ended in stalemate. The author considers that the Ottoman general, the Circassian 'Alī Saʿīd Pasha, 'despite the small stage on which he had operated, had shown himself one of the outstanding commanders of the First World War, as well as a man of honour and chivalry'.

374 **The two Yemens.**
R. L. Bidwell. Harlow, England: Longman; Boulder, Colorado: Westview Press, 1983. 350p. maps. bibliog.

An engaging, but never less than scholarly account of developments in both North and South Yemen during the 20th century (although the medieval and 19th-century background is sketched in). The author discusses tribal, social and economic affairs and well as the political current of events, and is particularly authoritative regarding Aden's run-up to independence, and the situation on both sides in the 1970s.

375 **Revolution zur Einheit: Jemens Kampf um die Unabhängigkeit.**
(Revolution for unity: Yemen's struggle for independence.)
Rudolf E. Bollinger. Hamburg, Germany: Hoffmann und Campe, 1984. 352p. maps.

The author, who travelled in both North and South Yemen, combines a description of personal experiences with a narrative of political events between 1967 and 1983. His insights are sometimes superficial, but his European perspective is often interesting, and counterpoints both Yemeni and Anglo-Saxon scholarship.

376 **Hadramawt: crisis and intervention, 1866-1881.**
Brinston Brown Collins. PhD dissertation, Princeton University, 1969. 362p. (Available from University Microfilms International, Ann Arbor, Michigan, order no. 708356).

The author ostensibly undertook his dissertation 'to test the hypothesis that small areas or countries exert considerable power upon the so-called powerful nations of the world'. Whether the author achieves his aim is a moot point, but the thesis does shed considerable light on the political and diplomatic manoeuverings of the Quʿayṭīs, the Kasādīs and, to a lesser extent, the Kathīrīs, and each side sought British support in their efforts to gain control over the South Arabian port of Shiḥr during the 1860s and 1870s. The author has made good use of both British archives and Yemeni manuscript sources to show how the British tried to remain neutral, but were inevitably dragged into the dispute and ended up having to take sides.

377 **An element of luck: to South Arabia and beyond.**
Michael Crouch. London: Radcliffe Press, 1993. 270p.

An informal memoir by a former political officer of his experiences in South Arabia between 1958 and 1967. Much of his time was spent in Mukallā and Radfān and he makes many interesting comments about Yemeni–British relations without ever entering the realm of high diplomacy.

378 **The Free Yemeni movement, 1935-1962.**
J. Leigh Douglas. Beirut: American University of Beirut, 1987. 287p. bibliog.

The posthumous publication of a very promising young scholar who was murdered during the Lebanese civil war. The author analyses the conflicting interests in North Yemeni affairs, and tries to assess the contributions of various individuals and organizations – collectively known as the Free Yemeni Movement – as they struggled to bring their country out of the isolation to which the rule of the Imams had condemned it. An impeccable piece of scholarship, using archival materials, Arabic and English published works, and a long series of interviews to study the political actions of the participants, their intellectual formation and their links with outside organizations.

379 **A fragment of the Yemeni past: ʿAlī Nāṣir al-Qardaʿī and the Shabwah incident.**

Paul Dresch. *Journal of Arabic Literature,* vol. 26, no. 3 (1995), p. 232-54.

Using orally transmitted poetry and prose, the author tries to disentangle the story of ʿAlī Nāṣir al-Qardaʿī (d. 1948), a tribal leader from Murād who was considered by the supporters of the Imam Yaḥyā (d. 1948) as 'a notorious tribal malcontent', but by his own people in the eastern part of North Yemen as 'a folk legend', and as witty, generous and courageous. He demonstrates the intrigues by which Imam Yaḥyā tried to curb ʿAlī Nāṣir, which culminated in the Shabwah incident of 1938, when ʿAlī Nāṣir led the Imam's forces against an important if remote part of the British Protectorate. It casts a fascinating light on the event from the Yemeni point of view, and shows that what the British regarded as a border incident, was in fact an episode in the power struggle between the Imam Yaḥyā and one of his opponents, which had serious repercussions for the history of North Yemen in the 1940s and beyond.

380 **Anglo-Ottoman confrontation in the Yemen, 1840-9.**

Caesar E. Farah. *Arabian Studies,* vol. 8 (1990), p. 137-69.

The author presents a detailed study, based on the Turkish archives in Istanbul, of the Ottoman occupation of the Tihāmah, which culminated in the deposition of the Imam in 1849, and the creation of new adminstrative ordinances, 'which, for all practical purposes, erected the Yemen into a vilayet'. The reader is able to follow the twists and turns of this turbulent period quite clearly, as the author has unearthed a surprising amount of data on both the actions and the motives of the Ottoman governor of Yemen, his superiors in Istanbul, the Imam in Ṣanʿāʾ, Captain Haines in Aden, Muḥammad ʿAlī in Egypt, the Turkish vali in Mecca and the British government in both London and India. The author has dealt with a slightly earlier period in Tihāmah history, 'Anglo-Ottoman confrontation in the Yemen: the first Mocha indident, 1817-22', in Professor R. B. Serjeant's presentation volume (*Arabian and Islamic Studies.* Edited by R. L. Bidwell, G. R. Smith. London; New York, Longman, 1983, p. 214-24).

381 **Aden under British rule, 1839-1967.**

R. J. Gavin. London: Hurst, 1975. 472p. bibliog.

A political history based solidly on British archives. It ignores Arab voices, except where they are represented in colonial papers, but is good at teasing out the complexities of Aden's division between imperial and Indian interests, and is particularly strong on the development of British administration during the nineteenth century, a period neglected by many other writers. The last few years of rule in Aden are dealt with in a surprisingly cursory fashion.

382 **Arabia without sultans.**

Fred Halliday. Harmondsworth, England: Penguin Books, 1979. Edition with postscript. 529p. maps.

Six chapters in this Marxist analysis of the recent history of the Arabian Peninsula deal with the two Yemens. The author pays particular attention to the forms of control used by the government, to economic factors and to the formation of classes, and this emphasis on often-neglected aspects of history is an important counterpart to the memoirs of British ministers and officials, particularly regarding Aden and the Ḥaḍramawt.

383 **Last sunset.**

Stephen Harper. London: Collins, 1978. 208p.

This is 'an attempt to record an Englishman's impression of the last twenty years of British imperial rule in the place it really ended' (i.e. Aden). The author concentrates on the military aspects of Britain's last years in the colony, frequently using the term 'terrorist gangsters', but also includes the diplomatic background. The author's point of view is clearly British but 'is, he hopes, informed by some sympathy for Arab aspirations' and the work presents an interesting contrast to the less personal but more rigorous analysis by Halliday (see above).

384 **Aden.**

Sir Tom Hickinbotham. London: Constable, 1958. 242p. map.

The author was appointed chairman of the Aden Port Trust in 1948, and in 1951 became governor of Aden, a post he held until 1956. This personal memoir reveals the relatively unstressed atmosphere of Aden in the early 1950s, and the author has much to say of interest regarding shipping, labour relations, life in the Protectorates, relations with North Yemen – particularly after the revolt of 1955 and again in the aftermath of the Suez Crisis – and the development of local politics.

385 **An account of the Arab tribes in the vicinity of Aden.**

F. M. Hunter, C. W. H. Sealey, A. H. E. Mosse. London: Darf Publishers, 1986. 356p.

A reprint of the edition first published in Bombay, India, in 1909, this survey was compiled for the use of the British administration in Aden. It lists all the treaties, engagements, and historical dealings of the tribes of Aden and the Ḥaḍramawt with the British forces, as well a list of the places visited by the Aden Troop between 1870 and 1880 and a list of 'Chiefs and other individuals of importance in the Aden Hinterland having relations with the Aden Residency (1907)'.

386 **Records of Yemen, 1798-1960.**

Edited by Doreen Ingrams, Leila Ingrams. Farnborough, England: Archive Editions, 1993. 16 vols.

Photographic reproductions of papers held by the India Office Library and Records and the Public Record Office, dealing with Aden, the Ḥaḍramawt and North Yemen. The early volumes deal mainly with treaties, boundary disputes and external relations (interspersed with the occasional travel narrative), but from the 1930s onwards, much more attention is paid to local political, social and economic issues, particularly in Aden. The first four volumes (to 1899) reproduce mainly handwritten documents, some of which are close to illegible, but from volume five onwards (1900-), most records are in typescript or printed format. Volume sixteen contains maps and views.

387 **Arabia and the isles.**

Harold Ingrams. London: John Murray, 1966. 3rd ed. 500p. maps.

Ingrams is probably the most famous and influential of all the officers who worked among the tribes in the Eastern Aden Protectorate. This book, after some initial chapters on his life in Zanzibar and Pemba, concentrates on his travels in Ḥaḍramawt, and his dealings with the shaykhs and tribal leaders there. At the end of the main section which was written in 1946, the author avows that 'Hadhramaut is an Arab country and Arab it must remain'. In the very long introduction to the third edition of 1966, the author goes on to bemoan the fact that the policy of 'non-interference in the internal affairs of state' current in the 1930s had been replaced after the Second World War with a much more direct form of administration which he calls 'out-and-out English colonialist thinking', and concludes with a pessimistic forecast for the future of Ḥaḍramī federation.

388 The Yemen: imams, rulers and revolutions.

Harold Ingrams. London: John Murray, 1963. 164p. map.

Partly a history of the last three Zaydī imams of North Yemen, and partly a survey of Anglo- or, rather, Adeni–Yemeni relations in which the author has a sometime personal involvement. Ingrams recounts negotiations on both sides, with one side out of touch with modern diplomacy and the other keen to introduce a pattern of administration previously unknown in (and, to the author's mind, wholly unsuitable for) the region. The author wrote his book just after the Yemeni civil war had broken out and during a period of increasingly strained relations in Aden, and, understandably, his views of Yemeni unity are pessimistic – 'When Egyptian Yemen and British Yemen disappear, as all the other foreign Yemens before them have disappeared, I have little doubt that al-Yemen will usually be as divided as it has been in the past'.

389 Kings of Arabia: the rise and set of the Turkish sovranty in the Arabian Peninsula.

Harold F. Jacob. London: Mills & Boon, 1923. 294p.

Colonel Jacob was First Assistant to the Resident of Aden, then Political Agent for the Aden hinterland. During the First World War he served as Chief Political Adviser on South-West Arabia to the High Commission in Egypt. As such, he was in a unique position to write a scholarly account of the Turks in Yemen, but, in fact, his book is shallow, tendentious and arrogant. Its value lies mainly in the insight it gives into the views of some of the British officials, as well as some practical details of Adeni–Yemeni relations.

390 The view from Steamer Point: being an account of three years in Aden.

Charles Hepburn Johnston. London: Collins, 1964. 224p.

Sir Charles Johnston was Governor in Aden from 1960 to 1963, and the main value in this slice of autobiography is as an admittedly partisan account of negotiations between Aden, the nationalist leaders, tribal shaykhs and the British government. In contrast to Harold Ingrams (see item no. 388), the author felt that 'the Arabs really care about unity . . . they have a feeling of brotherhood in their blood', and that 'the idea of merger [with Aden] to the half million inhabitants of the old Federation was a question of life and death'.

391 **Aux origines de l'implantation française en Mer Rouge: vie et mort d'Henri Lambert, Consul de France à Aden, 1859.** (On the origins of the French settlement in the Red Sea: the life and death of Henri Lambert, French Consul in Aden, 1859.)
Roger Joint Daguenet. Paris: L'Harmattan, 1992. 347p. bibliog. (Collections Racines du Présent).

A important study, based mainly on archival documents, of the role Henri Lambert played in establishing French rule in the Red Sea. Lambert arrived in Aden in 1855 and travelled by sea both to North Yemen (Mocha and Hodeida) and to the Somali coast. Based in Aden, Lambert sought to establish a French power-base in the region, but he roused the antagonism of several parties and was eventually murdered on board ship off Djibouti in 1859. The diplomatic consequences of Lambert's death, which involved the French, British and Ottoman authorities are lucidly disentangled by the author, and the result is a fascinating study of small-scale imperial rivalries in the Red Sea.

392 **The history of Aden, 1839-72.**
Z. H. Kour. London: Cass, 1981. 240p.

A straightforward narrative history of Aden, seen from the British point of view, using the Aden Residency Records, the Bombay Secret Proceedings, and the papers of various high officials in British India. There is little attempt to set the conquest of Aden against the general imperial strategy pursued by Britain, but the mass of factual detail collected by the author is considered mainly in the light of the activities of the British Resident.

393 **Some notes on the economy of Ottoman Yemen (1870-1918.)**
Sinan Kuneralp. *Studies on Turkish–Arab Relations,* vol. 3 (1988), p. 99-106.

A brief but interesting look at a neglected topic. The author discusses land and agriculture, industry (mainly weaving and dyeing), mineral wealth, trade including imports of cloth and crockery from Europe and exports of coffee, smuggling, the tax regime, and the control of the currency. The information is taken mainly from British consular reports and the works of European travellers, rather from the Ottoman archives in Istanbul.

394 **Yemen: unification and modernisation.**
Rafiq Latta, edited by John P. Cooper. London: Gulf Centre for Strategic Studies, 1994. 92p. (Contemporary Strategic Issues in the Arab Gulf).

A potted history of both Yemens which, while it gives due weight to both the tribal and religious factors in the pre-contemporary era, is mainly concerned with the political manoeuvrings of the post-independence period. The author analyses the course of both North and South Yemen in the 1970s and 1980s, culminating in the unification of 1990, which he views with some scepticism, citing unequal demographic weight, hostility between rival political leaders, and the fallout over the support given to Iraq in the Gulf War of 1990-91 as the chief problems faced by the new country.

395 **Shifting sands: the British in South Arabia.**
David Ledger. London: Peninsular Publishing, 1983. 232p. maps.

Although the author claims in his preface that 'this book does not pretend to be a history or an authority, but is an account of events as I saw them', the book itself is much more than a personal memoir. It tells the story of the final few months of British rule in Aden in a detailed and dramatic way, and is particularly good at disentangling the internal politics of the Arab groups involved in the liberation struggle.

396 **Eritrea e Yemen: tensioni italo-turche nel Mar Rosso, 1885-1911.**
(Eritrea and Yemen: Italian–Turkish tensions in the Red Sea, 1885-1911.)
Marco Lenci. Milan, Italy: Franco Angeli, 1990. 162p.

During the twenty-five years following the Treaty of Uccialli (1889), which gave Italy control of Eritrea, the Italians pursued a policy of confrontation with the Ottomans in the Red Sea, which culminated in the naval conflict of 1911-12, when Italy was officially at war with the Turks. This fine study is based mainly on Italian archival material, and tells the story from the Italian side. For a version of the war, based on British sources see 'The Turkish–Italian war in the Yemen, 1911-1912', by John Baldry (*Arabian Studies,* vol. 3 [1976], p. 51-65).

397 **South Arabia: arena of conflict.**
Tom Little. London: Pall Mall Press, 1968. 196p. maps.

An account of South Arabia's progress towards independence focusing on political issues, such as relations with the Imam in North Yemen, the growth of political movements in Aden and the Protectorates, and the administrative services provided by the British. The author does not seem to like the Protectorates much, quoting an Aden Information Department leaflet of 1961, which called the Ḥaḍramawt 'this largely barren land [which] has little to commend it', and he goes on to describe the inhabitants as 'eking out miserable existences made tolerable only by the habit of countless generations and the anarchical freedom which suits their temperament'.

398 **Mocha and the overland route to India.**
Eric Macro. *Proceedings of the Seminar for Arabian Studies,* vol. 12 (1982), p. 49-60.

A short article which discusses how the Bombay–Suez steamship route was planned and what effect this had on the Red Sea and South Arabian ports. The overland route was overland in name only, basically over the Suez Isthmus, and by far the greater part consisted in sea journeys, particularly the 1,600 miles from Suez to Bombay. In the early nineteenth century, many sites were proposed as coaling stations, but the increasing range of steamships left Aden and Mocha as the only real contenders. The author also looks at the provision for steamships and their passengers in Aden from its capture by the British in 1839 until the building of the Suez Canal.

399 **Yemen and the Western world.**
Eric Macro. London: Hurst, 1968. 150p. map. bibliog.

A record of European diplomatic and commercial contacts with Yemen and South Arabia. The volume begins with the activities of the Portuguese in the sixteenth century, moves through contact with the English and Dutch East India Companies over the next hundred years, to British, American and French maritime contacts in the nineteenth century. The twentieth century saw activities by the Italians, French, Germans, Americans, Japanese, Israel, and, latterly, the Soviet Union, all of which are chronicled by the author, along with the numerous border disputes between Aden and North Yemen. This is a somewhat patchy book (it had its genesis in a number of previously published articles), but it does contain a large amount of curious and important information about the Yemeni-oriented activities of states ignored by many other authors.

400 **Aden and Yemen (1905-1919).**
R. N. Mehra. Delhi: Agam Prakashan, 1988. 274p. maps. bibliog.

A well-balanced account of the international relations of Aden at the beginning of the twentieth century. Relying on British and Indian archives, the author tackles the vexed question of boundary disputes with Ottoman Yemen, treaties and agreements with the tribes of the hinterland, the activities of the French, Germans and Italians in the region, while also evaluating the 'continued neglect of developmental growth' in Aden by both the British and Indian governments. The volume concludes with the reprinting of seven articles by the author, five of which deal with Aden between 1837 and 1905, and two with the politics of South Yemen in the 1970s.

401 **The Yemeni opposition movement, 1918-1948.**
Abdualaziz K. al-Msoadi. PhD dissertation, Georgetown University, 1987. 298p. bibliog. (Available from University Microfilms International, Ann Arbor, Michigan, order no. 8816329).

Presented in the same year as Leigh Douglas's book (see item no. 378) was published, this work spends almost as much space describing the social and economic background to the reign of Imam Yaḥyā (d. 1948) as it does analysing the tribal revolts and uprisings which broke out during the period, and the forms in which the urban opposition manifested itself. It is a coherent, but not particularly original piece of scholarship.

402 **The war in the Yemen.**
Edgar O'Ballance. London: Faber & Faber, 1971. 218p. maps.

The standard chronicle of events during the Yemeni civil war of 1962-70. The author takes account of terrain, social conditions, personalities and foreign intervention in his account of the war, but eschews a deeper analysis of economic, religious and class factors, of the kind provided by Halliday (see item no. 382).

403 ***al-Īmān* and al-Imam: ideology and state in the Yemen, 1900-1948.**
Gerald Obermeyer. In: *Intellectual life in the Arab East, 1890-1939.* *Edited by* Marwan R. Buheiry. Beirut: American University of Beirut Press, 1981, p. 176-92.

A valuable and interesting study of the ideological foundations of the twentieth-century Zaydī state in North Yemen, seen principally through the pages of the state's official newspaper, *al-Īmān.* The author surveys the limited impact of the Ottoman occupation of Yemen, which failed to change 'the elementary structure of indigenous politics', which he sees as 'a dynamic pattern of opposition by tribes to domination by competing imams'. The author suggests that Imam Yaḥyā (d. 1948) was not as isolated from outside influences as has been claimed but that he was aware of technological and intellectual developments in the Arab World and beyond. The Imam's primary concern was to integrate the Zaydī community and create a political centre at Ṣanʿāʾ (constantly referred to in the official newspaper as *Markaz al-Khilāfah*, the Centre of the Caliphate), and the author sees the newspaper as the Imam's principal method of disseminating official ideas on law, economics and politics, and thereby countering the growing strength of nationalism displayed by the Free Yemeni Movement.

404 **Yemen enters the modern world: secret U.S. documents on the rise of the second power on the Arabian Peninsula.**
Edited by Ibrahim al-Rashid. Chapel Hill, North Carolina: Documentary Publications, 1984. 2 vols. (Documents on the History of Saudi Arabia, vol. 6).

A series of transcribed documents on the conditions in Yemen between 1945 and 1949 as seen through American diplomatic eyes. There are telegrams from US ministers and officers of the State Department, memoranda of conversations with Yemeni dignitaries, and occasional translations from Arab newspapers and periodicals, such as the text of the 'National Sacred Pact of the new constitutional government of the Yemen' published in *al-Ikhwān al-Muslimūn* on 20 February 1948.

405 **Yemen under the rule of the Imam Ahmad.**
Edited by Ibrahim al-Rashid. Chapel Hill, North Carolina: Documentary Publications, 1985. 194p. (Documents on the History of Arabia, vol. 7)

A companion volume to the above, covering documents prepared between 1950 and 1954. Many of the papers deal with relations between North Yemen and the tribes of the Aden Protectorates, but others look at the exiled opposition leader, Muḥammad Maḥmūd al-Zubayrī, or at the internal politics of the imamate state.

406 **Die Oppositionsbewegung im Jemen zur Zeit Imam Yahyas und der Putsch von 1948.** (The opposition movement in Yemen during the reign of Imam Yaḥyā and the 1948 coup.)
Ahmed Kaid al-Saidi. Berlin: Baalbek Verlag, 1981. 276p. bibliog.

After a long introduction describing at the historical development of North Yemen and the political power structure there, the author looks at the various groups who opposed Imam Yaḥyā: the *sayyids* (descendants of the Prophet), the judges, the merchants, the modernists, the landlords and the tribal leaders. He describes the methods they employed and analyses their attitude towards various key issues, such as the British in Aden, or Arab nationalism. He goes on to show how they came together in the 1948 coup and puts forward various reasons for the failure of the coup, as well as discussing its consequences. This is a solid, even stolid, piece of work, soundly based on Arab sources.

407 **Tribal warfare and foreign policy in Yemen, Aden and adjacent tribal kingdoms, 1920-1929.**
Edited by Reginald W. Sinclair. Salisbury, North Carolina: Documentary Publications, 1976. 2 vols. (Documents on the History of Southwest Arabia).

Facsimile reproductions of eighty-three American diplomatic documents chronicling mainly the attempt by the Imam of North Yemen to consolidate and expand his power in the face of numerous tribal revolts within Yemen. There are also numerous despatches which detail the sundry intrigues conducted by the Imam among the Arab tribes of the Aden Protectorates, and the book concludes with a series of consular messages about oil exploration in the kingdom.

408 **Yemen: revolution versus tradition.**
Robert W. Stookey. In: *The Arabian Peninsula: zone of ferment.* Edited by Robert W. Stookey. Stanford, California: Hoover Institution Press, 1984, p. 79-108.

A survey of social groupings, political parties, and the external relations of both Yemens from a historical perspective. The author sees the Yemens as sharing a common culture and history but that 'there were already significant differences in social structure and politics before the arrival of the British in Aden in 1839'.

409 **Shades of amber: a South Arabian episode.**
Sir Kennedy Trevaskis. London: Hutchinson, 1968. 256p. map.

The author, who was High Commissioner for Aden and the Protectorates between 1965 and 1967, here surveys the history of the area from 1951 – when he flew into Aden for the first time – to the departure of the British in 1967. This is an engaging memoir, which has considerable value as history, since the author discusses all the personalities he met and had dealings with in the territories, from Duncan Sandys to the Sharīf Ḥusayn of Bayḥān.

410 **The Middle East in revolution.**
Humphrey Trevelyan. London: Macmillan, 1970. 275p.

This is an account of three periods of extreme turbulence in the Arab world as experienced by the author: Egypt from August 1955 to the Suez Crisis of 1956; Iraq from December 1958 four months after the revolution until October 1961, after the failure of the Iraqi claim to Kuwait; and May to September 1967, when the author was the last British High Commissioner in Aden. The author's view of British policy is somewhat jaundiced, being described as 'a policy of cynicism and economy up till the nineteen-fifties' and, thereafter, echoing the words of Sir Charles Johnston (see item no. 390), as one of 'idealism and cash'. The author's negotiations with both main Adeni opposition parties are narrated in detail and with considerable sardonic humour, while the United Nations's mission is described as 'a sort of Mad Hatter's Tea Party'.

411 **The conventional war in Yemen.**
David Warburton. *Arab Studies Journal,* vol. 3, no. 1 (1995), p. 20-44.

A straightforward and very clear description of the war which erupted between the Northern and Southern parts of the unified Republic of Yemen in 1994. The war lasted two months and was eventually won by the Northern forces, but neither side's forces are considered to have performed particularly well. The Northern offensive was characterized by 'poor planning and clumsy execution', while the Southern defence was 'remarkably inept'.

412 **Sultans of Aden.**
Gordon Waterfield. London: John Murray, 1968. 267p. maps.

The story of S. B. Haines, the first, and, in many ways, the most important of the Political Residents of Aden, who was appointed in 1839, dismissed for financial irregularities in 1854, and died shortly after his release from a debtor's prison in 1860. It was Haines who commanded the force which captured the town, and he oversaw its transformation into an important fortress and entrepôt, as well as securing its hinterland for defensive purposes. The author has based his biography solidly on archival records.

413 **Modern Yemen, 1918-1966.**
Manfred W. Wenner. Baltimore, Maryland: The Johns Hopkins Press, 1967. 256p. bibliog. (The Johns Hopkins University Studies in Historical and Political Science, no. 85/1).

The author looks at the reigns of the Imams Yaḥyā (d. 1948) and Aḥmad (d. 1962) in North Yemen from the points of view of internal government, opposition movements and internal security and foreign relations, with a final chapter on the civil war (which was still raging when the book was published). This is a useful historical textbook, if a little dated now.

Ṣanʿāʾ: an Arabian Islamic city.
See item no. 59.

Tribes, government and history in Yemen.
See item no. 537.

Rulers and Residents: British relations with the Aden Protectorate, 1937-59.
See item no. 725.

Arabia's frontiers: the story of Britain's boundary drawing in the desert.
See item no. 728.

***Ṣanʿāʾ*: eine amtliche osmanische Provinzzeitung im Jemen.** (*Ṣanʿāʾ*: an official Ottoman provincial journal in Yemen.)
See item no. 910.

Population and Demography

414 **Fertility, mortality, migration and family planning in the Yemen Arab Republic.**
James Allman, Allan G. Hill. Population Studies, vol. 32, no. 1 (1978), p. 159-71.

Basing themselves on the preliminary results of the 1975 census and a further small sample survey carried out in 1976, the authors examine various aspects of Yemeni demography. They draw statistical and sociological conclusions about the low overall sex ratio (due to the labour migration of Yemeni males), the proportional age structure, infant mortality, and fertility (this last aspect is based mainly on the 1972 Ṣanʿāʾ survey). Their 1976 fieldwork at two health centres in the Yemen Arab Republic leads them on to further analysis of women's attitudes to breastfeeding, contraception and multiple births.

415 **Ottoman sources on Arabian population.**
Justin McCarthy. In: *Studies in the history of Arabia*. Vol. 1, *Sources for the history of Arabia.* Riyadh: Riyadh University Press, 1979, part 2, p. 113-33.

The author, who has worked extensively in the Ottoman archives on demographic issues, deals in this paper with the three Ottoman *vilayets* (provinces) which lay in the Arabian Peninsula: the Hijaz, Yemen and Basra (although the latter also covered part of Iraq). Although the population statistics for Arabia are the least complete and the least accurate for the whole Empire, yet 'despite their deficiences, they are valuable to the study of late nineteenth and early twentieth century history'. The author proceeds to describe how the statistics were issued, what their current bibliographical state is, what the difficulties are in interpreting the data, and for what purposes the existing material can be used.

416 **Population and development in the Republic of Yemen: proceedings of the first National Population Policy Conference, October 26-29, 1991, Ṣanʿāʾ.**

Ṣanʿāʾ: Ministry of Planning and Development, 1992. 2 vols.

These conference papers are the result of the Yemen government's attempts to determine a formal population policy. The conference itself was attended by 250 experts and discussed the results of deliberations by seventeen different task forces. These presented papers on safe motherhood, child welfare, family planning, women and development, housing, water resources, migration and many other subjects. The papers themselves, supported by a wide range of statistics, analyse existing problems in Yemen and propose solutions.

417 **Population geography of the Yemen Arab Republic: the major findings of the Population and Housing Census of February 1975 and of the Supplementary Demographic and Cartographic Surveys.**

Hans Steffen. Wiesbaden, Germany: Ludwig Reichert, 1979. 172p. and 132p. maps. (Beihefte zum Tübinger Atlas des Vorderen Orients, Reihe B, no. 39).

An invaluable study of the first official census of the Yemen Arab Republic (YAR). In the first part of the book, the author looks at the reliability and limitations of the census, at the administrative divisions of the YAR, at fertility, migration, population and family statistics, education, manpower, housing and household patterns and development problems resulting from the male labour migration. The second part of the work focuses in detail on three separate locations: Turbat al-Shamā'itayn in the south; Jabal ʿIyāl Yazīd north of Ṣanʿāʾ; and al-Luḥayyah in the Tihāmah. In these regional studies, the author is able to bring in other geographical elements such as land use and traffic routes, as well as studying the central demographic features of housing, household composition and rural population mobility.

418 **The population of Suqutra in the early Arabic sources.**

Ahmad Ubaydli. *Proceedings of the Seminar for Arabian Studies,* vol. 19 (1989), p. 137-54.

Not so much a study in demography, as an examination of the various races who visited and settled in Socotra, according to the literary evidence. The author looks at information on the Greeks, the Indians, and briefly at the Mahrah, the Ibadis and others. The information is presented in a somewhat haphazard manner, and is not related to the available archaeological evidence.

419 **The population situation in the ECWA region: Democratic Yemen.**

United Nations Economic and Social Commission for Western Asia. Beirut: ECWA, 1980. 23p. bibliog.

Based on the preliminary results of the 1973 census, and some subsequent small-scale sample surveys, this work details the population of the People's Democratic Republic of Yemen by age and sex, discusses the levels of fertility and mortality, and considers the consequences of the census results for education and the labour force.

Bibliography of population literature in the Arab world.

See item no. 937.

Minorities

420 **The Jews of the British Crown Colony of Aden: history, culture, and ethnic relations.**

Reuben Ahroni. Leiden, The Netherlands: Brill, 1994. 314p. bibliog. (Brill's Series in Jewish Studies, vol. 12).

The first, and, so far, only critical monograph devoted to the Jews of Aden. When the British conquered Aden in 1839, they found a small community of around 250 Jews in a total population of 600. By 1947, this had risen to 6,000 as Jews immigrated from Yemen, India, other countries in the Middle East, and Europe. This book looks at the history of the development of the Jewish colony, the 'salient dimensions of the religious, socioeconomic, cultural, and intellectual fabric of this community' and at the relationship between Jews and Arabs in Aden. The author also includes a short section on the Jews of Ḥabbān, a small town in central Ḥaḍramawt, who were, before emigration, 'considered the most exotic of all the Jewish communities on the Arabian Peninsula'.

421 **Yemenite Jewry: origins, culture and literature.**

Reuben Ahroni. Bloomington, Indiana: Indiana University Press, 1986. 227p. bibliog. (Jewish Literature and Culture).

A narrative history of the Jews of North Yemen from the earliest (biblical) times to the end of the Ottoman occupation in 1919. The author uses all the Jewish sources at his disposal, consisting of religious texts, historical chronicles, travel narratives, poetry and the Genizah documents, to give a rounded picture of the intellectual, social and historical development of one of Judaism's most isolated communities. Arabic sources such as the history (see van Koningsfeld, item no. 430) of Aḥmad ibn Nāṣir al-Zaydī (d. c. 1678) are, however, rarely mentioned.

422 **The magic carpet.**

Shlomo Barer. London: Secker & Warburg, 1952. 267p.

The author was an eyewitness to Operation Magic Carpet, which transported almost the entire Jewish community of North Yemen, Aden and the Ḥaḍramawt to Israel over the space of two years in 1949 and 1950. This book first recounts in diary form his experiences at Hashed transit camp near Aden, then moves on to a potted history of the Jews in Aden, before returning to Hashed and the author's relationship with the various authorities, British, Arab, and Israeli, involved in the exodus.

423 **Ethnologie der jemenitischen Juden.** (Ethnology of Yemeni Jews.)
Erich Brauer. Heidelberg, Germany: Carl Winter, 1934. 402p. maps.

Still the most substantial work to deal with the social and cultural life of the Jews of North Yemen, although the author never visited Yemen himself, and based his work on the reports of earlier travellers and many interviews with Yemeni immigrants in Palestine. The work includes chapters on the material culture of the Jews, family structures, economic activities, educational matters, magic and ritual, and the importance of Jewish festivals, the synagogue, the Jewish court and relations with the Muslim state. Since the community emigrated en masse to Israel in 1949-50, this book remains an important factual testimony to a way of life that has now disappeared.

424 **The Jews of the Middle East, 1860-1972.**
Hayyim J. Cohen. New York: John Wiley; Jerusalem: Israel Universities Press, 1973. 213p. bibliog.

A useful summary of the history of the Jews in the Arab World, Iran and Turkey (but not in the Balkans) over the past hundred years or so. The work includes chapters on demographic trends, economic transformations, educational progress and social changes; references to the Jews both of Aden and of the Yemen Arab Republic feature in every section.

425 **The Jews of Yemen in the nineteenth century: a portrait of a messianic community.**
Bat-Zion Eraqi Klorman. Leiden, The Netherlands: Brill, 1993. 209p. bibliog. (Brill's Series in Jewish Studies, vol. 6).

The bulk of this work is concerned with what the author calls 'the last and only known messianic movements in Jewish history in post-Sabbatian times', that is after the great religious movement that developed around the personality of Sabbatai Sevi in the latter half of the 17th century. The author looks at the repercussions of this phenomenon on Yemen, relying in the main on the published translation of Aḥmad ibn Nāṣir al-Zaydī (d. c. 1678) (q.v.), but then moves on to her original research which centres on the movements inspired by Shukr Kuhayl I (1861-65), Shukr Kuhayl II (1868-75) and Yosef ʿAbd Allāh (1888-95). The author concludes her study with an examination of the messianic hopes which permeated the lives of emigrants from Yemen to Palestine between 1881 and 1914. The interrelationship between Muslim and Jewish messianic and apocalyptic movements is also fully explored both in this book and in the author's earlier article, 'Jewish and Muslim messianism in Yemen' (*International Journal of Middle East Studies,* vol. 22, no. 2 [1990], p. 201-28).

426 **The Jews of Yemen.**
S. D. Goitein. In: *Religion in the Middle East.* Vol. 1: *Judaism and Christianity.* Edited by A. J. Arberry. Cambridge, England: Cambridge University Press, 1969, p. 226-39.

A brief article which looks at the social situation of Jews in North Yemen, and their economic and cultural, rather than historical development. The result is a vivid if rather compressed sketch of an ancient tradition.

427 **The preservation of Jewish ethnic identity in Yemen: segregation and integration as boundary maintenance mechanisms.**
Yael Katzir. *Comparative Studies in Society and History,* vol. 24, no. 2 (1982), p. 264-79.

The author, using a concept elaborated by Fredrik Barth, discusses the means whereby North Yemeni Jews maintained their distinct identity. These included the transmission of vocational and artisan skills from father to son, thus ensuring that the Jewish community preserved an essential economic role; full literacy in Hebrew for all males; and endogamous marriage with the father's brother's daughter. The shared elements of culture and language between Muslim and Jew enabled co-existence to continue, but were insufficient to break down the ethnic barriers between the two groups.

428 **The Jews of Yemen.**
Aviva Klein-Franke. In: *Yemen: 3000 years of art and civilisation in Arabia Felix.* Edited by Werner Daum. Innsbruck, Austria: Pinguin-Verlag; Frankfurt am Main, Germany: Umschau-Verlag, 1988, p. 265-80, 297-9.

Having begun with a survey of the history of the Jews in Yemen (both North and South) from biblical times to the 20th century, the author moves on to their intellectual, cultural and educational life. She looks at religious literature, especially the Kabbalah, and at the themes and subject matter of Yemeni Jewish poetry, finishing with the translation of a poem on *qāt* and coffee by the 17th-century poet Salim Shabbazi.

429 **Zum Rechtsstatus der Juden im Jemen.** (On the legal status of Jews in Yemen.)
Aviva Klein-Franke. *Die Welt des Islams,* new series, vol. 37, no. 2 (1996), p. 178-222.

A detailed documentary study of relations between the Muslims and the Jews in North Yemen. The author begins with a survey of the legislation on Jews from the time of the Prophet Muḥammad, before moving on briefly to the era of the second Ottoman occupation, which ended in 1919. Her main argument, however, centres around how the poll tax was administered during the reign of Imam Yaḥyā (1904-48) and it is based on documents, several of them reproduced in Arabic with German translation, from the collection of Rabbi Shalom Gamliel, who was leader of the Jewish community in Ṣanʿāʾ from 1935 until 1944. The author concludes that Imam Yaḥyā felt himself bound as spiritual leader of the Yemen to uphold the command of Muḥammad to protect the Jews, and that his policy towards his Jewish subjects was imbued with a deep sense of religious responsibility.

430 **Yemenite authorities and Jewish messianism: Aḥmad ibn Nāṣir al-Zaydī's account of the Sabbathian movement in seventeenth century Yemen and its aftermath.**
P. S. van Koningsveld, J. Sadan, Q. Al-Samarrai. Leiden, The Netherlands: Faculty of Theology, Leiden University, 1990. 206p. bibliog.

An edition, translation and extended study of an important Arabic source 'which casts new light on the vicissitudes of the Jewish messianic movement in 17th century Yemen, and especially on its interaction with the local Muslim authorities. The author, the Muslim scholar Aḥmad ibn Nāṣir ibn ʿAbd al-Ḥaqq al-Zaydī [d. c. 1678], quotes hitherto unknown court documents and reflects the authentic opinions of the Yemenite ruling élite.' The authors analyse the data offered by al-Zaydī, compare it with Hebrew versions of the events in question as collated by Yosef Tobi and offer some general conclusions on the social and legal position of Yemeni Jews in the seventeenth century.

431 **Les Juifs du Yémen: approche ethnologique.** (The Jews of Yemen: an ethnological approach.)
Liliane Kuczynski. In: *L'Arabie du Sud: histoire et civilisation.* (South Arabia: history and civilization.) Vol. 3: *Culture et institutions du Yémen* (Culture and institutions of Yemen.) Joseph Chelhod (et al.). Paris: Maisonneuve et Larose, 1985, p. 277-302.

Having praised the work of Erich Brauer (see item no. 423) on the social life and customs of the Jews of Yemen as 'without equal', the author goes on to examine more deeply 'certain aspects [of Jewish life] which have appeared to us as the most typical in comparison with other Jewish communities and with the Muslim milieu'. These aspects are Jewish houses, Jewish clothes, Jewish craftsmen, and Jewish education, and the author bases her information mainly on travellers of around a hundred years ago and the works of more recent scholars such as Erich Brauer (q.v.), Aviva Lancet-Müller and Aviva Klein-Franke (see items 428, 429).

432 **Jewish life in Habban: a tentative reconstruction.**
Laurence D. Loeb. In: *Studies in Jewish folklore: proceedings of a regional conference of the Association for Jewish Studies, held at Spertus College of Judaica, Chicago, May 1-3, 1977.* Edited by Frank Talmage. Cambridge, Massachusetts: Association for Jewish Studies, 1980, p. 201-17.

Although the author did not visit the community of Ḥabbān in South Arabia himself (the last directly observed description is by R. B. Serjeant in 1947, 'A Judeo-Arab house-deed from Ḥabbān, with notes of the former Jewish communities of the Wāḥidī Sultanate', *Journal of the Royal Asiatic Society* [October 1953], p. 117-31), he was able to interview many Habbanites in Israel who 'had very clear recollections of their life in South Yemen'. The author describes the history of Ḥabbān (inasmuch as it can be traced), the organization of the Jewish Quarter there, and the structure of the Jewish community in the town from the political, economic, educational and religious points of view.

433 **The Jews of Aden.**
London Museum of Jewish Life, Kadimah Youth Movement.
London: London Museum of Jewish Life, 1991. 48p.

Produced to accompany an exhibition held in the Museum in April 1991, this is a vivid, well-illustrated survey of all aspects of Jewish life in Aden, enhanced by extracts from oral history interviews with some of the 600 Adeni families now living in London.

434 **The Jews of Yemen: highlights of the Israel Museum collection.**
Ester Muchawsky-Schnapper. Jerusalem: The Israel Museum, 1994. 130p. bibliog.

The Israel Museum contains over 800 Yemenite items collected *in situ* by the German orientalist Carl Rathjens between 1928 and 1935, and has acquired further objects from Yemenite Jews living in Israel and from the collections of the Women's International Zionist Organization. This well-illustrated book describes over fifty Yemeni Jewish objects, mostly items of dress or personal adornment, but also ritual and ceremonial objects and pieces of material culture such as carpets, wickerwork and pottery. A selection of Rathjens' photographs of Yemeni Jewish life, together with some taken by the traveller Hermann Burchardt in the early part of the 20th century, have also been published in an exhibition catalogue, *The Jews of Sanʿa as seen by the researchers Hermann Burchardt and Carl Rathjens* (Tel Aviv, Israel: Beth Hatefutsoth, the Nahum Goldmann Museum of the Jewish Diaspora, 1982. unpaged).

435 **The Jews of the Yemen, 1800-1914.**
Yehuda Nini, translated from the Hebrew by H. Galai. Chur, Switzerland; Reading, England: Harwood Academic, 1991. 256p. bibliog.

Covers the same ground chronologically as Eraqi Klorman (see item no. 425), but devotes far less space to the messianic movements, and much more to the political events of the period, the geographical dispersal of Jewish settlement, the nature of community organization and contacts between the Jews of Yemen and elsewhere, including immigration into Palestine in the late Ottoman period. The work is based mainly on Hebrew sources, with a limited use of European travellers and even less of Arabic historical chronicles.

436 **Jewish minority experience in twentieth-century Yemen.**
Tudor Parfitt. In: *Nationalism, minorities and diasporas: identities and rights in the Middle East.* Edited by Kirsten E. Schulze, Martin Stokes, Colm Campbell. London: Tauris Academic, 1996, p. 117-43.

An excellent survey of the position of the Jews as a minority in North Yemen from the late Ottoman occupation until the foundation of the State of Israel in 1948. The author looks at the legal and social status of the Jews, their relations with the Imam and the tribes, their quarters in towns and cities, their economic circumstances and, briefly, their relations with outside bodies and powers. He shows clearly the civil disabilities under which the Jews laboured, and gives the lie to the assertion that the Jews' lot improved under the Ottomans, suggesting that 6,000 Jews (or eighty per cent of the pre-famine population) died in the 1904 seige of Ṣanʿāʾ by the Imam's forces.

437 **The road to redemption: the Jews of the Yemen, 1900-1950.**
Tudor Parfitt. Leiden, The Netherlands: Brill, 1996. 299p. bibliog. (Brill's Series in Jewish Studies, vol. 17).

One of the most interesting sections of this fascinating book is the first chapter which summarizes the controversy over the origin of the Yemeni Jewish community (were they converts or émigré Israelites?), but the book soon moves on to its central topic – the history of the Jews of North Yemen (and of Aden to a lesser extent) from the late Ottoman period until the exodus to Israel in 1949-50. The author, in addition to the standard works in Hebrew and English has made good use of the testimonies of various Jewish emissaries, secret or otherwise, who visited Yemen on behalf of the wider Jewish community, and, for the final phase, of the personal archive of Robin Gilbert, who was intimately involved in the transportation of the Yemeni Jews to Israel.

438 **On wings of eagles: the plight, exodus and homecoming of Oriental Jewry.**
Joseph B. Schechtman. New York; London: Thomas Yoseloff, 1961. 429p.

A useful summary of the recent history and emigration of the various Jewish communities in the Middle East. The first chapter deals with the Jews of North Yemen (p. 31-73), the second with the Jews of Aden and the Ḥaḍramawt (p. 74-86), and the final chapters with the problems of integrating the Oriental Jews into Israeli society (p. 339-98).

439 **The Hindu, Baniyān, merchants and traders.**
R. B. Serjeant. In: *Ṣanʿāʾ: an Arabian Islamic city.* Edited by R. B. Serjeant, Ronald Lewcock. London: World of Islam Festival Trust, 1983, p. 432-5.

Apart from the Jews (and visiting or colonizing Europeans and Turks), almost the only other minority group to have maintained a separate status in Yemen is the Hindu community of merchants known as the *Baniyān*. This article looks at references to their presence in Ṣanʿāʾ and elsewhere in North Yemen in Arabic chronicles and Western travel accounts. The bulk of the information comes from the 17th to 19th centuries, and indicates that the the *Baniyān* were treated with tolerance most of the time but little respect. For the author's account of the *Baniyān* presence in South Arabia in medieval times, see his article 'Yemeni merchants and trade in Yemen, 13th-16th centuries' (item no. 352).

440 **The Jews of Ṣanʿāʾ.**
A. Shivtiel, Wilfred Lockwood, R. B. Serjeant. In: *Ṣanʿāʾ: an Arabian Islamic city.* Edited by R. B. Serjeant, Ronald Lewcock. London: World of Islam Festival Trust, 1983, p. 391-400, 417-31.

A detailed study of Jews in Ṣanʿāʾ mainly from the 16th to the early 20th century and based on Arabic and Western rather than Hebrew sources. The authors look at relations with Muslims, conversion to Islam, the poll tax, sumptuary laws, types of occupation and forms of address between Muslims and Jews, as well as sketching in the political history and translating some typical documents, e.g. on arrangements for the ritual slaughter of animals. This is an interesting, but not complete, article, since it omits details of the Jewish community's activities outside its relationship with the majority Muslim population.

441 **The authority of the community of San'a in Yemenite Jewry.**
Yosef Tobi. In: *Jews among Muslims: communities in the precolonial Middle East.* Edited by Shlomo Deshen, Walter P. Zenner. Basingstoke, England: Macmillan, 1996, p. 232-43.

A slightly abbreviated version of a paper which first appeared in *Jewish societies in the Middle East: community, culture and authority* (Edited by Shlomo Deshen and Walter P. Zenner. Washington, DC: University Press of America, 1982, p. 235-50), this is an interesting study of the internal organization of the Jewish community, particularly regarding juridical authority. Using five 19th-century Hebrew documents, the author is able to demonstrate the tension between the rabbis of Ṣan'ā' and those of other communities, and how, in the end, the judgments of the Bet Din of the capital prevailed, even when the dispute concerned Jews outside the political control of the Imam of Yemen. The author extends his study briefly to the 20th century, when the Ottoman position of Hakimbaşi (or Head of the Jewish community throughout Yemen) was suppressed, but without diminishing the authority of the Chief Rabbi of Ṣan'ā' to any material degree.

442 **Histoire de la communauté juive du Yémen aux XIXe et XXe siècles.** (History of the Jewish community in Yemen in the 19th and 20th centuries.)
Yosef Tobi. In: *L'Arabie du Sud: histoire et civilisation.* (South Arabia: history and civilization.) Vol. 2: *La société yéménite de l'Hégire aux idéologies modernes.* (Yemeni society from the rise of Islam up to modern ideologies.) Paris: Maisonneuve et Larose, 1984, p. 119-37. bibliog.

An excellent summary of the various levels of Jewish community in Yemen, their relations with the Zaydī and Ottoman states, and the economic activities and social organization of the Jews throughout Yemen and South Arabia from the mid-18th century to the departure of the Ottomans in 1919.

Travels in Yemen.
See item no. 127.

Immagine dello Yemen. (A picture of Yemen.)
See item no. 128.

Les exilés du Yémen heureux. (The exiles of Arabia Felix.)
See item no. 163.

From Bustān al-'uqūl to Qiṣat al-batūl.
See item no. 502.

Inheritance rights of Jewish women and Moslem women in Yemen.
See item no. 589.

Jewish domestic architecture in San'a, Yemen.
See item no. 844.

The social structure of Jewish education in Yemen.
See item no. 848.

Tribulations and aspirations in Yemenite Hebrew literature.
See item no. 859.

Daughters of Yemen.
See item no. 861.

Tablet weaving by the Jews of Sanʿa (Yemen).
See item no. 876.

From the land of Sheba: tales of the Jews of Yemen.
See item no. 888.

Overseas Populations

443 **The Yemeni immigrant community of Detroit: background, emigration, and community life.**
Nabeel Abraham. In: *Arabs in the New World: studies on Arab-American communities.* Edited by Sameer Y. Abraham, Nabeel Abraham. Detroit, Michigan: Wayne State University, Center for Urban Studies, 1983, p. 110-34.

In this article, which is based on his PhD dissertation at the University of Michigan (1978), the author divides the 6,000 or so Yemenis into two groups: the larger group of temporary migrants, from a rural background, who work mainly in the car plants or on Great Lakes shipping, and whose aim is to make as much money as quickly as possible and then to return to Yemen; and a much smaller group, mostly from Aden, who possess some education and intend to settle in the United States. The non-settlers consciously minimize their interaction with the host society, refusing to learn English, and maintaining close links with their home villages. Some of the younger immigrants openly flout the behavioural norms of the Yemeni community, and become involved with drugs, alcohol or gambling, but provided they continue to fulfil their economic obligations to their families in Yemen, they are not fully ostracized. The author, however, notes a growing tension between the attractions of permanence and transience.

444 **Le Hadhramout et les colonies arabes dans l'archipel indien.** (The Ḥaḍramawt and the Arab colonies in the Indian archipelago.)
L. W. C. van den Berg. Farnborough, England: Gregg, 1969. 292p. maps.

A reprint of the edition published in Batavia (Jakarta) in 1886, this remains the classic work on the South Arabian emigrants to the Dutch East Indies (now Indonesia). The author gives details of the population, social structure, economic situation and customs and habits of the Ḥaḍramī Arabs, before passing on to the life of immigrants throughout the East Indies. The author gives a comprehensive account of numbers of immigrants (categorized by age and sex as well as residence), of their occupations and income, of their religion and culture, and of their political aspirations and their influence on the native population. The work concludes with a study of the Arabic spoken by the immigrants and some samples of letters written by them.

445 **Yemenite-Jewish migration and adaptation to the United States, 1905-1941.**

Dina Dahbahy-Miraglia. In: *Crossing the waters: Arabic-speaking immigration to the United States.* Edited by Eric J. Hooglund. Washington, DC: Smithsonian Institution, 1987, p. 119-31.

A survey of the early immigration of Yemeni Jews to the United States, based on the author's PhD dissertation at Columbia University, 1983. The Yemeni Jewish community in North America was always small, consisting in 1941 of around 100 adults and 150 children. The adults had all grown up in Palestine, to which their families had emigrated in the late 19th and early 20th centuries. Emigration overseas for Yemeni Jews began after the First World War and was triggered off in some cases by service in the Jewish Brigade, and the consequent prolonged exposure to non-Yemenis. Once in America, the families stuck together in the New York area, meeting at a minimum on a weekly basis, and marrying within the community. By the 1950s, however, the children, educated in America, were beginning to marry non-Yemenis and to migrate from their original New York homes. The Yemeni Jewish community, severely diluted, was in danger of disappearing, until the arrival of several thousand Yemeni Jews from Israel from 1959 onwards. This is an interesting and well-researched paper, although the author's knowledge of Yemen itself occasionally appears a little vague.

446 **Sojourners and settlers: the Yemeni immigrant experience.**

Edited by Jonathan Friedlander. Salt Lake City, Utah: University of Utah Press; Los Angeles, California: G. E. von Grunebaum Center for Near Eastern Studies, University of California at Los Angeles, 1988. 188p.

The most substantial book on Yemenis in North America, this work attempts to set the Yemeni experience against the wider context of immigration into the United States in the 20th century (Jon C. Swanson), and against the social conditions prevailing in Yemen in the 1960s and 1970s (chapters by Nikki R. Keddie, Manfred W. Wenner and Thomas B. Stevenson). Individual fieldwork studies look at Yemenis in the San Joaquin Valley in California (Ron Kelley) and in New York City (Shalom Staub, based on his PhD dissertation, University of Pennsylvania, 1985), and are essential complements to the original research of Nabeel Abraham in Detroit (see item no. 443). The volume concludes with a general sociological analysis of Yemeni immigrants (Georges Sabagh, Mehdi Bozorgmehr) and two photographic essays (Tony Maine, Milton Rogovin). Two of the chapters had earlier been published in slightly different form in *Middle East Report,* no. 139 (1986): 'Sojourners and settlers: Yemenis in America' (Jon C. Swanson, p. 5-21) and 'The Yemenis of the San Joaquin' (Ron Kelley, p. 22-36).

447 **Ginger and salt: Yemeni Jewish women in an Israeli town.**
Lisa Gilad. Boulder, Colorado: Westview Press, 1989. 274p. bibliog. (Women in Cross-Cultural Perspective Series).

The author conducted research in the Israeli town of Gadot in the early 1980s, investigating the lives of thirty-five women who had emigrated from North Yemen in 1949-50 and a further thirty-three unmarried women of Yemeni families, who had been born in Israel. The author looks at the changes in family composition, parental authority and responsibility, occupation and domestic labour, and residence patterns, and challenges the views held by other scholars like Herbert Lewis (see item no. 453) that a Yemeni ethnic revival is taking place in Israel, although she makes clear that Yemeni 'mother country imagery' is an important feature of life for the older generation of immigrants. This is a solid piece of ethnographic research, which shows the tensions inherent in immigrant life, and how at least one group of Israeli Yemenis are coming to terms with their change in status and life-styles.

448 **Arabs in exile: Yemeni migrants in urban Britain.**
Fred Halliday. London: Tauris, 1992. 166p. bibliog.

The longest-established of all Arab (and Muslim) immigrant communities in the United Kingdom are the settlers from both North and South Yemen, who, according to the author, are 'sharply contrasted in origin and social character from later Arab settlers'. The author looks at the history of Yemeni immigration, beginning with groups of sailors hired at Aden, who settled in ports like Cardiff, Liverpool, and South Shields from the 1880s onwards, and moving on after the war to migrants looking for work in the industrial cities of the North and Midlands of England (Birmingham, Sheffield, Rotherham and Manchester). In almost all cases, the Yemenis did not bring their families with them and intended to return to their home villages once they had made enough money, although changes in the British immigration laws in 1962 made travel to and from Yemen more difficult. The author concludes his study with an examination of Yemeni political movements and associations in Britain, and how the Yemeni community in the 1980s (perhaps about 12,000 strong) compares with other immigrant groups in Britain.

449 **Consequences of Hadrami migration to India: the Arab presence in Haydarabad.**
Omar Khalidi. *al-Darah/Addarah* (Riyadh), vol. 10, no. 3 (1984), p. 5-29.

The author follows the course of Ḥaḍramī immigration to the west coast of India from medieval times to the present. In the earlier period, immigration 'was more or less restricted to naval traders and peaceful *sufis* and holy men as preachers of Islam', but from the late 16th to the mid-19th century, Ḥaḍramī immigration was concentrated on soldiers who found employment in the armies of various Muslim and Maratha rulers of western, central and southern India. With the defeat of South Indian forces by the British in the third Anglo-Maratha war of 1817-18, many Ḥaḍramīs joined the armies of the Nizam of Hyderabad, where some became so wealthy that they were able to help launch both the Quʿayṭī and Kathīrī sultanates in Ḥaḍramawt in the mid-19th century. Most Ḥaḍramī migrants were young, unattached males who married local Hindu women (according to the author 'respectable Muslim families refused to marry their daughters to them') and they maintained a separate identity with their own form of law, nomenclature and occupations. Today, estimates of the descendants of the Ḥaḍramī migrants vary between 20,000 and 55,000, all of them congregated in a particular quarter of the southern Indian city of Hyderabad.

450 **The impact of Ḥaḍramī emigrants in the East Indies on Islamic modernism and social change in Ḥaḍramawt in the 20th century.**
Joseph Kostiner. In: *Islam in Asia.* Vol. 2: *Southeast and East Asia.* Edited by Raphael Israeli, Anthony H. Johns. Boulder, Colorado: Westview Press; Jerusalem: Magnes Press, 1984, p. 206-37.

The author surveys the reasons behind emigration from Ḥaḍramawt (endemic warfare; lack of opportunities for economic advancement) and looks at Ḥaḍramī social structures, before examining the impact of the Ḥaḍramī immigrants on East Indian society. He looks in particular at the conflict between the *Irshādīs*, who favoured a liberal interpretation of Islam and were influenced by modernist thinking, and those who wished to maintain the traditional right of the *Sayyids* (descendants of the Prophet) to mediate in disputes. This dispute in turn had a significant reaction on Ḥaḍramī society in the 1930s, as the *Sayyids* sought to bolster their position by cooperating with the British in establishing a general truce, while the *Irshādī* position, supporting Arab nationalist ideas, failed to make much of an impact in the Ḥaḍramawt. The author's conclusion is that '*Irshādī* influences were strong enough to affect the social situation. but it could not produce a new institutionalized consensus replacing the old religiously sanctioned social stratification'.

451 **The Arabs in Indonesia.**
Justus M. van der Kroef. *Middle East Journal,* vol. 7 (1953), p. 300-23.

An interesting look at the Ḥaḍramī Arabs of Indonesia from the local point of view, The author makes some reference to the social structure of Ḥaḍramawt, but is far more concerned to examine the social, political, economic and religious life of the Arab minority. The author sees the Arabs, who are looked up to by the majority of indigenous Indonesians for their 'superior' adherence to Islam as 'of all the minority groups now residing in Indonesia, the one best able to adjust itself to the changing realities of the country'. Moreover, he notes that since independence, the Ḥaḍramī minority had undergone 'a greater assimilation with the Indonesian population groups, more active participation in political life, the abandonment of distinct Hadhramite culture traits and a broadening of economic interests'.

452 **From Taʿizz to Tyneside: an Arab community in the North-East of England during the early twentieth century.**
Richard I. Lawless. Exeter, England: University of Exeter Press, 1995. 292p.

A serious work of local history basing itself on local and national archives and on the many reports found in the local newspaper. The author looks at the arrival of the Yemeni community, its social structure in South Shields, the competition for jobs and examines in detail three crises: the riots of 1930 caused by an attempt by the National Union of Seamen to discriminate against the Yemenis; mixed marriages and moral outrage; and slum clearance and the proposal to segregate the Arabs. The work concludes with an investigation of the religious and political associations active among the Yemenis of South Shields and elsewhere in England.

453 **After the eagles landed: the Yemenites of Israel.**
Herbert S. Lewis. Boulder, Colorado: Westview Press, 1989. 277p. bibliog.

A sociological analysis of the Yemenite community in a new town not far from Tel Aviv. The author looks at religious and social life, identity, values and attitudes, work and occupations, and how the Yemenis relate to their ancestral heritage. The author makes many telling points about ethnicity and contends that 'the Yemenites of Kiryat Eliahu, and of many other communities, seem to operate in terms of a distinctive cultural code, a set of ideas as to how a person is expected to behave', but this distinctive culture rarely comes alive in the book, as the author prefers to describe and analyse what he sees, rather than allowing the Yemenis to speak in their own terms.

454 **Migrations from the Ḥaḍramawt to East Africa and Indonesia, c. 1200 to 1900.**
B. G. Martin. *Research Bulletin, Centre of Arabic Documentation, University of Ibadan*, vol. 7 (1971), p. 1-21.

One of the few works to concentrate on Ḥaḍramī emigration to East Africa, this is a scholarly study based on Arabic, Swahili and archival European sources. The author shows how originally many Ḥaḍramīs moved to the Horn of Africa to participate in religious wars against the Christians of Ethiopia, and the sources constantly emphasize the Muslim character of these and later immigrants. Despite its title, this article deals mainly with immigration in the 16th and 17th centuries into Africa, and has relatively little to say on either Indonesia or modern times.

455 **Yemenite Jews: a photographic essay.**
Zion Mansour Ozeri. New York: Schocken Books, 1985. unpaged.

After a short introduction, in which the author describes his father's life in a village near Ṣanʿāʾ, and his own youth growing up in the new state of Israel, the photographic section of the book begins. This consists of seventy-two black-and-white studies of Yemeni Jews, old and young, male and female, in various towns and cities of Israel. The shots are well judged and show the contrasts and tensions of a community in a state of constant change.

456 **L'émigration yéménite.** (Yemeni emigration.)
Alain Rouaud. In: *L'Arabie du Sud: histoire et civilisation.* (South Arabia: history and civilization.) Vol. 2: *La société yéménite de l'Hégire aux idéologies modernes.* (Yemeni society from the rise of Islam to modern ideologies.) Paris: Maisonneuve et Larose, 1984, p. 227-50.

The only source which looks at overseas Yemeni communities as a whole. The information for each area is superficial, and the data on the United States, India and South-East Asia cannot compare with the sources quoted elsewhere in this chapter. The author does, however, supply hard-to-come-by information on Yemeni emigration to Ethiopia, Djibouti, Somalia, Madagascar, the Comoros Islands and Zanzibar, even if the figures are often tentative.

457 **Remarques sur quelques aspects de l'émigration hadrami en Insulinde.** (Remarks on some aspects of Hadrami emigration to the East Indies.)

Alain Rouaud. In: *Migrations, minorités et échanges en Océan Indien, XIXe-XXe siècle.* (Migrations, minorities and exchanges in the Indian Ocean, 19th-20th centuries.) Aix-en-Provence, France: Institut d'Histoire des Pays d'Outre-Mer, Université de Provence, 1978, p. 68-92.

A summary of the results of emigration from Ḥaḍramawt to the East Indies (including Singapore and Malaya), based almost exclusively on the magnum opus of van den Berg (see item no. 444). The author shows how the numbers of emigrants rose during the latter half of the 19th century (although there was a constant flow of returning emigrants to South Arabia), but he makes little attempt to analyse either the impact of the emigrants on Indonesian society or the nature of Arab immigrant society in South-East Asia.

458 **Changing health and changing culture: the Yemenite Jews in Israel.**

Michael A. Weingarten. Westport, Connecticut: Praeger, 1992. 187p. bibliog.

A first-rate socio-medical study of Yemeni Jews in Israel by a doctor whose practice lay in Rosh Haʿayin, home to around 13,000 Yemeni Jews. The author looks at family patterns, social problems such as alcoholism and smoking, psychiatric issues, 'plagues and pestilence', 'diseases of civilization', community health including child and maternal care and, perhaps most interestingly of all, how Yemenite Jews respond to illness and how their beliefs about health have changed. Where possible the author relates his discoveries to conditions prevailing in the Yemen his patients had left behind, and the result is a fascinating study of the physical effects of changing patterns of life-style.

Languages and Dialects

Arabic

459 **Die Dialekte der Gegend von Ṣaʿdah (Nord-Jemen.)**
(The dialects of the Ṣaʿdah region (North Yemen).)
Peter Behnstedt. Wiesbaden, Germany: Harrassowitz, 1987. 327p. maps. bibliog. (Semitica Viva, Band 1).

A detailed study of the dialects found around the northern Yemeni city of Ṣaʿdah, based on two visits to the region. Part one looks at the comparative phonology, morphology and vocabulary of around thirty locations in the province, while Parts two and three sketch the dialect spoken in al-Naḍīr in the Jabal Rāziḥ to the west of Ṣaʿdah, and dialect of al-Maṭṭah, a village to the north of the regional capital, inhabited by a branch of the Banū Munabbih. This is an important piece of fieldwork, and one can only regret that the author's third journey to the region to carry out more detailed studies was cut short.

460 **Die nordjemenitischen Dialekte.** (The North Yemeni dialects.)
Teil 1: **Atlas.** Teil 2: **Glossar, Alif-Dāl.** Teil 3: **Glossar, Dāl-Ġayn.**
Peter Behnstedt. Wiesbaden, Germany: Harrassowitz, 1985-96. 3 vols. (Jemen-Studien, Band 3).

The first volume consists of a linguistic atlas of the Yemeni Arabic spoken by men throughout the province of Ṣaʿdah in North Yemen. Different questions (168 in number) were asked ranging from the pronunciation of the *qāf* and how relative pronouns work, to the second person feminine singular of the verb, and the local words for frog, donkey and yesterday. The second and third volumes form a dictionary arranged alphabetically by root, which looks at all words found by the author in his fieldwork in North Yemen, with any occurrences noted by other scholars. A fourth volume should complete the work, which is complemented by the author's further researches into the linguistic material recorded by the 19th-century scholar Eduard Glaser, *Glossar der jemenitischen Dialektwörter in Eduard Glasers Tagebüchern*

(Dictionary of the Yemeni dialect words found in Eduard Glaser's diaries) (Vienna: Österreichische Akademie der Wissenschaften, 1993. 225p.).

461 **Note sull'arabo parlato al Baraddūn (Yemen del Nord).** (Notes on the Arabic spoken in al-Baraddūn in North Yemen.)
Lidia Bettini. In: *Studi Yemeniti* (Yemeni studies). Edited by Pelio Fronzaroli. Florence, Italy: Istituto de Linguistica e di Lingue Orientali, Università di Firenze, 1985, p. 117-59. (Quaderni di Semitistica, vol. 14).

Research based on fieldwork conducted between 1981 and 1984 in the village of al-Baraddūn, which is situated some way south of Ṣanʿāʾ in the South Central Highlands of North Yemen. The linguistic data were drawn from conversations with male informants of varying ages and cover many but not all aspects of the speech there. This paper gives considerable detail on the phonology of the dialect, and the pronominal and verbal forms used there, but has little to say on, for example, stress patterns or syntactical constructions.

462 **Jemenitisches Wörterbuch: arabisch–deutsch–englisch.** (Dictionary of Yemeni Arabic: Arabic–German–English.)
Jeffrey Deboo. Wiesbaden, Germany: Harrassowitz, 1989. 292p.

The introduction gives no indication of whether the author has conducted fieldwork in North Yemen and if so, where, or if this dictionary of North Yemeni Arabic is based on secondary sources. The author has arranged the text by Arabic lead word according to the order of the Latin alphabet. He tends to list only one variant of each Arabic word, although the atlas of Peter Behnstedt (see item no. 460) shows how many variations of pronunciation one can find, and he usually gives each Arabic word just one equivalent in German and English, as well as indicating where the term is most commonly used in Yemen. This is a useful preliminary study, although clearly much research remains to be done.

463 **Skizzen jemenitischer Dialekte.** (Sketches of Yemeni dialects.)
Werner Diem. Beirut; Wiesbaden, Germany: Franz Steiner, 1973. 166p. (Beiruter Texte und Studien, Band 13).

One of the first comprehensive studies on the Arabic dialects of North Yemen. The author proposes a preliminary classification into the dialects of the northern and southern plateaux, both of which are related to the dialects of Ṣanʿāʾ, the dialects of the coastal plain (the Tihāmah), and the dialects of the southern mountain range centered on Taʿizz and the related dialects of the Ḥujarīyah. The author at the time had no information on the dialects of the far north (since remedied by the work of Peter Behnstedt [see items 459, 460]), or of the northeast or the southeast, but this early study does show how complex the linguistic situation is in Yemen and provides valuable date for later dialectologists.

464 **Arabic Adeni reader.**
Habaka J. Feghali, edited by Alan S. Kaye. Wheaton, Maryland: Dunwoody Press, 1990. 265p.

A selection of forty-five texts in Adeni Arabic 'based on field tapes recorded by natives of Aden with different educational and social backgrounds'. Most of the narratives are on political and economic issues and fall, in their style and choice of vocabulary, between the stools of Modern Standard Arabic and full colloquial. The user will also not be helped by the comparative paucity of grammatical and syntactical notes.

465 **Arabic Adeni textbook.**
Habaka J. Feghali, edited by Alan S. Kaye. Wheaton, Maryland: Dunwoody Press, 1991. 233p.

More a series of dialogues with vocabulary than a textbook, this is designed to introduce the reader to 'culturally relevant and significant aspects of Adeni and Yemeni culture and civilization as a whole'. The book, however, makes little attempt to explain either the grammar or the syntax of Adeni Arabic and will be difficult for students to use on their own.

466 **Zur Phonologie und Phonetik des Ṣanʿānīschen.** (On the phonology and phonetics of Ṣanʿānī Arabic.)
Otto Jastrow. In: *Entwicklungsprozesse in der Arabischen Republik Jemen.* (Developmental processes in the Yemen Arab Republic.) Edited by Horst Kopp, Günther Schweizer. Wiesbaden, Germany: Reichert, 1984, p. 289-304. (Jemen-Studien, Band 1).

A brief investigation of certain phonetic peculiarities of Ṣanʿānī Arabic, including pausal glottalization, morphophonemic changes in verb endings and the voicing of dental stops in particular situations. The author also considers the question of whether Modern Standard Arabic has an influence on the pronunciation of Ṣanʿānī Arabic and finds that, in the main, dialectal phonology predominates.

467 **Dictionary of post-classical Yemeni Arabic.**
Moshe Piamenta. Leiden, The Netherlands: Brill, 1990-91. 2 vols.

A very substantial work, which began with the author's interest in the Arabic spoken and recorded by North Yemeni Jews, and eventually became transformed into a dictionary based on many forms of post-classical Yemeni Arabic, both Jewish and Muslim. The reliance on written texts and secondary works and the lack of fieldwork means that the dictionary does not show local variants in pronunciation and vocabulary in the way Peter Behnstedt's studies do (see items 459, 460), nor is any interest shown in the Arabic of Aden and the Ḥaḍramawt (R. B. Serjeant is quoted only once, and then for his work on Ṣanʿāʾ [item no. 59]), but this is, nonetheless, an important contribution to our understanding of the North Yemeni lexicon.

468 **Remarks on the spoken Arabic of Zabīd.**
Theodore Prochazka. *Zeitschrift für Arabische Linguistik,* vol. 17 (1987), p. 58-68.

A brief treatment of some of the aspects of Arabic spoken in Zabīd in the southern Tihāmah region of North Yemen. Aspects of the dialect described by the author are phonology, the verb system, negation, the personal and suffix pronouns, and adjectives, but the article itself is too short to be considered as anything more than a starting point for further study.

469 **Yemeni Arabic I–II.**
Hamdi A. Qafisheh. Tucson, Arizona: Department of Oriental Studies, University of Arizona, 1984. 2 vols. 690p.

A straightforward self-instructional guide to Ṣanʿānī Arabic, which is designed to teach the basics of the language through drills but apparently without the use of accompanying audio-tapes. The dialogues which form the forty drills cover a wide variety of subjects, but are basically rooted in the normal situations in which a visitor to the Yemen might find him or herself. The first volume was republished in 1990 in Beirut by Librairie du Liban.

470 **Yemeni Arabic reference grammar.**
Hamdi A. Qafisheh. Kensington, Maryland: Dunwoody Press, 1992. 308p.

A basic guide to Ṣanʿānī Arabic, this work is divided into sections on phonology (including sound changes and stress), morphology (verbs, nouns, noun-modifiers, pronouns and particles) and syntax (sentence types, clauses, phrase types, verbal phrases, concord and negation), followed by a selection of Arabic texts, with translation into English. The level of linguistic analysis is lower than in Janet C. E. Watson's grammar (see item no. 478), while the structure of the book and even the exact wording of the text is often an exact copy of the author's much earlier work, *A short reference grammar of Gulf Arabic* (Tucson, Arizona: University of Arizona Press, 1977. 274p.).

471 **L'arabo parlato a Ṣanʿāʾ: grammatica, testi, lessico.** (The Arabic spoken in Ṣanʿāʾ: grammar, texts, lexicon.)
Ettore Rossi. Rome: Istituto per l'Oriente, 1939. 250p.

Although the grammatical part of this work runs to only forty-six pages and is therefore highly concentrated, it has still not been entirely superseded. The same holds true for the collection of texts, which range from one-word greetings to entire description of weddings and popular songs and poetry, all presented in transcribed Ṣanʿānī Arabic with Italian translation. The dictionary section contains not only an Italian–Arabic lexicon, but also brief chapters explaining the most common terms used in various contexts, such as government, occupations, and food and drink.

472 **Les dialectes arabes de la Tihāma du Yémen: diversité et caractéristiques.** (The Arabic dialects of the Tihāmah in Yemen: variety and characteristics.)
Marie-Claude Siméone-Senelle, Martine Vanhove, Antoine Lonnet. In: *Actes des Premières Journées Internationales de Dialectologie Arabe de Paris.* (The Paris Proceedings of the first International Study Days of Arabic Dialectology.) Edited by Dominique Caubet, Martine Vanhove. Paris: Publications Langues 'O, 1994, p. 217-31.

Preliminary results from the Mission Française d'Enquête sur les Langues du Yémen (French Mission of Enquiry on the Languages of Yemen). The article looks at the comparative phonology, morphology (articles, pronouns, demonstratives, negation) and vocabulary in four villages lying on or near the Red Sea coast of North Yemen between Hodeida and Mocha. The authors' conclusion is that the region plays host to a huge variety of dialectal variety, even when studying comparatively limited geographical areas, and that the situation was probably even more complex in the past.

473 **Note sur le dialecte *qeltu* de Dhalaᶜ (Province de Lahej, Yémen).**
(Note on the *qeltu* dialect of Dhalaᶜ, in the Province of Laḥij, Yemen.)
Martine Vanhove. *Matériaux Arabes et Sudarabiques,* 1993, p. 175-99.

One of the rare studies of a dialect from South Yemen, this looks at the so-called *qeltu* dialect (characterized by its verbal morphology among other factors) of al-Ḍāliᶜ, capital of the former Sultanate of Laḥij, to the north of Aden. The author concentrates on verbal and pronominal forms, and draws parallels with some of the Northern Yemeni dialects described by Peter Behnstedt (see items 459, 460).

474 **Notes on the Arabic dialectal area of Yafiᶜ (Yemen.)**
Martine Vanhove. *Proceedings of the Seminar for Arabian Studies,* vol. 25 (1995), p. 141-52.

A preliminary study of another South Yemeni dialect (see the item above), this time spoken to the northeast of Aden. The author looks at wider issues than just the phonetics, morphology and vocabulary of the dialect, by considering whether it has been influenced by Himyarite (the presence of the verbal suffix k would indicate that this is probable) and how far her informants were conscious of the linguistic status of their dialect when speaking to her.

475 **Kaškaša with reference to modern Yemeni dialects.**
Janet C. E. Watson. *Zeitschrift für Arabische Linguistik,* vol. 24 (1992), p. 60-81.

An interesting article which bridges the gap between dialectology and Classical Arabic grammar. Using examples from her fieldwork in Yemen, the author investigates the phenomenon of *kashkashah* (which relates to the formation of particular pronominal suffixes) and how it was understood both by Classical Arab grammarians, and Western linguists.

476 **On the definition of dialect with reference to Yemeni dialects of Arabic.**
Janet C. E. Watson. In: *Arabic sociolingustics: issues and perspectives.* Edited by Yasir Suleiman. Richmond, Surrey: Curzon Press, 1994, p. 237-50.

The author examines what constitutes a dialect, both theoretically by looking at the Western literature on the subject, and concretely by drawing on her knowledge of Yemeni Arabic and 'the importance of native speakers' perception of dialects'. Her conclusion is that a dialect exists 'as a psychological reality in the minds of its speakers and in the minds of speakers of other dialects in relation to other dialects'.

477 **Ṣbahṭū!: a course in Ṣanʿānī Arabic.**
Janet C. E. Watson. Wiesbaden, Germany: Harrassowitz, 1996. 324p. (Semitica Viva: series didactica, vol. 3).

The most accurate and reliable guide available for anyone wishing to learn the Arabic of Ṣanʿāʾ. Not perhaps as user-friendly as it might be (there are no accompanying tapes, and the descriptive text is occasionally a little stiff), but this is an authoritative, comprehensive and detailed work.

478 **A syntax of Ṣanʿānī Arabic.**
Janet C. E. Watson. Wiesbaden, Germany: Harrassowitz, 1993, 454p. bibliog.

By far the most important recent work on the Arabic spoken in the Yemeni capital, this impressive study contains full discussions of all aspects of syntax. It is particularly suited to linguistic specialists, who will welcome its technical vocabulary and the enormous number of examples illustrating every possible form of syntactical usage.

Ancient South Arabian languages

479 **Glossaire des inscriptions de l'Arabie du Sud.** (Glossary of South Arabian inscriptions.)
Alessandra Avanzini. Florence, Italy: Istituto di Linguistica e di Lingue Orientali, Università di Firenze, 1977-80. 2 vols. (Quaderni di Semitistica, vol. 3).

A valuable if incomplete dictionary of the words found in South Arabian inscriptions recorded and published between 1950 and 1973. The first volume individualizes all the inscriptions bibliographically, but without giving the text, while the second volume comprises a partial glossary of the words found in these inscriptions. The dictionary section is organized according to the Semitic alphabet in transcription, and consists of words beginning with the letters *alif, ʿayn, bā, dāl, dhā, ḍāḍ, fā, gā, ghayn* and *ḥā;* within each entry all the occurrences of the word are noted, with the translation given by the scholar who had recorded the inscription in the first place. There is no indication of whether the author intends to complete her glossary for the remaining nineteen letters of the alphabet.

480 **Sabaic dictionary (English–French–Arabic) = Dictionnaire sabéen (anglais–français–arabe) = al-Muʿjam al-sabāʾī (bi-al-inglīzīyah wa-al-faransīyah wa-al-ʿarabīyah.)**
A. F. L. Beeston, M. A. Ghul, W. W. Müller, Jacques Ryckmans. Louvain, Belgium: Peeters; Beirut: Librairie du Liban, 1982. 173p.

A dictionary of words occurring in published South Arabian inscriptions, arranged according to the order of the Semitic alphabet (in transcription). While the reference to the source is always noted, the compilers have chosen to offer their own equivalent of the South Arabian word in English, French and Arabic, rather than just quote the translation given by the recorder of the inscription as Avanzini does (see above).

481 **Sabaic grammar.**
A. F. L. Beeston. Manchester, England: Journal of Semitic Studies, University of Manchester, 1984. 76p. bibliog. (Journal of Semitic Studies Monograph, no. 6).

A continuation of the author's earlier work on the subject, *A descriptive grammar of Epigraphic South Arabian* (London: Luzac, 1962. 80p.), this work covers clearly and concisely all the grammatical features of the most important of the ancient South Arabian languages (phonology; verbs; nouns; adjectives; numerals; and pronouns) as well as dealing with the basic syntax. A short appendix deals with the three non-Sabaic languages of what the author terms the 'Sayhadic group', namely Minaic, Qatabanic and Hadramitic.

482 **Dictionary of Old South Arabic: Sabaean dialect.**
Joan Copeland Biella. Chico, California: Scholars Press, 1982. 561p. bibliog. (Harvard Semitic Studies, no. 25).

Building on the work on Avanzini (q.v.) and others, the author has compiled a dictionary of Epigraphic Sabaean, based on all the many inscriptions available to her. The dictionary is arranged alphabetically by root, according to the order of the Hebrew alphabet, with additions. Under each root, the author cites the bibliographical details of the published inscription in which the root occurs, gives a translation in English, suggests cognates or equivalents in other Semitic languages, and quotes the translation of the relevant part of the inscription, based on that of the person who published the inscription in the first place. This is an important and useful reference work.

483 **An index and concordance of pre-Islamic Arabian names and inscriptions.**
G. Lankester Harding. Toronto, Canada: University of Toronto Press, 1971. 943p. bibliog.

An impressive work of reference, this study attempts to list all words and names found in published South Arabian inscriptions. It is arranged by root according to the order of the Arabic alphabet, gives the Arabic cognate and English equivalent of most words (but not all, many are designated 'root unknown'), and lists the number of occurrences of the root in the seven Epigraphic South Arabian languages. A final section offers a concordance of inscriptions by language for Lihyanite, Safaitic, Thamudic and South Arabian.

484 **Altsüdarabische Grammatik.** (Grammar of Old South Arabian.)
Maria Höfner. Leipzig, Germany: Harrassowitz, 1943. (Porta Linguarum Orientalium, Band 24).

Despite its age, this is still a useful reference grammar. It covers the script, phonology, pronouns and verbs, nouns, numerals, adjectives and particles of the Old South Arabian languages, before moving on to a brief discussion of syntactic questions. The work was reprinted in Osnabrück, Germany, by Zeller in 1976.

485 **The migration of the script and the formation of the state in South Arabia.**

Ernst Axel Knauf. *Proceedings of the Seminar for Arabian Studies*, vol. 19 (1989), p. 79-91.

The author studies the link between the introduction of the South Arabian script into the country in the 8th century BC and the relationship the South Arabian kingdoms developed with the ancient world economy systems. He sees the alphabet as 'the survivor of a Proto-Canaanite alphabet which had died out in Palestine around 1200 BC', and explains the four-century gap in its use in South Arabia, as a result of the gradual transformation of Yemen into an urban culture with trading links to other states. Only then, he argues, would the Himyarites and others have needed to write and to leave monuments to posterity.

486 **Ancient Yemen: some general trends of evolution of the Sabaic language and Sabaean culture.**

Andrej Vitalyevich Korotayev. Oxford, England: Oxford University Press on behalf of the University of Manchester, 1995. 130p. bibliog. (Journal of Semitic Studies Supplement, vol. 5).

A collection of four separate studies; the first is a quantitative analysis of the titles of persons found in Sabaean inscriptions; the second looks at the supposition of 'the probable transformation of the names of certain ancient administrative posts into the names of some Middle Sabaean clan groups'; while the third is a quantitative analysis of Sabaic possessive pronominal suffixes. The fourth and final chapter moves away from language and investigates some factors in the decline of the early Sabaean state and the political characteristics of its successors.

487 **Die Konstruktion mit /fa-/ im Altsüdarabischen: syntaktische und epigraphische Untersuchungen.** (Constructions with /fa-/ in Old South Arabian: syntactic and epigraphic investigations.)

Norbert Nebes. Wiesbaden, Germany: Harrassowitz, 1995. 302p. bibliog. (Veröffentlichung der Orientalischen Kommission, Band 40).

An extremely detailed analysis of the particle *fa* and its usage in the ancient South Arabian languages. In contradistinction to North (Classical) Arabic, where *fa* and *wa* are used to join coordinate clauses, */fa-/* in Old South Arabian plays a much more complex role, which the author describes in great detail, with many examples drawn from the epigraphic literature.

488 **Lexicon of inscriptional Qatabanian.**

Stephen D. Ricks. Rome: Pontificio Istituto Biblico, 1989. 241p. (Studia Pohl, vol. 14).

The first major lexicon devoted to an Ancient South Arabian language, other than Sabaean, this work is patterned on the dictionaries of Alessandra Avanzini, Joan Copeland Biella and A. F. L. Beeston (see items 479, 480, 482). Arranged by root according to the order of the Hebrew alphabet (with additions), this work quotes every inscription which includes the root and offers a single word translation, and usually an example (in English translation) of the use of the word/root in context.

489 **Inventaire des inscriptions sudarabiques = Inventario delle iscrizioni sudarabiche.** (Inventory of South Arabian inscriptions.) Vol. 1: **Inabba', Haram, al-Kāfir, Kamna et al-Ḥarāshif.** Compiled by Christian Robin. Vol. 2: **Shaqab al-Manassa.** Compiled by Gherardo Gnoli. Vol. 4: **As-Sawda.** Compiled by Alessandra Avanzini. Paris: Académie des Inscriptions et Belles-Lettres; Rome: IsMEO (Istituto Italiano per il Medio e Estremo Oriente), 1992-95. 4 vols.

Three volumes have so far been published in this ongoing joint epigraphic venture between French and Italian institutions (vol. 1 in two parts in French, and vols 2 and 4 in Italian). The purpose of the series is to publish the epigraphic South Arabian text, the transcription, the translation and commentary of all the inscriptions from a particular site. Many of them are published for the first time as a result of the French and Italian Archaeological Missions to Yemen, and more volumes are in preparation.

490 **Ṣayhadica: recherches sur les inscriptions de l'Arabie préislamique offertes par ses collègues au professeur A. F. L. Beeston.** (Ṣayhadica: researches on the inscriptions of pre-Islamic Arabia offered to Professor A. F. L. Beeston by his colleagues.) Edited by Christian Robin, Muḥammad Bāfaqīh. Paris: Geuthner, 1987. 180p.

Twelve papers in English, French, German, Italian and Arabic dealing with South Arabian inscriptions in their widest sense. Three papers tackle specifically linguistic issues: Alessandra Avanzini looks (in English) at 'construction inscriptions', bringing the concept of 'the linguistic event' developed by ethnolinguists to bear on epigraphy; Norbert Nebes examines (in German) the construction of sentences in Sabaean when subject or object are dependent on an infinitive; while A. G. Lundin makes some additions (in English) to the Sabaic dictionary of A. F. L. Beeston and others (see item no. 480).

491 **Die Personennamen in den altsabäischen Inschriften: ein Beitrag zur altsüdarabischen Namengebung.** (Personal names in Ancient Sabaean inscriptions: a contribution to Old South Arabian nomenclature.) Salem Ahmad Tairan. Hildesheim, Germany: Olms, 1992. 265p. bibliog. (Texte und Studien zur Orientalistik, Band 8).

An index, arranged in the order of the Arabic alphabet, of all the personal names found in published Sabaean inscriptions. For each root, the author gives the epigraphic reference where the name is found, the geographical location where the inscription was recorded, and a thorough comparative analysis of the name-elements with appropriate translations into German.

Modern South Arabian languages

492 **Studien zur Laut- und Formenlehre der Mehri-Sprache in Südarabien.** (Studies in the phonology and morphology of the Mehri language in South Arabia.)
Maximilian Bittner. Vienna: Hölder, 1909-15. 7 vols. (Sitzungsberichte, Kaiserliche Akademie der Wissenschaften, Philosophisch-Historische Klasse, vols 162/5, 172/5, 174/4, 176/1, 178/2-3).

Although now somewhat antiquated, these still represent important contributions to our knowledge of the most widespread of the modern South Arabian languages. The author also published on Soqotri, *Vorstudien zur Grammatik and zum Wörterbuch der Soqotri-Sprache* (Preliminary studies of the grammar and vocabulary of the Soqotri language) (Vienna: Hölder, 1913-22. 3 vols) and, unreliably, on the related Sheri or Jibbāli language of neighbouring Dhofar, *Studien zur Šhauri-Sprache in den Bergen von Dofar am Persischen Meerbusen* (Studies in the Shkhauri language of Dhofar on the Persian Gulf) (Vienna: Hölder, 1915-17. 4 vols).

493 **Mehri lexicon and English–Mehri word-list.**
T. M. Johnstone. London: School of Oriental and African Studies, 1987. 676p.

A posthumous publication based on the typescript delivered by the author to the publishers in 1983, this is the last of Johnstone's great lexicographical contributions to the modern South Arabian languages (the others: *Ḥarsūsi lexicon and English–Ḥarsūsi word-list* (London: Oxford University Press, 1977. 181p.) and *Jibbāli lexicon* (London: Oxford University Press, 1981. 328p.) deal with languages no longer spoken in the Republic of Yemen). The work is based on extensive fieldwork and careful cross-checking with native informants, and given the decline in Mehri speakers both the Eastern part of South Yemen and in Dhofar, is likely to remain forever the standard work in its field.

494 **The modern South Arabian languages.**
T. M. Johnstone. *Afroasiatic Linguistics,* vol. 1, no. 5 (1975), p. 93-121.

A very useful comparative and descriptive survey of Mehri, Harsusi, Sheri (Jibbāli) and Socotri. The author looks at the consonantal system, analyses the morphology of the verb (tenses, conjugation), and of the noun, followed by a study of adjectives, numerals, demonstratives and pronouns. The article concludes with a description of case-markers and a short note on syntax.

495 **Südarabische Expedition.** (South Arabian expedition.)
Kaiserliche Akademie der Wissenschaften. Vienna: Hölder, 1900-11. 10 vols.

An immensely important collection of South Arabian and other texts given in transcription and German translation, which have often been used as the basis for later grammars and dictionaries. The relevant volumes are no. 3: *Die Mehri-Sprache in Südarabien: Texte und Wörterbuch* (The Mehri language in South Arabia: texts and dictionary), by Alfred Jahn (1902); nos. 4, 6 and 7: *Die Mehri und Soqotri Sprache: Texte, Soqotri-Texte, Shauri-Texte* (The Mehri and Socotri language: texts, Soqotri texts, Shkhauri (Jibbāli) texts), by David Heinrich Müller (1902, 1905, 1907); and no. 9: *Mehri- und Hadrami-texte gesammelt im Jahre 1902 in Gischin von Dr. Wilhelm Hein* (Mehri and Ḥaḍramī texts collected in 1902 in Gishin by Dr. Wilhelm Hein), edited by David Heinrich Müller (1909). The other volumes in the set deal with Somali (nos. 1, 2 and 5) and the Arabic dialect of Dhofar (nos. 8 and 10).

496 **Lexique soqotri (subarabique moderne) avec comparaisons et explications étymologiques.** (Socotri lexicon (Modern South Arabian) with etymological comparisons and explanations.)
Wolf Leslau. Paris: Klincksieck, 1938. 501p. (Collection Linguistique publiée par la Société de Linguistique de Paris, vol. 41).

Although based on the texts collected by David Heinrich Müller (q.v.) and Maximilian Bittner (q.v.), rather than personal fieldwork, this still remains the most important single work in the field of Socotri lexicography.

497 **The parts of the body in the modern South Arabic languages.**
Wolf Leslau. *Language,* vol. 21 (1945), p. 230-49.

A word-list of the parts of the body in Mehri, Sheri (Jibbāli) and Soqotri, arranged in various sections according to the order of the Semitic alphabet. The first section contains words common to all Semitic languages, the last contains words found only in the modern South Arabian languages, while in between are sections with various combinations of languages, such as one of words common to South Arabian and Ethiopic. The article concludes with an alphabetical list of the parts of the body in English with their various South Arabian equivalents.

498 **The modern South Arabian languages in the P. D. R. of Yemen.**
Antoine Lonnet. *Proceedings of the Seminar for Arabian Studies,* vol. 15 (1985), p. 49-55.

The author describes the present-day geographical distribution of the speakers of Mehri, how widely and in what circumstances it is spoken, and the estimated number of speakers within the borders of South Yemen (about 60,000). The author is, however, concerned about the low status of Mehri in the eyes of Arabic speakers and the Mahrī themselves. He concludes his article with the briefest of descriptions of Hobyot, a South Arabian language spoken on the borders of South Yemen and Oman, which he considers 'cannot be considered a mere dialect of either Mehri or Jibbali'.

499 **Matériaux arabes et sudarabiques.** (Arabic and South Arabian materials.)
Paris: Association GELLAS, Université Paris III, 1983- . annual.

The only periodical which has a regular section devoted to work on the modern South Arabian Languages, this has many contributions by Marie-Claude Siméone-Senelle and Antoine Lonnet, such as their continuation of Wolf Leslau's study of parts of the body (see item no. 497), 'Lexique des noms des parties du corps dans les langues sudarabiques modernes' (Lexicon of the names of the parts of the body in the modern South Arabian languages), published in the volumes for 1985-86 (p. 259-304) and 1988-89 (p. 191-253).

500 **Comparative vocabulary of Southern Arabic: Mehri, Gibbali and Soqotri.**
Aki'o Nakano. Tokyo: Institute for the Study of Languages and Cultures of Asia and Africa, 1986. 182p. (Studia Culturae Islamicae, no. 29).

The author collected linguistic data from various native informants, mostly based in Aden, but does not seem to have ventured far into the territories actually occupied by the speakers of the languages under investigation. The 1,156 entries for individual words are arranged under twenty-eight subject headings, but the divergence from the terms found by T. M. Johnstone (q.v.) and Wolf Leslau (q.v.) is considerable. The author has not incorporated the recent European scholarship exemplified by the articles in *Matériaux arabes et sudarabiques* (see above) into his dictionary, and these omissions, together with an inadequate level of English, make this a work to be used with caution.

501 **Four strange tongues from South Arabia: the Hadara group.**
Bertram Thomas. London: Humphrey Milford, 1937. 105p.

Originally published in the *Proceedings of the British Academy,* vol. 23 (1937), this is a comparative study of the four living South Arabian tongues spoken on the mainland of the Arabian Peninsula, principally in Dhofar and Eastern South Arabia: Shahari (Jibbāli), Mehri, Harsusi and Botahari. The author looks at the grammar, vocabulary and personal name-giving for all four languages, and, despite the lack of modern scholarly apparatus, the fact that the author collected the data himself, makes this still a work of considerable importance.

Southern Arabia.
See item no. 120.

An archaeological journey to Yemen, March–May 1947.
See item no. 231.

Sabaean inscriptions from Maḥram Bilqîs (Mârib).
See item no. 235.

Corpus des inscriptions et antiquités sud-arabes. (Corpus of South Arabian inscriptions and antiquities.)
See item no. 246.

Etudes sud-arabes: recueil offert à Jacques Ryckmans. (South Arabian studies: collection offered to Jacques Ryckmans.)
See item no. 288.

L'Arabie antique de Karib'îl à Mahomet. (Ancient Arabia from Karib'il to Muḥammad.)
See item no. 303.

Salām tahiyah: greetings from the highlands of Yemen.
See item no. 531.

L'habitat traditionnel à Ṣanʿāʾ: sémantique de la maison. (Traditional housing in Ṣanʿāʾ: the semantics of the house.)
See item no. 842.

Religion

502 **From Bustān al-ʿuqūl to Qiṣat al-batūl: some aspects of Jewish–Muslim religious polemic in Yemen.**
Reuben Ahroni. *Hebrew Union College Annual,* vol. 52 (1981), p. 311-60.

This is a serious and scholarly article of great interest, in which the author examines two polemical works written in Arabic to defend Judaism against Muslim attacks. The first part of the article looks at the sixth chapter of the 12th-century author Nathan'el Ibn Fayyūmī's *Bustān al-ʿuqūl,* which goes further than most medieval Jewish works in acknowledging that Muḥammad was indeed a prophet and messenger of God, but considers that his mission was confined to the Arabs. This form of reasoning was an ingenious device, allowing the Jews of Yemen to retain their own faith, while at the same time, not denying Muḥammad's prophethood, and thereby risking the death penalty. The second work studied (published for the first time in the article) is a poem in Judaeo-Arabic by an unknown author of unknown date. It discusses the day-to-day manifestations of Jewish social and religious life and 'brings into sharp focus the contrasting mentalities of Jew and Muslim'.

503 **Judaism and Christianity in pre-Islamic Yemen.**
A. F. L. Beeston. In: *L'Arabie du Sud: histoire et civilisation.* (South Arabia: history and civilization.) Vol. 1: *Le peuple yéménite et ses racines.* (The people of Yemen and their roots.) Paris: Maisonneuve et Larose, 1984, p. 271-78.

The author look at the epigraphic and literary evidence for the manifestations of Christianity and, to a lesser extent, Judaism, between the 4th and 6th centuries AD. He looks at not only the history of the communities and their relationship with other groups in South Arabia, but also at their religious convictions and rituals, in so far as these can be determined.

504 **The religions of pre-Islamic Yemen.**
A. F. L. Beeston. In: *L'Arabie du Sud: histoire et civilisation.* (South Arabia: history and civilization.) Vol. 1: *Le peuple yéménite et ses racines.* (The people of Yemen and their roots.) Paris: Maisonneuve et Larose, 1984, p. 259-69.

The author shows how until the 4th century AD the inscriptions are uniformly polytheistic, invocations being 'addressed to a large number of named deities and more generally to "all gods and goddesses"'. Within the South Arabian pantheon, however, some names stand out more prominently than others, in particular the male deity ʿAthtar and the gods who were patrons of one or other of the great tribal confederations. At another level, there were tutelary deities of the village or clan and of the family, and familial gods, characterized by the term 'sun'. The author rejects as 'much too simplistic' the theory that all the major figures in the South Arabian pantheon were celestial bodies, and that ʿAthtar was the Venus-star and the federal deities moon gods, but does not deny some association with heavenly bodies. None of the gods seems to have had particular attributes beyond the bestowal of blessings, in particular the provision of rain, and there is little evidence of a priestly caste, although ritual hunts and pilgrimages were common. In the 4th and 5th centuries the pantheon disappears, to be replaced by a unique God called 'the Merciful', which the author feels was not derived from either Christianity or Judaism, but rather 'the faith of the *ḥunafā*'', or proto-monotheists.

505 **A pre-Islamic rite in South Arabia.**
Werner Daum. *Journal of the Royal Asiatic Society* (1987), p. 5-14.

The author describes an unusual ritual connected with a particular saint, al-Shamsī, whose tomb in found near Bājil in the Tihāmah in North Yemen. He shows that the cult has numerous pre-Islamic features, including the use of a solar calendar and a matrilocal marriage system.

506 **Ursemitische Religion.** (Ancient Semitic religion.)
Werner Daum. Stuttgart, Germany: Kohlhammer, 1985. 223p.

The whole of the first part of this scholarly work (p. 14-107) deals with the religion of South Arabia. The author describes the ancient South Arabian pantheon and then looks at the links between modern South Arabian folktales and pre-Islamic myths, in particular tales of female sacrifice, of Afrit and Jarjuf, and of the young hero. Further chapters deal with the ritual hunt and pilgrimages to saints' tombs, the work concluding with a survey of ancient marriage customs.

507 **Die Ausbreitung der šāfiʿitischen Rechtsschule von den Anfängen bis zum 8./14. Jahrhundert.** (The spread of the Shāfiʿī school of law from its beginnings to the 8th/14th century.)
Heinz Halm. Wiesbaden, Germany: Reichert, 1974. 340p. bibliog. (Beihefte zum Tübinger Atlas des Vorderen Orients, Reihe B, no. 4).

A historical and geographical analysis of the spread of the Shāfiʿī school of law, which today predominates in South Yemen and is significant in large portions of North Yemen. Basing himself mainly on the biographical dictionary of ʿUmar ibn ʿAlī al-Jaʿdī (d. 1190) and the historical works of Ibn al-Mujāwir (d. 1291) and ʿAlī ibn al-Ḥasan al-Khazrajī (d. 1410), the author traces the establishment of judgeships and *madrasahs* (Islamic colleges) in both North Yemen and Aden and the relationship of the legal scholars to the political authorities. This is useful as a historical overview, but it has little to say on the social impact of Shāfiʿism or its particular legal doctrines.

508 **Evolution of the organizational structure of the Fāṭimī daʿwah: the Yemeni and Persian contribution.**

ʿAbbas Hamdani. *Arabian Studies,* vol. 3 (1976), p. 85-114.

A scholarly examination, based on the Arabic texts, of how the Fāṭimid (or Ismāʿīlī) sect organized its propaganda and missionary activities in Yemen and Iran between the 9th and 11th centuries. The *daʿwah,* or missionary movement, was not interested in mass conversions, but 'aimed at creating a class of the élite', and functioned as a closed fraternity with a system of initiation and its own internal secrecy and discipline. The author also discusses the metaphysical evolution of Fāṭimi doctrine, in particular the hierarchy of the cosmos, and how this was mirrored by the way in which the Fāṭimis structured their *daʿwah.*

509 **The Ṭayyibī-Fāṭimid community of the Yaman at the time of the Ayyubid conquest of Southern Arabia.**

ʿAbbas Hamdani. *Arabian Studies,* vol. 7 (1985), p. 151-8.

A brief study of the organization, history and personnel of one of the last independent Fāṭimi (or Ismāʿīlī) communities in the Yemen, the Ṭayyibī *daʿwah* (missionary movement) based around Ḥarāz in the latter half of the 12th century. Based on a contemporary Fāṭimi document, the author is able to establish all the names of the officers of the *daʿwah* and their order of precedence, their organizational structure, and their method of political accommodation with the Sunnī Ayyūbids and the Shīʿī Zaydīs.

510 **The cult of saints in Ḥaḍramawt: an overview.**

Alexander Knysh. *New Arabian Studies,* vol. 1 (1993), p. 137-52.

The author was a member of the Soviet–Yemeni Historical and Archaeological Mission between 1986 and 1989, and was able to conduct extensive fieldwork on saints and their shrines in Ḥaḍramawt. The author describes how one becomes a saint, the physical location and appearance of their tombs, the nature of and reasons for pilgrimages to the tombs, the development of *ṣūfī* (mystical) ceremonies called *haḍārāt* associated with the tombs, and the opposition to the veneration of holy men both from the orthodox *fuqahā'* (or legal scholars) and from Marxist ideologues from the Yemeni Socialist Party of the People's Democratic Republic.

511 **Takfīr und Ǧihād bei den Zaiditen des Jemen.**

(Takfīr and *jihād* among the Zaydīs of Yemen.)

Hans Kruse. *Die Welt des Islams,* new series, vols 23-24 (1984), p. 424-57.

After a general survey of the principles of *takfīr* (accusation of unbelief) and *jihād* (holy war), the author looks at how the Zaydīs used these concepts in their dealings with other branches of Islam. Using the works of Muḥammad ibn ʿAlī al-Shawkānī (d. 1834) and Muḥammad ibn Muḥammad Zabārah, the author shows how the Shāfiʿī population of North Yemen was never treated by the Zaydī imams as infidel, which was an accusation limited firstly in the 12th century to 'sinners' (probably the remnants of the Qarmaṭī community), secondly to the Ismāʿīlīs, and thirdly to the Ottomans. The latter part of this important work examines the Zaydīs' official attitude to the second Ottoman occupation (1849-1919), and how the Zaydīs sought to enlist the support of the tribes against the Turks through the declaration of holy war against the Ottomans in 1890-91.

512 **al-Hādī ilā 'l-Ḥaḳḳ.**
Wilferd Madelung. *The Encyclopaedia of Islam,* new edition. Leiden, The Netherlands: Brill, 1982, fascicules 5-6 of the Supplement, p. 334-5.

A brief account of the founder of the Zaydī Imamate in Yemen, al-Hādī ilā al-Ḥaqq (d. 911), which concentrates on his life, rather than on his doctrines.

513 **Imām al-Qāsim ibn Ibrāhīm and Muʿtazilism.**
Wilferd Madelung. In: *On both sides of al-Mandab: Ethiopian, South-Arabic and Islamic studies presented to Oscar Löfgren on his ninetieth birthday, 13 May 1988, by colleagues and friends.* Edited by Ulla Ehrensvärd, Christopher Toll. Istanbul, Turkey: Swedish Research Institute in Istanbul, 1989, p. 39-48.

A study of the theological views of al-Qāsim ibn Ibrāhīm al-Rassī (d. 860), the grandfather of the founder of the Zaydī state, al-Hādī ilā al-Ḥaqq (d. 911). The author is of the opinion that al-Qāsim 'saw himself, and acted, primarily as a religious leader, not as a systematic theologian', and that he was not essentially influenced by the Muʿtazilī school of rationalist thinking, a view that the author had developed at greater length in his *Der Imām al-Qāsim ibn Ibrāhīm und die Glaubenslehre der Zaiditen* (The Imām al-Qāsim ibn Ibrāhīm and the theology of the Zaydīs) (Berlin: De Gruyter, 1965. 271p. bibliog.), which studied not only the thinking of al-Qāsim himself, but also his influence on later Zaydī theology (up to the 12th century). The view of al-Qāsim as anti-Muʿtazilī has recently been challenged by Binyamin Abrahamov (q.v. under al-Rassī, items 515, 518).

514 **Islam in Yemen.**
Wilferd Madelung. In: *Yemen: 3000 years of art and civilisation.* Edited by Werner Daum. Innsbruck, Austria: Pinguin-Verlag; Frankfurt am Main, Germany: Umschau-Verlag, 1988, p. 174-7.

Although brief, this is one of the few works to tackle all forms of Islam prevalent in North Yemen from the early school of Islamic scholarship in 8th-century Ṣanʿāʾ, through the spread of orthodox (Sunnī) Islam of the Shāfiʿī and Ḥanafī schools, and the challenge mounted by the Shīʿī sects of Zaydism and Ismāʿīlism, to the relevance of the *madrasah* (Islamic college) and *ṣūfī* orders in Yemen. A tantalising glimpse of a general religious history of Yemen which is still sorely needed.

515 **al-Rassī, al-Ḳāsim ibn Ibrāhīm.**
Wilferd Madelung. In: *The Encyclopaedia of Islam,* new edition. Leiden, The Netherlands: Brill, 1993, vol. 8, p. 453-4.

A biography of al-Qāsim ibn Ibrāhīm al-Rassī (d. 860), 'Zaydī *imām* and founder of the legal and theological school later prevalent among the Zaydīs in the Yemen'. The author sums up al-Qāsim's religious teaching as being in partial agreement with the Muʿtazilah, since al-Qāsim stressed the overriding authority of the Qur'ān, and 'disassociated God from evil acts and affirmed human free will'. The author has written several more biographical articles of prominent Yemeni imams in *The Encyclopaedia of Islam*, new edition, notably 'al-Manṣūr Billāh', a Zaydī imam who died in 1003 (vol. 6, p. 435-6), and 'Manṣūr al-Yaman', also known as Ibn Ḥawshab, the founder of the Ismāʿīlī *daʿwah* in Yemen (vol. 6, p. 438-9).

516 **Le daʿwa fatimide au Yémen.** (The Fatimid *daʿwah* in Yemen.)
Jean Moncelon. *Chroniques Yéménites,* vol. 3 (1995), p. 26-37.

The author describes the rise of Ismāʿīlism in Yemen, from its beginnings in the 9th century, through its 'golden age' under the Ṣulayḥids (1037-1138), the Ṭayyibī *daʿwah* of the 12th century, and the gradual decline in the medieval period, particularly after the Zaydī persecutions of the 16th century. The author appends a useful list of fifty-nine Ismāʿīlī *dāʿīs* (or leaders of the community) and a brief glossary of technical terms.

517 **Zur religiösen und sozialen Gliederung der Bevölkerung in der Arabischen Republik Jemen (Nordjemen).** (On the religious and social structure of the population in the Yemen Arab Republic (North Yemen).)
Ulrich Pietrusky. *Mitteilungen der Geographischen Gesellschaft in München,* vol. 67 (1982), p. 125-54.

One of the few attempts at a general sociological analysis of all religious groups in North Yemen, this article begins with a survey of the position of the Zaydīs, the Shāfiʿīs, the Ismāʿīlīs and the Jews in 19th- and 20th-century Yemen, and continues with a description of the tribes and the hierarchy of social groups in the contemporary state. This article is more useful for its numerical information, its charts and its survey of the existing literature, than for any new insights it brings, since the author has done no fieldwork and offers few, if any, opinions of his own.

518 **Al-Ḳāsim ibn Ibrāhīm on the proof of God's existence: Kitāb al-Dalīl al-Kabīr.**
al-Qāsim ibn Ibrāhīm al-Rassī (d. 860), edited and translated by Binyamin Abrahamov. Leiden, The Netherlands: Brill, 1990. 200p. bibliog. (Islamic Philosophy and Theology: Texts and Studies, vol. 5).

Important, not only for the edition and translation of one al-Qāsim's fundamental texts, but for its lengthy discussion of al-Qāsim's theology in the introduction (p. 1-60). In this section of the book, the editor looks at how influenced al-Qāsim was by the Muʿtazilī school of rationalist thinking, and takes issue with Wilferd Madelung (q.v.) on a number of theological questions, but does not attempt to estimate al-Qāsim's influence on later Zaydī thinking. Abrahamov has also edited and translated another Arabic theological text by al-Qāsim in the same series, *Anthropomorphism and interpretation of the Qur'an in the theology of al-Qāsim ibn Ibrāhīm: Kitab al-Mustarshid* (al-Qāsim ibn Ibrāhīm al-Rassī [d. 860]. Edited and translated by Binyamin Abrahamov. Leiden, The Netherlands, Brill, 1996. 152p. bibliog. [Islamic Philosophy, Theology and Science: Texts and Studies, vol. 26]).

519 **Éléments de bibliographie sur le zaydisme.** (Bibliographical references on Zaydism.)
Étienne Renaud. *IBLA,* no. 146 (1980), p. 309-21.

A bibliographical survey of edited and published texts in Arabic by Zaydī authors plus a short list of Western-language books and articles about Zaydism. The author divides his survey into biographical sources, legal works, and other categories and admits that this bibliography is still seriously incomplete, particularly considering the mass of still unpublished works.

520 **Histoire de la pensée religieuse au Yémen.** (The history of religious thought in Yemen.)
Etienne Renaud. In: *L'Arabie du Sud: histoire et civilisation.* (South Arabia: history and civilization.) Vol. 2: *La société yéménite de l'Hégire aux idéologies modernes.* (Yemeni society from the rise of Islam up to modern ideologies.) Paris: Maisonneuve et Larose, 1984, p. 57-68.

A brief overview of the development of Zaydī theology (which the author sees as heavily influenced by Muʿtazilism), of the spread of the Ḥanafī and Shāfiʿī law schools in North Yemen, and of the impact of the Ismāʿīlīs during the medieval period. The author makes some interesting remarks about the sociology of Yemeni religion, but does not really develop these, and he also does not carry the story forward beyond the 15th century. Nevertheless, this still remains a useful if rather succinct study.

521 **The old South Arabian religion.**
Jacques Ryckmans. In: *Yemen: 3000 years of art and civilization.* Edited by Werner Daum. Innsbruck, Austria: Pinguin-Verlag; Frankfurt am Main, Germany: Umschau-Verlag, 1988. p. 107-10.

The author looks not only at the evidence furnished by inscriptions but also at archaeological data, describing temples and their cultic furniture, as well as the gods and the rituals associated with them. He looks in particular at the South Arabian pantheon, at the sphere of the sacred (the *ḥaram),* at magic, funerary customs, and how the individual saw and served the gods.

522 **Hūd and other pre-Islamic prophets of Hadramawt.**
R. B. Serjeant. *Le Muséon,* vol. 67 (1954), p. 121-79.

Reprinted in *Studies in Arabian history and civilisation* (London: Variorum, 1981 [q.v.]), this is a detailed investigation of the rituals surrounding the pilgrimage to the tomb of Hūd, the prophet mentioned in the Qur'ān, who, according to the author, 'is reckoned in Ḥaḍramawt only second to Muḥammad himself'. The author discusses the historical evidence for the tomb, the links with pre-Islamic practices, the poetry recited during the pilgrimage to the tomb, and the rituals surrounding other similar shrines, such Mawlā Maṭar and Hādūn ibn Hūd.

523 **The Zaydis.**

R. B. Serjeant. In: *Religion in the Middle East: three religions in concord and conflict.* Edited by A. J. Arberry. Vol. 2: *Islam.* Cambridge, England: Cambridge University Press, 1969, p. 285-301.

A survey of Zaydī history and doctrine, which looks initially at the theological development of the school, and moves on to the political and territorial growth of the Zaydī state in North Yemen, and concludes with the conflict within Yemen between the theocratic state of the Imams Yaḥyā (d. 1948) and Ahmad (d. 1962) and the secular and liberal opposition to their rule.

524 **Memorials of the Hon. Ion Keith-Falconer, the late Lord Almoner's Professor of Arabic in the University of Cambridge, and missionary to the Mohammadans of Southern Arabia.**

Robert Sinker. Cambridge, England: Deighton, Bell; London: George Bell, 1903. 258p.

Ever since the arrival of Islam, Christianity has found it hard to maintain a foothold in the Arabian Peninsula. When the British conquered Aden in 1839, they found no indigenous Christians, but a Roman Catholic mission was soon established in 1840. It was fifty years, however, before a Protestant mission was founded in the Aden Protectorate. This was the work of the Arabist and Free Church of Scotland missionary, Ion Keith-Falconer, who arrived in Aden in 1885 and soon began a mission school and a hospital in Shaykh ʿUthmān. Both survived his early death in 1887 and this work chronicles, often in Keith-Falconer's own words, the struggles the mission faced during his time in Aden, and continues the story until the early years of this century. The almost contemporary visit to and description of Ṣanʿāʾ by the American Protestant missionary, Samuel J. Zwemer, who went to the capital of North Yemen to investigate the possibility of establishing a mission there (the mission was eventually established in Basrah, Iraq) is succinctly analysed by Jerzy Zdanowski, 'The trip of Samuel J. Zwemer to Sanʿa in 1891 and the question of establishing a station of the Arabian Mission' (*Hemispheres: Studies in Cultures and Societies* [Warsaw], vol. 10 [1995], p. 155-60).

525 **Linking groups in the networks of eighteenth-century revivalist scholars: the Mizjaji family of Yemen.**

John O. Voll. In: *Eighteenth-century renewal and reform in Islam.* Edited by Nehemia Levtzion, John O. Voll. Syracuse, New York: Syracuse University Press, 1987, p. 69-92.

The Mizjajī family were a relatively cohesive unit, living around Zabīd in the Tihāmah in the 18th century. Members of the Ḥanafī school, the family had a solid scholarly reputation based on their knowledge of *ḥadīth* (Islamic traditions) and their participation in the Naqshabandīyah *ṭarīqah* (mystical order). Most male members of the Mizjajīs performed the pilgrimage and studied in the Holy Cities of Arabia, thereby meeting many important scholars from other regions, as well as being acquainted with scholars based in Yemen such as Muḥammad Murtaḍā al-Zabīdī (d. 1791) and the Ahdal family. The author suggests that the Mijzajī family participated in revivalism (viewed by the author as 'part of the long tradition of the fundamentalist mode of the Islamic experience'), as a result of their special interest in both *ḥadīth* studies and sufism, but the evidence provided is neither conclusive nor completely convincing.

Saba'.
See item no. 284.

A history of the Jews of Arabia from ancient times . . .
See item no. 297.

The martyrs of Najrân: new documents.
See item no. 307.

Christianity among the Arabs in pre-Islamic times.
See item no. 310.

Social Conditions and Organization

General

526 **Qabyala: the tribal concept in the Central Highlands of the Yemen Arab Republic.**
Najwa Adra. PhD dissertation, Temple University, 1982. 312p. bibliog. (Available from: University Microfilms International, Ann Arbor, Michigan, order no. 8311676).

The author analyses the concept of tribalism and what it means to be a member of a tribe, basing herself on field work conducted in al-Ahjur, which lies about thirty miles northwest of Ṣanʿāʾ. She looks at *qabyalah,* or tribal values, the tribal economy, customary law, tribal organization (using the segmentary model), and concludes with an investigation of two kinds of tribal dancing (*barʿah* and *liʿbah*), and how these symbolize the cooperation and individuality inherent in tribal culture. A résumé of her thesis was published as 'The concept of tribe in rural Yemen', in *Arab society: social science perspectives*. Edited by Saad Eddin Ibrahim and Nicholas S. Hopkins (Cairo: American University in Cairo Press, 1985, p. 275-85; first published in 1977 as *Arab society in transition*).

527 **Adolescents and culture in Yemen.**
Nadeem Muhamed Ashuraey. EdD dissertation, Boston University, 1986. 343p. bibliog. (Available from University Microfilms International, Ann Arbor, Michigan, order no. 8615314).

An exploration of the feelings and thoughts of North Yemeni male and female youth towards relationships, the family, sexuality, society, education and themselves. This is a complex study which finds that the major psychological concerns of the adolescents in the survey were their relationships with others. 'Very few participants [in the interviews] thought of themselves in individualistic terms and very few spoke about their personal characteristics'. The author also found that many feared separation from their loved ones or betrayal by them, and that some females found it difficult to reconcile their future career choices or their sexuality with their own images of the ideal Muslim. Finally, the author discerned a potential identity crisis in the future caused by the new channels of information from the outside wold and the consequent challenges to existing social values.

528 **Une tribu sédentaire: la tribu des hauts plateaux yéménites.**
(A sedentary tribe: the tribe in highland Yemen.)
Geneviève Bédoucha. *L'Homme,* no. 102 (1987), p. 139-50.

A theoretical study which looks at the characteristics of the Yemeni tribe. The author examines the differences between North and South Yemeni kinship systems and, basing herself on fieldwork conducted in Ṣaʿdah in the north of the Yemen Arab Republic, concludes that 'linking oneself back to a common ancestor and defending the same honour with respect to possession of territory' are ways in which a group is defined. The author also notes frequent changes of tribal membership which 'emphasize the fraternization resulting from political alliances to the detriment of real genealogical filiation'.

529 **"Peaks of Yemen I summon": poetry as cultural practice in a North Yemeni tribe.**
Steven C. Caton. Berkeley, California: University of California Press, 1990. 351p. 2 maps. bibliog.

The author has made the field of the ethnography of Yemeni poetry his own, and this extensive investigation of the topic is based on the fieldwork he conducted for his PhD dissertation in Khawlān al-Ṭiyāl, to the southeast of Ṣanʿāʾ. He focuses on the entire system of poetic discourse and the way in which it interacts with the social practices and cultural beliefs of a particular group of Yemeni tribesmen. This is a ground-breaking study of considerable originality, described by a colleague as 'technically the most impressive work an outsider has done on Yemen'. His approach has found echoes for the Hadramawt in the work of the Russian scholar, Mikhail Rodionov (see item no. 550).

530 **The poetic construction of self.**
Steven C. Caton. *Anthropological Quarterly,* vol. 5, no. 4 (1985), p. 141-51.

The author uses a model developed by George Herbert Mead to study the oral verse genre called *balah,* which is performed at North Yemeni marriage ceremonies. He concludes that 'a balah is not only a game of poetry, for on a deeper level of analysis it is also a game of honour' and that 'the creation of an oral poem is considered to be a glorious deed of challenge and counter-challenge'.

531 **Salām tahiyah: greetings from the highlands of Yemen.**
Steven C. Caton. *American Ethnologist,* vol. 13 (1986), p. 290-308.

The author analyses concepts of honour and piety through the greetings employed between different social categories in a highland area of the Yemen area of the Yemen Arab Republic. This is an interesting and subtle look at a little-studied area of sociolinguistics.

532 **L'Arabie du Sud: histoire et civilisation.** (South Arabia: history and civilisation.) Vol. 3: **Culture et institutions du Yémen.** (Culture and institutions of Yemen.)
Joseph Chelhod (et al.). Paris: Maisonneuve et Larose, 1985. 432p. maps. (Islam d'Hier et d'Aujourd'hui, vol. 25).

Most of this volume is written by Joseph Chelhod and it brings together the anthropological and sociological data he published in article format mainly in the 1970s. He tackles tribal organization, kinship systems, tribal law, marriage ceremonies and cultural processes surrounding *qāt* consumption in both North and South Yemen, and places his data in a historical framework. The other contributions to the book are quoted in their relevant chapters, as are the first two volumes of the title, which were both edited by Chelhod (see item no. 264).

533 **Die Beduinen in Südarabien: eine ethnologische Studie zur Entwicklung der Kamelhirtenkultur in Arabien.** (The Bedouin in South Arabia: an ethnological study of the development of the camel-herding culture in Arabia.)
Walter Dostal. Vienna: Ferdinand Berger, 1967. 199p. bibliog. (Wiener Beiträge zur Kulturgeschichte und Linguistik, Band 16).

The author undertook extensive field studies in the Eastern Aden Protectorate in the early 1960s to investigate aspects of the camel-herding nomads of the region. He discusses the various tribes of the region, their historical evolution, their customs, and the influence of the British administration on their *Weltanschauung*. He also describes the material culture associated with camel-herding but pays relatively little attention to herding itself or its economic aspects.

534 **Egalität und Klassengesellschaft in Südarabien: anthropologische Untersuchungen zur sozialen Evolution.** (Equality and class structure in South Arabia: anthropological studies in social development.)
Walter Dostal. Vienna: Ferdinand Berger, 1983. 457p. maps. bibliog. (Wiener Beiträge zur Kulturgeschichte und Linguistik, Band 20).

Over half the book is devoted to a study of the Banū Ḥushaysh of the Yemen Arab Republic (the rest is given over to the Banū Shiḥūḥ and the Banū Shumaylī of the United Arab Emirates). The author concentrates his researches on the class structure of the tribe, who live in the Central Highlands to the east of Ṣanʿāʾ, and divides them into five social categories, paying particular attention to the *muzayyinīn* or socially inferior occupational groups. He looks at forms of production, the weekly market, and household and political organization, and the book as a whole makes an important contribution to our understanding of social stratification among Yemeni tribes.

535 **Guaranty of market at Ḥūth.**
Paul Dresch. *Arabian Studies,* vol. 8 (1990), p. 63-91.

The author explores the opposition between Islamic law and tribal law through a 1928 document (given in its Arabic original and English translation), which guarantees the market in Ḥūth, a North Yemeni town important in the Zaydī tradition. Through the document, the author is able to clarify the details of political accommodation between the Imams and the tribes, which are more flexible than the rhetorically stated opposition might imply. For comparative purposes, the reader can consult 'The special features of the Yemeni weekly market system: an attempt at an anthropological interpretation', by Walter Dostal (*New Arabian Studies,* vol. 3 [1996], p. 50-7), which translates and comments on a document on market regulations drawn up in the 1920s by the Zahrān tribes of the North Yemen/Saudi Arabia border.

536 **The position of shaykhs among the northern tribes of Yemen.**
Paul Dresch. *Man,* new series, vol. 19, no. 1 (1984), p. 31-49.

Using North Yemen as an example, the author takes issue with the theory that tribal societies can be conceived of as a balance of power between equal and opposite elements and asserts that the domains of shaykhs do not necessarily coincide neatly with tribal divisions. He shows how shaykhs operate within Yemeni society, how they exercise authority and what the limits of this authority are. Dresch uses both historical and contemporary examples to illlustrate his views, which are clear, coherent and authoritatively argued.

537 **Tribes, government and history in Yemen.**
Paul Dresch. Oxford, England: Clarendon Press, 1989. 440p. maps. bibliog.

One of the most interesting recent books on North Yemen, this work combines ethnography with historiography as it attempts to place tribalism within the framework of Yemeni history. The first third of the book identifies key concepts in tribal culture (*ʿarḍ, sayyid, hijrah,* etc.) and discusses the salient ideas by which the tribesman's world is organized, while the second third shows what place the tribes have had in the affairs of the country from medieval times to the 1950s (paying particular attention to Zaydī history). The final portion of the book looks at the position of tribes and tribalism in contemporary Yemen, and evaluates the changes which tribal structures are currently undergoing. R. B. Serjeant has appended some typically scholarly observations to Dresch's book in his review article, 'The Zaydī tribes of the Yemen: a new field study' (*Bulletin of the School of Oriental and African Studies,* vol. 55, no. 1 [1992], p. 16-21).

538 **The tribes of Ḥāshid and Bakīl as historical and geographical entities.**
Paul Dresch. In: *Arabicus Felix Luminosus Britannicus: essays in honour of A. F. L. Beeston on his eightieth birthday.* Edited by Alan Jones. Reading, England: Ithaca Press for the Board of the Faculty of Oriental Studies, Oxford University, 1991, p. 8-24.

In this article, the author continues his study of the interplay between tribalism and history in North Yemen. Using the work of the early historian and geographer al-Ḥasan ibn Aḥmad al-Hamdānī (d. c. 945), the author looks at tribal geography, and the reasons for changes in tribal boundaries and of the relation of groups of people to collective names. The author's conclusion is that 'the tribal categories as such remain geographically fixed while men or families move between them'.

539 **Market, mosque and mafraj: social inequality in a Yemeni town.**
Tomas Gerholm. Stockholm: Department of Social Anthropology, University of Stockholm, 1977. 217p. bibliog. (Stockholm Studies in Social Anthropology, vol. 5).

The first major study to look at social stratification in North Yemen, this work examines wealth and status in the mountain town of Manākhah, which is situated midway between Hodeida and Ṣanʿāʾ. He uncovers no evidence of class consciousness, but finds instead that a keen sense of status groups is present, which divides the local society into a hierarchy which 'is ambiguous and open to negotiation on several points'. He demonstrates how this hierarchy penetrates everyday life, by conducting analyses of typical social situations in which townsmen find themselves on a daily basis, i.e. the market place, the mosque, and the *mafraj,* or living-room where men chew *qāt.*

540 **Beiträge zur Ethnographie der Provinz Ṣaʿda (Nordjemen): Aspekte der traditionellen materiellen Kultur in bäuerlichen Stammesgesellschaften.** (Contributions to the ethnography of Ṣaʿdah Province, North Yemen: aspects of traditional material culture in peasant tribal societies.)
André Gingrich, Johann Heiss. Vienna: Österreichische Akademie der Wissenschaften, 1986. 186p. bibliog. (Sitzungsberichte, Österreichische Akademie der Wissenschaften, Philosophisch-Historische Klasse, Band 462).

The authors look mainly at the tools, dwellings and techniques of peasants in three areas in the region of Ṣaʿdah, each zone distinguished by different forms of agriculture. They find that the rising incomes, the departure of Jewish artisans, and the massive emigration of labour have introduced many changes to Yemeni society, although these are unevenly distributed, affecting the town more than the countryside. They also detect a decline in local craft industry, but maintain that economic development has had much more effect on the purchase of consumer goods and on trade, than on methods of agricultural and craft production.

541 **Südwestarabische Sternenkalender: eine ethnologische Studie zu Struktur, Kontext und regionalem Vergleich des tribalen Agrarkalenders der Munebbih in Jemen.** (South-West Arabian star calendars: an ethnological study of the structure and context of the tribal agricultural calendar of the Munabbih in Yemen with a regional comparison.)
André Gingrich. Vienna: WUV-Universitätsverlag, 1994. 350p. bibliog. (Wiener Beiträge zur Ethnologie und Anthropologie, Band 7).

The author has spent a decade studying the way in which Yemeni tribes use the stars for both chronology and agriculture, and this work is a summation of his researches among the Munabbih tribe who live in North-West Yemen beyond Ṣaʿdah. Through his understanding of material culture and cosmological concepts, the author shows how knowledge about stars has been passed on from generation to generation (ultimately going back to pre-Islamic times), and links today's tribesmen to the world of nature, work and agricultural ritual in timeless fashion.

542 **The flower of paradise: the institutionalized use of the drug qat in North Yemen.**

John G. Kennedy. Dordrecht, The Netherlands; Lancaster, England: Reidel, 1987. 268p. bibliog.

A highly praised interdisciplinary study of *qāt* (*Catha edulis*) based on a two-year field study of users in North Yemen, backed up by a team of historians, anthropologists, doctors and biochemists. The author looks at the history of *qāt* chewing, its importance as a social institution, the effects reported by users, the agriculture and economics of *qāt* production, the pharmacology of the plant, and, finally, the effects of *qāt* on health and whether it can be considered an addictive drug. The author comes to the conclusion that the prolonged use of *qāt* can have negative effects on health, but he also provides convincing evidence to show that in general its harmful effects are mild, that it is not a major contributor to the economic backwardness of the country and that the cultivation of *qāt* is not associated with the decline of coffee production.

543 **Were there any truly matrilineal lineages in the Arabian Peninsula.**

Andrey Vitalyevich Korotayev. *Proceedings of the Seminar for Arabian Studies,* vol. 25 (1995), p. 83-98.

The author studies the question of lineage through the ample epigraphic evidence from pre-Islamic South Arabia. He looks at the work of other scholars on the topic and claims that the Banu MḪBḌM was a 'distinctly autonomous well integrated corporate matrilineage', whose probable area of habitation was around Marib and Nashān within the territory of the Banū Amīr. In conclusion, he finds that although patrilineal lineages were in the majority in South Arabia, 'the answer to the question posed by the title of this paper is "yes"; this "yes" is, of course, now much less emphatic than it was little more than a century ago'.

544 **Tribes at the core: legitimacy, structure and power in Zaydi Yemen.**

Jeffrey R. Meissner. PhD dissertation, Columbia University, 1987. 448p. bibliog. (Available from University Microfilms International, Ann Arbor, Michigan, order no. 8710208).

After a long introduction, in which the author places Zaydism in its historical context, attention is shifted to social structure and social status. The author investigates how the possession of a particular social status correlates with descent, occupation and tribal conceptions of honour, and concludes with an in-depth study of the relationship between the Zaydī state and elements within the social structure, especially the *sayyids* (descendants of the Prophet) and the *qāḍīs* (Islamic judges).

545 **Tournaments of value: sociability and hierarchy in a Yemeni town.**

Anne Meneley. Toronto, Canada: University of Toronto Press, 1996. 216p. bibliog.

Based on her PhD dissertation at New York University (1993), the author examines the range of social events in Zabīd, such as visits, weddings and funerals, and through these she studies the interactions between the different social classes. She looks at how ideal concepts such as modesty and respect are grounded in reality, how women manage their affairs with men and with each other, and at the role of anger and emotional display in group sociability. This is a solid piece of anthropological research, unencumbered by theoretical issues and historical and comparative perspectives.

546 **Adapting to wealth: social change in a Yemeni highland community.**

Timothy Morris. PhD dissertation, London University, 1985. 353p. bibliog. (Available from British Thesis Service, British Library, Boston Spa, West Yorkshire, England, order no. DX191910).

The author conducted fieldwork in a (never identified) small town in the North-West highlands of the Yemen Arab Republic. In this work, he describes the social structure of the town and assesses the effects on it of economic change and labour migration, which he concludes 'have blurred what are still regarded as immutable boundaries'. Additional chapters describe the market-place, the relationship between townsmen, shaykh and the local administration, and social practices and customs, ranging from the evil eye to modern health care. The author returned to Yemen as an aid worker and published a somewhat jaundiced account of his experiences there the second time round (see item no. 597).

547 **Domestic government: kinship, community and polity in North Yemen.**

Martha Mundy. London; New York: Tauris, 1995. 317p. bibliog. (Society and Culture in the Modern Middle East).

One of the most important recent studies on Yemeni society. The author, an Arabist and anthropologist, focuses on one community, Wādī Ḍahr, a valley of irrigated agriculture on the Ṣanʿāʾ plateau. She examines the relationship between the state and the community: law, justice and the resolution of disputes; how the village economy functions, particularly with regard to property rights; gender relations and the family; and, finally, the shifting nature of kinship and marriage alliances. This is a work of impressive scholarship, based on three-and-a-half years of field study, and a wide array of primary and secondary sources.

548 **Island of the phoenix: an ethnographic study of the people of Socotra.**

Vitalij V. Naumkin, translated from the Russian by Valery A. Epstein. Reading, England: Ithaca Press, 1993. 421p. bibliog. (Middle East Cultures Series, no. 16).

The most detailed study ever undertaken of the culture of the inhabitants of Socotra and the neighbouring island of ʿAbd al-Kūrī. The author began his fieldwork in the 1970s and his researches continued into the 1980s, culminating in five successive seasons between 1983 and 1987 as part of the joint Yemeni–Soviet expedition. The author looks at most aspects of Socotran society apart from language and includes chapters on history, geography and archaeology in his survey. He concentrates his fire, however, on ethnography and provides extensive analyses of the physical anthropology, material culture, economic sytems, kinship and family structures, and the folk customs and rituals of the islanders.

549 **Tribe, family and state in Mahra and Socotra: traditional identities in the changing world.**

Vitalij V. Naumkin. *Proceedings of the Seminar for Arabian Studies*, vol. 25 (1995), p. 99-105.

The author looks at the ways in which society in Mahra and Socotra differ from other areas of South Arabia. He finds a strict social hierarchy in Mahra, linked to blood feud and bellicosity, but less rigid divisions in Socotra, where the tribes were not so militant. Both areas favoured patrilineal marriages, particularly in Socotra, where historically marriage between children of brothers had been 'a categorical imperative'. Although this tradition had begun to weaken, a 1984 survey of Socotran men showed that over seventy per cent had married relatives and fellow tribeswomen. Women were freer in both Mahra and Socotra, in movement, tasks, and marriage and divorce, and the author concludes, that, while modernization has weakened some of the rigid social structures, 'the astonishingly great ability of old institutions and values to survive and to continue functioning effectively is still noticeable'.

550 **Poetry and power in Hadramawt.**

Mikhail Rodionov. *New Arabian Studies*, vol. 3 (1996), p. 118-33.

An interesting parallel from South Yemen to the work pursued by Steven C. Caton (see items 529, 530) on the ethnography of poetry. Rodionov conducted his researches independently of Caton but employed similar techniques and came to similar conclusions, namely that 'local power is based not only on material force but also, and particularly, on spiritual authority. One vital means of expressing the latter is through persuasion, especially when mediators are attempting to resolve a conflict. In this context, the role of the poet and the social function of poetry can hardly be overstated'. This article looks at the role poetry plays in conflict resolution and in a wider political context in Ḥaḍramawt both during the British occupation and today.

551 **Das Qāt: Geschichte und Gebrauch des Genussmittels *Catha edulis* Forsk. in der Arabischen Republik Jemen.** (*Qāt*: the history and use of the luxury item *Catha edulis* Forsk. in the Yemen Arab Republic.)

Armin Schopen. Wiesbaden, Germany: Franz Steiner, 1978. 237p. bibliog. (Arbeiten aus dem Seminar für Völkerkunde der Johann Wolfgang-Goethe-Universität, Frankfurt am Main, Band 8).

The first serious academic study of the cultivation and use of *qāt* in North Yemen. The author lists the main zones of cultivation of *qāt,* how it is sold and the chemical and pharmacological constituents of the drug. The major part of the work, however, is devoted to the social impact of *qāt*, and particularly interesting are the author's descriptions of chewing sessions on particular occasions such as engagement parties, weddings, births, circumcisions, and during illness and death. The work concludes with the Arabic text and German translation of two Yemeni treatises on *qāt.*

552 **Ḥaram and ḥawṭah, the sacred enclave in Arabia.**
R. B. Serjeant. In: *Mélanges Taha Husain offerts par ces amis et ses disciples à l'occasion de son 70ième anniversaire = Ilā Ṭāhā Ḥusayn.* (A miscellany for Taha Husayn, offered by his friends and pupils on the occasion of his 70th birthday.) Edited by Abdurrahman Badawi. Cairo: Dār al-Maʾārif, 1962, p. 41-58.

Although the bulk of this seminal article deals with relations between the Prophet Muhammad, the local tribes and the sacred spaces of Mecca, the first few pages discuss the existence of sacred enclaves in contemporary South Arabia. The author describes the conditions attached to two *ḥawṭahs* in Hadramawt and the role of customary law in protecting the enclave and its guardian (usually known as the Manṣab).

553 **The Saiyids of Hadramawt.**
R. B. Serjeant. London: University of London, School of Oriental and African Studies, 1957. 29p.

A historical survey of the ʿAlawī Sayyids of Hadramawt, an aristocratic group, who claim descent from the Prophet Muḥammad. The author discusses the religious role of the *sayyids* including the institution of the *ḥawṭah,* or sacred enclave, and their importance in the domains of law and sufism. He goes on to describe the migration of *sayyids* to Africa, India and South-East Asia, and how increasing modernization and secularization have weakened the influence of *sayyid* families both within and outside Hadramawt.

554 **Social stratification in Arabia.**
R. B. Serjeant. In: *The Islamic city: selected papers from the colloquium held at the Middle East Centre, Faculty of Oriental Studies, Cambridge, United Kingdom, from 19 to 23 July, 1976.* Edited by R. B. Serjeant. Paris: UNESCO, 1980, p. 126-47.

The author approaches the question of social structure both as historian and arabist, and contributes a great deal of valuable data on classes and occupations in both North and South Yemen. He is able to show from personal experience which occupations are the most respected in both Ṣanʿāʾ and Tarīm, and that both *sayyids* (descendants of the Prophet) and *qāḍīs* (arbiters or Islamic judges) work honourably as blacksmiths and carpenters in the Yemeni capital. On the basis of written documents as well as numerous visits, the author goes on to explain the complex administration, customs and social structure of towns like Shiḥr and Tarīm.

555 **South Arabia.**
R. B. Serjeant. In: *Commoners, climbers and notables: a sampler of studies on social ranking in the Middle East.* Edited by C. A. O. van Nieuwenhuijze. Leiden, The Netherlands: Brill, 1977, p. 226-47.

An exposé of the social structure existing in both North and South Yemen up to the 1960s. The author asserts that 'Arabian society is as stratified and inegalitarian as that of most European countries, and the transition from one class to another vastly more difficult', and proceeds to show how customary law has established the principle of *kafāʾah* (equivalence of social status) to determine who was of sufficient degree to marry. He discusses the various classes such as the aristorcratic *sayyids* and *sharīfs* (descendants of the Prophet), the middle-ranking *miskīns* and *muzayyin* (shopkeepers, artisans and other lower-class occupations), and various groups at the bottom of the class structure such as the *dawshān* and the *akhdām*. He emphasizes, however, that the tribesman has scant respect for the townsman, and that 'whatever form of government has existed in Southern Arabia, the real power lies with the large arms-bearing tribes'.

556 **South Arabian hunt.**
R. B. Serjeant. London: Luzac, 1976. 143p.

The author looks at the ritual hunt from various angles: personal experience; historical references; legal texts; and poetical descriptions. The result is an authoritative study, replete with the quality and quantity of detail for which the author was famous. Influenced by this work, the Russian ethnographer Mikhail Rodionov has described the contemporary ceremonial procession surrounding the hunt in three South Arabian villages in, 'The ibex hunt ceremony in Hadramawt today' (*New Arabian Studies*, vol. 2 [1994], p. 123-9).

557 **The rise of Nāṣir al-Nims: a tribal commentary on being and becoming a shaykh.**
Andrew J. Shryock. *Journal of Anthropological Research*, vol. 46, no. 2 (1990), p. 153-76.

Through the oral biography of Nāṣir al-Nims, a shaykh of the Murād tribe in North Yemen, the author investigates how tribal authority is acquired and maintained, and also, in what it consists. He uses comparisons from the work of other anthropologists to show that it is through the mediation of disputes that a man becomes more than just an ordinary tribesman and he concludes that 'the standing of men like Nāṣir depends almost wholly upon their ability to create a form of hierarchy – that entailed by arbitration and guaranty'.

558 **Social change in a Yemeni highlands town.**
Thomas B. Stevenson. Salt Lake City, Utah: University of Utah Press, 1985. 190p. bibliog.

An ethnographic survey of life in ʿAmrān, a small town to the north of Ṣanʿāʾ. The author looks at tribal affiliation, kinship, occupation, and marriage patterns, and, in the most interesting chapter, how ʿAmrānīs perceive social change and modifications to status.

559 **Development and change in highland Yemen.**
Charles F. Swagman. Salt Lake City, Utah: University of Utah Press, 1988. 200p. bibliog.

The author conducted research in two neighbouring, but separate towns in the western highlands of the Yemen Arab Republic. He studied both communities from a developmental perspective and concluded that the difference in attitude to the local development associations was dependent on whether the community was truly tribal or not, and therefore capable of corporate action. This is an innovative and important contribution to our understanding of the psychology of social change.

560 **Doing development anthropology: personal experience in the Yemen Arab Republic.**

Charles F. Swagman. In: *Anthropology and development in North Africa and the Middle East.* Edited by Muneera Salem-Murdock, Michael M. Horowitz, Monica Sella. Boulder, Colorado; Oxford, England: Westview Press, 1990, p. 279-91.

Swagman describes his experiences as a development anthropologist working on two different projects in North Yemen. In the Ḥarāz Afforestation Project (q.v. under Ladj), he was hired to conduct an attitude survey of local farmers and to assess their willingness to participate in a tree-planting programme. Although his report recommended action which did not accord fully with the planners' intentions, and was therefore not acted upon for four years, the author feels that his role was clearly defined and his contribution worthwhile. By way of contrast, his participation in the Dhamār Governorate Health Services Programme is deemed a failure, since the research goals were ill-defined, and the results met with indifference from the technical experts, and with little support from the local management. The author describes a conflict between the planners in Europe and the field management in very much the same terms as Timothy Morris (see item no. 597), and recommends that 'matching expectations to performance' and focusing 'on action rather than applied research' can minimize role conflicts for the development anthropologist.

561 **Tribe, tribute and trade: social class formation in highland Yemen.**

Richard Tutwiler. PhD dissertation, State University of New York at Binghamton, 1987. 584p. bibliog. (Available from University Microfilms International, Ann Arbor, Michigan, order no. 8710921).

A very detailed investigation of the formation of social class in Jabal al-Maḥwīt, a highland area to the west of Ṣanʿāʾ. The author looks at class structure not so much in terms of hierarchy, but in neo-Marxist economic terms, relating each class to 'modes of production'. He finds that the civil war of 1962-69 was a turning point, since 'after 1962, the economy of the region was transformed by commodity relations, and new commercial classes emerged as a result of class struggle'. The author provides ample evidence for changing economic relations as he investigates the situation of particular groups like smallholders and wholesale merchants. This is an original study using a perspective rarely found, and not always appreciated, among scholars of North Yemen.

562 **Affluence and the concept of the tribe in the Central Highlands of the Yemen Arab Republic.**

Daniel Martin Varisco, Najwa Adra. In: *Affluence and cultural survival: 1981 proceedings of the American Ethnological Society.* Edited by Richard F. Salisbury, Elizabeth Tooker. Washington, DC: American Ethnological Society, 1984, p. 134-49.

The authors argue that the remittances sent home by migrant Yemeni workes have reduced rather than enhanced the disparity between social categories, since the basis of social organization, the tribe, has 'maintained an egalitarian tribal focus while operating within a stratified model of social structure'. The authors explain social structure, stratification and the significance of customary law in al-Ahjur, a valley in the central highlands of North Yemen, before examining the impact of relative affluence. Although their research is incomplete and was undertaken while the significance of the new wealth was still being absorbed by Yemenis, their view that 'the tribal code is flexible enough to serve in the transition to a broader cultural identity' has been shown to generally valid.

563 **On the meaning of chewing: the significance of qāt (*Catha edulis*) in the Yemen Arab Republic.**
Daniel Martin Varisco. *International Journal of Middle Eastern Studies,* vol. 18, no. 1 (1986), p. 1-13.

An investigation of the sociology of *qāt,* based on fieldwork undertaken in the late 1970s in al-Ahjur, in the central highlands of North Yemen.The author concludes that, despite official government disapproval, *qāt* chewing is a positive affirmation of Yemeni identity, which can be afforded by almost everyone. He claims that 'at a time when identity is not clearly defined, any Yemeni may chew as one way of affirming both the value of his heritage and his own sense of self-worth'.

564 **Perceptions of social inequality in the Yemen Arab Republic.**
Delores M. Walters. PhD dissertation, New York University, 1987. 400p. bibliog. (Available from University Microfilms International, Ann Arbor, Michigan, order no. 8801582).

Although somewhat overburdened with theory, and not always coherently structured, this remains a valuable contribution to our knowledge of Yemeni society, in that it focuses on the *akhdām,* which is one of the lowest status groups in North Yemen, and, consequently, one conventionally ignored by anthropologists. The author based her investigations on two separate sites, and her research shows the interaction of ethnicity and class in a society usually considered hierarchical but ethnically homogeneous.

565 **Qat in Yemen: consumption and social change.**
Shelagh Weir. London: British Museum Publications, 1985. 191p. bibliog.

The author conducts a thorough survey of the literature on *qāt,* and provides detailed information on its cultivation and use. She is strongest on the social significance of *qāt* chewing and relies on studies by John G. Kennedy (see item no. 542) for evidence of the physiological consequences of *qāt* consumption.

566 **Yemen Sanaa.**
Peuples Méditerranéens/Mediterranean Peoples, no. 46 (1989). 167p.

A special issue of this multilingual journal, devoted to papers given at a conference organized by Gilbert Grandguillaume and Franck Mermier and held in Paris in 1988. Three of the contributions are in English: in 'Keeping the Imam's peace: a response to tribal disorder in the late 1950s', Paul Dresch discusses a document describing the intervention of the Imam's regular army in a tribal dispute; in 'Irrigation and society in a Yemeni valley: on the life and death of a bountiful source', Martha Mundy looks at the historical character of local tradition as it relates to a particular watercourse in Wādī Ḍahr; and in 'The guest meal among the Munebbih: some considerations on tradition and change in ʿ*aish wa milh* in Northwestern Yemen', André Gingrich continues his anthropological investigations among the Banū Munabbih. Among the French papers,

Franck Mermier looks in two separate contributions at urban life in Ṣanʿāʾ and at the effect of the importation of manufactured goods on craftsmen, Jean Lambert analyses the change in status of Yemeni musicians, and Jean-Charles Depaule examines the the changing styles of architecture in Ṣanʿāʾ. Papers by Mona Ghamess on women's education, by Philippe Panerai on the Islamic city, and by Gilbert Grandguillaume on social change in Yemen complete the conference contributions.

Women's studies

567 **Down-playing gender: H̱atm rituals in Ṣanʿāʾ.**
Gabriele vom Bruck. *Quaderni di Studi Arabi,* vol. 12 (1994), p. 161-82.

One of the few studies of gender as opposed to women alone, this article looks at the *khatm* ritual, whereby children between the ages of seven and twelve celebrate completing the reading of the Qur'ān without making any mistakes. The author considers the *khatm* ritual to have been 'the most important celebration performed for children before marriage in pre-revolutionary Yemen', and claims that 'gender difference finds little expression in social practice at the age where the *ẖatm* is performed'. This is an important study which breaks with ethnographic tradition in suggesting that in pre-pubescent children, gender is not always linked to power, since girls who succeeded in reading the Qur'ān were considered superior to both boys and girls who failed to do so, thus emphasizing the moral authority of religious knowledge, rather than masculine power over the female.

568 **Enacting tradition: the legitimation of marriage practices among Yemeni sādah.**
Gabriele vom Bruck. *Cambridge Anthropology,* vol. 16, no. 2 (1992/93), p. 54-68.

An interesting article combining anthropology with legal theory and practice. The author surveys the problems faced by North Yemeni women from the *sādah* (who claim descent from the Prophet), if they contemplate marriage outside their social group. She looks at Zaydī legal precepts, contemporary ethnographies, case law and actual practice in the period up to the revolution of 1962 and after.

569 **Re-defining identity: women in Ṣanʿāʾ.**
Gabriele vom Bruck. In: *Yemen: 3000 years of art and civilisation in Arabia Felix.* Edited by Werner Daum. Innsbruck, Austria: Pinguin-Verlag; Frankfurt am Main, Germany: Umschau-Verlag, 1988, p. 396-408.

A brief survey, using official Yemeni government sources, of the present-day condition of women in North Yemen. The author looks at marriage and divorce, education, work and social activities.

570 **Bibliography on women in Yemen.**
Joke Buringa, edited by Marta Colburn. Westbury, New York: American Institute for Yemeni Studies, 1992. 158p. (Yemen Development Series, no. 2).

A comprehensive survey of mainly English-language books, articles and reports on women in both Yemens. It is particularly strong on technical reports covering health and related issues (nutrition, family planning, etc.) and is a first-rate source for the academic and development specialist.

571 **Espaces et matériels de la vie féminine sur les hauts plateaux du Yémen.** (Space and material culture in women's lives in highland Yemen.)
Dominique Champault. In: *L'Arabie du Sud: histoire et civilisation.* (South Arabia: history and civilization.) Vol. 3: *Culture et institutions du Yémen.* (Culture and institutions of Yemen.) Joseph Chelhod (et al.). Paris: Maisonneuve et Larose, 1985, p. 185-230.

The author pays little attention to women's interaction with men, preferring instead to concentrate on how women spend their time in the home and outside it. She looks at the kitchen, how it is equipped, and all the various kinds of food prepared there, then moves on to other rooms such as the *mafraj al-ḥarīm* or living-room, the toilet and the stable. Women's social activities like visiting and going to the *ḥammām,* or public baths, are considered, as well as jobs which require women to leave the house – such as harvesting, fetching water and wood, and paid employment (rare in rural areas, and confined to the *muzayyin* class). Finally, Champault looks at areas normally forbidden to women (the market and mosque), at women's dress, the veil, and at the recent changes wrought by consumerism and changing customs.

572 **Femmes du Yémen.** (Women of Yemen.)
Blandine Destremau. Paris: Editions Peuples du Monde, 1990. 302p.

The author spent twelve months in an unnamed village in north-western Yemen between 1985 and 1987. In this work, she gives us a detailed description of the typical life of a rural Yemeni woman. The usual subjects are covered – dress, cooking, marriage, children, health, veiling, etc. – but some less common themes are dealt with as well, such as the role of the media and the female economy. This book is more than just a travel narrative, as the descriptions are always placed in a historical and social context, and the work has considerable academic value.

573 **Women of ʿAmrān: a Middle Eastern ethnographic study.**
Susan Dorsky. Salt Lake City, Utah: University of Utah Press, 1986. 230p. bibliog.

Dorsky lived in ʿAmrān, a small town north of Ṣanʿāʾ, for sixteen months, during which time she made many friends among the women of the neighbourhood. In this book, she describes their lives, concentrating on marriage and family life, and provides a vivid picture of traditional Yemeni society, unencumbered by technical anthropological language.

574 **Vies de femmes au Yémen: récits de Nagiba.** (Women's lives in Yemen: accounts by Nagiba.)
Claudie Fayein. Paris: L'Harmattan, 1990. 103p.

Claudie Fayein, whose first stay in North Yemen is recounted in *A French doctor in the Yemen* (q.v.), returned to Ṣanʿāʾ in 1990. There she became reacquainted with Nagiba, a Frenchwoman married to a Yemeni, and together they conducted 200 interviews with local women. This book contains a brief selection of the women's testimony, which centres on questions of marriage and health, and complements the work undertaken earlier by Joseph Chelhod (q.v.).

575 **Ein Leben in der Unsichtbarkeit: Frauen in Jemen.** (A life of invisibility: women in Yemen.)
Gisela Frese-Weghöft. Reinbek bei Hamburg, Germany: Rowohlt, 1986. 184p.

The author, who spent two-and-a-half years in a small North Yemeni town as an aid worker, describes her life among the local women. This is a collection of entertaining anecdotes, rather than a scholarly study.

576 **Attitudes of government employees toward women's employment in Yemen.**
Mohammed Ali Al-Haziazi. PhD dissertation, University of Pittsburgh, 1992. 229p. bibliog. (Available from University Microfilms International, Ann Arbor, Michigan, order no. 92264494).

After discussing the role and status of women in united Yemen, as well as general theories of female participation in the labour force, the author analyses the data he collected by means of a questionnaire distributed to a sample of 400 male and female government employees. His findings are that respondents had neutral or slighly negative attitudes to women's employment, but that guardian disapproval, lack of childcare facilities, local interpretation of Islamic injunctions, and women's general level of education are the greatest barriers to women and jobs.

577 **Women and development in the Republic of Yemen.**
Helen Lackner. In: *Gender and development in the Arab world: women's economic participation – patterns and policies.* Edited by Nabil F. Khoury, Valentine M. Moghadam. London: Zed Books; Tokyo: United Nations University Press, 1995, p. 71-96.

After a substantial introduction, explaining the background to the unification of Yemen in 1990, and outlining the differences between North and South, the author turns to the status of women in the new republic. She shows how the Personal Status Law of 1992 has reintroduced *sharīʿah* (Islamic) law to women from the south, permitting polygyny, male repudiation of a wife, and accepting male authority within the family. She also describes women's activities in both the rural and urban sectors, their participation in education, health and population policy, and the labour force. However, much of her statistical information is based on documents published in 1990 or before, and for a more up-to-date analyis, the reader should consult the 1995 article by Maxine Molyneux (see item no. 583).

578 **Brides for sale? Human trade in North Yemen.**
Eileen Macdonald. Edinburgh, Scotland: Mainstream Publishing, 1988. 216p.

A journalist's account of Nadia and Zana Muhsen from Birmingham who were sold as child brides by their Yemen-born father to men from his home village. Their life in Yemen is described in graphic and emotional terms, as well as their attempts to return to Britain. Zana's story of her eight years in Muqbanah (North Yemen) and her eventual escape in the early 1990s are told in *Sold: a story of modern day slavery* (Zana Muhsen with Andrew Crofts. London: Futura, 1991. 216p.; also published in paperback – London: Warner Books, 1994. 229p.). The mother's equally harrowing tale and her attempts (so far unsuccessful) to free her second daughter Nadia are recounted in *Without mercy: a woman's struggle against modern slavery* (Miriam Ali with Jana Wain. London: Little, Brown & Company, 1995. 314p.).

579 **Food and gender in a Yemeni community.**
Ianthe Maclagan. In: *Culinary cultures of the Middle East.* Edited by Sami Zubaida, Richard Tapper. London: Tauris, 1994, p. 159-72.

The author carried out fieldwork from 1981 to 1983 in a small town in the western highlands of North Yemen, looking at how food can be used as a means of exploring male–female (and female–female) relations. She sees men's and women's obligations as being defined mainly in terms of food, since women have a theoretical right to be kept by men all their lives, and their own obligations are often structured around food preparation. When men were absent from the household, women's meals and their daily routine changed dramatically. In addition, the refusal to prepare food is an essential weapon in every married woman's armoury, while cooperative cooking cements friendship among women. The author traces an analogy between men's relationship to women, and the tribesmen's to butchers, in that 'both have avenues of action open to them because they are supposed to be "weak" and in the positions of servers'.

580 **Changing veils: women and modernisation in North Yemen.**
Carla Makhlouf. London: Croom Helm, 1979. 103p. bibliog.

The author, an Arabic-speaking social anthropologist, carried out fieldwork in Ṣanʿāʾ in 1974 and 1976. She interviewed a representative sample of forty women, and supplemented their information by visits to as many institutions in the capital as possible. Newspaper articles, television programmes, contemporary poetry and legal texts are also used to provide the reader with a rounded portrait of the types of social change being faced by urban Yemeni women. The author summarized her findings as 'Women and social change in urban North Yemen' (in: *Women's status and fertility in the Muslim world.* Edited by James Allman. New York: London: Praeger, 1978, p. 333-47).

581 **The law, the state and socialist policies with regard to women: the case of the People's Democratic Republic of Yemen, 1967-1990.**
Maxine Molyneux. In: *Women, Islam and the state.* Edited by Deniz Kandiyoti. Basingstoke, England: Macmillan, 1991, p. 237-71.

According to Molyneux, 'this chapter examines the legal reforms introduced in Democratic Yemen, after it gained independence from Britain in 1967, and focuses on attempts to improve the juridical position of women in accordance both with its egalitarian principles, and with its commitment to the revolutionary socialist transformation of state and society'. This is a thorough and scholarly study seen from a Marxist perspective and based on field trips undertaken in 1977 and 1984. It updates the author's earlier 'Legal reform and socialist revolution in Democratic Yemen: women and family', *International Journal of the Sociology of Law,* vol. 13 (1985), p. 147-72.

582 **State policies and the position of women workers in the People's Democratic Republic of Yemen, 1967-77.**

Maxine Molyneux. Geneva, Switzerland: International Labour Office, 1982. 87p. bibliog. (Women, Work and Development, no. 3).

A survey, based on extensive fieldwork carried out in both Aden and the remoter regions of South Yemen. It covers literacy, education, family status and political participation, as well as employment; the last topic is divided into the manufacturing, agricultural and professional sectors. The text is replete with statistics, taken both from official publications and from the author's personal analysis of the home and work conditions of 120 female factory workers. The data on state policies can be supplemented by the author's 'State policy and the position of women in South-Yemen' (*Peuples Méditerranéens/Mediterranean Peoples,* vol. 12 [1980], p. 33-49), which consists mainly of interviews with three senior members of the General Union of Yemeni Women, the official woman's organization of the People's Democratic Republic of Yemen (PDRY).

583 **Women's rights and political contingency: the case of Yemen, 1990-1994.**

Maxine Molyneux. *Middle East Journal,* vol. 49, no. 3 (1995), p. 418-31.

An impressive survey of the legal changes caused by unification, with particular reference to family law. The author shows that many of the provisions of the 1974 Family Law Act of the People's Democratic Republic of Yemen, having been eroded under the last year of the socialist government, were allowed to fall into complete disuse during the transitional period (1990-94). Bride prices rose, unilateral divorce became common, and men entering into polygamous union in the South were not prosecuted. In addition, many women factory workers in Aden were dismissed. The author sees the victory of the North in the 1994 civil war as the precursor of new Islamic legislation which will further undermine women's rights, pointing out that the new constitution intended to make the *sharīʿah* (Islamic law) the basis for all leglislation, and that in 1995 all schools were to become single-sex.

584 **Women's inheritance of land in highland Yemen.**

Martha Mundy. *Arabian Studies,* vol. 5 (1979), p. 161-87.

The author bases her analysis on anthropological observation and interview, local tax records and legal judgments, and a knowledge of Islamic legal theory. What becomes clear is that most claims by women are subject to much negotiation between the male heirs and a male agent acting on the woman's behalf. The article is also illuminating on the agricultural economy of North Yemen and the landholding patterns of the communities studied.

585 **Women and development in Yemen Arab Republic.**
Cynthia Myntti. Eschborn, Germany: German Agency for Technical Cooperation, 1979. 169p. bibliog.

An extensive survey of North Yemeni women, which looks at their work and social roles, the organization of the household, education, health and the legal institutions affecting women, such as marriage, divorce, inheritance and bride-money. The author has based her information on fieldwork, official publications, and a wide variety of developmental reports prepared for international aid organizations. The author goes on to evaluate how women can participate in and profit from development projects (a number of which are singled out for comment), and the book concludes with a complete translation of the provisions of the YAR (Yemen Arab Republic) Labour Law of 1970 and the YAR Family Law of 1978.

586 **Women, work, population and development in the Yemen Arab Republic.**
Cynthia Myntti. In: *Women, employment and development in the Arab world.* Edited by Julinda Abu Nasr, Nabil F. Khoury, Henry T. Azzam. Berlin: Mouton Publishers, 1985, p. 39-59. (New Babylon: Studies in the Social Sciences, no. 41).

A straighforward survey of women's employment in North Yemen, based on the 1975 census and subsequent legislation. The author found that ninety per cent of women lived in rural areas, and, although only two per cent of them were literate, they performed a crucial, albeit unwaged role in the agricultural economy. In the three major towns of Ṣanʿāʾ, Taʿizz and Hodeida, on the other hand, only four per cent of the total labour force were female, of which by far the highest group was cleaners and street sweepers, occupations performed exclusively by the *akhdām,* one of the lowest social classes in North Yemen.

587 **Rasūlid women: power and patronage.**
Noha Sadek. *Proceedings of the Seminar for Arabian Studies,* vol. 19 (1989), p. 121-36.

Based on part of her 1990 PhD dissertation at the University of Toronto (*Patronage and architecture in Rasūlīd Yemen 626-858 A. H./1229-1454 A. D.)* the first half of this short article looks at references to women of the ruling classes during the Rasūlid period (1229-1454). The author is able to establish that women participated in political decisions and that they were often financially independent. The second half of the article looks at their role as patrons of architecture, and pays particular attention to one building in Taʿizz, the *madrasah* (teaching mosque) al-Muʿtabīyah, which was built by Jihat Jamāl al-Dīn Muʿtab (d. 1393), the wife of Sultan al-Ashraf Ismāʿīl (d. 1400) and mother of his successor al-Nāṣir Aḥmad (d. 1424).

588 **Yemenite women: employment and future challenges.**
Thaira A. Shaalan. In: *Women of the Arab world: the coming challenge: the papers of the Arab Women's Solidarity Association Conference.* Edited by Nahid Toubia, translated by Nahed El Gamal. London: Zed Books, 1988, p. 117-23.

Using the censuses of 1975 and 1986, along with other statistical material, the author examines the participation of women in the civil service and in agricultural production in North Yemen. She shows that, despite the existence of egalitarian labour laws, fewer than twelve per cent of the civil service workforce was composed of women in 1983. In agriculture, on the other hand, women formed the bulk of the workforce, but had little or no say in decision-making.

589 **Inheritance rights of Jewish women and Moslem women in Yemen.** Yosef Tobi. *Proceedings of the Seminar for Arabian Studies,* vol. 24 (1994), p. 201-8.

Using court records, the author traces the influence of Islamic law on Jewish women's inheritance in North Yemen. In both Islam and Judaism, he finds a conflict between the different law codes, with the *halakha* (Jewish law) 'discriminating against women, as opposed to Islamic law, which favoured them'. However, 'among the Moslems, the tendency was to follow the *ʿurf* (customary law) and not the rules of the *sharīʿa* (Islamic law), but where the Imam Yaḥyā (d. 1948) wielded most power, the *sharīʿa* overshadowed the *ʿurf.* In contrast, even though the tendency among the Jews was to follow the *halakha,* the Imam's policy toward the Jews was a liberal one and he did not try to force Islamic law on them'. This is an important study, not only of the theoretical aspects of women's rights in Yemen, but, more importantly, of the neglected subject of the actual practice of courts and families alike.

Yemen – zwischen Reisebeschreibung und Feldforschung . . . (Yemen – between travel narrative and field study . . .)
See item no. 104.

Eduard Glaser – Forschungen im Yemen . . . (Eduard Glaser – explorations in Yemen . . .)
See item no. 124.

Some features of social structure in Saba.
See item no. 285.

Women of the *zār* and middle-class sensibilities in colonial Aden, 1923-1932.
See item no. 689.

Muslim women throughout the world: a bibliography.
See item no. 927.

Cultural anthropology of the Middle East: a bibliography.
See item no. 936.

Social Services, Health and Welfare

590 **Feeding patterns, growth and mortality among pre-school children in PDR Yemen.**
Gunnel Bågenholm. Gothenburg, Sweden: Department of Pediatrics, Gothenburg University, 1988. 66p. bibliog.

An investigation into the feeding patterns of over 3,000 children below the age of seven, chosen from all parts of Aden city and surrounding villages. The conclusions are that bottle-feeding was used from an early age in all levels of the sample, that the infant, child and under-five mortality rates were high and that muscle and fat stores of the sample children were small compared with the control group. The author's report is followed by the text of two unpublished studies on infant mortality and child tissue depletion in South Yemen by Gunnel Bågenholm and A. A. A. Nashir, and reproductions of three articles, previously published in 1987 and 1988, by Gunnel Bågenholm, A. A. A. Nashir and K. Kristiansson on child feeding habits and malnutrition in South Yemen.

591 **Infant feeding in the Yemen Arab Republic.**
James Firebrace. London: Catholic Institute for International Relations, 1981. 47p.

An expanded and updated version of the author's *Imported milk powders and bottle feeding: the evidence from the Yemen Arab Republic* (Geneva, Switzerland: World Health Organization, 1979), this short study looks at the reasons behind the rise in use of infant formulas and milk powders, and recommends action to be taken against the practice. The author shows how direct and indirect promotional methods by European companies have changed mothers' attitudes to breast-feeding, leading to the exacerbation of 'Yemen's already severe problems of infant malnutrition'.

592 **Contraception, marital fertility, and breast-feeding in the Yemen Arab Republic.**
H. J. Goldberg (et al.). *Journal of Biosocial Science,* vol. 15 (1983), p. 67-82.

The information contained in this extensive survey comes from the Yemen Arab Republic National Nutrition Survey of 1979, sponsored by the World Bank, USAID and the government of Yemen. Households were sampled in rural areas of seven of North Yemen's ten provinces and compared with data collected in Ṣanʿāʾ. The findings were that the levels of contraception in rural areas is very low (about three per cent), but considerably higher in the capital, while fertility was higher in Ṣanʿāʾ than in the villages. Infant and child mortality was high everywhere, while breast-feeding was widespread with over ninety per cent of both urban and rural children being breast-fed. One unusual piece of information to surface was that 'young female children in Ṣanʿāʾ were appreciably more likely to have been breast-fed than young male children', a trend not found in rural areas.

593 **Ambition and reality: planning for health and basic health services in the Yemen Arab Republic.**
Jens Herrmann. Frankfurt am Main, Germany: Peter Lang, 1979. 135p. bibliog. (Medizin in Entwicklungsländern, no. 2).

The first chapter examines North Yemen from a wide variety of angles: history, economics, agriculture, education and cultural patterns, while the second chapter presents a detailed analysis of the organization of the Yemeni health service, followed by a survey of morbidity patterns. The conclusions deal with the problems foreseen in the Yemen government's Basic Health Services/Primary Health Care Programme, which range from over-reliance on foreign assistance to the overburdening of health workers 'with too many tasks, functions and responsibilities'.

594 **Republic of Yemen: health sector review.**
International Bank for Reconstruction and Development. Washington, DC: World Bank, 1994. 74p. bibliog. (World Bank Country Studies).

A survey of the existing health-care system in united Yemen with recommendations for improvements. The report examines health care from the top down, although the investigating team were 'aware of problems in the public perception of medical attention', and visited at least one public health centre which dealt with only four patients during the entire day of the visit. Nevertheless, this is useful summary of official government policy, replete with statistics and charts.

595 **A baseline health study of three areas in Al Jaʿfarīyah district.**
Catherine Johnson, Marion O'Reilly, Douglas Soutar. Raymah, Yemen Arab Republic: Raymah Health Project; Ṣanʿāʾ: British Organisation for Community Development, 1985. 106p.

A report on one of several projects mounted by European, American and other governments and aid organizations to improve basic health care in both Yemens. This report, funded by Oxfam UK, was produced as a by-product of a training programme for thirteen primary health-care workers in the Raymah mountains to the south-west of

Ṣanʿāʾ, and contains a survey of 300 under-fives, and the results of a questionnaire to seventy-two women regarding infant feeding practices and nutrition. In fact, the general social information about the region, and about prevalent illnesses and traditional and non-traditional methods of treatment is particularly interesting, while the data on breast-feeding and childhood morbidity has been carefully gathered and adds to the reports of James Firebrace (see item no. 591) and Dianna Melrose (see below).

596 **The great health robbery: baby milk and medicines in Yemen.**
Dianna Melrose. Oxford, England: Oxfam, 1981. 50p.

A survey of health services in North Yemen based on data gathered through the Raymah Health Project, run by the Catholic Institute for International Relations. The author's passionate descriptions of the results of feeding babies with powdered rather than breast milk make for grim reading, as do her revelations about the amount of money spent on imported drugs. The author is not unaware of the often unreasonable expectations that Yemeni villagers have of Western medicine, but recommends action to be taken by the government of the Yemen Arab Republic, by the British government, and by ordinary members of the public.

597 **The despairing developer: diary of an aid worker in the Middle East.**
Timothy Morris. London: Tauris, 1991. 287p.

The day-to-day story of an aid worker struggling to improve primary health care in the northern regions of the Yemen Arab Republic. The author, who had a PhD in social anthropology (see item no. 546) and who had already mastered the dialect of the Tihāmah, began with high hopes, but the project gradually became bogged down in clashes between the aid workers and central government, between different aid organizations and between different groups in the region itself. In the end, no male or female health-care workers were trained, and grassroots initiatives to raise money and build health centres were discouraged by officials. Vaccines were not distributed, donated drugs were sold for profit and untrained injectionists held key posts in hospitals. Meanwhile the author and his fellow aid workers were reduced to an endless round of paperwork and analyses of 'objectives', while the agency in London produced glossy annual reports describing the continued success of the project. A briefer but no less damning account of the author's experiences is given in 'Eze-vu success through evaluation: lessons from a primary health-care project in North Yemen', in *Practising development: social science perspectives.* Edited by Johan Pottier. London: Routledge, 1993, p. 205-15. A similar clash in objectives is recounted by Charles F. Swagman (see item no. 560).

598 **Breastfeeding patterns and promotion of infant formula in the Republic of Yemen.**
Abdulrahman O. Musaiger. *Journal of Tropical Paediatrics,* vol. 39, no. 1 (1993), p. 59-64.

A substantial but by no means complete literature review on the subject of breast-feeding in both North and South Yemen. The author establishes that the first researches were carried out in the early 1970s and have continued ever since. Research shows that, over the past twenty years, there has been a marked decline in breast-feeding, widespread adoption of infant formulas, and disagreement over the most appropriate age at which to introduce babies to solid food.

599 **Hegemony and healing in rural North Yemen.**
Cynthia Myntti. *Social Science and Medicine,* vol. 27, no. 5 (1988), p. 515-20.

Basing herself on research carried out in a village in the southern highlands of North Yemen, the author examines how different groups use alternative medical strategies to tackle illness. She shows how some choose the classical Arabic tradition, others folk or spiritual healing, while some prefer a Western health-care system approach, and discusses in what way the choice is dependent on affordability, knowledge, and what is considered socially appropriate.

600 **Notes on mystical healers in the Ḥugariyyah.**
Cynthia Myntti. *Arabian Studies,* vol. 8 (1990), p. 171-6.

A brief study of the way in which mystical healers gain access to extra-human powers through their unique relationship with the *jinn.* The author describes cases from the Ḥujarīyah district in North Yemen, giving examples of both the *Ṣāḥib al-Kitāb,* who had acquired the power to heal through his literacy, and the *Majnūn,* who was said to have lived for seven years in a cave inhabited by *jinn,* and to have taken a *jinniyah* bride.

601 **Social determinants of child health in Yemen.**
Cynthia Myntti. *Social Science and Medicine,* vol. 37, no. 2 (1993), p. 233-40.

The author conducted research in a village in the southern highlands of North Yemen between 1988 and 1989, to determine why a minority of the families there carried most of the burden of child illness and death. She used quantitative measures to map child health in conjunction with the resident doctor and nurses, and in this article she describes five case-studies. She found that the survey and the structured interviews failed to offer clues as to why separate groups of women should have such different experiences regarding the health of their children, but suggests that 'it is the interaction of chronic economic problems, social isolation and a mother's inability to cope – the psychological dimension – that has a negative effect on child health'.

602 **Field data on folk medicine from the Hadramawt.**
Mikhail Rodionov. *Proceedings of the Seminar for Arabian Studies,* vol. 26 (1996), p. 125-33.

The author has studied both the oral and the written traditions on medicine in Hadramawt, and finds 'that there is no clear-cut opposition between the oral and the written discourse, the two being interdependent and complementary'. He discovered more than a dozen medical manuscripts in various Ḥaḍramī archives, and found that many of his informants had more than a vague notion of their contents. However, the 'first medicine' is not drugs or surgery, but rather magico-therapeutic formulae, supplemented by dietary stimulants like honey, goat-meat broth and the fresh juice of aloes. Blood-letting is also practised extensively but cauterization is known as the 'last medicine'.

603 **Die Nata'iğ al-fikar des Šaʿbān ibn Sālim aṣ-Ṣanʿānī: eine jemenitische Gesundheitsfibel aus dem frühen 18. Jahrhundert.** (The Natā'ij al-fikar of Shaʿbān ibn Sālim al-Ṣanʿānī: a Yemeni health primer from the early 18th century.)
Shaʿbān ibn Sālim al-Ṣanʿānī (1655-1736). Edited and translated into German by Armin Schopen, Oliver Kahl. Wiesbaden, Germany: Harrassowitz, 1993. 365p. bibliog.

The coffee trade brought considerable wealth to North Yemen in the 18th century, and brought into relief the significant agricultural resources of the country. This work is an edition of a lengthy Arabic poem, with German translation, introduction, and notes. The poem itself deals with forty-four different products which had medicinal uses, such as grapes, sesame and rice, and describes their cultivation and their use for cooking and for health. The poem also deals with the seasons, eating and drinking in general, sleeping and waking and physical activities, and gives a fascinating insight into Yemeni culture of the period.

604 **Traditionelle Heilmittel in Jemen.** (Traditional medicines in Yemen.)
Armin Schopen. Wiesbaden, Germany: Steiner, 1983. 256p. map. bibliog.

A list of all the *materia medica* which the author could find during field researches in North Yemen in 1978 and 1979. The drugs and plants are arranged in a single list according to the order of the Arabic alphabet and under each item, the botanical name is given, followed by the German equivalent, the place(s) where the drug is found, how and for what purpose it is used, and any references to the drug in the classical Arab pharmacologies. This list is followed by a collection of thirty complex remedies, giving their constituents and their use.

605 **Aloe and dragon's blood: some medicinal and traditional uses on the island of Socotra.**
Marie-Claude Siméone-Senelle. *New Arabian Studies,* vol. 2 (1994), p. 186-98.

The author, who participated in several French expeditions to Socotra, describes the medicinal use of the various kinds of aloe found on Socotra, and of the resin of the famous Dragon's Blood tree. In a similar article in French, 'Magie et pratiques thérapeutiques dans l'île de Soqotra: le médecin-guérisseur' (Magic and therapeutic practices on the island of Socotra: the medicine-man) (*Proceedings of the Seminar for Arabian Studies,* vol. 25 [1995], p. 117-26), she discusses different kinds of herbal drugs, various pseudo-surgical interventions like blood-letting and cauterization, and the use of magic (which, under official prohibition, is gradually disappearing from use) for medicinal purposes. For this study, the author makes use of ethnographic and linguistic texts collected by earlier travellers (notably David Heinrich Müller [q.v.]), as well as personal research.

606 **Fija': fright and illness in Highland Yemen.**
Charles F. Swagman. *Social Science and Medicine,* vol. 28, no. 4, (1989), p. 381-8.

The author examines the occurrence of *fija',* or illness consequent on a sudden fright, within the tradition of folk medicine in North Yemen. Assessing six separate cases, he concludes that men are much less liable to complain of *fija'* than women, because they are much more exposed to alternative traditions, and because the idea of succumbing to illness as a result of fright contradicts the male ideal of the courageous tribesman.

607 **Health problems of Yemen and its populations: a bibliographic review.**
Michel C. Thuriaux. Coconut Grove, Florida: Field Research Projects, 1983. 145p.

An extremely thorough survey of the literature of health, illness, medicine and disease as it relates to North Yemen. The work is divided, firstly, into a bibliographical survey of the various diseases prevalent in Yemen – such as schistosomiasis, leprosy, malaria, and more general disorders of various organs – as well as chapters on demography, *qāt*, animal bites and stings, and health services, and, secondly, an alphabetical list of all the references, which cover Western European languages, Russian, and a few books and articles in Hebrew and Arabic.

608 **Cultural change, growth and feeding of children in an isolated rural region of Yemen.**
Peter Underwood, Barrie Margetts. *Social Science and Medicine,* vol. 25, no. 1 (1987), p. 1-7.

Two Australian health professionals studied the growth and feeding patterns of children from Raymah, a mountainous region, south-west of Ṣanʿāʾ in North Yemen. They examined 318 children and found that children from the small town of al-Jabīn grew more poorly and had a higher mortality than those from the immediate rural hinterland. The authors hypothesize that 'the continuation of increasing availability of milks and bottles [in towns] and the changing social roles and activities of urban women' led to less breast-feeding in towns and consequently, poorer infant health. Only 7.5 per cent of rural children suffered from marasma, in contradistinction to 28 per cent found in al-Jabīn. In general, however, infections and malnutrition were widespread throughout the region.

609 **New spells for old: expectations and realities of Western medicine in a remote tribal village in Yemen, Arabia.**
Peter Underwood, Zdenka Underwood. In: *Changing disease patterns and human behaviour.* Edited by N. F. Stanley, R. A. Joske. London: Academic Press, 1980, p. 271-97.

For many Yemenis, their first contact with Western medicine is through the *ṣāḥī,* an untrained practitioner, whose one qualification is his ability to give an injection. The authors investigate this frightening phenomenon, which they link to the local belief in the external causation of disease, and conclude that the Western cure-oriented intervention by the *ṣāḥīs* is positively harmful, because it can do nothing to prevent disease and masks the real causes. Since traditional medicine in the town in the highlands of North Yemen where they conducted their survey, 'enjoys neither special prestige or great popularity', the authors suggest training the *ṣāḥīs* in primary health care, particularly the importance of nutrition and immunization, which they see as the key to improving health standards in the Yemen. They consider direct attempts to introduce Western preventive medicine, thus ignoring the local cultural factors, as doomed to failure.

610 **Impact of selected macroeconomic and social policies on poverty: the case of Egypt, Jordan and the Republic of Yemen.**
United Nations Economic and Social Commission for Western Asia. New York: ESCWA, 1995. 140p. bibliog.

This report looks in considerable detail at the incidence and determinants of poverty, at food security and the poor, and at other basic needs of the poor in three Arab states, including Yemen. It concludes with an analysis of the impact of the current economic reform programmes, at housing, health, education, population and human resources, and at agricultural and food subsidies, which are all considered in depth, and with the aid of the latest statistics. The recommendations in the case of Yemen are for a safety net for the poor covering food and basic needs, an improved human resources base, and continuing basic health services, but restricted to the lowest-income groups.

611 **Evolution of rational drug prescribing in Democratic Yemen.**
Godfrey J. A. Walker (et al.). *Social Science and Medicine,* vol. 31, no. 7 (1990), p. 823-8.

The government of the People's Democratic Republic of Yemen began an essential drugs programme in 1984, whereby every month quantities of thirty separate drugs were delivered in pre-packed kits to health units and standard treatment schedules were agreed. This article evaluates the programme and finds that the health workers at the units prescribed drugs more rationally than at health centres and hospitals, where patients often received irrational types and quantities of drugs.

A French doctor in the Yemen.
See item no. 160.

Le Yémen: pays de la Reine de Saba. (Yemen: the country of the Queen of Sheba.)
See item no. 193.

Repertory of drugs and medicinal plants of Yemen.
See item no. 201.

Fertility, mortality, migration and family planning in the Yemen Arab Republic.
See item no. 414.

Politics

North Yemen (Yemen Arab Republic)

612 **Prelude to unification: the Yemen Arab Republic, 1962-1990.**
Robert D. Burrowes. *International Journal of Middle East Studies,* vol. 23 (1991), p. 483-506.

The author analyses the moves towards state-building achieved by the Yemen Arab Republic (YAR) over the past twenty-five years. Numerous problems beset Yemen at the end of the civil war in 1969: a distortion of the relationship between the tribes and the government; a lack of administrative capacity; and a disorganized army. After a tentative start, real progress towards a strong state was achieved by President ʿAlī ʿAbd Allāh Ṣāliḥ through the creation of the General People's Congress, which broadened the base for popular participation in the regime.The author goes on to discuss the 1970 constitution, socio-economic developments, and the recent relationship between the YAR and the People's Democratic Republic of Yemen (PDRY).

613 **State-building and political construction in the Yemen Arab Republic, 1962-1977.**
Robert D. Burrowes. In: *Ideology and power in the Middle East: Studies in Honor of George Lenczowski.* Edited by Peter J. Chelkowski, Robert J. Pranger. Durham, North Carolina: Duke University Press, 1988, p. 210-38.

This is mainly a narrative study of the achievements of President ʿAbd al-Raḥmān al-Iryānī, whose rule from 1967 to 1974 was marked by a return to traditional and tribal Yemeni values, and by the drafting of the 1970 constitution, and of President Ibrāhīm Muḥammad al-Ḥamdī, who fostered the development work begun by his predecessor, re-organized and re-equipped the armed forces, and continued the reform of the political system.

614 **The Yemen Arab Republic: the politics of development, 1962-1986.**
Robert D. Burrowes. Boulder, Colorado: Westview Press; London: Croom Helm, 1987. 173p. maps.

In this book, Burrowes is able to examine in much more depth the concerns over socio-economic development and state-building, which he has dealt with in his articles (see above). In addition, he examines closely the regime's administrative reforms, its foreign policy, and its economic problems, some of the latter alleviated by the discovery of oil in early 1984. Most of the data are based on original sources such as radio broadcasts, newspaper reports and interviews with leading politicians.

615 **The Yemen Arab Republic's legacy and Yemeni unification.**
Robert D. Burrowes. *Arab Studies Quarterly,* vol. 14, no. 4 (1992), p. 41-68.

In the first part of this paper, the author covers much of the same ground as he did in his 1991 article (see item no. 612). In the second part, he describes the steps to unification taken by the leaders of the two Yemens, and analyses the capacity of the unified state to make and carry out public policy in the economic, military and social spheres.

616 **Autonomy and secondhand oil dependency of the Yemen Arab Republic.**
Sheila Carapico. *Arab Studies Quarterly,* vol. 10. no. 2 (1988), p. 193-213.

The author analyses the changes which have taken place in the political and social structure of the YAR from a socialist point of view and with the assistance of dependency theory. She finds that the dependence of the Yemen economy on the export of labour and the resulting remittances has led to a centralization of political authority, to the dominance of the bourgeois class, and to the government's encouragement of private capital to finance new, productive enterprises.

617 **Imams and tribes: the writing and acting of history in Upper Yemen.**
Paul Dresch. In: *Tribes and state formation in the Middle East.* Edited by Philip S. Khoury, Joseph Kostiner. London: Tauris, 1991, p. 252-87.

A sophisticated study of the role of the tribe inside a wider political society with examples taken from the northern part of the Yemen Arab Republic over a long historical perspective. The author relates tribes to the Zaydī state, especially to the concept of the 'just imam', as well as to non-Zaydī dynasties like the Rasūlids (1229-1454), concentrating on ideas of legitimacy and state formation. He goes on to look at the Qāsimī dynasty which held power from the seventeenth to the nineteenth centuries and finishes by an examination of the nation-state in Yemen in the 1970s. Throughout the article, the author warns of the dangers of using Western concepts of the state to analyse the Yemeni model, and he pays particular attention to the very terms used to define the concepts themselves, words such as *dawlah* and *ummah.*

618 **Yemen: the search for a modern state.**
J. E. Peterson. London: Croom Helm, 1982. 221p. bibliog.

An analysis of the shape of North Yemeni politics since the departure of the Ottomans in 1919. The book is stronger in its analysis of the politics of the Imamate, than for the period of republican rule which is presented in a rather fragmentary fashion, although the author's understanding of development issues is a strong point.

619 **Yemen: traditionalism vs. modernity.**
Mohammed Ahmad Zabarah. New York: Praeger, 1982. 154p. bibliog.

The author divides his study into four sections: the isolationist era before 1948, which is examined in terms of the historical factors which influenced the imamate regime to adopt an isolationist policy; the focus during the transitional period of Imam Aḥmad up to 1962 is on the influx of modern ideas, especially those generated by Arab nationalism; during the civil war period (1962-70), the author studies the effects of the involvement of external powers; while the fourth part evaluates the recent socio-economic and political changes under the new republican government. This work is a convenient overview of developments in the political structure of North Yemen since 1920, but its analysis should have been much sharper and more critical.

South Yemen (People's Democratic Republic of Yemen)

620 **The People's Democratic Republic of Yemen: the transformation of society.**
Ziad Mahmoud Abu-Amr. PhD dissertation, Georgetown University, 1986. 252p. (Available from University Microfilms International, Ann Arbor, Michigan, order no. 8726450).

This is a detailed description of the political programme of what at the time was the only Marxist state in the Middle East. The author describes the legacy of the British (here the influence of Fred Halliday [q.v.] is very evident), and discusses both the various political groups formed by Arabs during the period of British rule, and the parties which emerged on independence. He goes on to identify the areas where the government planned to change society, but is reliant on official statistics and plans to prove his case. Perhaps the most interesting chapter of the thesis is the last, which analyses the reasons why the PDRY chose a Marxist line and why they stuck to it.

621 **Südjemen – Kampf um einen progresiven Entwicklungsweg.** (South Yemen: the struggle for a progressive path to development.)
Armin Börner, Mario Kessler, Muḥammad as-Suhari. In: *Die Araber an der Wende zum 21. Jahrhundert: Studien zu Evolution und Revolution in Nordafrika und Nahost.* (The Arabs at the turn of the 21st century: studies in evolution and revolution in North Africa and the Middle East.) Edited by Günter Barthel, Helmut Nimschowski. Berlin: Akademie-Verlag, 1987, p. 223-37.

Interesting in its strict application of Marxist ideology to the political formation of the People's Democratic Republic of Yemen. The authors begin with the nationalist struggle against the British, before surveying the first decade of independence. Although the authors point out many of the difficulties faced by the regime in its attempt to transform society and the economy along communist lines, they still maintain that 'it is possible to motivate and mobilize the workforce to strive for social goals', a claim which history has shown to be unrealizable, at least for South Yemen.

622 **The politics of stratification; a study of political change in a South Arabian town.**
Abdalla S. Bujra. Oxford, England: Clarendon Press, 1971. 201p. map. bibliog.

An excellent anthropo-political field study of a particular family (the ʿAṭṭas) and their role in the small Ḥaḍramī town of Ḥurayḍah, near Shibām. The work looks at the religious status of the ʿAṭṭas, their domination of local education, and their administrative and legal role, especially the expansion of their power through the local council. It also studies kinship ties, marriage and mobility, economic (particularly agricultural) organization and the distribution of wealth, and concludes with an analysis of political alignments in 'the expanding ideological arena of 1960-63'.

623 **Oil strike and leadership struggle in South Yemen: 1986 and beyond.**
Robert D. Burrowes. *Middle East Journal,* vol. 43, no. 3 (1989), p. 437-54.

An interesting and informative analysis of events in South Yemen between 1986 and 1988, concentrating on plans to begin oil production in the Shabwah field with Russian help; on relations with North Yemen, and on the political effects of the leadership struggle in 1986, after which 'by one count some fifty of the roughly seventy-five members of the Yemeni Socialist Party Central Committee – most of a core of a generation of leaders used to working together and running the country – were dead, wounded, missing, jailed or in exile'.

624 **Islam and the state in South Yemen: the uneasy co-existence.**
Norman Cigar. *Middle Eastern Studies,* vol. 26, no. 2 (1990), p. 185-203.

Basing himself mainly on local newspapers, the author has attempted to define the attitude of the South Yemen government towards Islam, showing how the state has 'been careful to ensure its continuing control over the clerics and to monitor religious expression' and to assess the impact on the state of what the author calls Islamic revivalism. He demonstrates how the regime and the revivalists are opposed on many key issues, and considers that the revivalists are much better placed than the regime to win the hearts and minds of the traditional Muslims, particularly young people, who make up by far the largest proportion of the population.

625 **State and society in South Yemen.**
Norman Cigar. *Problems of Communism,* vol. 34, no. 3 (1985), p. 41-58.

The author looks at how the government of the People's Democratic Republic of Yemen is confronting several issues in its attempt to restructure society: social groups, including tribes; religious groups; the family; women; youth; and culture. He claims that in pursuing its plans to transform society, the government has relied primarily on three tools: education, the YSP (the Yemeni Socialist Party, the only legal forum for political activity) and the state's administrative machinery, including the mass organizations, but that 'social transformation has not been noticeably more rapid in the PDRY than elsewhere in the Arab world; in some respects . . . South Yemen's society, with the exception of Aden, is still more "traditional" than that in some of the other Arab states'.

626 **Radical political ideologies and concepts of property in Libya and South Yemen.**
Marius Deeb. *Middle East Journal,* vol. 40, no. 3 (1986), p. 445-61.

The author examines the social basis of the National Liberation Front of South Yemen and its ideological roots. He contrasts the Party's attitude towards the ownership of agricultural land – favouring cooperatives but not outlawing privately owned farms of limited size – with that of al-Qadhdhāfī's Libya, which supported personal and 'socialist' property. He also looks at South Yemen's business nationalization plan, when the incorporation of thirty-six private enterprises into the state in 1969 led to the flight of capital, the emigration of merchants and businessmen, and rising unemployment. The author sees the radical ideology of South Yemen as unlikely to last long 'because of the lack of a socio-economic basis necessary for it to be relevant to South Yemenite society'.

627 **Catastrophe in South Yemen.**
Fred Halliday. *Middle East Report,* no. 139 (1986), p. 37-9.

A brief but trenchant analysis of the causes of the civil war which devastated the People's Democratic Republic of Yemen in January 1986, resulting in the deaths of thousands of people. Halliday looks at the course of both Yemeni policies and Yemeni political manoeuvrings since independence in 1967, and concludes that the civil war was largely a self-inflicted catastrophe. 'The South Yemeni crisis is another case of that broader political problem of highly centralized political systems in socialist states where politics is very much confined within the leadership and all sorts of disagreements can expand and acquire an explosive potential out of all proportion to their substantive significance. Conflicts then spill over into wider circles of highly politicized but inexperienced and undisciplined youth, who quickly escalate the struggle'.

628 **Yemen's unfinished revolution: socialism in the South.**
Fred Halliday. *MERIP Reports,* no. 81 (1979), p. 3-20.

The author describes the economic and social problems confronting the government of the People's Republic on gaining independence from Britain in 1967, and analyses the progress made since then. He considers that the PDRY is the only Arab country where an 'incontestable' social revolution has taken place, mainly by socializing the means of production and 'the outright expropriation of the indigenous landowners and bourgeoisie'. He looks at the government's economic achievements (and its failures, such as the bank nationalization of 1969), examines the social transformation in detail, and describes the changes in the party machinery and political structure. Finally, he discusses regional relations and the factional fighting which resulted in the execution of President Sālim Rubayʿ ʿAlī in 1978.

629 **The People's Democratic Republic of Yemen: politics, economics and society: the politics of socialist transformation.**
Tareq Y. Ismael, Jacqueline S. Ismael. London: Pinter, 1986. 183p. map. bibliog. (Marxist Regimes Series).

Basing themselves on newspaper reports, studies from international organizations such as the United Nations, the World Bank, and the Food and Agriculture Organization, and a small number of secondary works, the authors give a lucid description of the first ten years of independence in the PDRY. The book discusses the structure of government, the ruling party, and economic, social and foreign policy. The authors agree with Halliday (see above), that the government has succeeded in 'the transformation of the institutions of the state into a socialist structure', but that 'a precarious balance exists between domestic and foreign policy that results from the potential tensions of revolutionary commitment versus internal development'.

630 **Arab radical politics: al-Qawmiyyun al-Arab and the Marxists in the turmoil of South Yemen, 1963-1967.**
Joseph Kostiner. *Middle Eastern Studies,* vol. 17, no. 4 (1981), p. 454-77.

Having described how, at the beginning of the 1960s, Aden had both established political parties and a well-organized trade union movement, the author goes on to discuss *al-Qawmīyūn al-ʿArab,* a radical pan-Arab movement, which opened its first branches in both North and South Yemen in 1956. Originally a Palestinian student political group, 'the movement was characterised by student leadership, support of Palestinian communities, recruitment of local elements and penetration into local societies'. Disputing radical leadership with the Communists and the Baʿth Party, *al-Qawmīyūn al-ʿArab* was active in the National Liberation Front (NLF), whose declared aim was 'to promote struggle, embracing and uniting all the national forces in the South'. The author also sees the organization initially as carrying out their activities in support of Nasserist aims. However, he criticizes the movement as failing in the fields of strategy and propaganda, and at making no effort to widen participation and power-sharing with the masses. As a result, a crisis developed in the NLF, and between 1965 and 1967, the leaders of *al-Qawmīyūn al-ʿArab* faction were gradually ousted in favour of a more Marxist and anti-Nasserist grouping, which came to constitute the basis for South Yemen's first independent government.

631 **The struggle for South Yemen.**

Joseph Kostiner. London: Croom Helm, 1984. 195p. maps. bibliog.

This work is a much more detailed version of the article above on *al-Qawmīyūn al-ʿArab* (q.v.), both being based on the author's MA thesis at the University of Haifa. This book concentrates on the activities of the National Liberation Front (NLF) and its rivals between 1963 and 1967, and shows how the NLF triumphed over *al-Qawmīyūn al-ʿArab* and the Front for the Liberation of Occupied South Yemen (FLOSY).

632 **P. D. R. Yemen: outpost of socialist development in Arabia.**

Helen Lackner. London: Ithaca Press, 1985. 219p. maps. bibliog.

Basing herself mainly on the daily reports of the Aden News Agency and the official publications of both the government and the ruling party, the author has produced a detailed, factual, but somewhat uncritical analysis of recent political, economic and social developments in independent South Yemen.

633 **Moscow and Aden: coping with a coup.**

David Pollock. *Problems of Communism,* vol. 35, no. 3 (May-June 1986), p. 50-70.

The South Yemeni crisis of early 1986, as Head of State ʿAlī Nāṣir Muḥammad was forced into exile, is here put under the microscope. With the help of extensive press reports, the author considers both why the President fell, and what the complexion of the new government will be, but the real focus of his article is the Soviet reaction to the coup, and the regional repercussions resulting from it.

634 **Marxism in Arabia: South Yemen twenty years after independence.**

Volker Stanzel. *Aussenpolitik,* vol. 39, no. 3 (1988), p. 265-77.

An interesting analysis by a former West German chargé d'affaires in Aden of the PDRY's political and economic development. Stanzel finds there to be a considerable discrepancy between political objectives and actual achievements since a Marxist political superstructure governs a private sector which accounts for fifty per cent of the Gross Domestic Product (GDP), a third of the employed male population consists of economic migrants, and the social and religious structure has hardly changed since pre-independence days. Progress has been made in some fields, particularly education and health care, but the author questions whether these are directly attributable to the ideological programme of the government.

635 **Ideology versus pragmatism in South Yemen, 1968-1986.**

Manfred W. Wenner. In: *Ideology and power in the Middle East: Studies in Honor of George Lenczowski.* Edited by Peter J. Chelkowski, Robert J. Pranger. Durham, North Carolina: Duke University Press, 1988, p. 259-73.

The author identifies a number of marked changes in the government's views since 1967, paying particular attention to the crises of 1978, when Sālim Rubayʿ ʿAlī was executed, and 1986, when Head of State ʿAlī Nāṣir Muḥammad was forced into exile.

Unified Yemen (Republic of Yemen)

636 **Yemen: another case of unification.**
Ursula Braun. *Aussenpolitik,* vol. 43 (1992), p. 174-84.

The author surveys the situation in the united Yemen of 1991 from the points of view of the new constitution, administrative and political reform, economic prospects and the aftermath of the Gulf War of 1990-91. She sees grave problems ahead both in the resentment felt by many Southerners over what they perceive to be an unequal division of resources, and in the tribal and religious structure of the North which seems impervious to change. Her article appears to be based on Western newspaper reports rather than fieldwork or interviews.

637 **Elections and mass politics in Yemen.**
Sheila Carapico. *Midde East Report,* no. 185 (1993), p. 2-6.

The author looks at the political conditions which led to the elections, at the general state of party politics in the unified country, at the involvement of the United States in the elections, and at post-election developments. In the same issue of the journal, 'The Yemeni elections close up' (p. 8-12), Renaud Detalle studies how the elections were actually conducted on the ground, and at what the future holds for the opposition parties.

638 **From ballot box to battlefield: the war of the two ʿAlis.**
Sheila Carapico. *Middle East Report,* no. 190 (1994), p. 24-7.

An open and honest article analysing the reasons why united Yemen degenerated into civil war in 1994. In the author's words, 'in the end, it boiled down to both military leaderships' rejection of pluralism and dialogue. Simply put, each side wanted its maximum domain'. The author shows how both North and South supported the National Dialogue Committee of Political Forces officially, but how its recommendations were ignored in practice, particularly by the military element and by *al-Iṣlāḥ's* Islamist ideologue, ʿAbd al-Majīd al-Zindānī. The intransigence of both sides was supported by Saudi Arabia, which was ready to back anyone willing to break up the new unity and the democratic political structure.

639 **Yemen between civility and civil war.**
Sheila Carapico. In: *Civil society in the Middle East.* Edited by Augustus Richard Norton. Leiden, The Netherlands: Brill, 1996, vol. 2, p. 287-316.

A first-rate piece of primary research on the dynamics of pluralism between the formal declaration of unity in 1990 and the outbreak of the civil war in 1994. The author looks at relationships between the tribes and central government, the religious organizations, especially *al-Iṣlāḥ,* welfare and regional organizations, and formal civic organizations, such as those in the field of human rights or cultural affairs. The main stratagems used to defuse tensions were conferences (tribal, religious and others), the press – which became much freer – and the creation of a National Dialogue Committee in 1993. The author concludes that despite complaints from Yemeni intellectuals that 'by and large there was no civil society in Yemen' only freedom of speech, 'the evidence illuminates a civil-society-in-the-making', and she is cautiously optimistic about 'the protection of society from the arbitrary abuses of state power and the creation of an autonomous space for political expression'.

640 **Yémen: les élections législatives du 27 avril, 1993.** (Yemen: the general election of 27 April 1993.)
Renaud Detalle. *Monde Arabe/Maghreb Machrek,* no. 141 (July-Aug. 1993), p. 3-26.

A detailed and knowledgeable survey of the political manoeuvrings preceding the elections of 1993, although the author's prediction that 'the country will remain en route to a careful democratization and one without risk for the current élite' proved to be misfounded. Nevertheless, this is still the best guide to the course and results of the first-ever democratic election campaign to be held in the Arabian Peninsula.

641 **A daily plebiscite: nation and state in Yemen.**
Paul Dresch. *Revue du Monde Musulman et de la Méditerranée,* no. 67 (1993), p. 67-77.

A brief article, emphasizing the complex nature of Yemeni society, and discussing the difficulty of defining a state in a Yemeni context. The author also analyses the relationship between government, political power, tribalism and regionalism.

642 **Stereotypes and political styles: Islamists and tribesfolk in Yemen.**
Paul Dresch, Bernard Haykel. *International Journal of Middle East Studies,* vol. 27, no. 4 (1995), p. 405-31.

A detailed study of the *al-Iṣlāḥ* party, which performed well in the 1993 elections, winning over sixty seats. The authors look at the 'rhetorical axes which define Iṣlāḥ', by studying the views expressed by its leaders in interviews and speeches, and by attempting to analyse the party's appeal among Yemenis. They conclude that it is more a party of the establishment centre than a radical or fundamentalist one, but that its public identity 'depends on terms and arguments centered elsewhere than Yemen and they misrepresent, to many Yemenis as to others, what is happening'. This is a sophisticated piece of linguistic and socio-political analysis.

643 **The unification of Yemen: process, politics, and prospects.**
Charles Dunbar. *Middle East Journal,* vol. 46, no. 3 (1992), p. 456-76.

The author, who was US ambassador to the Yemen Arab Republic from 1988 to 1990, and to unified Yemen from 1990 to 1991, was in a unique position to observe the political dynamics of the unification process and to gauge its success. He identifies key issues in creating the climate for unification as being the dysfunctional economy of South Yemen, and the accommodation achieved in the North between tribe and state. He sees the economic pressure caused by returnees from Saudi Arabia after the Gulf War of 1990-91 as the greatest threat to the new unified regime, along with poor Saudi–Yemeni relations, but he concludes, 'it is hard to conceive of any set of circumstances that would produce significant pressure for north and south to separate'.

644 **The wrong place, the wrong time: why Yemeni unity failed.**
Michael C. Dunn. *Middle East Policy,* vol. 3, no. 2 (1994), p. 148-56.

A senior American analyst gives nine reasons why the Yemeni unification of 1990 led to civil war in 1994. He suggests that the Yemeni authorities proceeded too fast, ignored regional differences, and relied on the pre-unity leadership, which resulted in an unworkable coalition. He emphasizes the failure to unite the two armies as a key factor, and proposes a federal structure as the system best suited to reconciling political hostility between North and South.

645 **Yemeni unity: past and future.**
F. Gregory Gause. *Middle East Journal,* vol. 42, no. 1 (1988), p. 33-47.

A straightforward narrative of recent developments in both the internal politics of both Yemens and their relations with one another. On the future of Yemeni unity the author refused to be drawn, asserting on the one hand, that numerous obstacles stood in its way, notably Saudi Arabia and 'powerful tribal shaykhs in the North', but that, nonetheless, 'the commitment to Yemeni unity on both sides of the border remains strong'.

646 **The first Yemeni parliamentary elections in 1993: practising democracy.**
Iris Glosemeyer. *Orient* (Opladen, Germany), vol. 34 (1993), p. 439-51.

A detailed study of the conduct of the elections held in the Republic of Yemen in April 1993. Glosemeyer outlines the constitutional position, the electoral laws, the registration of candidates and voters, the actual procedures followed on election day, foreign observers and foreign assistance, the election results, and the problems accompanying the elections, including challenges to individual ballots and candidates. The author's report is not as dry as that produced by the National Democratic Institute for International Affairs (see item no. 657), but often focuses on problems peculiar to Yemen, such as the problems inherent in tribal constituencies and the fact that forcing voters to be photographed in order to register made it impossible for many women to participate in the electoral process.

647 **Liberalisierung und Demokratisierung in der Republik Jemen, 1990-1994: Einführung und Dokumente.** (Liberalization and democratization in the Republic of Yemen, 1990-1994: introduction and documents.)
Iris Glosemeyer. Hamburg, Germany: Deutsches Orient-Institut, 1995. 311p. bibliog. (Aktueller Informationsdienst Moderner Orient, no. 14).

The author takes us through the the growth of political participation and pluralism from the foundation of the unified Republic in 1990 to the elections of 1993 and their aftermath. Her facts and her analyses are well presented, but the main interest of the work is the detailed chronology of events during the four years of democracy, information on political parties and newspapers, and, above all, the thirty-six documents (mostly in Arabic but some in English) dealing with the new Yemeni constitution; the manifestos and other publications of the main political parties; the laws governing politics, the press and the elections; parliamentary resolutions; and newspaper reports on political meetings and other activities.

648 **Regional consequences of the conflict in Yemen: a seminar held on 28th June, 1994, by the Gulf Centre for Strategic Studies.**
Gulf Centre for Strategic Studies. London: Gulf Centre for Strategic Studies, 1994. 106p. (Contemporary Strategic Issues in the Arab Gulf).

A hastily convened seminar (the fighting in Yemen did not finish till more than a week after the Seminar had taken place), which has the value of immediacy and the drawback of lack of long-term analysis. The papers by Omar al-Hassan and John P. Cooper, discussing respectively the attempts by the Gulf Cooperation Council (GCC) and the United Nations (UN) to mediate in the dispute between North and South, are useful if cursory, while Andrew Rathmell's military analysis of the war is, again, a helpful, if interim assessment (for a full account, see the article by David Warburton [item no. 411]). The main value of the collection lies in the appendix, which contains the full text of four important documents by the GCC and the UN.

649 **Yemen: the politics of unity.**
Siobhan Hall. London: Gulf Centre for Strategic Studies, 1991. 47p. bibliog. (Contemporary Strategic Issues in the Arab Gulf).

A factual, if analytically weak account of both internal and external political developments in both Yemens from the mid-1960s to unity in 1990. The full translation of the new draft constitution in the appendix is, however, extremely useful.

650 **The third inter-Yemeni war and its consequences.**
Fred Halliday. *Asian Affairs,* vol. 26 (old series vol. 82), no. 2 (1985), p. 131-40.

A typically incisive article which sees the union of 1990 as 'the continuation of rivalry by other means, not an actual agreement to merge', and the commitment to free speech which followed union as 'a means of increasing the space for public criticism of the other side'. The author surveys briefly the history of relations between North and South, before analysing the factors behind the 1994 civil war, which he characterizes as 'a means whereby the Northern regime, seeking to offset the crisis it has provoked within the country, imposed its will on the South'. His forecast for the future of united Yemen is deeply pessimistic: 'a deepening Yemeni economic and social crisis, political instability within the northern regime and opposition to the northern conquest in the South'.

651 **Bipolarity, rational calculation, and war in Yemen.**
Michael C. Hudson. *Arab Studies Journal,* vol. 3, no. 1 (1995), p. 9-19.

Hudson demonstrates that the two governments of North and South Yemen 'went into the merger lacking good faith and trust in each other', and that although there was 'an efflorescence of public activity and civil society', this was insufficient to override the logic driving the two power centres to war. He views the disputes from the point of view of both parties and suggests that it was the emergence of a new player on the stage, the Islamic Reform Grouping *(al-Iṣlāḥ),* which precipitated the open conflict.

652 **Unhappy Yemen: watching the slide toward civil war.**
Michael C. Hudson. *Middle East Insight,* vol. 10, nos. 4-5 (1994), p. 10-19.

The author describes the process whereby unity was achieved between 1989 and 1990, and the factors which led to the civil war of 1994. He emphasizes the enthusiasm of the ordinary people for unity and the fact that neither the leadership of North or South was popular. In addition, the wave of democratization in Europe may have persuaded the leadership of the People's Democratic Republic that 'the prospects of prosperity through unity, pluralistic power-sharing, oil, and international investment seemed more attractive than the old single-party command economy alternative'. However, reality turned out to be different, as returning migrants from Saudi Arabia after the Gulf War put enormous pressure on the economy and social services, while 'four years after unity there were still two separate, sovereign, and mutually antagonistic establishments ruling in the country'.

653 **Human rights in Yemen during and after the 1994 war.**
Human Rights Watch/Middle East. Washington, DC: Human Rights Watch, 1994. 31p. (Newsletter/Human Rights Watch/Middle East, vol. 6, no. 1).

The report, written by Sheila Carapico and Jemera Rone, sketches in the background to the civil war, highlighting the failure to merge the two armies and security establishments, and the imbalance in representation caused by the rise of *al-Iṣlāḥ* party, as the main causes for the secession of South Yemen. The report then details the infringements of human rights during and after the conflict: indiscriminate shelling and Scud attacks; the destruction of Aden's water supply; illegal detentions and arbitrary arrests; torture and ill-treatment of detainees; and severe restrictions on the press. The report makes nine recommendations, designed to reintroduce the rule of law and the restoration of civil rights in the country.

654 **Yemen: the tortuous quest for unity, 1990-94.**
Joseph Kostiner. London: Royal Institute of International Affairs, 1996. 132p. map. bibliog. (Chatham House Papers).

The most thorough study available for the political developments of united Yemen, although it is still too early to draw any conclusions from the civil war of 1994. The author examines relations among the leadership groups of North and South, and looks at the growth of new institutions in the economic and administrative spheres, at foreign relations and the influence of regional developments, at the process of democratization, and how the 'relative strength of the North has led to the formulation of a new concept of unification, one based on Northern force and dominance'.

655 **Les islamistes yéménites et les élections.** (The Yemeni Islamists and the elections.)
Bernard Lefresne. *Monde Arabe/Maghreb Machrek,* no. 141 (July-Aug. 1993), p. 27-36. maps.

Basing himself on newspaper reports and interviews and on the party's own public literature, the author examines the role played by the pro-Saudi *al-Iṣlāḥ* party in the Yemeni elections of 1993. He finds that the Party favoured national symbols (unity, the Revolution, the Republic) in its publicity, while also 'playing the card of responsibility, of moderation and of patriotism'. Furthermore, the fact that so many of its members are tribal or religious dignitaries enabled the Party to enter into a relationship of power with the government.

656 **Yemen: steps toward civil society.**
Middle East Watch. New York: Middle East Watch, 1992. 26p. (Newsletter/Middle East Watch, vol. 4, no. 10).

This report was written by George Lerner for Middle East Watch (which became Human Rights Watch/Middle East [see item no. 653] in 1993). It examines how, in the aftermath of union in 1990 and in the run-up to elections in 1993, the political situation in Yemen was fluid and changeable. Many aspects of political repression had been eased: most Yemenis formerly living in exile had returned home; most, but not all, political prisoners had been released; freedom of expression and association were in evidence with over 100 newspapers and magazines flourishing and over forty political parties in operation. However, the author strikes a note of caution: in some areas of politics such as foreign policy criticism was forbidden; the political parties law had not been enacted; and low-level political violence continued with over a dozen members of the Yemeni Socialist Party having been killed in twelve months.

657 **Promoting popular participation in Yemen's 1993 elections.**
National Democratic Institute for International Affairs. Washington, DC: National Democratic Institute, 1994. 152p.

In 1993, the NDI was invited to assist the National Yemeni Committee for Free Elections (NCFE) in training volunteers to help in Yemen's first free elections, which were held in 1993. Much of this report deals with the NCFE and its administration, but considerable information is also included on the elections themselves – the NDI found that the illiteracy of the majority of voters contributed to some malpractice, and that there were duplicate ballot papers in circulation – and on women's participation in the political process.

658 **Yemeni unification: the end of marxism in Arabia.**
Gerd Nonneman. In: *The Middle East in the New World Order.* Edited by Haifaa A. Jawad. Basingstoke, England: Macmillan, 1994, p. 53-69.

The author adduces the economic reasons behind the 1990 unification of the two Yemens, and looks at the economic results of the merger. He sees the key economic factors in the future success of the country as lying in the development of the hydrocarbon sector, the role of the migrant workers ejected from Saudi Arabia after the Gulf War of 1990-91, and the level of international aid. This is a somewhat unbalanced article, based on a limited range of secondary sources, and one which makes little attempt to analyse the political and social dimensions of unification.

659 **The Yemeni War of 1994: causes and consequences.**
Edited by Jamal S. al-Suwaidi. London: Saqi Books, 1995. 124p. bibliog.

This book contains papers by Michael C. Hudson, Paul Dresch, Charles Dunbar, Robert D. Burrowes and Mark Katz, given originally at a symposium organized by the Emirates Center for Strategic Studies and Research in March 1994. Dresch looks at the tribal factor in a much wider context than just the civil war (in which they did not participate directly), analysing the relationship between tribal conferences, civil society and party politics in North Yemen. Dunbar suggests that the most likely direction that Yemen will take in the future is the maintenance of the status quo, with President Ṣāliḥ seeking national reconciliation, while rewarding the armed forces and pursuing an authoritarian programme. Both Katz and Burrowes look at the foreign policy implications of the civil war, paying particular attention to Saudi Arabia and the Gulf States. All the contributors, as well as the editor, emphasize the necessity for economic development to cement national cohesion, but none is overly optimistic about the country's chances of achieving success in this sphere. The paper by Michael Hudson has been published separately (see item no. 652), while for a military account of the war, see the article by David Warburton (item no. 411).

660 **Islamism and tribalism in Yemen.**

Eric Watkins. In: *Islamic fundamentalism.* Edited by Abdel Salam Sidahmed, Anoushiravan Ehteshami. Boulder, Colorado: Westview Press, 1996, p. 215-25.

An interesting if incomplete study of the roles played by three shaykhs, ʿAbd Allāh ibn Ḥusayn al-Aḥmar, ʿAbd al-Majīd al-Zindānī and Ṭāriq al-Faḍlī, in the recent politics of Yemen. The author looks at the historical roots of the disaffection of both the al-Aḥmar and al-Faḍlī families, and attempts to chart the relationship between *al-Iṣlāḥ*, the Islamic Jihād Organization and the Muslim Brotherhood in Yemen. The author concludes that 'in retrospect, it can be seen that tribalist forces, in alliance with the central government, encouraged, controlled and directed the growth of Islamist forces in Yemen, both to secure and to extend their own positions of power throughout the country'.

661 **National integration and national security: the case of Yemen.**

Manfred W. Wenner. In: *The Many faces of national security in the Arab World.* Edited by Bahgat Korany, Paul Noble, Rex Brynen. Basingstoke, England: Macmillan, 1993, p. 169-84.

The author identifies a twofold threat to national security: Saudi manipulation of border conflicts and tribal elements, and economic weaknesses, arising from a dependency on aid, the inability to control smuggling, and the return of hundreds of thousands of expatriate workers during and after the Gulf Crisis of 1990-91. The author suggests that unification will not bring greater stability, since he sees amalgamation consuming more resources than forecast, while creating insurmountable problems of resource allocation.

662 **Yemen.**

Manfred W. Wenner. In: *Political parties of the Middle East and North Africa.* Edited by Frank Tachau. Westport, Connecticut: Greenwood Press, 1994, p. 611-39.

After an introduction outlining the growth of political associations and parties from the 1930s in both North and South Yemen, the author looks at the constitutional and legal framework for party politics in the unified republic, and discusses the results of the 1993 elections. He then lists thirty-six political parties, operating both historically and currently in Yemen, giving details of the name of the party in both English and

Arabic (and any former name), the date of foundation, the history of the party and its leaders, where it draws its major support from, and its estimated membership (if known). This is a very useful factual adjunct to the many political analyses listed in this chapter.

The Free Yemeni movement, 1935-1962.
See item no. 378.

Arabia without sultans.
See item no. 382.

Les islamistes yéménites à travers leur presse . . . (Yemeni Islamists through their press . . .)
See item no. 908.

Law and Constitution

663 **Law and justice in contemporary Yemen: the People's Democratic Republic of Yemen and the Yemen Arab Republic.**

S. H. Amin. Glasgow, Scotland: Royston, 1987. 159p. maps. bibliog.

After a brief introduction to the history and social and economic structure of both Yemens, the author looks at the constitution of South Yemen (promulgated in 1970 and amended in 1978), and the development of the legal system both under the British and in the contemporary period. He goes on to survey the constitutions of the Yemen Arab Republic, its criminal, family and commercial law, and the organization of the judiciary. The author relies very much on written sources rather than fieldwork, pays no attention to customary or tribal law, and underestimates the Islamic sensibilities of North Yemen society, and as a result, has produced a work which is not as authoritative as it might have been.

664 **Arab Law Quarterly.**

London: Lloyds of London (vols 1-2); London: Graham and Trotman (vols. 3-9); London; The Hague: Kluwer Law International, (vol. 10-), 1985- . annual.

Apart from critical studies analysing both Islamic and secular law (listed separately in this chapter where appropriate), most issues of this important journal carry translations of recent legislation passed by individual Arab governments. Recent examples concerning Yemen are: 'Law by Republican Decree no. 22 of 1992 concerning arbitration' (vol. 10, no. 2 [1995], p. 150-64); 'Law no. 19 of 1994 concerning intellectual property rights' (vol. 10, no. 2 [1995], p. 165-90); and 'Law no. 4 of 1993 concerning free zones' (vol. 10, no. 3 [1995], p. 267-77). Other new periodicals on Middle Eastern and Islamic law which contain relevant material are the *Middle East Commercial Law Review* (London: Sweet & Maxwell, 1995- . 6 issues per year): 'Yemen's maritime law of 1994', by A. Haberbeck (vol. 1, no. 4 [1995], p. 135-8); and 'Investment in the Republic of Yemen', by John McHugo (vol. 1, no. 6 [1995], p. 193-7), and *Islamic Law and Society* (Leiden, The Netherlands: Brill, 1994- . 3 issues per year): '*Ibrā*' in highland Yemen: two Jewish divorce settlements', by I. Hollander (vol. 2, no. 1 [1995], p. 1-23); 'Three recent decisions of the Yemeni

Supreme Court', by Chibli Mallat (vol. 2, no. 1 [1995], p. 71-91); and 'A Ṣanaʿa court: the family and the ability to negotiate', by Anna Würth (vol. 2, no. 3 [1995], p. 320-40), which shows how marital disputes in Ṣanʿāʾ are being increasingly settled by the courts rather than local mediators.

665 **Le système juridique traditionnel.** (The traditional legal system.)
Joseph Chelhod. In: *L'Arabie du Sud: histoire et civilisation.* (South Arabia: history and civilization.) Vol. 3: *Culture et institutions du Yémen.* (Culture and institutions of Yemen.) Paris: Maisonneuve et Larose, 1985, p. 125-81.

Divided into three sections: *La société yéménite et le droit* (Yemeni society and the law); *Aspects du coutumier yéménite de type bédouin* (Aspects of Yemeni tribal customary law); and *Le droit intertribal* (Inter-tribal law), this is an important study of the relationship between society and law in North Yemen, particularly the values placed on the law, and how the law is administered. The author has no interest in the textual or religious aspects of Yemeni law (the differences between Zaydī and Shāfiʿī law are scarcely mentioned), but looks at legal matters with the eye of an anthropologist. The first part of this study was first published in slightly different form but with the same title in *L'Homme,* vol. 15, no. 2 (1975), p. 67-86.

666 **Islam and personal law in the Yemens.**
Gulshan Dhanani. *International Studies* (New Delhi), vol. 22 (1985), p. 19-32.

The author looks at the attempts both North and South Yemen have made to modernize their codes of personal law, but much of the article is concerned with introducing the two countries, while the actual legal section is dependent both for fact and interpretation on the works of other scholars.

667 **Die Arabische Republik Jemen: zur Verfassung und Verwaltung eines Entwicklungslandes.** (The Yemen Arab Republic: on the constitution and administration of a developing country.)
Ralf Dreyer. Bochum, Germany: Studienverlag Brockmeyer, 1983. 212p. bibliog.

By far the most comprehensive study of the constitutional development of North Yemen, this work considers in some detail the political system operating under the Imamate, opposition to the Imam including the embryonic constitutional movement, and the Imam's own position under Zaydī law. The author passes fairly quickly over the civil war period of 1962-70, but devotes a good deal of space to delineating and analysing the legal, political and social moves towards a permanent constitution for the Republic, concluding his study in 1974 when the *Majlis al-Shūrā* (Consultative Assembly) was abolished by the President.

668 **Company law in Yemen.**
Geralyn M. Fallon. *Arab Law Quarterly,* vol. 7 (1992), p. 237-48.

A description of the law of commercial companies promulgated in 1991, which superseded the respective commercial codes of former North and South Yemen. The author describes the six forms of business permitted in unified Yemen (general partnership, limited partnership, joint venture, joint stock company, company limited by shares, limited liability company), but without critical comments or analysis.

669 **The taxation of companies and individuals in Yemen.**
Geralyn M. Fallon. *Arab Law Quarterly,* vol. 8, no. 1 (1993), p. 37-45.

The Yemen Income Tax Law of 1991 replaced the previous tax regimes of North and South Yemen, and this article looks at the taxation of individuals, the taxation of companies and other taxes, such as *zakāt* (alms), business profit tax, real-estate revenue tax and stamp duty. The author has not always been able to establish how the new tax laws are applied in practice.

670 **Arbitration in the Yemen Arab Republic.**
Isam Muḥammad Ghanem. Braunton, Devon, England: Merlin Books, 1988. 22p.

One of many books and articles (the author lists his own bibliography on p. 19-22) on Yemen, Islam, forensic medicine, law and poetry produced by this prolific scholar, who was originally a magistrate in Aden. This particular pamphlet looks at customary law in North Yemen and its relationship with Law no. 33 of 1981 covering arbitration. It is discursive, sometimes unnecessarily personal, but still full of useful information.

671 **Commercial litigation in the Yemen Arab Republic with special reference to marine insurance.**
Isam Muḥammad Ghanem. *Arab Law Quarterly,* vol. 2 (1987), p. 230-64.

The author looks at Command Council Resolution no. 4 of 1976 setting up commercial courts, the law of civil procedure embodied in Law no. 42 of 1981, and several other pieces of legislation which cover the operation of foreign companies in North Yemen, such as the law on trade marks, on agency, on freedom of contract, and on insurance. He also takes the reader through various relevant cases, based on published cases decided between 1976 and 1985, and his own experiences as an advocate in Ṣanʿāʾ and a legal translator in Hodeida.

672 **Zaydi scholastics in Yemeni commercial and shipping disputes.**
Isam Muḥammad Ghanem. Dubai, United Arab Emirates: Express Printing Services, 1989. 186p.

After an extensive study of Zaydī principles of authority and constitutional developments in North Yemen up to and including *al-Mīthāq al-Waṭanī* (National Charter) of 1980-82, the author examines the provisions on commercial law enshrined in Yemeni legislation from 1962 to 1981. The work concludes with a survey of the provisions for natural justice in Islamic law and how these apply to the Yemen Arab Republic. Like many of the author's works, the organization of the text leaves much to be desired, but there is a hard core of useful information and analysis awaiting the persistent reader.

673 **Al-Shawkānī and the jurisprudential unity of Yemen.**
Bernard Haykel. *Revue du Monde Musulman et de la Méditerranée,* no. 67 (1993), p. 53-65.

The author suggests that Muḥammad ibn ʿAlī al-Shawkānī (d. 1834) has exercised a great deal of influence over both the Zaydī and Shāfiʿī sects for the past 150 years. During his lifetime, al-Shawkānī was supported by the Qāsimī Zaydī imams of the Yemen, since 'his legal promulgations gave doctrinal legitimation to an Imamate that was no longer doctrinally in tune with Zaydī orthodoxy', while his works also 'found great appeal among the Shāfiʿīs who formed the vast majority of the Imam's subjects by the second half of the 18th century'. The Ḥamīd al-Dīn imams who ruled North Yemen from 1918 to 1962 had a pragmatic attitude towards al-Shawkānī and had a number of his works published in Egypt. On the other hand, the views of al-Shawkānī was used against the imams by Muḥammad Maḥmūd al-Zubayrī (d. 1965), a leader of the Yemeni liberals, and it is no surprise to find that 'Yemeni law in the republican period was also influenced by al-Shawkānī's jurisprudential opinions and methodology'. This impressive article, based on original Arabic sources, shows how al-Shawkānī 'was able to bridge the gap between Zaydīs and Shāfiʿīs because of a legal methodology which insisted on *ijtihād* [individual legal opinion] but drew textual proof for the *sunna* [customary practice] from Sunnī *ḥadīth* sources'.

674 **Constitutional proposals for South Arabia.**
Sir Ralph Hone, Sir Gawain Bell. Aden: Federation of South Arabia, 1966. 187p. map.

A fascinating, if ultimately futile document, in which two seasoned British diplomats wrestle with the impossible task of creating an effective constitution for a new federal republic, which would unite the city and port of Aden with the states of the Federation of South Arabia (formerly the Eastern and Western Aden Protectorates). The authors use as a model a Western, federal structure, which makes almost no mention of God or Islam, but which concentrates on human rights and duties. The result is an excellent theoretical model for a United Republic of South Arabia, but one which the anti-imperialist heirs to the British protectorate wanted nothing to do with. In his memoirs (see item no. 371), Sir Gawain Bell sketches in the background to the formulation of the constitutional proposals.

675 **Legal systems and basic law in Yemen.**
H. A. Al-Hubaishi. London: Sphinx Publishing, 1988. 248p.

A fairly systematic study of the laws of the Yemen Arab Republic (with an excursus on the laws prevailing in the People's Democratic Republic). After an historical introduction, the author summarizes the provisions of the constitution, and the codes governing private, criminal, commercial and family law, concluding with an overview of the judicial system, and the legal profession. There is no attempt by the author to explain, criticize or defend any laws, to cite particular examples of their operation, or give the reader any understanding of the social or political reasons for enacting certain laws, so that this book can be used only as a ready reference for the existing code.

676 **Business laws of Yemen.**

Abdulla M. A. Maktari, John McHugo. London: Graham and Trotman, 1995. 300p. (Arab and Islamic Laws Series).

The two authors have translated from the Official Gazette of the Republic of Yemen the constitution promulgated on 28 September 1994; the 1991 laws governing investment, social insurance, income tax and commercial companies; the 1992 laws on arbitration and the activities of foreign companies; and the 1993 laws on free zones. A second volume of legal translations is promised in the introduction.

677 **Water rights and irrigation practices in Laḥj: a study of the application of customary and sharīʿah law in South-West Arabia.**

Abdulla M. A. Maktari. Cambridge, England: Cambridge University Press, 1971. 202p. bibliog. (University of Cambridge Oriental Publications, no. 21).

A seminal work, originally produced as the author's PhD dissertation at the University of Cambridge under Professor R. B. Serjeant. It first looks at the legal position of water and water rights, from the point of view of both the classical Shāfiʿī jurists, and local *fatwās* (legal opinions) pronounced by lawyers from Yemen and the Hadramawt. Part two looks at how irrigation actually works in Laḥij (to the north of Aden), at the codification of customary law, and at the proceedings of the agricultural court. If there is a fault to be found with this book, it is that it does not summarize the relationship between customary and *sharīʿah* (Islamic) law, but leaves readers to draw their own conclusions from among the wealth of detail.

678 **The calligraphic state: textual domination and history in a Muslim society.**

Brinkley M. Messick. Berkeley, California: University of California Press, 1993. 341p. bibliog. (Comparative Studies on Muslim Societies, no. 16).

An exemplary work combining a historical account of the sources of modern Yemeni law (Shāfiʿī, Zaydī and Ottoman), an exploration of how the law actually functions in terms of courts and officials, and an analysis of the role of written legal documents in a fundamentally oral society. The author has used two periods of fieldwork in Ibb in North Yemen to observe the law in action and has tested his observations against both legal theory and historical reality as revealed in texts, to produce a first-rate work on the sociology of law.

679 **Kissing hands and knees: hegemony and hierarchy in shariʿa discourse.**

Brinkley M. Messick. *Law and Society Review,* vol. 22, no. 4 (1988), p. 637-59.

Using examples from Yemeni society and citing the Yemeni jurist Muḥammad ibn ʿAlī al-Shawkānī (d. 1834), the author looks at the legal relationship between ignorance and knowledge, and at what obligations the *ʿāmmah,* or uneducated populace, had towards Islam. This is a complex but rewarding article, which deals with some fundamental aspects of Islamic law in a Yemeni context.

680 **Legal documents and the concept of 'restricted literacy' in a traditional society.**
Brinkley M. Messick. *International Journal of the Sociology of Language,* vol. 42 (1983), p. 41-52.

In a brief but wide-ranging article, the author looks at the place of written documents in a society which is not only no more than partially literate, but is also legally dependent on oral testimony. Taking into account the theoretical and practical work of Jack Goody, the tension between oral and written culture is examined within the context of a small town in North Yemen. The author tackles the same subject from a different and less theoretical angle in 'Literacy and the law: documents and document specialists in Yemen' (in: *Law and Islam in the Middle East.* Edited by Daisy Hilse Dwyer. New York: Bergin & Garvey, 1990, p. 60-76).

681 **The mufti: the text and the world: legal interpretation in Yemen.**
Brinkley M. Messick. *Man,* new series, vol. 21, no. 1 (1986), p. 102-19.

A *muftī* is a Muslim jurist 'who delivers a non-binding type of legal opinion known as a *fatwa*', and who occupies 'a niche between the jurist as teacher and the jurist as judge'. In this article, the author looks at the functions of the Muftī of Ibb, a small town in North Yemen, both in historical and in contemporary terms, and, in particular, at the techniques used in arriving at a legal judgment. The author continues his investigation of the role of the Yemeni *muftī* in 'Media muftis: radio fatwas in Yemen' (in: *Islamic legal interpretation: muftis and their fatwas.* Edited by Muḥammad Khalid Masud, Brinkley M. Messick, David S. Powers. Cambridge, Massachusetts; London: Harvard University Press, 1996, p. 310-20), in which conventional and radio *fatwās* issued in the 1980s and 1990s are compared with respect to both content and style.

682 **Prosecution in Yemen: the introduction of the Niyāba.**
Brinkley M. Messick. *International Journal of Middle East Studies,* vol. 15 (1983), p. 507-18.

In Islamic law, no office of public prosecutions is known, and 'litigation before a sharīʿa (Islamic law) court requires the initiation of an action by a private claimant'. However, as the author points out, both the judge and the *muḥtasib* (market inspector) have areas of public responsibility, and some Arab legal codes have built on this latter aspect of law to create the *niyābah,* 'an agency of investigation and prosection, with jurisdiction in criminal cases and other areas of "public' rights'. The new organization was formally instituted in the Yemen Arab Republic in 1977, and in this article, the author reviews the work of the *niyābah* of Ibb, its procedures and its success. He sees it as an organ of limited effectiveness, often peripheral to the outcome of a case, but one which 'may become a stratagem in the hands of disputants as they maneuver in an overal process that ends in a *ṣulḥ* [settlement]'.

683 **Ṭāġūt, man' and šarī'a: the realms of law in tribal Arabia.**
Gerald J. Obermeyer. In: *Studia Arabica et Islamica: Festschrift for Iḥsān 'Abbās on his sixtieth birthday.* Edited by Wadad al-Qadi. Beirut: American University of Beirut, 1981, p. 365-71.

Drawing on work done by Iḥsān 'Abbās on the relationship between pre-Islamic idol worship and the reality of tribal politics in Arabia, the author looks at the conception of law used by the Banū Murād tribe of Marib in North Yemen. He examines concepts such as *ṭāghūt* and *ḥukm al-man'*, which he sees as being organized mainly around the idea of collective responsibility and as relying on a cultural concept of honour for its legitimacy. He goes on to study whether *ṭāghūt* or retaliatory action taken by the whole tribe with the aim of correct behaviour is in conflict with the *sharī'ah* or Islamic law, and concludes that neither *man'* nor *ṭāghūt* is in conflict with *sharī'ah* doctrine but 'that both compete for control over man's political behaviour'.

684 **Il diritto consuetudinario delle tribù arabe del Yemen.** (The customary law of the Arab tribes in Yemen.)
Ettore Rossi. *Rivista degli Studi Orientali,* vol. 23 (1948), p. 1-36.

A very detailed investigation of tribal law in Yemen, in which the author first describes the information on customary law and tribal organization found in the writings of Joseph Halévy, Eduard Glaser and Ḥayyīm Ḥabshūsh (qq.v.). He then analyses in depth a Zaydī *fatwā* (legal opinion) on the *ḥukm al-ṭāghūt* (customary law) which accuses bedouin of excluding women from inheritance, and thus forcing cousin-to-cousin marriage and violating Qur'ānic norms on retaliatory punishments. He contrasts three accusations with data from several manuscripts dealing with tribal law and finds that there is little in them which contradicts the *sharī'ah* (or Islamic law) from the point of view of ritual dogma. In practice, the greatest deviations from Islamic law have come in the field of retaliation, and, while it is clear that the base of tribal law is *'urf* (custom), based on principles of *sharaf* (honour), the author finds that the writings on customary law are 'animated by the spirit of Islam'.

685 **Customary and sharī'ah law in Arabian society.**
R. B. Serjeant. Aldershot, England: Variorum, 1991. unpaged.

A collection of seventeen articles, previously published between 1951 and 1989, of which five deal with some aspect of law in North Yemen or South Arabia: 'A Judeo-Arab house-deed from Ḥabbān (with notes on the former Jewish communities of the Wāḥidī Sultanate'; 'Forms of plea: a Šāfi'ī manual from al-Šiḥr'; 'Two tribal law cases (documents), Wāḥidī Sultanate, South-West Arabia'; 'Recent marriage legislation from al-Mukallā, with notes on marriage customs'; and 'Maritime customary law off the Arabian coasts'. To this can be added the article 'Customary law among the fishermen of al-Shiḥr', first published in *Middle East studies and libraries; a felicitation volume for Professor J. D. Pearson* (Edited B. C. Bloomfield. London: Mansell, 1980, p. 192-203).

686 **Arbitration in the Yemen Arab Republic.**
Saeed Hassan Sobhi. In: *Arab comparative & commercial law: the international approach.* Vol. 1: *The shariʿa and its relevance to modern international disputes; the settlement of disputes through arbitration; joint ventures.* London: Graham and Trotman; International Bar Association, 1987, p. 207-22.

A translation, with introduction and notes, of Law no. 33 of 1981 on arbitration, from the Civil Code of the Yemen Arab Republic.

687 **The Yemeni constitution and its religious orientation.**
Al-Tayib Zein al-Abdin. *Arabian Studies,* vol. 3 (1976), p. 115-25.

The Yemen Arab Republic's first permanent constitution after the civil war of 1962-70 was finally promulgated in 1971, and the author shows how various groups, notably the *ʿulamā'* (religious scholars) and the *shabāb* (young politicians), were influential in drafting the wording of the text. He is especially interested in examining the Islamic tenets of the constitution both in theory and practice, considering that 'the religious causes have not really prevented the Government from doing what it wants', and that 'the concept of a Constitution that divides powers and regulates procedures is unfamiliar to the Yemeni people', who preferred the 'simple, direct and decisive way of administration' of the Imamate.

The law, the state and socialist policies with regard to women . . .
See item no. 581.

Women's rights and political contingency . . .
See item no. 583.

Women's inheritance of land in highland Yemen.
See item no. 584.

Inheritance rights of Jewish women and Moslem women in Yemen.
See item no. 589.

Yemen: the politics of unity.
See item no. 649.

Transactions in Ibb . . .
See item no. 751.

A bibliography of Islamic law, 1980-1993.
See item no. 938.

Administration

688 **Die Entwicklung der administrativen Gliederung und der Verwaltungszentren in der Arabischen Republik Jemen (Nordjemen).** (The development of the administrative structure and the centres of local government in the Yemen Arab Republic (North Yemen).)

Volker Höhfeld. *Orient* (Opladen, Germany), vol. 19, no. 2 (1978), p. 22-61. maps. bibliog.

A scholarly and important article, which looks at the historical pattern of administrative divisions in North Yemen, which have been influenced by the split between Shīʿī and Sunnī areas, by the Ottoman administration of the 19th century, and, above all, by the continuing influence of tribal leaders. The author sees 'the principal centres of the present-day administrative units as being still based on the old tribal foci', with 'their position within the hierarchy of tribal settlement determining their rank as administrative centres'. The author also looks at the influence of agriculture and economics on the development of local administration, and provides his article with an abstract in English.

689 **Women of the *zār* and middle-class sensibilities in colonial Aden, 1923-1932.**

Lidwien Kapteijns, Jay Spaulding. *Sudanic Africa,* vol. 5 (1994), p. 7-38.

Based on the Aden Residency Records preserved in the India Office Library and Records in London, this is a fascinating study of how the British administration in Aden dealt with competing interests among Adenis regarding local customs. The practice of the *zār* (a female ceremony for the casting out of spirits and which involved music) had been imported into Aden and Yemen in general from the Horn of Africa and, in 1923, the British in Aden received a petition from well-known local *ʿulamā'* (religious scholars) that 'the *zār* was against religion and contained all kinds of disapproved acts'. The authors trace the tortuous development of the case, as government officials, Jewish Adeni lawyers, local male middle-class leaders of the community, and, most interestingly, 'lower-class Northeast African Muslim women not under any apparent male authority' all made representations to the colonial authorities, resulting finally in a definitive ban on the *zār* in 1932, after nine years of debate. The authors publish and translate specimen documents in Arabic both by women supporting the ceremony and by men opposed to it.

690 **The evaluation of an administrative co-operation project in North Yemen and its significance for German aid policy.**
Klaus König, Friedrich Bolay. *Public Administration and Development,* vol. 2 (1982), p. 225-37.

An evaluation of a project which operated within the framework of the National Institute of Public Administration in Ṣanʿāʾ. The authors describe the complex system obtaining in North Yemen at the time of their survey, where 'pre-islamic structures are combined with islamic traditions, personalistic with territorial elements, and administrative establishments from the time of the Turkish occupation with those of the "imamate" constitution', and go on to discuss recent innovations such as the Local Development Associations. They analyse the project which developed three kinds of courses, ranging from ten months to three days, and which, *in toto,* reached twenty per cent of the key administrative personnel of the Yemen Arab Republic. The paper concludes by looking at German aid policy and argues the merits of providing aid in support of training to improve the quality of public administration. For an examination of how Yemeni civil servants see themselves, especially regarding their involvement in public policy formulation, see the dissertation by Khaled Mohsen al-Akwaʿa, *The policy role of the senior civil servants in the Government of Yemen* (PhD dissertation, Portland State University, 1996. 232p. bibliog.) (Available from University Microfilms International, Ann Arbor, Michigan, order no. 9701101).

691 **The history of *ʿuzlah* and *mikhlāf* in North Yemen.**
Hiroshi Matsumoto. *Proceedings of the Seminar for Arabian Studies,* vol. 24 (1994), p. 175-82.

Using medieval geographical and historical texts, the author looks in great detail at the administrative divisions of North Yemen and how they correspond to the distribution of tribes. He attempts to define the administrative terms *mikhlāf* and *ʿuzlah,* both of which relate to geographical areas smaller than the *nāhiyah* or district, and which he views as terms used by the Himyarite culture in the southern highlands. He also touches on the process of conversion taking place from 'the traditional and indigenous regional divisions to the modern rural administrative divisions'. His hypothesis about the relationship between tribes and administrative districts is stated but not worked out, and given the difficulty of assembling historical data on the subject, may never be more than a theory.

692 **Bureaucratic corruption as a consequence of the Gulf migration: the case of North Yemen.**
Nabil Ahmed Sultan. *Crime, Law and Social Change,* vol. 19, no. 4 (1993), p. 379-93.

An article-length version of the author's PhD dissertation at the University of Liverpool (1991), this empirical investigation into corruption shows how remittances from abroad caused gross excess domestic demand, rapid inflation, a dramatic growth in investment in land, housing and construction, and a major increase in the government's development programme. Government and municipal employees' salaries failed to keep up with inflation (declining as much as fifty-six per cent in real terms between 1971 and 1988) at a time when their services were in ever-greater demand, and officials often resorted to taking bribes as a way of making ends meet. The situation was exacerbated by divisions between the Shāfiʿīs who controlled the commercial sector and the Zaydīs who dominated the political process, clientelism and corruption in the government, and weak policing of the bureaucracy. The author sees the return of so many migrants as anti-inflationary in the long run, with consequently less pressure on officials to resort to corruption, although on the other hand pressure on housing and other services is currently so great that supplementing one's income illegally has become even easier. However, Sultan remains cautiously optimistic, hoping that the newly freed press and a future growth in living standards from oil and gas sales, will help curb the worst excesses of the bureaucracy.

693 **Colonial policing in Aden, 1937-1967.**

John Willis. *Arab Studies Journal,* vol. 5, no. 1 (1997), p. 57-91.

The author comes to the issue of colonial administration from the viewpoint of Michel Foucault and Timothy Mitchell, emphasizing that the role of the police in Aden was not only to prevent crime and arrest criminals, but to police 'an appearance of order both in the individual and in the structure of the city'. The police force enforced laws 'aimed at creating the modern, moral citizen and the ordered, clean city', by outlawing brothels and gambling, banning *qāt,* controlling the movement of traffic, arresting beggars, confiscating weapons, killing dogs, and removing unauthorized vendors. This article looks at the recruitment, composition and training of the Aden Police Force, and at the duties they were expected to carry out. The stress is not so much on crime (although this *is* dealt with in some detail), as on the 'policing of morality', the regulation of traffic and urban discipline, and the maintenance of public order. Based on original sources, and with a theoretical framework, this is an useful contribution to our understanding of the British attitude towards colonial rule.

Aden under British rule, 1839-1967.

See item no. 381.

Arabia and the isles.

See item no. 387.

Foreign Relations

694 **International boundaries of Saudi Arabia.**
Abdul-Razzak S. Abu Dawood, P. P. Karan. New Delhi: Galaxy Publications, 1990. 95p. maps.

The objectives of this study are twofold: to examine the movement of people and goods across the boundaries of Saudi Arabia; and to describe the historical evolution of Saudi boundaries. For the second part, the authors look at the historical growth of the Saudi state, and the treaties which define its borders, including those with North and South Yemen. For the first part, the authors conducted a sample survey of interviews with travellers leaving or entering Saudi Arabia at official points of entry in two months in 1982 and 1983, and give figures for frequency of trip, purpose of trip, length of stay and mode of transport. It is instructive to see that North Yemenis are the largest category of visitors to Saudi Arabia, making up eighteen per cent of border crossings, with South Yemenis accounting for just over six per cent, although it was found that many of the latter travelled via North Yemen because of the 'topographic difficulties in the Saudi–South Yemen boundary area'.

695 **Yemen and the United States: a study of a small power and super-state relationship, 1962-1994.**
Ahmed Noman Kassim Almadhagi. London: Tauris, 1996. 234p. bibliog. (Library of Modern Middle East Studies, no. 2).

A factually useful, if analytically rather weak, study of US–North Yemen relations. The strategic dimension of American policy, particularly regarding its rivalry with the Soviet Union in the Indian Ocean is underplayed, while Yemeni opposition to the Allies' attack on Occupied Kuwait and Iraq in the Second Gulf War, is touched upon but not developed. On the other hand, the coverage of developments since unification is welcome, especially regarding the United States' attitude both towards the civil war of 1994 and the preceding economic crisis.

696 **The Saudi–Egyptian conflict over North Yemen, 1962-1970.**
Saeed M. Badeeb. Boulder, Colorado: Westview Press; Washington, DC: American-Arab Affairs Council, 1986. 148p. bibliog.

The author ascribes the involvement of both Saudi Arabia and Egypt in the Yemen civil war of 1962-70 to inter-Arab rivalry on the part of Egypt (which he does not analyse in much detail), and the desire to maintain internal security on the part of Saudi Arabia. He describes the military and diplomatic manoeuvrings of both parties (and several others, including the United Nations) during the civil war, and discusses the lessons learnt by both sides. This is a useful, but not particularly profound work, which is stronger on Saudi Arabia than it is on Egypt or North Yemen.

697 **The end of empire in the Middle East: Britain's relinquishment of power in her last three Arab dependencies.**
Glen Balfour-Paul. Cambridge, England: Cambridge University Press, 1991. 278p. maps bibliog. (Cambridge Middle East Library, no. 25).

An interesting account by a former diplomat (now a university academic) of the ending of British rule in the Sudan, in South Arabia and Aden, and in the states of the Arab Gulf. Britain's relinquishment of power in South Arabia (discussed on p. 49-95, and in the final chapter) was in many ways the most complicated, and certainly the bloodiest of the three examples of decolonization analysed here, but all the episodes show a confusion in strategic thinking on the part of the Foreign Office, and, in the case of Aden, a great uncertainty over what the future should hold.

698 **China and the People's Democratic Republic of Yemen: a report.**
Translated, edited and introduced by Hashim S. H. Behbehani. London: KPI, 1985. 68p.

Formal diplomatic links between the People's Republic of China and South Yemen were established on 31 January 1968, and this work records the minutes of the meetings between officials of the Chinese government and the first delegation from South Yemen to visit China in September 1968. The Chinese side stressed the need for South Yemen to remain independent of other power blocs, for it to maintain its commitment to Marxist-Leninist thought, for it to rely on the support of the workers and not the army, and for it not to expect any substantial support from China.

699 **United Nations Yemen Observation Mission.**
Karl Th. Birgisson. In: *The evolution of UN peacekeeping: case studies and comparative analysis.* Edited by William J. Durch. Basingstoke, England: Macmillan, 1994, p. 206-18.

The United Nations first became involved in the Yemeni civil war of 1962-70 when the Yemeni Mission in New York wrote a letter to the Secretary-General in November 1962. The United Nations, through Ralph Bunche and Ellsworth Bunker, worked out a disengagement agreement between Egypt and Saudi Arabia in 1963, which, with the support of the Great Powers, resulted in the establishment of the United Nations Yemen Observation Mission or UNYOM. The Mission was sent to North Yemen in the middle of 1963 to monitor Saudi and Egyptian compliance with the disengagement agreement. However, short of all operational basics such as personnel, equipment and funding, as well as local support, the Mission 'floundered for fourteen months under very adverse conditions and was withdrawn'.

700 **Soviet use of proxies in the Third World: the case of Yemen.**
Richard E. Bissell. *Soviet Studies,* vol. 30 (1978), p. 87-106.

The author examines the relationship between the Soviet Union and the Yemen Arab Republic during the late 1960s, particularly the period of 1967-68 when the civil war was drawing to a close. He finds that the ties with Yemen became less significant over time, because of: more attractive naval bases in Somalia; continued hostility from Saudi Arabia; the closure of the Suez Canal in 1967; and the inability of the Yemeni government to develop a viable plan of economic development. 'Regional factors proved more influential than the projected might of a superpower', is the author's conclusion, although the emergence of an alternative proxy, in the newly independent Marxist state of South Yemen is hardly mentioned.

701 **Nord- und Südjemen im Spannungsfeld interner, regionaler und globaler Gegensätze.** (North and South Yemen in an area of tension between internal, regional and global conflicts.)
Ursula Braun. Bonn: Forschungsinstitut der Deutschen Gesellschaft für Auswärtige Politik, 1981. 81p. (Arbeitspapiere zur Internationalen Politik, no. 19).

A straightforward appraisal of the internal and external politics of both Yemens, and the attitudes towards the two states of the Soviet Union, the United States, China and Europe. The author also evaluates the chances of a union of the two countries, and while her analysis is sound, it is a reflection of the world situation obtaining at the beginning of the 1980s, and, not surprisingly, in no way anticipates the fall of international communism later in the decade.

702 **Soviet–South Yemeni relations: the Gorbachev years.**
Norman Cigar. *Journal of South Asian and Middle Eastern Studies,* vol. 12, no. 4 (1989), p. 3-38.

Basing himself on a thorough reading of both the Soviet and the South Yemeni press, the author analyses the Soviet reaction to the 1986 leadership struggle, the effect of the Soviets' determination to reduce their economic support to the Third World, and their attitude towards economic liberalization. The main goal of Soviet policy, according to the author, was to prevent another political upheaval in the PDRY, and to this end they worked towards rebuilding the Yemeni Socialist Party, diluting the strength of the military and persuading the Yemenis to adopt *perestroika* ('a codeword for Moscow's general pressure on Aden to reform its political system by opening it up, somewhat, to other forces, to reduce its relative domestic isolation and to stabilize the situation').

703 **Saudi Arabia's hegemonic policy and economic development in the Yemen Arab Republic.**
Giovanni Donini. *Arab Studies Quarterly,* vol. 1, no. 4 (1979), p. 299-308.

A critique of Saudi aid policy in general, and towards the Yemen Arab Republic in particular. It is argued that Saudi aid for North Yemen's first Five-Year Development Plan (1976/77-1980/81), estimated at one billion dollars, makes no provision for agrarian reform, nor does it make any commitment to eradicate *qāt*, (which the author calls 'this obnoxious shrub'). The author recommends the development by the Saudis of an indigenous working class, which would enable them to dispense with Yemeni labour, and end the maintenance of 'the YAR in a state of economic subservience rendered more acceptable by generous handouts which, together with the income from Yemeni emigrants, effectively reduce local pressures aiming at independent economic development'.

704 **Soviet interests in the Arabian Peninsula: the Aden Pact and other paper tigers.**
Michael C. Dunn. *American-Arab Affairs,* vol. 8 (1984), p. 92-8.

The author examines the failure of the Aden Treaty Tripartite Alliance (the Aden Pact), which was created in 1981 between South Yemen, Ethiopia and Libya. He points out various difficulties in holding the alliance together, of which the most significant was that only one country, the People's Democratic Republic of Yemen, was under the control of the Alliance's sponsor, the Soviet Union, and even then 'periodic bursts of violence inside the ruling elite occasionally force the Soviets to reassess who their real friends are there'. The author goes on to suggest that the Soviet Union supported South Yemen's rapprochement with Oman in the hope that it might reduce South Yemen's pariah status and thereby ease the Soviet Union's economic burden of aid.

705 **Eritrea–Yemen dispute over the Ḥanish Islands.**
Daniel J. Dzurek. *IBRU Boundary and Security Bulletin* (Durham, England), vol. 4, no. 1 (1996), p. 70-7.

In late 1995, forces belonging to Eritrea and Yemen clashed over the possession of the Ḥanish Islands, a group of at least twenty-three rocky outcrops in the southern Red Sea. This article analyses the claims of both sides to sovereignty over the islands, describes the genesis of the dispute, and discusses the nature of the fighting and the attempts at mediation by Ethiopia, Egypt and France. The author concludes by speculating whether the current conflict will lead to general negotiations over maritime boundaries.

706 **Saudi–Yemeni relations: domestic structures and foreign influence.**
F. Gregory Gause. New York: Columbia University Press, 1990. 233p. maps. bibliog.

A chronological and analytical survey of relations between Saudi Arabia and both North and South Yemen, from the beginning of the civil war in 1962 to 1982. The author looks at several factors which often influence the effectiveness of foreign policy (power differentials, economic relations and ideological affinities) in an atttempt to explain why the Saudi government has had much more success in the North than in the South, but concludes that it is the weakness of the North's control over its society which has enabled the Saudis to 'develop client relations with powerful autonomous groups' in North Yemen, i.e. with some of the major tribes, in a way that has not been possible in the South.

707 **The Kennedy administration and the Egyptian–Saudi conflict in Yemen: co-opting Arab nationalism.**

Fawaz A. Gerges. *Middle East Journal,* vol. 49, no. 2 (1995), p. 292-311.

This article argues that the Egyptian intervention in Yemen in 1962 was directly related to the 1961 breakup of Egypt's union with Syria, and to Nasser's determination to pursue his claim to be the leader of Arab nationalism. The author sees Egypt's strategy as being defensive rather than offensive, but also as being a major miscalculation, resulting in a drawn-out war 'which exacted a heavy toll on Egypt's economy and had damaging effects on its army'. On the Saudi side, any threat to the stability of North Yemen posed the gravest problems of security 'because of its possible spillover effect', and the Saudis looked to Washington for help. Kennedy, however, was anxious to remain on good terms with Nasser, given Egypt's dominant position in the Arab world, and viewed 'the confrontation as an inter-Arab dispute and not as a communist-inspired one'. The United States, therefore, attempted to broker a ceasefire between the warring sides, until relations with Egypt took a turn for the worse under the new administration of Lyndon Johnson. For a narrow blow-by-blow account of the sort of diplomacy the Americans employed, see the short study by Christopher J. McMullen (item no. 714) of Ellsworth Bunker's efforts at mediation.

708 **Revolution and foreign policy: the case of South Yemen, 1967-1987.**

Fred Halliday. Cambridge, England: Cambridge University Press, 1990. 315p. bibliog. (Cambridge Middle East Library, no. 21).

The author looks at the foreign policy of South Yemen both as a Third World state and as a revolutionary one. He establishes the domestic political context of South Yemen's foreign relations and shows the centrality of both the ruling party and the president to the making of foreign policy. Relations with the major Western states (Great Britain, the United States, France and West Germany) are analysed, as are the ties binding South Yemen to the Soviet Union, and, to a lesser extent, the People's Republic of China. Central to the book is an examination of how South Yemen saw itself as part of a divided country, and how it pursued a revolutionary policy with its neighbours, not only towards North Yemen, but also towards Saudi Arabia and Oman as well, although this policy was modified as the 1980s wore on. This is a highly analytical, well-documented study, which is still the most important in its field.

709 **North Yemen between East and West.**

Mark N. Katz. *American-Arab Affairs,* vol. 8 (1984), p. 99-107.

After a gallop through Yemeni history, the author looks at North Yemeni foreign policy, principally towards Saudi Arabia, the United States and South Yemen. He also deals with some aspects of North Yemen's recent political history, considering that the 'internal threat [to its security] is of greater concern than the external one, since the Saleh regime is both unpopular and weak'. However, despite his unpopularity and weakness, and the upheavals of unification and civil war, President Ṣāliḥ is still in power.

710 **Russia and Arabia: Soviet foreign policy toward the Arabian Peninsula.**
Mark N. Katz. Baltimore, Maryland: Johns Hopkins University Press, 1986. 279p. map. bibliog.

Separate chapters, based mainly on press and broadcasting reports, survey the development of Soviet policy towards North and South Yemen. Considerable attention is paid to military and economic assistance, as well as to the strategic advantages that are perceived both by the Yemeni governments and by the Soviet Union. In the case of the North, the author sees South Yemen as 'the primary threat to North Yemen security', with Ṣanʿāʾ therefore maintaining good relations with Moscow to ensure no overt Soviet support for the South, should war break out between the two Yemens. The Soviet Union, for its part, wants good relations with the Yemen Arab Republic to protect its interests in Aden and 'to prevent Saudi and American influence from becoming predominant'. The South is seen very much as a Soviet satellite, as a military and naval base, and as an (unsuccessful) centre from which to spread Marxist revolution in the Peninsula.

711 **Yemeni unity and Saudi security.**
Mark N. Katz. *Middle East Policy,* vol. 1, no. 1 (1992), p. 117-35.

The author surveys Saudi–Yemeni relations over the past twenty years, concentrating on the aftermath of the Gulf War of 1990-91 and the immediate post-war future. He sees Saudi–Yemeni enmity as 'likely to be a permanent feature of the international relations of the Arabian Peninsula', with Yemen angry over the expulsion of so many of its migrant workers, and the Saudis unhappy about Yemeni support for Iraq during the Gulf War. The author, however, overestimates the degree of cohesion in Yemen brought about by the union of 1990, and underestimates the internal difficulties facing the new regime; both of these factors lend an air of unreality to his predictions.

712 **Imperial outpost – Aden: its place in British strategic policy.**
Gillian King. London: Oxford University Press, 1964. 93p. maps. (Chatham House Essays).

Produced for the Royal Institute of International Affairs, this short book asks 'whether it is in the long-term British interest to maintain a sovereign base in Aden'. The author sees the essence of British foreign policy in the Arabian Peninsula as being defined by the 1962 White Paper on Defence, which stated categorically that Britain must protect her oil interests in the Arab Gulf, and she looks at the options open to the British government in furthering this policy. She concludes that 'the base [in Aden] is badly placed for any independent role that the United Kingdom could legitimately expect to play [and that] forces from home or from Singapore could better meet such dwindling obligations as remain her sole responsibility at strategic level'.

713 **South Yemen's revolutionary strategy, 1970-1985: from insurgency to bloc politics.**
Joseph Kostiner. Boulder, Colorado: Westview Press: Jerusalem: The Jerusalem Post, 1990. 122p. maps. (JCSS Study, no. 14).

A sophisticated analysis of the revolutionary policy pursued by South Yemen towards its immediate neighbours. The author looks at the aims of the campaigns in Dhofar and North Yemen, at the tactics adopted, at the achievements of the guerrillas, and at the reasons for the change in policy in both areas. The author evaluates South Yemen's success as mixed: while no regime was overthrown, he considers that Aden's security was enhanced, and while aid from China declined, and 'disillusionment with Soviet technical and financial aid was also evident', financial assistance from the Gulf states kept flowing at least until the end of 1985.

714 **Resolution of the Yemen Crisis, 1963: a case study in mediation.**
Christopher J. McMullen. Washington, DC: Institute for the Study of Diplomacy, Georgetown University, 1980. 51p.

An interesting contrast to the wider analysis of Fawaz Gerges (see item no. 707), this short work focuses on the day-to-day peace brokering of Ellsworth Bunker, the United States special envoy to King Faysal during the first few months of the Yemeni civil war in 1963. It shows in great detail both the concerns of the State Department, the perceived positions of both Saudi Arabia and Egypt, and the techniques used by Ambassador Bunker to achieve a settlement, albeit a partial and temporary one.

715 **Politics and the Soviet presence in the People's Democratic Republic of Yemen: internal vulnerabilities and regional challenges.**
Laurie Mylroie. Santa Monica, California: Rand, 1983. 72p. bibliog.

By analysing the internal politics of the People's Democratic Republic of Yemen, the author attempts to evaluate the relationship between the government and its Arab neighbours, as well as its ties to the Soviet Union. The author sees economic pressure as being the prime mover behind the regime's internal politics as well as its external politics, which had entered on a period of détente. However, 'given the volatility and violence of political change in Aden', the author hesitates in making any firm predictions over South Yemen's future. This report was commissioned by the United States Air Force as part of the Rand project 'Enhancing U.S. leverage in Persian Gulf/Middle East conflicts', and while its analysis of internal Yemeni affairs is hardly profound, its significance lies in the demonstrable importance America attached at that time to South-West Asia.

716 **Moscow and the Arabian Peninsula.**
Stephen Page. *American-Arab Affairs,* vol. 8 (1984), p. 83-91.

A straightforward survey of the relationship between the Soviet Union and the countries of the Arabian Peninsula between 1967 and 1985, concentrating on military and strategic issues relating to both North and South Yemen. The author sees the kernel of Soviet policy towards North Yemen as lying in 'encouraging Sanaa to keep its distance from Saudi Arabia and the United States', while the primary Soviet interest in South Yemen is 'to preserve the security of the country and of the Yemeni Socialist Party regime'.

717 **The Soviet Union and the Yemens: influence in asymmetrical relationships.**
Stephen Page. New York: Praeger, 1985. 225p. bibliog. (Studies of Influence in International Relations).

A well-documented and well-argued study of the relationship between the Soviet Union and North and South Yemen, between 1967 and 1984. The author concludes that while the Soviet Union had developed both economic and military ties to the Yemens, which enabled it 'to persuade governments in the area to take actions to which the latter were predisposed anyway', it is 'less clear that the Soviets have the ability to affect any or every event that they wish, much less to achieve desirable outcomes for events consistently'. The policy aims towards North Yemen are seen to be quite modest: for the Yemen Arab Republic not to be actively hostile to South Yemen and not to move closer to Saudi Arabia or the United States. The policy aims towards South Yemen have been more comprehensive, and while the People's Republic has adopted a socialist orientation, and has in general supported international goals, 'Moscow has not been able to influence Aden's policies in the direction of its own interests when those interests are perceived by a major faction in the ruling group to be inconsistent with the PDRY's interests'.

718 **The silent demise of democracy: the role of the Clinton administration in the 1994 Yemeni Civil War.**
Carlos A. Parodi, Elizabeth Rexford, Elizabeth Van Wie Davis. *Arab Studies Quarterly,* vol. 16, no. 4 (1994), p. 65-76.

The authors analyse the conditions which led to the Yemeni civil war of 1994, which they ascribe primarily to northern aggression, in the form of political assassinations, economic discrimination, and the perpetuation of standing armies, fuelled by the interference of Saudi Arabia through its manipulation of *al-Iṣlāḥ* party. Nevertheless, they find the seeds of democracy in the transformation of the South and the elections of 1993, both of which alarmed Saudi Arabia. As they consider 'the cornerstone of U.S. foreign policy on the Arabian Peninsula is its partnership with Saudi Arabia', they show that Clinton's policy of backing President Ṣāliḥ and opposing secession, was no defence of 'democracy', but rather the promotion of events which 'effectively eliminated the major democratic threat to the conservative ruling families of the Arabian Peninsula'. Although they may overstate their case, the authors do have a clear-sighted vision of the realities of politics both within and outside Yemen.

719 **Conflict in the Yemens and superpower involvement.**
J. E. Peterson. Washington, DC: Center for Contemporary Arab Studies, Georgetown University, 1981. 38p.

A well-balanced and succinct account of internal politics in both North and South Yemen and their repercussions on foreign policy by a historian and political scientist who understands the social and tribal composition of both countries. Much of this pamphlet is concerned with relations between the two states, and the consequences of the fighting in 1972 and 1979.

720 **Britain, Aden and South Arabia: abandoning empire.**
Karl Pieragostini. Basingstoke, England: Macmillan, 1991. 256p. maps. bibliog.

Using American diplomatic sources, newspaper reports, and interviews with numerous British politicians and colonial officers, the author attempts to answer the question of why Britain invested so much energy and money on Aden and the Federation of South Arabia, and then promptly decided to withdraw. Although somewhat theoretical and occasionally repetitive, Pieragostini shows how decisions about the importance of Aden were not based on a consensus, but on a shifting coalition of players, which included the Foreign Office, the Colonial Office, the Ministry of Defence, the Army and the Royal Air Force. The decisive change in policy came about as a result of the 'shift of the Ministry of Defence from an alliance with the Colonial Office during the Conservative Government to one with the Foreign Office under Labour'.

721 **Die Aden-Grenze in der Südarabienfrage (1900-1967).** (The Aden border in the South Arabian question, 1900-1967.)
Jens Plass, Ulrich Gehrke. Opladen, Germany: Leske, 1967. 345p. maps. bibliog.

The authors have divided the work between them, Jens Plass tackling 'Die Adener Grenzkommission, 1901-1907' (The Aden Boundary Commission, 1901-1907), and Ulrich Gehrke 'Überblick über die englisch–jemenitischen Beziehungen under dem Gesichtspunkt des Süd-Jemenanspruchs, 1900-1967' (Overview of British–Yemeni relations, from the point of view of the claim to South Yemen, 1900-1967). Both authors base their sections on the British archives, and while Jens Plass gives a clear account of diplomatic manoeuvrings around rival territorial claims, Ulrich Gehrke surveys the numerous attempts the British made to create a federated state, and the support and opposition this created among the South Arabian population.

722 **The Egyptian policy in the Arab world: intervention in Yemen, 1962-67: case study.**
Ali Abdel Rahman Rahmy. Washington, DC: University Press of America, 1983. 391p. bibliog.

The author, who served as a major in the Egyptian Army during the Yemen campaign, looks at Nasser's motives in committing major Egyptian resources to foreign military intervention, at the differing international responses to Egyptian involvement, at the military campaign itself and its probable cost, and at the disengagement process. This is a useful work, based on access to what few Egyptian documents are available, with the added attraction of a documentary and diplomatic appendix.

723 **Le contentieux territorial entre le Yémen et l'Arabie Saoudite: vers une solution?** (The territorial dispute between Yemen and Saudi Arabia: towards a solution?)
Mohamed A. Al-Saqqaf. *Monde Arabe Maghreb Machrek,* no. 149 (1995), p. 56-71.

In February 1995, Yemen and Saudi Arabia signed the Mecca Agreement, which set up an arrangement for defining their border. Yemen agreed to accept the terms of the 1934 Treaty of Ṭā'if, thus finally abandoning any claims to the Saudi province of ʿAsīr. The author looks at the historical background to the dispute between the two states, before examining the different attitudes among Yemeni political parties towards the accord.

724 **South-West Arabia.**
Edited by Richard N. Schofield. Slough, England: Archive Editions, 1993. 6 vols. (Arabian Geopolitics: Regional Documentary Studies, set 1).

A selection of facsimile reports from British official papers (Colonial Office, Foreign Office, War Office and India Office), which include: in volume one, documents on relations and border disputes between the Aden Protectorates and the Imamate of Yemen, 1901-62; in volume two, documents on relations and border disputes between the Aden Protectorates and Saudi Arabia, 1913-61; in volume three, historical documents on relations between the British and the Ottoman Empire in South-West Arabia, 1802-1918; in volume four, documents on the absorption of ʿAsīr into Saudi Arabia between 1913 and 1934, and the British role in this; in volume five, documents on British relations with the Ḥaḍramī tribes of the Aden Protectorates, 1855-1966; and in volume six, documents on French and Italian involvement in South-West Arabia, 1809-1939, and documents on oil exploration rights between 1913 and 1961.

725 **Rulers and Residents: British relations with the Aden Protectorate, 1937-59.**

Simon C. Smith. *Middle Eastern Studies,* vol. 31, no. 3 (1995), p. 509-23.

The author sees the relations which Britain formed with the Protectorate rulers as having 'a significant impact on the viability of Britain's whole position in South-West Arabia'. Britain's initial policy was to hand over control to the indigenous rulers, and when it was criticized for 'presiding over an unprogressive and anachronistic imperial system', its closer relationship with the shaykhs in the 1950s, 'preserved the façade of traditional rule while undermining its foundations', since 'by associating themselves so closely with the colonial power, the rulers weakened the tribal links with their followers'. Consequently, Britain was saddled with an alliance with tribal shaykhs who were unable to deliver the loyalty of their subjects. This well-researched article traces the development of Britain's policies clearly and concisely, and shows why Britain was unable to sustain her position in South Arabia.

726 **Russian policy in the Middle East: from messianism to pragmatism.**

Alexei Vassiliev. Reading, England: Ithaca Press, 1993. 384p.

Chapter five, entitled 'An exotic flower of Arabia', includes extracts from interviews with four senior Soviet officials about Moscow's attitude to and effect on the People's Democratic Republic of Yemen. R. A. Ulyanovsky, Deputy Secretary of the Central Committee of the Communist Party of the Soviet Union, saw the primary purpose of Soviet policy as supporting a progressive government and counterbalancing American naval strategy, but a more balanced view, which includes the admission of strategic and economic mistakes, is expressed by the other three interviewees, who include two former Soviet ambassadors to the Yemens.

727 **Politics in the Yemens and the Horn of Africa: constraints on a superpower.**

Paul R. Viotti. In: *The Soviet Union and the Middle East in the 1980s: opportunities, constraints and dilemmas.* Edited by Mark V. Kauppi, R. Craig Nation. Lexington, Massachusetts: Heath, 1983, p. 211-26.

The author places Soviet policy within a strategic, regional framework, before examining in detail Moscow's attitude to both Yemens and to conflict between them. He finds Soviet policy flexible, cautious, and 'constrained by the realities of a tribal and highly personalized politics endemic to the region'. Viotti suggests that 'central government institutions in the South exercise somewhat greater sway over the countryside [than in North Yemen]', and that Moscow should 'guard against any reestablishment by Aden of close links with London'.

728 **Arabia's frontiers: the story of Britain's boundary drawing in the desert.**
John C. Wilkinson. London: Tauris, 1991. 422p. maps. bibliog.

Yemen looms large in this clear and coherent survey of border disputes in the Arabian Peninsula. The Yemeni section begins with an examination of relations between Aden and Ottoman Yemen before the First World War, then moves on to inter-war relations (the Treaty of Ṣanʿāʾ of 1934, the dispute over Shabwah), and concludes with oil exploration and the unification of Yemen in 1990. This is a sound survey, marrying history and geography with both personalities and power relations.

729 **In the direction of the Gulf: the Soviet Union and the Persian Gulf.**
Aryeh Yodfat, Mordechai Abir. London: Cass, 1977. 167p. maps. bibliog.

Despite its title, this work contains a chapter on South Yemen entitled 'South Yemen – the Cuba of the Middle East', which surveys Soviet–South Yemeni relations between 1967 and 1976. The authors consider that the Soviet Union approved of Yemeni support for rebellions in Dhofar and North Yemen, since it found it 'convenient to have someone else engage in subversion with only indirect Soviet support', but were disturbed by the South Yemen government 'maintaining its political and ideological independence'. Aryeh Yodfat gives us a further instalment, dealing with relations between 1976 and 1980 in *The Soviet Union and the Arabian Peninsula: Soviet policy towards the Persian Gulf and Arabia* (London: Croom Helm; New York: St. Martin's Press, 1983. 190p. bibliog.).

A Yemenite embassy to Ethiopia, 1647-1649.
See item no. 334.

Records of Yemen, 1798-1960.
See item no. 386.

Aux origines de l'implantation française en Mer Rouge . . . (On the origins of the French settlement in the Red Sea . . .)
See item no. 391.

Eritrea e Yemen . . . (Eritrea and Yemen . . .)
See item no. 396.

Yemen and the Western world.
See item no. 399.

Aden and Yemen (1905-1919).
See item no. 400.

Moscow and Aden: coping with a coup.
See item no. 633.

The Yemeni war of 1994: causes and consequences.
See item no. 659.

Economics, Finance and Banking

730 **Economic prospects in a United Yemen.**
Jonathan Addleton. *Journal of South Asian and Middle Eastern Studies,* vol. 14, no. 4 (1991), p. 2-14.

The author surveys the unified economy in all its major aspects: national accounts, service sector; agriculture; manufacturing; oil and gas production and exploration. He sees the Gulf War of 1990-91 and the subsequent inflow of half a million returning migrants from Saudi Arabia as the crucial factor in determining Yemen's economic future. Long-term donor relationships are threatened; remittance income has declined dramatically; sanctions have damaged Yemen's small but significant trade relationship with Iraq and Kuwait; and new private investment does not seem to be forthcoming. Despite several positive factors in Yemen's favour, such as its entrepreneurial spirit and its large labour force, the author claims that 'more than ever, Yemen's own economic future now hinges on the successful development of its oil and gas reserves'.

731 **Economic stabilization policies in the Yemen Republic: a general equilibrium approach.**
Mohamed Ahmed Al-Afandi. PhD dissertation, University of Colorado at Boulder, 1991. 294p. bibliog. (Available from University Microfilms International, Ann Arbor, Michigan, order no. 9132537).

The author examines the effectiveness of the fiscal, monetary and exchange-rate policies adopted voluntarily by the North Yemen government in the 1980s. To do so, he develops a technical macroeconomic model reflecting the basic structure of the economy of Yemen, which shows that monetarist policies are relatively effective but have significant disadvantages. He suggests that 'supply–demand policies combined with smaller devaluation are the superior stabilization strategies for the case of Yemen', provided they do not violate the religious and social principles which govern the country.

732 **Economic planning in Yemen Arab Republic: the dependency problem.**
Abdul-Karim Ahmed Amer. PhD dissertation, Colorado State University, 1985. 197p. bibliog. (Available from University Microfilms International, Ann Arbor, Michigan, order no. 8527806).

The author appraises the structure of the first three YAR development plans and tests their effectiveness against a general macroeconomic model of the economy. His three principal findings are: that economic planning by itself was not responsible for the recent economic growth in North Yemen; that economic growth is generated externally through foreign aid and workers' remittances from abroad; and that 'the Yemeni economy will remain dependent on other economies for growth and development in the foreseeable future'. The thesis was also published in Ṣanʿāʾ in 1986 by Dar Azal.

733 **The Arab economies: structure and outlook.**
Arab Banking Corporation. Manama, Bahrain: Arab Banking Corporation, 1994. 4th rev. ed. 166p.

A succinct survey of Arab economies, this edition deals with the Republic of Yemen on pages 157-64. The authors see the hydrocarbon sector and Yemen's relationship with Saudi Arabia as crucial to economic development, although they also emphasize Yemen's agricultural potential, the weakness of the private sector and the necessity of ensuring an equitable distribution of resources throughout the country.

734 **Migration, balance of payments and economic growth: the case of the Yemen Arab Republic.**
Saif Mahyuob Al-Asaly. PhD dissertation, University of South Carolina, 1990. 176p. bibliog. (Available from University Microfilms International, Ann Arbor, Michigan, order no. 9029158).

Using economic theory and macroeconomic models, the author examines the effect on the YAR of large-scale labour migration. The author concludes that if migration is permanent, its positive elements outweigh the negative ones, but that (as has proved the case following the Gulf War of 1990-91) 'the real danger of migration lies in the difficulties and the pain which the country will endure if migration is temporary'. He goes on to show when large number of migrants return, the capital–labour ratio will fall, as well as income per worker and the general standard of living.

735 **Autonomy and secondhand oil dependency of the Yemen Arab Republic.**
Sheila Carapico. *Arab Studies Quarterly*, vol. 10, no. 2 (1988), p. 193-213.

The author combines a comprehensive survey of Yemeni economic development between 1962 and 1986 with a penetrating Marxist analysis of class formation, state autonomy and external dependency. She shows how remittances from external workers fuelled a consumer boom and inflation in the 1970s, but that development projects in that period were poorly coordinated while government departments ran up serious deficits in their current accounts. In the early 1980s, however, the government introduced austerity measures, practised genuine economic policy and discovered oil, thereby creating greater internal hegemony and reducing economic dependency. The author now identifies the bourgeoisie as the dominant class, but one with 'in marxist terms, no direct class relation to working people', since it is a commercial class rather than one which employs labour.

736 **The economic dimension of Yemeni unity.**
Sheila Carapico. *Middle East Report,* no. 184 (1993), p. 9-14.

The author suggests that 'at best, the North's capitalist orientation and the South's socialism represented tendencies or goals, for both were really "mixed" economies', with convergent patterns, the explanation for which lay in the development projects supported by foreign donors. The constitution of 1991 called for a mixed economy based on Islamic social justice, a developed public sector, the preservation of private ownership and 'scientific planning which leads to the establishment of public corporations engaged in exploiting the national and public resources, developing capabilities of and opportunities for the public, private and mixed sectors'. Before the economic benefits of unification could be realized, however, the aftermath of the Gulf War of 1990-91 drove Yemeni migrants back to their home country, thereby completely disrupting Yemen's economic plans.

737 **The political economy of self-help: development cooperatives in the Yemen Arab Republic.**
Sheila Carapico. PhD dissertation, State University of New York at Binghamton, 1984. 356p. bibliog. (Available from University Microfilms Internation, Ann Arbor, Michigan, order no. 8408393).

The author surveys the economy of North Yemen on the eve of the civil war of 1962-70 and contrasts it with the transformations wrought in the 1970s by the widely dispersed, virtually untaxed cash wealth which reached the country in the form of remittances from migrant workers. Given the lack of basic services supplied by central government, much of this wealth flowed into semi-formal cooperative movements. Using documentary and interview materials, the author shows that the 'appearance and gradual institutionalization of "development cooperation" before, during and after the Revolution were closely related to broader trends in the transformation of the traditional political economy'. The cooperative projects were a major factor in the extension of the primary infrastructure in the 1970s, and were spread throughout the whole country, encompassing all regions and rural areas as well as cities and small towns. The author summarized her dissertation in 'Self-help and development planning in the Yemen Arab Republic' (in: *Public participation in development planning and management: cases from Africa and Asia.* Edited by Jean-Claude García-Zamor. Boulder, Colorado: Westview Press, 1985, p. 203-34), emphasizing the modus operandi of the cooperatives and their relationship to central government.

738 **The price of wealth: business and state in labor remittance and oil economies.**
Kiren Aziz Chaudhry. *International Organization,* vol. 43, no. 1 (1989), p. 101-45.

Focusing on Saudi Arabia and North Yemen, the author seeks to 'demonstrate that the type, volume and control of different kinds of capital inflows decisively influence the ability of state bureaucracies to respond to economic crises'. He argues that divergent patterns of social change in the two states enabled the Yemeni government to institute a whole new set of economic measures, while the Saudis were unable to replace external capital with domestic revenue. The author claims that 'in times of crisis, the financial autonomy of the Saudi state did not translate into the ability to implement economic reform, nor did the financial independence of the Yemeni private sector enhance its ability to resists such economic reforms'. The article as a whole is an interesting marriage between practice and theory; in the sections on Yemen, the author is strongest on currency dealings and the banking infrastructure and weakest on the impact of tribalism and the distribution of labour migrants.

739 **Tendances et perspectives de l'économie yéménite.** (Trends and prospects of the Yemeni economy.)
Blandine Destremau. *Revue du Monde Musulman et de la Méditerranée*, no. 67 (1993), p. 109-19.

After a critical look at how the economies of both North and South Yemen performed before unification in 1990, the author looks at the results of the first two years of the unified economy: reduction in aid from Gulf states after the Gulf War of 1990-91 and a similar drying up of workers' remittances; an agricultural sector restricted by drought in the North and floods in the South; industry starved of investment; and a heavy burden of external debt. The author sees oil as Yemen's principal resource, but is uncertain (with justification, as it turned out) about the capacity of the government to create a genuine climate of unity.

740 **Development of aid programs to Yemen.**
Margarita Dobert. *American-Arab Affairs,* vol. 8 (1984), p. 108-16.

After a general survey of the North Yemen economy, the author looks at particular projects sponsored by the United States government: the Ibb Secondary Agricultural Institute and similar horticultural stations; bursaries for study in the United States; reconstruction assistance in Dhamār to repair the earthquake damage; water and sewerage projects for Taʿizz; and military aid and other projects in the field of education and primary health care. The author suggests that local expectations of these projects are too high, and that aid applied indirectly through the local development associations is the most effective. However, for political and security reasons, most government aid programmes operate through the central administration, which is the least successful channel, since 'directing activities from the top tends to weaken the unique self-reliance of Yemeni villagers'.

741 **Arabian Peninsula: Bahrain, Kuwait, Oman, Qatar, Saudi Arabia, United Arab Emirates, North and South Yemen: economic structure and analysis.**
Economist Intelligence Unit. London: EIU, 1988. 204p. maps.

A summary of the economies of both Yemens can be found on pages 166-200. It deals with currency, national accounts, employment, agriculture, the manufacturing sector, finance and banking, foreign trade, and external payments and debt. Both chapters have numerous statistical tables, which are fuller and more up to date for North than for South Yemen.

742 **Country profile: Oman, the Yemens.**
Economist Intelligence Unit. London: EIU, 1991- . annual.

This replaces the *Annual Supplement to the Country Report: Bahrain, Qatar, Oman, the Yemens,* which first came out in 1986. Each volume devotes around forty pages to Yemen and is a thorough review of all sections of the economy from manufacturing and construction to currency, the national accounts, and external payments and debt.

743 **Country report: Oman, the Yemens.**
Economist Intelligence Unit. London: EIU, 1991- . quarterly.

This replaces *Country report: Bahrain, Qatar, Oman, the Yemens* (1986-90), which itself replaced the *Quarterly Economic Review: Bahrain, Qatar, Oman, the Yemens* (1978-85). Each quarterly survey devotes around twelve to fifteen pages to the politics and economics of Yemen (particularly the hydrocarbon sector in recent years), and much of the report is taken up with forecasting the short-term outlook for the country. Both this publication and its stable companion (see above) make full use of the available official statistics.

744 **La transition en Arabie du Sud: économie, société, culture.**
(The transition of South Arabia: economy, society, culture.)
Groupe de Recherches sur le Maghreb et le Moyen-Orient. Paris: Laboratoire Tiers-Monde Afrique, Université de Paris VII, 1993. 173p. (Cahiers du GREMAMO, no. 11).

The nine articles (eight in French, one in English) tackle mainly economic issues. Blandine Destremau looks at the crisis of the Gulf War which followed hard on unification in 1990, and which forced thousands of Yemeni migrants to return. This caused budgetary deficits, a balance-of-payments crisis and a reduced standard of living particularly in the South, although growing tourism and the oil reserves are bright spots on the horizon. In a another paper, she looks at the economy of *qāt* production, while Ali Shamsuldin looks at the negative effects *qāt* chewing has on the economic and social development of Yemen. He also examines trade relations between the two states in the two decades prior to the union. Marion Farouk-Sluglett reports (in English) on sixteen months of fieldwork in the northern Tihāmah, where she investigated labour, cash management and agricultural production, and two authors look at the political consequences of unification: Mohammed Al Saqqaf on the new constitution and Jacques Couland on the forthcoming elections. The remaining articles deal with Islam and slavery, and the role of France in the Indian Ocean and Red Sea (1840-1922).

745 **A comparative study of the economies of the Yemen Arab Republic and the People's Democratic Republic of Yemen (1970-1988.)**
Ali Saleh Al-Hagari. PhD dissertation, University of Nebraska–Lincoln, 1992. 185p. bibliog. (Available from University Microfilms International, Ann Arbor, Michigan, order no. 9233390).

A very narrow study based on a comparison of the development plans of both countries and how these square with various economic theories. The author ignores the private sector, migrant workers and cooperatives in favour of an exclusive analysis of the state sector and recommends in conclusion that 'the unified nation should adopt a export-led industrialization strategy with emphasis on the use of labor-intensive technology'.

746 **Development potential and policies in the South Arabian countries: Yemen Arab Republic, People's Democratic Republic of Yemen, Sultanate of Oman.**
Michael Hofmann. Berlin: German Development Institute, 1982. 152p. maps. bibliog.

A straightforward survey of the economies of both Yemens, making full use of statistical data in its survey of structural changes, sectoral developments (industry, agriculture, fisheries) and foreign aid. The author ignores social and political factors in his generally pessimistic forecast of progress.

747 **Economic liberalization and privatization in socialist Arab countries: Algeria, Egypt, Syria and Yemen as examples.**
Edited by Hans Hopfinger. Gotha, Germany: Justus Perthes Verlag, 1996. 263p. (Nahost und Nordafrika: Studien zu Politik und Wirtschaft, Neuerer Geschichte, Geographie und Gesellschaft, vol. 1).

The results of a conference held in Germany in 1994, this collective work contains three papers on Yemen: Jaffer Hamed on 'The requirements of the economic policy in the Republic of Yemen after unification with special view to liberalization and privatization', which discusses the objectives of a private sector policy in general; Ali A. al-Bahr on 'Privatization and liberalization in Yemeni political programs and practice', which looks briefly at privatization in action; and the best of the three, Karl-Josef Theobald on 'Trends in privatization in the industrial sector in Yemen and case study of the Yemeni Textile Corporation – Aden', which contrasts the situation before and after unification and offers a valuable case-study, based on the author's fieldwork.

748 **People's Democratic Republic of Yemen: a review of economic and social development.**
International Bank for Reconstruction and Development. Washington, DC: Europe, Middle East and North Africa Regional Office, World Bank, 1979. 169p.

A wide-ranging survey of most aspects of the economy and society of the PDRY: national income, balance of payments; agriculture, fisheries, manufacturing and mining; transport and communications; employment and migration; food, nutrition and health; education; and housing, as well as an analysis of how government decisions are made and executed. The World Bank team praises the equalizing of income distribution, the education and health programmes, domestic resource mobilization, and the economic growth in most sectors apart from agriculture. Causes for concern are productivity, skill shortages and the efficient utilization of labour, foreign investment, economic coordination and urban/rural disparities.

749 **Yemen Arab Republic: development of a traditional economy.**
International Bank for Reconstruction and Development. Washington, DC: Europe, Middle East and North Africa Regional Office, World Bank, 1979. 303p. bibliog.

A comprehensive look at the economy of North Yemen, emphasizing transport; agriculture; industry; the food supply; education; trade; human resource management; public sector planning; and financial management. The main question-marks surrounding economic development were found to be the manpower shortage; inflation; the rational allocation of investment resources; the maintenance of capital stock; productivity; and education.

750 **The economic development of the Yemen Arab Republic.**
Ragaei El Mallakh. London: Croom Helm, 1986. 196p. bibliog.

The only monograph devoted exclusively to the economic development of either of the two Yemens, this is a rather uneven work based very heavily on printed sources. No attempt is made to place the economy in its social context, key areas such as the cooperative movement, taxation and external debt are ignored, and the findings of numerous research projects such the Yemen Research Program administered by Cornell University are notably absent from the 'Selected Bibliography'. However, it does summarize existing data in a number of areas, notably manpower and human resource development, industry and trade.

751 **Transactions in Ibb: economy and society in a Yemeni highland town.**
Brinkley M. Messick. PhD dissertation, Princeton University, 1978. 490p. bibliog. (Available from University Microfilms International, Ann Arbor, Michigan, order no. 7818379).

Having collected copies of around a thousand, mostly legal, documents, the author set about analysing the various kinds of economic activity undertaken in Ibb, an ancient and important provincial capital in the south of the Yemen Arab Republic. He studied landlord-and-tenant relations, harvest appraisal and grain storage; trading and market activity, the government sector, including the treasury (*al-mālīyah*), the municipal administration (*al-baladīyah*), and pious endowments (*awqāf*); and, finally, private ownership and wealth. These transactions are tied in with class structure and concepts of wealth and poverty to provide a rich and complex anthropologico-legal study of material transactions.

752 **Yemeni workers abroad: the impact on women.**
Cynthia Myntti. *MERIP Reports,* vol. 14, no. 5 (no. 124, June 1984), p. 11-16.

A study of the division of labour in a village in the Ḥujarīyah district of the Yemen Arab Republic and of the changes which have occurred both historically and currently as a result of male migration. The author finds that the main beneficiaries are younger men, who benefit from the absence of many adult males, and middle-class women, who have used the remittances from migrants to buy consumer goods and lighten the work-load. Poorer women, however, still find themselves at the bottom of the economic pile and have to hire out their labour for the most menial of tasks, while upper-class women aspire to a life of leisure, and are thereby more subject to sexual seclusion, rarely making appearances in public.

753 **Oman and Yemen.**

Gerd Nonneman. In: *Economic and political liberalization in the Middle East.* Edited by Tim Niblock, Emma Murphy. London: British Academic Press, 1993, p. 256-77.

The author looks at economic developments from the mid-1980s to unification in 1990 in the light of both the published development plans as well as actual practice. The author characterizes the problems in both North and South Yemen as stemming 'from a dearth of resources and the lack of central control over parts of both territory and economy'. In the North, austerity measures adopted in the 1980s led to an increase in state control, while the opposite occurred in the South, as the government tried to encourage foreign investment by developing the free market. On unification, official economic policy 'laid stress on freedom of economic action and the attraction of local as well as foreign private investment', but the results have been patchy, since investors have been put off by 'a perceived lack of social, political and institutional stability' and by a lack of skilled labour and sophisticated infrastructure.

754 **The cooperative movement of Yemen and issues of regional development.**

Edited by Muḥammad Ahmad Al-Saidi. New York: The Professors World Peace Academy, Middle East Division, 1992. 104p.

The first three contributions to this work deal with the cooperative movement in Yemen and were originally presented to a seminar organized by the Yemen Economic Society in Ṣanʿāʾ in May 1985. (The other three papers deal with countries outside the Middle East.) Dirar Abduldaim presents a factual account of the beginnings of the cooperative movement, stressing the role of the annual conferences of the Confederation of Yemeni Development Associations. Eberhart Lutz looks at the legislative framework of the local development associations (LDAs) and the attitude of the government towards them between 1973 and 1976. Fritz Piepenburg updates his conference paper and looks at developments after 1985 and how the government to some extent took over the internal running of the LDAs, which improved coordination but 'gnawed at the very foundation of the self-help idea'.

755 **The two Yemens: ideology and variations in socioeconomic development.**

M. A. Mohamed Salih. In: *The least developed and the oil-rich Arab countries: dependence, interdependence or patronage?* Edited by Kunibert Raffer, M. A. Mohamed Salih. Basingstoke, England: Macmillan, 1992, p. 203-15.

A survey of the economies of the two Yemens by a Sudanese social anthropologist, which reaches the conclusion that ideological differences in the governments of the two countries have produced few significant variations in socioeconomic performance. The author characterizes both economies as 'shambolic', suffering from 'slow or negative economic growth, a balance of payments deficit and poor foreign trade performance, all culminating in staggering economic and political crises'. The author bases his conclusions mainly on official statistics, although he does use some secondary sources by Western authors (whose names he has an unfortunate tendency to misquote, thus rendering the references to their works unrecognizable).

756 **Emigration and economic development: the case of the Yemen Arab Republic.**

Jon C. Swanson. Boulder, Colorado: Westview Press, 1979. 104p. bibliog.

A somewhat brief, but interesting and well-argued investigation, based on the author's PhD dissertation at Wayne State University in 1978, of the effect of remittances on three separate villages in North Yemen. The findings were that those left behind in the villages had higher standards of living, that migration had led to an inflation in land prices and a crystallization of land ownership patterns, and that higher daily wages and labour shortages had led to declining agricultural production. The author also looks at urban investments by migrants, but makes no mention of cooperative ventures.

757 **Rural society and participatory development: case studies of two villages in the Yemen Arab Republic.**

Jon C. Swanson, Mary Hebert. Ithaca, New York: Yemen Research Program, Center for International Studies, Cornell University, 1981. 281p. bibliog.

Between 1980 and 1981, Jon Swanson and Mary Hebert stayed for eight months in respectively Banī ʿAwwām in Ḥajjah province and Maghlāf in Hodeida province. During their residence, in the words of the introduction they 'examined the decision-making process relating to innovation and development', paying particularly close attention to issues surrounding resource management and central land tenure, emigration, crops and cropping strategies, and occupations. This study shows how two quite different villages function on a social, economic and agricultural level and provides a great many valuable data. The same can be said of most of the publications associated with the Yemen Research Program, especially those by John M. Cohen and David B. Lewis and the wide-ranging survey by S. Tjip Walker: *Emerging rural patterns in the Yemen Arab Republic: results of a 21-community cross-sectional study* (1983).

758 **Ta awun Mahwit: a case study of a local development association in highland Yemen.**

Richard Tutwiler. In: *Local politics and development in the Middle East.* Edited by Louis J. Cantori, Iliya Harik. Boulder, Colorado: Westview Press, 1984, p. 166-92. (Westview Special Studies on the Middle East).

One of the most penetrating studies in the field, this article takes a close look at the composition, financing and functioning of a North Yemeni cooperative, in this case the Taʿāwun Maḥwīt, based in a small provincial capital lying between Ṣanʿāʾ and Hodeida. The author shows how the cooperative arranged for two roads to be built to al-Maḥwīt, how it dealt with criticisms from other villages and factions, and what its other achievements have been. Of equal interest, is the author's ability to place the members of the cooperative and the cooperative itself as a corporate entity within Yemen's complex social structure and within the debate between the *shabāb,* or young men, and the *shaybāt,* or old men. In conclusion, the author examines the social, administrative and financial challenges facing the cooperative as it faced elections in 1978.

759 **Labour migration and key aspects of its economic and social impact on a Yemeni highland community.**
Shelagh Weir. In: *The Middle Eastern village: changing economic and social relations.* Edited by Richard Lawless. London: Croom Helm, 1987, p. 273-96.

The author examines the effects of migration on al-Jabal (a fictitious name), a small town situated in the mountainous al-Rāziḥ province near the Saudi border. One of the major changes recorded was the great increase in *qāt* cultivation, while sorghum diminished, coffee production remained stable, and the banana crop actually increased; there was also an increase in wage labour, and a corresponding decrease in some female agricultural tasks, as fewer livestock animals were reared. The second area of transformation was the dramatic growth in trade as large numbers of Jabalī men entered the commercial sector for the first time and as the motor road constructed in 1978 enabled different and larger amounts of goods to be brought to the town. Life was greatly altered by the appearance of these new goods, while women's work in servicing the household was reduced by the eradication of flour-grinding and wood-collecting. By 1980, about half the adult male population of the town was involved in some aspect of trade, which had become a 'respectable' occupation.

760 **The impact of external financial resources on the economic growth in North Yemen during the period 1963-1983.**
Zaid Ali Zabara. PhD dissertation, Howard University, 1986. 270p. bibliog. (Available from University Microfilms International, Ann Arbor, Michigan, order no. 8701904).

The author uses simple and multiple regression analysis to test whether 'external capital inflow affects all aspects of the economy and not just investment ventures'. He studies consumption, investment, savings, trade and external aid (little attention is paid to workers' remittances from abroad), and concludes that the inflow of external funds does make a sizeable contribution to the Gross Domestic Product (GDP) and has a positive and significant impact on the structural changes observed in North Yemen's economy between 1963 and 1983.

Yemeni unification: the end of marxism in Arabia.
See item no. 658.

Trade and Industry

761 **Textiles in Yemen: historical references to trade and commerce in textiles in Yemen from antiquity to modern times.**
John Baldry. London: British Museum, 1982. 107p. maps. (Occasional Paper, no. 27).

The author shows how, despite scattered references to textiles in pre-Islamic times, the clothing industry in Yemen did not become important until ʿAbbāsid times, when the Red Sea regained its predominance as a major trade route. Aden also became an important port of transhipment, as merchants trading with India and China by sea required warehousing facilities on the South Arabian coast. Aden retained its importance as European traders arrived on the scene for the first time in the 15th century, and there are numerous records showing goods from Surat in India being shipped in British and Muscati vessels to Aden and Mocha up to the 19th century. The history of the indigenous textile industry is also described at length, using both Arabic and European sources, and the author concludes with a survey of the cotton trade in North Yemen in the 20th century up to and including the construction in 1979 of a new cotton mill near Hodeida on behalf of the People's Republic of China.

762 **The indigo industry of the Yemen.**
Jenny Balfour-Paul. *Arabian Studies,* vol. 8 (1990), p. 39-62.

An important article, which given an eye-witness account of the last family workshops producing the indigo dye in both North Yemen (Zabīd), and South Yemen (al-Bayḍā'). The author describes the extraction of the dye, the cloth and its preparation, and the dyeing process itself as well as workshop organization and management. All this is set in a historical context, which shows that 'although the whole indigo craft today stands low in public esteem, this was not always so'. A complementary article by Hanne Schönig describes the fabrication of gall-ink (*khiḍāb)* in both a traditional and a modern way, 'Traditional cosmetics of women: the black dye *hiḍāb:* traditional and modern ways of fabrication' (*Proceedings of the Seminar for Arabian Studies,* vol. 26 [1996], p. 135-44).

763 **Kaffee aus Arabien: der Bedeutungswandel eines Weltwirtschaftsgutes und seine siedlungsgeographische Konsequenz an der Trockengrenze der Ökumene.** (Coffee from Arabia: the change in importance of an element in the world economy and its consequences for settlement on the edge of the arid zone.) Hans Becker, Volker Höhfeld, Horst Kopp. Wiesbaden, Germany: Franz Steiner, 1979. 78p. bibliog. (Erdkundliches Wissen, vol. 46).

The authors focus on Mocha and its role in the coffee trade in the 17th and 18th centuries. They show how 'despite the enormous annual quantities traded by European merchants – exclusively via Mocha . . . they exported only a very small proportion of Yemen's annual coffee crop. The biggest proportion was exported by non-European merchants who always used the co-existing traditional routes'. Further chapters look at the instability of Red Sea settlements as a consequence of the fluctuations in the coffee trade, while the final chapters examine the present-day situation and importance of Mocha and the role of coffee in the economy of North Yemen.

764 **The diary of a Mocha coffee agent.** P. C. Boxhall. *Arabian Studies,* vol. 1 (1974), p. 102-18.

The author transcribes entries from the official Diary of Transactions maintained in 1733 by Francis Dickinson, Commissary for Affairs for the East India Company in Mocha. The entries recorded show clearly that Mocha was only a point of transhipment, with most of the coffee coming from Bayt al-Faqīh, and that the Company's ships and their agent were subject to excessive and unpredictable demands in customs dues from the Imam's servants.

765 **Energy consumption in Yemen: economics and policy (1970-1990.)** Abdulkarim Ali Dahan. PhD dissertation, University of Arizona, 1996. 147p. bibliog. (Available from University Microfilms International, Ann Arbor, Michigan, order no. 9713384).

One of the few quantitative studies of the economy of North Yemen, this thesis analyses the relationship between energy (electricity use and petroleum consumption) and economic development and develops a model for determining both the demand for energy and the values of petroleum consumption for the years 1991-2000. The author concludes by making some limited recommendations regarding energy conservation.

766 **Observations on the measures of capacity in present-day northern Yemen.** W. J. Donaldson. *New Arabian Studies,* vol. 3 (1996), p. 33-49.

Traditional weights and measures tend to be complex, because the number of different units tends to be large, and the variations in the absolute size of these units is considerable, even within a relatively small geographical area. North Yemen is no exception to this rule, and the author takes us through some of the bewildering units of capacity which were used until very recently in different parts of the country, highlighting the difficulties of 'establishing the absolute magnitude of local standards'.

767 **Trade and shipping in the Red Sea region.**
J. M. Doviak, Gary Gimson. In: *The Red Sea: prospects for stability.* Edited by Abdel Majid Farid. London: Croom Helm; New York: St. Martin's Press, 1984, p. 18-35.

The article looks at trading patterns in the early 1980s for Egypt, Ethiopia, Israel, Jordan, Sudan and the Yemen Arab Republic, while extending the survey to Djibouti and the People's Democratic Republic of Yemen, when considering shipping and ports. The authors see little prospect of either of the Yemens developing a shipping industry, since they preferred instead to invest in port, bunkering and transhipment facilities. Most of the statistical information is taken from the *Seatrade Arab Shipping Guide* (Colchester, England: Seatrade House), which was published annually between 1978 and 1991 as a supplement to *Seatrade Weekly* and *Seatrade Business Review.*

768 **Antonin Besse of Aden: the founder of St. Antony's College, Oxford.**
David Footman. Basingstoke, England: Macmillan in association with St. Antony's College, Oxford, 1986. 258p. maps. (St. Antony's/ Macmillan Series).

Using private papers, the author traces the biography of Antonin Besse, who began life in 1877 in an impoverished southern French family, and died – in 1951 – a millionaire and the owner of the largest trading enterprise in South Arabia. After some years in the French army, Besse arrived in Aden in 1899 as a junior employee of a French firm trading in coffee. He branched out on his own in 1902, and thanks to an advantageous marriage, he was able to invest capital into a growing business. The turning points in his life came in 1922, when he divorced his first wife and married the Englishwomen Hilda Crowther, and in 1923 when he was awarded the agency in petroleum products by the Shell Petroleum Company. From that point on, he never looked back, and by expanding his activities to the Horn of Africa, he was able to profit from the Ethiopian War of 1936 and the Second World War. In 1948, he employed over 2,000 people, and owned four ships and fifteen dhows, making him by far the most important businessman in the region. He used his fortune for educational purposes and died in 1951 on a visit to Gordonstoun School in Scotland. This is an interesting and well-written work, which contains, in an appendix, long extracts from Besse's own 68-page review of his company's trading activities.

769 **Ansätze industrieller Entwicklung in einem arabischen Entwicklungsland ohne Erdöl-Ressourcen: die Jemenitische Arabische Republik (Nordjemen).** (Attempts at industrial development in a developing Arab country without petroleum resources: the Yemen Arab Republic (North Yemen).)
Hans Gebhardt. *Orient* (Opladen, Germany), vol. 25, no. 4 (1984), p. 516-36.

An extremely thorough survey of the conditions for industrial development in North Yemen. The author shows how the trading and service sectors of the economy boomed in the 1970s, fuelled by the remittances from Yemenis working abroad. By contrast, industry stagnated, except for the construction sector. In 1980, industrial enterprises of any sort with more than ten employees were concentrated in the main centres of

Ṣanᶜāʾ, Hodeida and Taᶜizz, while five of North Yemen's ten provinces had no medium-sized factories at all. The most significant areas for industry after the construction sector, were food, quarrying, metal-working and some small-scale chemical production. Some of this was financed by the state, but most of the enterprises were based in the private sector, with almost no foreign capital inflow, despite a very liberal investment law. The author sees the factors preventing the growth of North Yemen's industrial capacity as difficult to overcome, and suggests the imposition of import restrictions, the encouragement of investment and the setting up of a chain of special advisory bureaux.

770 **Arabie du Sud: le commerce comme facteur dynamisant des changements économiques et sociaux.** (South Arabia: trade as a dynamic factor in economic and social change.)
Groupe de Recherches sur le Maghreb et le Moyen Orient. Paris: A.U.P.A., GREMAMO, 1991. 225p. (Cahiers du GREMAMO, no. 10).

The results of a conference held in Paris in October 1990, in which scholars from France, the Yemens, Britain, Italy and elsewhere gave sixteen presentations on different aspects of Yemeni trade. Four of the contributions are in English: Shelagh Weir discusses the structure of markets and the protection of trade in the Jabal Rāziḥ (North-West Yemen); Ahmed Zayn Aidrous examines the role of commerce in the various agreements concluded between the British and the tribal leaders of the Hadramout in the 19th century; Massimo Campanini looks as much as the influence of Nasserism on North Yemen as he does at trade in his paper; while Ahmed al-Kasir suggests that recent changes in the social structure of North Yemen will lead to the growth of the 'national market'. Other interesting papers in French look at Franco-British rivalries over Shaykh Saᶜīd opposite Perim Island (Claudine Veillon), at markets in Ṣanᶜāʾ (Franck Mermier), at the role of trade in relations between the two Yemens (Soad Zerrouki) and at numerous social issues, such as changes in the tribal structure in South Yemen (Fawwaz Traboulsi).

771 **Socio-cultural and managerial behaviour of Yemeni entrepreneurs.**
Omar Osman Mohammed. *Orient* (Opladen, Germany), vol. 36, no. 2 (1995), p. 287-304.

The author examines the cultural divide between the Yemeni way of doing business and the Western, basing his research on intensive discussions with Yemeni civil servants, on the analysis of the business behaviour of twenty-eight Yemeni entrepreneurs, and on secondary literature produced by Arab research institutes. Business enterprises in Yemen are almost exclusively family affairs, with leadership vested in the head of the family, and no fixed organizational structure or job descriptions for other family members. Traditional leadership is seen as being in decline, although the older generations still dominate decision-making and prefer to negotiate face to face rather than through or with an agent. The author also looks at the role the government plays as entrepreneur, and considers how many senior civil servants apply what the author calls 'the Yemeni patriarchal social order' to public administration, thus undermining their subordinates, creating confusion in chains of command, and resorting to ad hoc solutions. The author concludes by showing the intimate relationship between the public and private sector in Yemen, and by giving some general advice to Westerners regarding the Yemeni business environment.

772 **Indo-Yemen trade relations: past and present.**
H. S. Al-Mulassi. *Anvesak,* vol. 24, no. 2 (1994), p. 125-46.

After a brief survey of trade between India and South Arabia in ancient times, the author moves on to commercial relations between North and South Yemen from 1970 until unification in 1990, and shows statistically that India was an important trading partner of both countries, but more particularly North Yemen, and that the balance-of-trade account was always in India's favour. The same situation holds true for trade between India and the new Republic of Yemen, with the latter importing foodstuffs, live animals, raw materials, and some manufactured goods such as textiles, bicycles, and articles in leather and wood. Yemen's exports to India were modest and consisted mainly of petroleum oil and scrap. Price is not always the determining factor in Yemen's choice of trading partner, as the author demonstrates by showing the standardized dollar value of the tea, rice and sugar imported by Yemen from a variety of countries. The author feels that the new investment law (No. 22 of 1991) and the creation of Aden as a free zone will stimulate more trade between the two countries, with particular benefits to India.

773 **Le café du Yémen et l'Égypte (XVII-XVIII siècles.)** (Yemeni coffee and Egypt: 17th-18th centuries.)
André Raymond. *Chroniques Yéménites,* vol. 3 (1995), p. 16-25.

A brief survey of the coffee trade between Yemen and Egypt. Coffee seems to have been used in Yemen for the first time in the 15th century, and to have been linked to certain *ṣūfī* (mystical) rituals. Its use had reached both Cairo and Mecca by the early 16th century, Istanbul in 1554, and Europe by the latter half of the 17th century. The author describes in details the means by which coffee from Mocha was brought to Egypt, and shows how the importation of Yemeni coffee was the most important commercial activity in Ottoman Egypt. In the latter part of the 18th century, coffee represented one-third of all imports into Egypt by value, and although much of it was used locally, a substantial amount was re-exported to Europe. By the end of the century, however, the competition from coffee grown by the colonial powers in Java and the French Antilles, and the arrival of European merchants in Mocha, had markedly affected Egyptian imports, and by 1789 Egyptian merchants importing coffee from Yemen had shrunk to half the number found a century earlier.

774 **Development of petroleum sector and prospects in Yemen.**
Muhammad Ahmad Al-Saidi. In: *Energy Watchers II.* Edited by Dorothea H. El-Mallakh. Boulder, Colorado: International Research Center for Energy and Economic Development, 1991, p. 27-9.

A brief summary of the programme for exploiting Yemeni oil reserves, as seen by the Secretary-General of the Supreme Council for Oil and Mineral Resources.

775 **Energy production and consumption in the Yemen Arab Republic.**
Abdulaziz Y. Saqqaf. *Journal of Energy and Development,* vol. 11, no. 1 (1986), p. 105-18.

Although overtaken by both political and economic events, this is still a useful survey of the historical development of North Yemen's energy demands. The author makes full use of specialized World Bank, United Nations Development Programme and official Yemeni government reports to look at petroleum production, refining capacity and oil exploration, at household energy consumption, at the demands of industry and agriculture, and at energy supply (including domestic fuelwood).

776 **Le Yémen et la Mer Rouge: actes du Colloque organizé au Sénat, 29-30 novembre, 1993 par le Centre Culturel Yéménite et l'Association France-Yémen.** (Yemen and the Red Sea: proceedings of the Colloquium organized by the Yemeni Cultural Centre and the Franco-Yemeni Association and held in the Senate on 29-30 November 1993.)
Edited by Yves Thoraval, Chawki Abdelamir, André Nied. Paris: L'Harmattan, 1995. 104p.

A collection of twelve short papers, of which half deal with trade with Yemen or in the Red Sea in general. Christian Lochon looks at the role of coffee in Franco-Yemeni relations, a topic which is put into a broader context by Philippe Haudrière who examines the general economic relations between France (and French India) and Yemen in the 18th century. Even wider in scope and the longest article in the collection is Michel Tuchscherer's excellent survey of Red Sea trade around 1700 (itself a summary of a longer survey published in volume five of *Res Orientalis* [Bures-sur-Yvette, France, 1993]). While the other contributions are interesting, none are more than eight pages long.

777 **People's Democratic Republic of Yemen: enhancing industrial productive capacity.**
United Nations Industrial Development Organization. Vienna: UNIDO, 1989. 135p. (Industrial Development Review Series).

The most comprehensive factual analysis of South Yemen's industrial base prior to unification in 1990. This work looks at the structure and performance of the industrial sector, and all the relevant industries, from fish processing to oil refinery, at the development strategy adopted by the government since 1971, and at the resources (or their lack) which underpin the economy. Identified as major problems are the poor infrastructure, a major skills shortage, water shortage, and a lack of inward investment.

778 **Yemen Arab Republic: diversifying the industrial base.**
United Nations Industrial Development Organization. Vienna: UNIDO, 1989. 147p. (Industrial Development Review Series).

This work, like its companion for South Yemen listed above, is the most important source of factual information on industrial development and prospects for North Yemen, prior to unification. It covers the same fields, such as ownership and investment patterns, and employment and productivity, and goes on to analyse the problems facing individual industries, the development strategy of the government since 1973, and the difficulties which the country will have to tackle in the 1990s such as a severe shortage of skills.

779 **Yemen commercial directory.**
Ṣanʿāʾ: Chamber of Commerce and Industry, 1995. 97p.

A list of companies operating from Ṣanʿāʾ, arranged alphabetically under broad categories of activity from accounting to watches. The most significant areas are building materials, spare parts for cars and oil supply services. This recent publication replaces the similarly structured but bilingual (English–Arabic) *Yemen business directory for trade and industry guide* (Damascus: Ekrama, 1985-86. 220p. [English text] and 212p. [Arabic text]).

Frankincense and myrrh: a study of the Arabian incense trade.
See item no. 291.

The Periplus of the Erythraean Sea.
See item no. 299.

Cauwa ende comptanten . . .
See item no. 320.

Yemeni merchants and trade in Yemen, 13th-16th centuries.
See item no. 352.

Have you anything to declare? . . .
See item no. 358.

Some notes on the economy of Ottoman Yemen (1870-1918).
See item no. 393.

Labour migration and key aspects of its economic and social impact . . .
See item no. 759.

Agriculture, Irrigation and Fisheries

780 **The training and visit agricultural extension system in the Tihama Plain region of Yemen: perceptions of contact farmers and extension workers.**

Tarek K. M. Aghabri. PhD dissertation, Michigan State University, 1989. 196p. bibliog. (Available from: University Microfilms International, Ann Arbor, Michigan, order no. 9111557).

The government of North Yemen, aware of the huge growth in food imports, set up an agricultural extension system in the early 1970s. Its mission consisted in giving technical advice, overseeing the introduction of new crops, and providing farmers with new knowledge and modern skills. This survey of the service found that extension workers were satisfied with the training they received, while contact farmers in general found the technical content of the programme 'informative, helpful, timely, relevant and suitable for their needs', although their perception differed according to their educational level. A more theoretical work, which looks more at leadership and motivation among agricultural extension agents in the Tihāmah is: *The management of rural development: the role of agricultural extension agents in the Yemen Arab Republic* (Mohammed Belhaj. PhD dissertation, Texas Technical University, 1989. 319p. bibliog. Available from University Microfilms International, Ann Arbor, Michigan, order no. 8920889).

781 **Water, risk and environmental management: agriculture and irrigation in South Yemen (PDRY.)**

Colin Barnes. *New Arabian Studies,* vol. 1 (1993), p. 124-36.

The author worked in 1985 on a design programme for the rehabilitation of flood protection and irrigation structures in the eight wadis which, together, contain over eighty per cent of the cultivated land in South Yemen. Although the author considers that 'in conventional economic terms, if one includes the costs of environmental protection and the annual land preparation and flood protection works, neither spate nor irrigated agriculture give particularly good returns', he still believes that investment in agriculture and the protection of water resources should continue.

782 **Sozialer Umbruch und Kulturlandschaftswandel in Südarabien: agrargeographische Untersuchungen im Umland von Ṣanʿāʾ (Arabische Republic Jemen).** (Social change and cultural landscape in South Arabia: agricultural and geographical investigations in the hinterland of Ṣanʿāʾ (Yemen Arab Republic).)
Emil Betzler. Wiesbaden, Germany: Reichert, 1987. 295p. bibliog. (Jemen-Studien, Band 5).

An excellent survey of structural changes in seven villages near Ṣanʿāʾ. The author shows how innovations in agriculture have been stimulated by the growth of the capital city, by better communications and by the more marked presence of Ṣanʿānī merchants, and how a 'transition is taking place from subsistence agriculture with strong tribal influence to a market-oriented form of agricultural production'. The author looks in particular at agricultural techniques, and at types of land property, concluding that social hierarchy is now dictated by the private property owned by a tribesman, which was not formerly the case. He warns about the over-exploitation of water resources and over-reliance on *qāt* production, but forecasts a productive future 'given the emotional relationship of the Yemen farmers with their land, as well as the high social respect of agriculture in the Yemen society'.

783 **Les pêcheurs de Shihr: transmission du savoir et identité sociale.** (The fishermen of Shiḥr: transmission of knowledge and social identity.)
Sylvaine Camelin. *Chroniques Yéménites,* vol. 3 (1995), p. 38-56.

An interesting study of how local fishermen from Shiḥr in South Yemen operate, both as a professional group and as individuals. The author describes the various elements in each crew, how the boat is organized, and the qualities and training required to become a *rabbān,* or captain. His role is spelled out in detail, as are the transformations in fishing techniques since independence in 1967.

784 **Yemeni agriculture and economic change: case studies of two highland regions.**
Sheila Carapico, Richard Tutwiler. Ṣanʿāʾ: American Institute for Yemeni Studies, 1981. 191p. maps. bibliog. (Yemen Development Series, no. 1).

An important factual survey of agriculture, livestock-rearing and land-owning practices in the regions of Ibb and ʿAmrān to the south and north of Ṣanʿāʾ respectively. The authors also look at the local markets, and at the problems of maintaining a steady labour force, and find that capital absorption rather than access to capital is one of the main problems. They conclude that 'commercialization has come to Yemen, changing the economic structure of the nation and its society irretrievably'.

785 **Runoff agriculture: a case study about the Yemeni highlands.**
Helmut Eger. Wiesbaden, Germany: Reichert, 1987. 238p. maps. bibliog. (Jemen-Studien, Band, 7).

The author conducted extensive investigations into runoff agriculture around ʿAmrān to the north of Ṣanʿāʾ in North Yemen. The main focus of the study is *sawāqī* (rather than *sayl)* irrigation, whereby rainwater from areas not used for agriculture is conveyed via unlined canals to the adjacent cropped areas. The author examines crops and crop distribution, the rainwater harvesting systems, the prevailing situation regarding land ownership, farm size, and land fragmentation, the agricultural labour force and farm equipment. He identifies certain constraints in the further development of runoff agriculture and makes detailed recommendations for future production.

786 **Implications of labor displacement for production relations in Yemen.**

Yakin Ertürk. In: *Population displacement and resettlement: development and conflict in the Middle East.* Edited by Seteney Shami. New York: Center for Migration Studies, 1994, p. 107-20.

Despite its title, this article is more a report on agricultural conditions in the Tihāmah of North Yemen than a contribution to labour studies. The author carried out fieldwork in small villages, and studied irrigation, cropping patterns, sharecropping arrangements, and social differentiation He found that 'although agriculture in the Tihāma still remains subsistence-oriented, it has become more diverse and market-oriented in the past 20 years'. Remittances from migrants enabled small farmers to invest in lift-pumps, which means a relatively predictable income but also problems of cash scarcity and rising costs for diesel fuel and spare parts. On the other hand, sharecroppers suffered from an increasing loss of their ability to determine the terms of their agreements with landlords, while landless labourers were faced with a shrinking job market. Given periodic droughts, sand dune encroachments and poor infrastructure, the outlook for small farmers in the province is bleak.

787 **Fisheries development in the North West Indian Ocean: the impact of commercial fishing arrangements.**

Khaled Hariri. London: Ithaca Press, 1985. 158p. maps. bibliog.

A very thorough analysis of the literature regarding fishing policies in the Red Sea, Gulf of Aden, Arabian Sea and Arab Gulf. The author's approach enables him to study the political and economic aspects of the fishing industry comprehensively, although his lack of fieldwork does not always allow him to criticize official statistics and policy statements or to describe local fishing methods as they are actually used.

788 **Irrigation farming in the ancient oasis of Marib.**

Ingrid Hehmeyer. *Proceedings of the Seminar for Arabian Studies,* vol. 19 (1989), p. 33-44.

The author describes the three systems of irrigation practised in ancient Marib: *sayl* (spate) irrigation by submersion, *sayl* irrigation by controlled flooding, and wells and cisterns. Seasonal crops were cultivated twice a year, the ground being ploughed before the *sayl* with a wooden hook plough, and fertilized with ash or organic manure. Cereals, pulses, vegetables and other garden crops were grown. In addition, the inhabitants practised sophisticated arboriculture, using basin irrigation from wells and cisterns in the dry season. In this way, date palms, fruit trees, vines and other trees were successfully cultivated.

789 **A beekeeping project in the Yemen Arab Republic.**
Elbert R. Jaycox, Jan Karpowicz. *Arabian Studies,* vol. 8 (1990), p. 1-10.

Following the earthquake in Dhamār in 1982, a small bee-keeping team from the United States visited the area to help re-establish the local hives. They went to ten locations in the Dhamār province, as well as contacting the teaching apiary at Ibb Agricultural Institute, which was supported by the New Mexico State University. This article describes the team's experiences in Yemen, but leaves unanswered (as they acknowledge) many questions regarding the biology and behaviour of Yemeni honey bees.

790 **The demands and limitations of sustainable water use in arid regions: a discussion of "sustainable development" taking the Wādī Markhah (Republic of Yemen) as an example.**
Stefan Kohler. *Applied Geography and Development,* vol. 47 (1996), p. 23-36.

The author has conducted research into recent changes in irrigation techniques in the Wādī Markhah, a valley on the former border between North and South Yemen, at the eastern edge of the highlands where the mountains and the desert meet. Traditional irrigation used the spring and summer floods, thus maintaining the water table and keeping the soil fertile, but also restricted the number of fields that could be cultivated. This system gradually gave way in the 1970s to pump irrigation, which tapped directly into the groundwater, and greatly increased the area under cultivation. Although this change has brought short-term benefits, the author considers that pump irrigation is antagonistic to sustainable development in the long run, since it lowers the water table, degrades the quality of the soil, and uses more energy than the traditional methods. He sees the farmers of Wādī Markhah as caught in a dilemma, since they can escape from their current state of underdevelopment only by 'growing more agricultural products for markets outside the region', which policy relies 'on the year-round availability of irrigation', yet this policy will inevitably result in the over-exploitation of the available groundwater resources and the consequent destruction of the region's economic base. He suggests using both flood and pump irrigation, thus combining the best in modern and ancient technologies.

791 **Agrargeographie der Arabischen Republik Jemen: Landnutzung und agrarsoziale Verhältnisse in einem islamisch-orientalischen Entwicklungsland mit alter bäuerlicher Kultur.** (The agrarian geography of the Yemen Arab Republic: land use and agrarian social relations in an Eastern Islamic developing country with an ancient farming culture.)
Horst Kopp. Erlangen, Germany: Selbstverlag der Fränkischen Geographischen Gesellschaft in Kommission bei Palm & Enke, 1981. 281p. maps. bibliog. (Erlanger Geographische Arbeiten, Sonderband 11).

The author carried out extensive fieldwork between 1974 and 1976, identifying five large agricultural areas in North Yemen. Each was distinguished by differing climate, hydrology and soil conditions, which permitted a variety of crops to be cultivated, under varying forms of land use and irrigation system. Kopp suggests that improvements in Yemeni agriculture will be achieved only through greater capital investment and higher labour intensity

792 **Entwicklungsprozesse in der Arabischen Republik Jemen.** (Developmental processes in the Yemen Arab Republic.)
Edited by Horst Kopp, Günther Schweizer. Wiesbaden, Germany: Reichert, 1984. 305p. maps. (Jemen-Studien, Band 1).

A collection of seventeen articles, mostly in German, reflecting the many development and research projects being undertaken by German academics in the Yemen Arab Republic. For example, Hans Gebhardt discusses the development of roadside markets, Helmut Eger looks at rainwater harvesting, Emil Betzler summarizes his work on agricultural development in the Ṣanʿāʾ hinterland, Horst Kopp examines animal husbandry and the use of wood in the region of al-Ṭūr, Rudolf Straub investigates soils in the Tihāmah, Ulrich Deil studies vegetation patterns in the Tihāmah, while Klaus Müller-Hohenstein takes us through some preliminary research on geobotany and range management in the whole republic.

793 **Agrarstruktureller Wandel in Ḥarāz-Gebirge (Arabische Republik Jemen): zur Problematik von Projektplanungen in kleinräumig-differenzierten ländlichen Regionen.** (Agrarian structural change in the Ḥarāz Mountains (Yemen Arab Republic): on the problems of project planning in highly diversified rural regions.)
Georg Ladj. Wiesbaden, Germany: Reichert, 1992. 384p. maps. bibliog. (Jemen-Studien, Band 11).

In some ways, this sums up the development dilemma, as it investigates why the Ḥarāz Afforestation Project in North Yemen failed. Traditional agriculture in Ḥarāz was based on subsistence production, and was well integrated into the tribal culture with labour being provided through the extended family. However, with the emigration of so many men to Saudi Arabia in the 1970s, the situation changed completely. The traditional subsistence economy has been almost totally monetarized, the social and productive unit is more and more the nuclear family, and while there has been a considerable rise in land prices everywhere, the forms of cultivation differ widely, with some villages dependent on remittances, and others fully occupied with terrace cultivation. Ladj concludes that the lesson for development planners is to understand diversity and not to consider projects on too large a scale. For an anthropological perspective on the Project by an American expert, see the article by Charles F. Swagman (item no. 560).

794 **Land reform or socialist agriculture?: rural development in PDRY Yemen, 1967-1982.**
Jim R. Lewis. In: *The socialist Third World: urban development and territorial planning.* Edited by Dean Forbes, Nigel Thrift. Oxford, England: Blackwell, 1987, p. 169-93.

The author studies the development of agricultural production against the programme of agrarian reform instituted by the South Yemen government shortly after independence. He gives several reasons for the limited success in increasing production and argues that central planning has not been effective in determining the nature and character of production. He concludes that 'what has happened in the past fifteen years has represented the first steps towards a socialist transformation and not the transformation itself'.

795 **Coffee in Yemen: a practical guide.**
J. Brian D. Robinson. Berlin: Klaus Schwarz, 1993. 87p.

A manual of coffee production produced on behalf of the Deutsche Gesellschaft für Technische Zusammerarbeit (German Agency for Technical Cooperation) for use in Rural Development Project Al-Maḥwīt Province. It covers environmental conditions, seedling production, field planting, pruning, weeding, irrigation, manure and fertilizer, harvesting and processing and a guide to pests, diseases and other disorders. As a teaching manual, it cannot be bettered.

796 **Land-cover studies and crop acreage estimates from aerial photographs and satellite imagery: a case study from Taʿizz-Turbah, Yemen Arab Republic.**
Rudolf Schoch. Zurich, Switzerland: Remote Sensing Section, Department of Geography, University of Zurich, 1982. 253p. maps.

Using aerial photographs, topographical maps, photo-maps and Landsat imagery, the author has undertaken a survey to see whether remote-sensing techniques can yield useful results with regard to the complex agricultural and land-use situation in the south of the Yemen Arab Republic. The author discusses farm characteristics, cropping patterns and water use, and the changes in land cover noted between 1972 and 1980. He concludes that the current pump irrigation is benefiting only a small minority of farmers and that 'there should be a careful investigation to see if an enforced development of the rainfed area would not generate higher profits in the long run'.

797 **The cultivation of cereals in mediaeval Yemen.**
R. B. Serjeant. *Arabian Studies,* vol. 1 (1974), p. 25-74.

An important contribution to our understanding of agriculture under the Rasūlids (1229-1454), this article consists of a general introduction to various aspects of cereal cultivation in South Arabia and to agricultural almanacs and calendars, followed by a translation with extensive notes of the chapter on cereals from *Bughyat al-fallāḥīn* written by the Rasūlid sultan ʿAbbās ibn ʿAlī al-Malik al-Afḍal (d. c. 1376). Nine kinds of cereals are dealt with by the medieval author (two kinds of wheat, barley, millet, rice, lucerne, sesame, kinib and ṭahaf-millet), and the translator assures us from his personal knowledge that everything described by al-Malik al-Afḍal can still be seen in South Arabia today.

798 **Farmers and fishermen in Arabia: studies in customary law and practice.**
R. B. Serjeant, edited by G. R. Smith. Aldershot, England: Variorum, 1995. unpaged.

An important collection of articles previously published between 1954 and 1993 of which seven deal with agriculture in North Yemen and the Ḥaḍramawt. Two papers, 'The cultivation of cereals in mediaeval Yemen' and 'Observations on irrigation in South-West Arabia', have been described separately (see items 797, 799), but among the other contributions, the following are relevant: 'Star calendars and an almanac from South-West Arabia', 'A Socotran star calendar', 'A *maqāmah* on palm-protection (*shirāḥah*)', 'A Yemeni agricultural poem' and 'Some irrigation systems in Hadramawt'. Apart from the last-mentioned, all the other four are based on literary productions from within South Arabian culture itself.

799 **Observations on irrigation in South West Arabia.**

R. B. Serjeant. *Proceedings of the Seminar for Arabian Studies,* vol. 18 (1988), p. 145-53.

The author collected his information on irrigation from poetry, from folklore, from his work on law books, legal opinions and customary law, and from his experiences when working on four occasions as a consultant to engineering firms. He discusses the methods for conducting spate water on to cultivable land in both North and South Yemen, and goes on to look at the historical evidence for barrages in Ḥaḍramawt, and at well irrigation there, before concluding with some observations on the *ghayl*, or underground canalization of springs, which can be found in Ṣanʿāʾ and elsewhere.

800 **The making of palm vinegar at al-Ḥiswah (near Aden) and some other crafts related to palm trees.**

Martine Vanhove. *New Arabian Studies,* vol. 2 (1994), p. 175-85.

A description, based on a native informant, of the production of vinegar and wine from a particular grove of palm trees near Aden. The author, who is a linguist by training, appends a list of technical terms, either words previously unrecorded or which have taken on specialized meanings. All relate to the doush palm tree and its by-products.

801 **The adaptive dynamics of water allocation in al-Ahjur, Yemen Arab Republic.**

Daniel Martin Varisco. PhD dissertation, University of Pennsylvania, 1982. 690p. bibliog. (Available from University Microfilm International, Ann Arbor, Michigan, order no. 8307372).

The author argues that tribal social organization is 'an adaptive and dynamic social reponse to constraints of water as a resource in the central highlands of the Yemen Arab Republic'. He shows how irrigators cooperate in the use of spring water flow according to traditional arrangements validated by customary tribal law, and in this thesis he makes an important contribution to our understanding of the relationship between customary law, tribal organization and natural resources in the Yemen.

802 **The agricultural marker stars in Yemeni folklore.**

Daniel Martin Varisco. *Asian Folklore Studies,* vol. 52, no. 1 (1993), p. 119-42.

This study focuses on a traditional star calendar used in highland Yemen to define the seasons and the timing of agricultural activities. The author regards the calendar's division into twenty-eight distinct periods linked to the lunar stations as a relatively recent variation on a number of local regional star lists, and goes on to describe how the markers functioned and compares them with a different version recorded in a 17th-century text. This and twelve other articles on Yemeni agriculture are reprinted in the author's collected essays entitled *Medieval folk astronomy in Arabia and Yemen* (Aldershot, England: Variorum, 1997. unpaged).

803 **The future of terrace farming in Yemen: a development dilemma.**
Daniel Martin Varisco. *Agriculture and Human Values,* vol. 8 (1991), p. 166-72.

The author highlights the dangers facing the continuation of terrace farming in the highlands of North Yemen: excessive irrigation which has resulted in serious environmental degradation and increasingly destructive floods; the dramatic decline in the water table; the 'skyrocketing demand for fuelwood' and the consequent reduction in tree cover; the insistence by the government on increased productivity and state support for unsuitable crops; international projects which have 'neither the information nor the expertise to switch to a sustainable agriculture program'; and, lastly, the raised expectations of Yemeni farmers themselves. The author argues that the government should harness the local knowledge of agriculture and the environment, and that indigenous expertise can be grafted on to modern methods and technology to save the remaining terraces.

804 **Land use and agricultural development in the Yemen Arab Republic.**
Daniel Martin Varisco. In: *Anthropology and development in North Africa and the Middle East.* Edited by Muneera Salem-Murdock, Michael M. Horowitz, Monica Sella. Boulder, Colorado; Oxford, England: Westview Press, 1990, p. 292-311.

A succinct but penetrating analysis of land use and, above all, land tenure in North Yemen. The author looks at the balance between private, communal, state and *waqf* (endowment) land, and discusses the important regional variations, particularly regarding sharecropping and tenancy arrangements, using the survey data produced by aid agencies and the Yemeni Ministry of Agriculture and Fisheries. He concludes his article with some caustic observations on the role of the anthropologist in development projects, echoing the experiences of Timothy Morris (see items 546, 597) and Charles F. Swagman (see item no. 560).

805 **Medieval agricultural texts from Rasūlid Yemen.**
Daniel Martin Varisco. *Manuscripts of the Middle East,* vol. 4 (1989), p. 150-4.

An annotated bibliography of the major texts from the Rasūlid era (1229-1454) dealing with agriculture. The author describes three general agricultural texts, seven agricultural almanacs, three records of tax data, a veterinary treatise and a brief anonymous excerpt from a larger work concerning planting times relevant to Wādī Zabīd. Very few of the works listed are available in critical (or, indeed, any) editions, although a few have been either fully or partially translated into English by R. B. Serjeant and Daniel Martin Varisco (qq.v.).

806 **Medieval agriculture and Islamic science: the almanac of a Yemeni sultan.**
Daniel Martin Varisco. Seattle, Washington; London: University of Washington Press, 1994. 349p. bibliog.

The author has edited and translated the almanac chapter from the astronomical treatise *al-Tabṣirah fī ʿilm al-nujūm* by ʿUmar ibn Yūsuf al-Malik al-Ashraf (d. 1296), but more important even than the original text are the author's copious historical, geographical, botanical, agricultural and bibliographical notes which are a mine of information for students of both medieval and contemporary Yemen, and show the relevance of the author's opening remark, 'The study of a medieval almanac as part of a living tradition can be accomplished in Yemen better than perhaps anywhere else in the Arab world'.

807 **The production of sorghum (dhurah) in Highland Yemen.**
Daniel Martin Varisco. *Arabian Studies,* vol. 7 (1985), p. 53-88.

Using historical texts and ethnographic data gathered during an eighteen-month residence in al-Ahjur, the author studies the techniques and vocabulary of sorghum cultivation and processing in North Yemen. Sorghum is a cereal grain, similar to millet, and is 'generally recognised as the staple crop of the region'. The author describes the field preparation, planting, growing cycle, leaf stripping, harvesting and processing of sorghum, as well as the food products made from it. He observes that 'despite its many benefits, sorghum appears to be on the decline in the Yemen', facing competition from maize, imported rice and wheat, and cash crops of which the most popular is *qāt.*

808 **A Rasūlid agricultural almanac for 808/1405-6:**
Daniel Martin Varisco. *New Arabian Studies,* vol. 1 (1993), p. 108-23.

A translation without much annotation or introduction of an anonymous Yemeni almanac dating from the beginning of the 15th century AD. Apart from agricultural information, such as 'first planting of turnip' and 'last harvest of wheat in the mountains', the short work also contains a considerable amount of astronomical and zodiacal lore.

809 **A royal crop register from Rasūlid Yemen.**
Daniel Martin Varisco. *Journal of the Economic and Social History of the Orient,* vol. 34 (1991), p. 1-22.

This article contains a translation of a brief register of crops for tax purposes, compiled for (or by) ʿAbbās ibn ʿAlī al-Malik al-Afḍal (d. c. 1376) in 1372. The work functions as an agricultural gazetteer for most of the coastal region (the Tihāmah) and the southern highlands of North Yemen, listing, as it does, all the crops and crop varieties grown in the areas under scrutiny. The dominant crop is sorghum, but wheat, date palms, sesame, cotton, grapes and fruit trees feature under specific regions, as well as many vegetables, flowers, herbs and pulses in the section entitled 'On what is planted but not restricted to a certain area'.

810 ***Sayl* and *ghayl*: the ecology of water allocation in Yemen.**
Daniel Martin Varisco. *Human Ecology,* vol. 11, no. 4 (1983), p. 365-83.

The author compares the two main types of water allocation system in North Yemen: seasonal flood (*sayl*) found in the coastal area and the foothills, and spring flow (*ghayl*), which is significant in the highlands. Together these systems are used for around fifteen per cent of Yemen's cultivated area. The author describes how both systems work in practice, outlining the legal principles operating in *sayl* irrigation, the ecological constraints and the relationship between water allocation and tribal organization. He finds that 'tribal organization in Yemen is well adapted to the allocation of spring flow in the highlands, but undergoes stress in the context of coastal flow systems', since the allocative roles generated by the flood systems 'often have major decision-making responsibilities'.

811 **The politics of water scarcity: irrigation and water supply in the mountains of the Yemen Republic.**
Linden Vincent. London: Overseas Development Institute, International Irrigation Management Institute, 1990. 28p. bibliog.

A description of the difficulties facing the villagers and local administration over the allocation of scarce water resources in al-Jabīn in the Raymah mountains of North Yemen. The author points out the significance of Islamic law and customary practices and how they have come into conflict with the growing authority of central government. The author recommends strengthening the power of villagers relative to their micro-level institutions, and increasing their incentives for cooperation in 'project rehabilitation, water reallocation and the resolution of territorial disputes'.

Wirtschafts- und sozialgeographische Untersuchungen . . . (Studies in the social and economic geography . . .)
See item no. 35.

Doing development anthropology . . .
See item no. 560.

Die Natā'iǧ al-fikar des Šaʿbān ibn Sālim aṣ-Ṣanʿānī . . .
See item no. 603.

Water rights and irrigation practices in Laḥj . . .
See item no. 677.

Employment, Manpower and Trade Unions

812 **Arab manpower: the crisis of development.**
J. S. Birks, C. A. Sinclair. London: Croom Helm, 1980. 391p. bibliog.

Historically important as a survey of the situation in the 1970s, this work is a country-by-country survey of the whole Arab world. The Yemen Arab Republic is dealt with on pages 244-55, and the People's Democratic Republic of Yemen on pages 256-65. North Yemen is seen as having benefited from workers' remittances, but the authors warn against the unrealistic attitudes and aspirations of the workforce and against the inability of either private capital or government to strengthen the productive base of the economy. On the other hand, South Yemen is seen as a resource-poor state with development problems of the same qualitative order as Egypt.

813 **International and return migration: the experience of Yemen.**
ESCWA Secretariat. *Population Bulletin of ESCWA,* nos. 41/42 (1993/94), p. 107-51.

Based on official figures, this is an impressive survey of the characteristics of Yemeni migrants and their fate after their expulsion from Saudi Arabia in 1990. The first half of the article details the age/sex distribution of the returnees, their educational achievement, work profile before, during and after migration, and the impact of their remittances on the economy of both North and South Yemen. The latter part of the report considers the social and economic impact of the returnees, and forecasts that 'most of the returnees will continue to suffer in the immediate future, given their slow absorption into an already depressed economy, their negative savings and high propensity towards consumption, and high population growth in general'.

814 **Return to Yemen: the end of the old migration order in the Arab world.**
Allan M. Findlay. In: *Population migration and the changing world.* Edited by W. T. S. Gould, A. M. Findlay. Chichester, England: Wiley, 1994, p. 205-23.

The author sets the expulsion of Yemeni workers in 1990 both against their position in the general Saudi labour market of the 1980s and against the mass migration created by the Gulf War of 1990-91 as a whole. He sees the Gulf crisis as marking the end of the old migration order for some states, notably Yemen and Jordan, and the beginning of a new phase of labour market development in the oil states. The author agrees with the widely held views that the generally low level of both education and capital among returnees will place a huge burden on Yemen's fragile economy and concludes that the changing situation of Arab oil states in the 1990s has led to one set of migrant-supplying countries being replaced by another, which operates only to the benefit of the labour-importing countries, by exerting continued downward pressure on wages and conditions.

815 **Yemeni exodus from Saudi-Arabia: the Gulf conflict and the ceasing of the workers' emigration.**
Rainer Hartmann. *Journal of South Asian and Middle Eastern Studies,* vol. 19, no. 2 (1995), p. 38-52.

It is estimated that around one million Yemeni migrant workers returned from Saudi Arabia and the Gulf States as a consequence of the Gulf War of 1990-91 with devastating effects on the economy: loss of remittances added up to more than 300 million US dollars, while the property left behind by returning migrants was worth many times that amount. The labour market in Yemen became extremely overloaded, with unemployment rising to thirty-five per cent by 1992. A fraction of the returnees had a profession or a qualification or had invested in the Yemeni economy during their stay in Saudi Arabia, but over forty per cent were illiterate and were forced to live in squatter camps, with over fifty per cent being unable to find accommodation in their home villages. Shanty towns and slums mushroomed (Hodeida saw a five-fold increase in its population over a two-year period), crime rose, food shortages were commonplace. The author of this report is pessimistic about the future for unified Yemen, and sees political stability and a change in the economic policy of dependency as prerequisites for growth.

816 **Republic of Yemen: human development, societal needs and human capital response.**
International Bank for Reconstruction and Development. Washington, DC: World Bank, 1992. unpaged.

This report covers all aspects of human resource management, concentrating on population, health, labour force and employment. Within these areas, there are numerous specific studies, ranging from quality assurance in education to modern sector employment and urbanization trends.

817 **Critique of trade union rights in countries affiliated with the League of Arab States.**
Jewish Labor Committee. New York: Jewish Labor Committee, 1989- . annual.

An annual survey of labour relations and trade union law in Arab countries. Each survey devotes at least a page to Yemen, and for some years (1989-92 inclusive), the Committee issued a *Documentation Supplement*, which included relevant passages from reports by the International Labour Organization and the United States Country Reports Human Rights Practices.

818 **Les rapatriés de la Crise du Golfe au Yémen: Hodeida quatre ans après.** (The returnees from the Gulf Crisis to Yemen: Hodeida four years later.)
Marc Lucet. *Monde Arabe Maghreb Machrek,* no. 148 (1995), p. 28-42.

In early 1994, the author conducted research in Hodeida, the capital of the Tihāmah which is the region which has absorbed almost fifty per cent of the returnees from Saudi Arabia. He found that despite governmental declarations about reintegrating the return migrants, more than 100,000 people in Hodeida alone were still living in shanty towns, and functioning economically on the extreme margins of Yemeni society. The author examines the organization of the shanty towns and the role played by the *ʿaqīl* (local boss) of each neighbourhood, and he discovers that the general attitude of Yemenis towards the poorest sector of the *Mughtaribūn* (returnees) is extremely negative, exacerbated by the darker skin colour of many of the migrants.

819 **Le marché du travail yéménite après l'unification.** (The Yemeni labour market after unification.)
Muḥammad ʿAbd al-Wahid al-Maytami. *Revue du Monde Musulman et de la Méditerranée,* no. 67 (1993), p. 121-9.

The author sees the migration of workers before the Gulf War of 1990-91 as a mixed blessing, since it unleashed a sudden inflation in wages in the 1970s as well as being responsible for a reduction in the amount of land under cultivation. The unforeseen return of the million or so workers from Saudi Arabia in 1990 has caused even graver problems. Almost half the returnees are illiterate, with only three per cent possessing a good educational qualification or sufficient capital. In addition, the 1980s saw a large number of rural migrants arriving in the towns, with Ṣanʿāʾ multiplying its population by a factor of nine between 1962 and 1986. The result of both factors is serious overcrowding, and a lack of adequate food supplies. Finally, the addition of almost 100,000 extra pupils after the war has stretched the education system to breaking point. The author sees only a dark future ahead with fewer job opportunities available than new arrivals on the labour market, and few possibilities of expanding what the author calls 'the modern sector'.

820 **Arbeitsemigration, Binnenwanderung und Wirtschaftsentwicklung in der Arabischen Republik Jemen.** (Worker emigration, internal migration and economic development in the Yemen Arab Republic). Günter Meyer. Wiesbaden, Germany: Reichert, 1986. 318p. maps. bibliog. (Jemen-Studien, Band 2).

The most important contribution to the whole subject of migration in North Yemen before unification. The author looks at the historical development of labour emigration, at the effects on the economy (rise in investment, imports and consumerism, high inflation, serious manpower shortages) and on internal migration. He then takes the building sector in 1983 as a case-study, showing that more than half the firms were less than three years old, and over eighty-five per cent of the owners had moved into towns from the countryside. The author also found that the overwhelming majority of wage-earners from a rural background lived alone or with male relatives in town, while almost half of the owners also left their families behind in their home villages. The author has both summarized and brought his research up to date using 1986 data in 'Migration, religion and economic development in the building sector of Sanaa and Cairo' (in: *Urban development in the Muslim world.* Edited by Hooshang Amirahmadi, Salah S. El-Shakhs. New Brunswick, New Jersey: Center for Urban Policy Research, 1993, p. 164-82).

821 **Yemeni workers come home: reabsorbing one** million migrants. Thomas B. Stevenson. *Middle East Report*, no. 181 (1993), p. 15-20.

The author highlights the problems facing Yemeni migrants returning to their home country after the Gulf War of 1990-91. Although he does offer many statistics – including quoting the official government survey as saying that while fifty-two per cent of returnees had been agricultural workers before migrating, fewer than four per cent intended to return to farming – the interest in this article lies in the human stories which he tells to illustrate the difficulties facing the returnees and how they are trying to solve them.

822 **The socio-economic impact of the involuntary mass return to Yemen in 1990.** Nicholas Van Hear. *Journal of Refugee Studies,* vol. 7, no. 1 (1994), p. 18-38.

The author conducted interviews with 110 returnees in six regions of unified Yemen to determine both household and individual experiences, and he then compared his data with official surveys and with information gathered by international non-governmental organizations such as the World Bank and the United Nations Development Programme. The returnees were found to have originally come from every region in Yemen with the Tihāmah providing the highest proportion. The group as a whole included wealthy merchants and bankers, those engaged in services and retailing, and a lumpenproletariat making a living in the lower reaches of the informal sector. Many of the last-named group had been abroad for long periods – up to forty years in some cases. All returnees suffered a decline in their standard of living, particularly those who had been abroad for many years, and had 'lost meaningful social and economic ties with Yemen'. The most successful at reintegrating themselves were Ḥaḍramīs of the merchant class. This excellent article is by far the most sophisticated analysis we have of the results of the Gulf War of 1990-91 on the Yemeni labour market.

Attitudes of government employees towards women's employment in Yemen.
See item no. 576.

State policies and the position of women workers . . .
See item no. 582.

Migration, balance of payments, and economic growth . . .
See item no. 734.

Yemeni workers abroad: the impact on women.
See item no. 752.

Emigration and economic development . . .
See item no. 756.

Labour migration and key aspects of its economic and social impact . . .
See item no. 759.

Statistics

Guides to statistics

823 **Official publications on the Middle East: a selective guide to the statistical sources.**
C. H. Bleaney. Durham, England: Middle East Libraries Committee, 1985. 32p. (Middle East Libraries Committee Research Guides, no. 1).

Although now dated, this is still a useful guide to statistical sources for both North and South Yemen. It covers country-by-country statistical sources, development plans and censuses, and lists the publications of relevant international and regional organizations, as well as bibliographical guides to world statistics and details of the major collections of Middle Eastern statistical material held in British libraries.

824 **ACCIS guide to United Nations information sources on international trade and development finance.**
United Nations, Advisory Committee for the Co-ordination of Information Systems. New York: United Nations, 1990. 192p.

Covers the functions, programmes and information sources by and about thirty-five United Nations bodies, including the International Monetary Fund and the World Bank, as well as selected other regional organizations such as the Council of Arab Economic Unity. This is the third of a series of four guides produced by ACCIS, the other volumes covering health (1992. 227p.), food and agriculture (1987. 124p.) and the environment (1988. 141p.).

Official statistics

825 **Statistical yearbook.**

People's Democratic Republic of Yemen, Ministry of Planning. Aden: Ministry of Planning, 1980-90. annual.

In English and Arabic. Volumes list statistics on climate and physical features, population, labour force, education, health, information, culture and tourism, agriculture and fishing, industry, transport and communications, foreign trade, prices and the national accounts.

826 **Statistical year-book.**

Republic of Yemen, Ministry of Planning. Ṣanʿāʾ: Ministry of Planning, 1991- . annual.

This publication in English and Arabic supersedes the separate *Statistical yearbooks* of both North and South Yemen, which are listed separately (see items 825, 827). The latest issue (1996) contains eighteen sets of tables covering population, education, health, vital statistics, migration, labour force, criminal and judicial matters, social and personal services, information and tourism, agriculture, industry, transport and communications, the building trade, investment, prices, finance, foreign trade and the national accounts.

827 **Statistical year book.**

Yemen Arab Republic, Central Planning Organisation. Ṣanʿāʾ: Central Planning Organisation, 1970/71-90. annual.

In English and Arabic. Each volume contains statistical tables on climate and physical geography, population, health, education, social issues, agriculture, industry, transport and communications, foreign trade, finance, prices and the national accounts.

Architecture

828 **Les maisons tours de Sanaa.** (The tower houses of Ṣanʿāʾ.)
Paul Bonnenfant. Paris: Presses du CNRS, 1989. 237p.

A photographic survey of the wonderful variety of houses in Ṣanʿāʾ, including pictures of chimneys, windows, plasterwork, doors, stained glass, and the interiors of the rooms. The text puts the images into context and the book as a whole is an excellent introduction to the social and architectural formation of the capital of North Yemen.

829 **Sanaa: architecture domestique et société.** (Ṣanʿāʾ: domestic architecture and society.)
Edited by Paul Bonnenfant. Paris: Presses du CNRS, 1995. 644p. bibliog.

The most important work on Ṣanʿāʾ since the magisterial magnum opus edited by R. B. Serjeant and Ronald Lewcock (q.v.), this well-illustrated book contains twenty-four chapters most of which are connected with the architecture or architectural details of the house in Ṣanʿāʾ. Among the most interesting are four surveys of individual houses by Paul Bonnenfant and papers on the materials used in house construction – stone, brick, plaster, glass and *qaḍāḍ* (mortar). Other important contributions deal with urban gardens, specific rooms, social events taking place in the house – including musical events – and the influence of neighbours and notables. The book limits itself strictly to its title and does not discuss in any depth public architecture, religious endowments, town planning, or conservation.

830 **The town as a garden: the case of Yemen.**
Rita Ceccherini (et al.). *Environmental Design,* no. 2 (1986), p. 48-55.

An imaginative (some might say fanciful) account of the spatial relationship between water, gardens and buildings in Yemen. The authors see the highland settlements of North Yemen as concentrating residential, public and religious functions in a small area, with the tower house performing a control function over the market garden and water supply. In Ṣanʿāʾ, the history of gardens expresses the 'eternal' presence of nature in the city and their positioning 'bears out the hypothesis of the progressive densifying of tower houses which incorporated the cultivated areas within them, presumably so as to satisfy the basic needs of subsistence'. Most gardens now belong to mosques and religious associations and the authors explore these further spatial relationships in some depth.

831 **Studies in Arabian architecture.**

Paolo M. Costa. Aldershot, England: Variorum, 1994. unpaged.

A collection of nine previously published articles, which includes three papers on Yemen. The author's work on the Great Mosque of Ṣanʿāʾ is here translated into English for the first time (it was originally published in Italian in 1974). and deals with the author's conservation work on the mosque, the 'inventory of ancient materials' found in it and an analysis of the historical evolution of the building's architecture. A companion piece is the author's paper, first published in 1983, on the Mosque of al-Janad in Ta'izz, while his 1992 article 'Problems of style and iconography in the South-Arabian sculpture' looks at how specific iconographic motifs have been used by ancient South Arabian craftsmen and how these motifs persisted into Islamic times.

832 **Yemen: land of builders.**

Paolo M. Costa, Ennio Vicario. London: Academy Editions, 1977. 174p.

A photographic study of four towns in Yemen – Ṣaʿdah in the North, Manākhah in the Central Highlands, Zabīd in the Southern Tihāmah and the capital Ṣanʿāʾ – before the construction boom and road-building began to change the urban landscape irreversibly. The text is equally informative and the book is a testimony to the imagination and skill of the traditional builders of North Yemen. The work, based on an Italian original, was also published in Milan, Italy (Rizzoli International Publications, 1977. 177p.) as *Arabia Felix: a land of builders.*

833 **The valley of mud brick architecture: Shibām, Tarīm & Wādī Ḥaḍramūt.**

Salma Samar Damluji. Reading, England: Garnet Publishing, 1992. 472p. maps.

After a historical introduction, the author concentrates on the mud-brick architecture found in the towns of the Wādī Ḥaḍramawt. She describes the buildings, the construction techniques, the materials used for building, and the contemporary situation regarding town planning and urban expansion. The work as a whole is very well illustrated with photographs, plans and line-drawings and contains a useful glossary of technical terms and some fascinating interviews with local craftsmen.

834 **A Yemen reality: architecture sculptured in mud and stone.**

Salma Samar Damluji. Reading, England: Garnet Publishing, 1991. 355p. map.

A companion piece to the author's academic study listed above, this is a collection of excellent colour photographs, illustrating buildings and their inhabitants in a dozen cities and wadis in South Yemen.

835 **The architecture of the Rasūlids.**
Barbara Finster. In: *Yemen: 3000 years of art and civilisation in Arabia Felix.* Edited by Werner Daum. Innsbruck, Austria: Pinguin-Verlag; Frankfurt am Main, Germany: Umschau-Verlag, 1988, p. 254-64.

The author sees the architecture produced during the rule of the Rasūlids (1229-1454) as both original and 'a modernisation of traditional elements'. Unfortunately, none of the great mosques of Rasūlid times have been preserved, but several smaller mosques, *madrasahs* (teaching mosques) and other buildings survive in Ibb, Taʿizz, Zabīd and elsewhere. Finster describes the characteristic elements of the architecture of the time and its details, and provides a list of all known buildings (whether preserved or not) erected under the Rasūlids.

836 **An outline of the history of Islamic religious architecture in Yemen.**
Barbara Finster. *Muqarnas,* vol. 9 (1992), p. 124-47.

The best survey we have of the development of the mosque and the *madrasah* (teaching mosque) in Yemen from the earliest Islamic times to the 17th century. The author sees the architecture of North Yemen as traditionalist but yet receptive to decoration of all kinds, and divided between Zaydī and Sunnī styles and influences. Perhaps the greatest contribution of Yemen to Islamic architecture in general is in the survival of so many coffered ceilings, although the author also sees Yemeni minarets as 'original creations peculiar to the country' as are the paintings in the cupolas of the Rasūlid (1229-1454) *madrasahs.* Finster has also published a series of four articles in German on individual Yemeni religious buildings in the first volume of *Archäologische Berichte aus dem Yemen,* produced by the Deutsches Archäologisches Institut Ṣanʿāʾ (q.v.) and some shorter papers in English such as 'Cubical Yemeni mosques' (*Proceedings of the Seminar for Arabian Studies,* vol. 21 [1991], p. 49-68).

837 **Contribution à l'étude de l'architecture de montagne en République Arabe du Yémen.** (A contribution to the study of highland architecture in the Yemen Arab Republic.)
Lucien Golvin. In: *L'Arabie du Sud: histoire et civilisation.* (South Arabia: history and civlization.) Vol. 3: *Culture et institutions du Yémen.* (Culture and institutions of Yemen.) Joseph Chelhod (et al.). Paris: Maisonneuve et Larose, 1985, p. 303-28.

An illustrated look at the characteristics of architecture in the highlands of North Yemen from Ṣaʿdah in the North to Ibb in the South. The author pays particular attention to architectural details such as stained glass and bull's-eye windows, to the materials used for construction, and to the relationship between man, space and habitation.

838 **Thulâ: architecture et urbanisme d'une cité de haute montagne en République Arabe du Yémen.** (Thula: architecture and town planning in a highland town in the Yemen Arab Republic.)
Lucien Golvin, Marie-Christine Fromont (et al.). Paris: Éditions Recherche sur les Civilisations, 1984. 242p. maps.

Thulā is a small town to the north-west of Ṣanʿāʾ, typical of many situated in the highland regions of North Yemen. This work is a description and analysis of all the significant buildings in the town accompanied by numerous black-and-white photographs. The authors examine the nine mosques, two *madrasahs* (teaching mosques) and some smaller religious buildings, before moving on the secular constructions such as the baths, markets, grain warehouses, and the *funduq* or caravanserai. They also investigate construction techniques and architectural details of all types, but their survey of town planning is more descriptive than analytical and does not use geographical concepts to analyse the town's development. Nevertheless, this is an example of meticulous scholarship, which documents a typical North Yemeni town before the changes of the past two decades became too apparent.

839 **L'architecture au Yémen du Nord.** (The architecture of North Yemen.)
Suzanne Hirschi, Max Hirschi. Paris: Berger-Levrault, 1983. 350p. bibliog.

An interesting work which focuses on the urban development in eight towns and villages of North Yemen, as well as describing individual buildings . The authors are not interested so much in the historical study of major buildings, as in the analysis of domestic architecture and the spatial organization of houses; they also deal with construction techniques and materials. The whole work is accompanied by photographs and explanatory line-drawings, and is a good example of the study of architecture on a human rather than a monumental scale.

840 **The old walled city of Ṣanʿāʾ.**
Ronald Lewcock. Paris: UNESCO, 1986. 124p. bibliog.

A satisfying mix of history (from pre-Islamic times to the present), social description, architectural analysis (both of major public and typical private buildings) and conservation strategy. The author recommends the retention of the traditional street pattern, the market gardens and the diversity of small-scale crafts and artisanal activities as a way of maintaining the dynamism, character and colour of the city.

841 **Wādī Ḥaḍramawt and the walled city of Shibām.**
Ronald Lewcock. Paris: UNESCO, 1986. 135p. bibliog.

In 1984, the city of Shibām and 'the sites of cultural and natural value in the valley of Wādī Ḥaḍramawt' were placed on the World Heritage List, and this work records the history and architecture of the city and its surroundings, and the conservation measures needed to protect it. This is an important and scholarly survey of a unique region and its culture.

842 **L'habitat traditionnel à Ṣanʿāʾ: sémantique de la maison.**
(Traditional housing in Ṣanʿāʾ: the semantics of the house.)
Samia Naïm-Sanbar. *Journal Asiatique,* vol. 275, no. 2 (1987), p. 79-113.

The author adopts a linguistic approach to the terms used to designate rooms in the traditional Ṣanʿānī house. Terms such as *daynah, maṭbakh* and *hijrah* are examined in detail in all their lexical variants.

843 **The architecture of the Ṭāhirid dynasty of the Yemen.**
Venetia Porter. *Proceedings of the Seminar for Arabian Studies,* vol. 19 (1989), p. 105-20.

The Italian traveller Ludovico de Varthema (q.v.) visited al-Miqrānah, the capital of the Ṭāhirids (1454-1517) in 1502 – fifteen years before it was plundered by the Egyptians – and described it as the strongest city in the world. The author uses Varthema's account and the relevant Arabic historical and geographical texts to piece together the architectural history of the Yemen during the latter half of the 15th century, before moving on to a detailed examination of the buildings which have survived until today. She sees the Ṭāhirids as more inward looking and isolationist than the Rasūlids (1229-1454), although the architecture of both dynasties borrowed elements from abroad and 'the Ṭāhirid and the Rasūlid mosques before them draw on a general vocabulary of architecture and architectural decoration current in the medieval Islamic world'.

844 **Jewish domestic architecture in Sanʿa, Yemen.**
Carl Rathjens, edited with an appendix relating to Jewish houses in Ṣanʿāʾ by S. D. Goitein. Jerusalem: Israel Oriental Society, 1957. 80p. (Oriental Notes and Studies, no. 7).

An important study, based on several visits to the Jewish quarter of Ṣanʿāʾ between 1927 and 1938. Using one Jewish building as an example, the author is able to show that the main feature that distinguished it from its Muslim neighbours is the *hijrah* or open court on the uppermost floor around which the living quarters, the kitchen and other rooms were grouped. Other distinctive features were the network of storerooms (Muslim merchants kept their wares in specially guarded warehouses), provision for erecting a tabernacle on the roof, and the designation of a ground-floor room for distilling home-made brandy. In many other details, however, Jewish houses resembled their Muslim counterparts.

845 **Art of building in Yemen.**
Fernando Varanda. London: Art and Archaeology Research Papers; Cambridge, Massachusetts: MIT Press, 1982. 292p. maps.

The author, who spent two years in the Yemen Arab Republic between 1973 and 1975 working for a United Nations Development Programme Town Planning project, has created a lavishly illustrated record of North Yemeni urban and rural architecture. Among areas not often dealt in other books, but considered here in some detail, are town walls and guard towers, the architecture of water, and the architecture (and inhabitants) of the Tihāmah. This is an interesting work, far more sophisticated and scholarly than most photographic albums.

Development and urban metamorphosis . . .
See item no. 49.

Ṣanʿāʾ: an Arabian Islamic city.
See item no. 59.

Rasūlid women: power and patronage.
See item no. 587.

A bibliography of the arts and crafts of Islam up to 1st January, 1960.
See item no. 925.

Education and Culture

846 **Education data quality in the Third World: a five country study.** David W. Chapman. *International Review of Education,* vol. 37, no. 3 (1991), p. 365-80.

An examination of the extent to which ministry-level decision-makers in North Yemen, Nepal, Botswana, Liberia and Somalia had confidence in the quality of the educational data available to them. All ministry officials assigned considerable importance to the role of data in decision-making and all estimated that the data regarding school enrolments were seriously flawed. The perception of ministries was that the only way to improve national data systems was 'to improve incentives and training available at school level'.

847 **Childhood and education in highland North Yemen.** Susan Dorsky, Thomas B. Stevenson. In: *Children in the Muslim Middle East.* Edited by Elizabeth Warnock Fernea. Austin, Texas: University of Texas Press, 1995, p. 309-24.

Based mainly on fieldwork conducted in ʿAmrān in the late 1970s, and updated by two later visits, this article describes, in its first half, Yemeni attitudes to children – in a rather general way. The second half focuses on education in ʿAmrān and compares male with female education, and the formal with both the informal and the religious sectors. Perhaps the most interesting section is the postscript, when the authors conducted follow-up interviews in 1992 with persons who had been schoolchildren when they first arrived in ʿAmrān in 1978.

848 **The social structure of Jewish education in Yemen.** S. D. Goitein. In: *Jews among Muslims: communities in the precolonial Middle East.* Edited by Shlomo Deshen, Walter P. Zenner. Basingstoke, England: Macmillan, 1996, p. 217-31.

Abridged from 'Jewish education in Yemen as an archetype of traditional Jewish education' (in: *Between past and future: essays and studies on aspects of immigrant absorption in Israel.* Edited by Carl Frankenstein. Jerusalem: Henrietta Szold Foundation, 1953, p. 109-46) and originally published in: *Jewish societies in the Middle East: communities, culture and authority* (Edited by Shlomo Deshen and Walter P. Zenner. Washington, DC: University Press of America, 1982, p. 211-33). The author shows how the education of Jewish boys in Yemen was carried out within the synagogue, by the synagogue and for the synagogue. The syllabus was of direct relevance to the life of the religious community and consisted in learning by heart prayers and readings from the Torah, and studying appropriate passages from the Prophets. Boys continued learning from their fathers after gaining independence, just as girls learnt basic religious teachings from their mothers, although, as a rule, women did not learn to read or attend the synagogue. Goitein explains the educational process in considerable detail, but makes no attempt to place it a historical or geographical context.

849 **Cultural policy in the Yemen Arab Republic.**
Abdul-Rahman al-Haddad. Paris: UNESCO, 1982. 74p. (Studies and Documents on Cultural Policies).

An interesting document which shows how the government of North Yemen has attempted to formulate cultural policy around the goals of the Revolution, and to use it both to reduce the legacy of the period of the Imams, and to promote unity with South Yemen. Details are given of policy regarding the national heritage, education, international cultural links, the press, radio and television, publishing, the popular arts including music, museums and antiquities, and the Ministry of Information and Culture, the Ministry of Education and other government agencies and research centres.

850 **School and education: formation and development.**
Hamid al-Iriyani. In: *Yemen: 3000 years of art and civilisation in Arabia Felix.* Edited by Werner Daum. Innsbruck, Austria: Pinguin-Verlag; Frankfurt am Main, Germany: Umschau-Verlag, 1988, p. 375-88.

A very brief survey of 20th-century education in North Yemen, which has little good to say about the rule of Imams Yaḥyā (d. 1948) and Aḥmad (d. 1962), and praises the policies of the current government.

851 **The encyclopedia of comparative education and national systems of education.**
Edited by T. Neville Postlethwaite. Oxford, England: Pergamon Press, 1988. 777p.

On pages 723-6, V. G. Desa runs through some basic statistics on the Yemen Arab Republic, while on pages 726-9, S. A. K. al-Noban does the same for the People's Democratic Republic of Yemen. Neither author includes data beyond 1981 and the entries themselves, though informative, are bland and uncritical.

852 **Higher education in the Republic of Yemen: the University of Sana'a.**

Viswanathan Selvaratnam, Omporn L. Regel. Washington, DC: World Bank, 1991. 48p. (Policy, Research and External Affairs Working Papers, no. 676).

A clear exposition of the development and current status of the University of Ṣanʿāʾ. The authors note many problems associated with the university: high student–staff ratios, high drop-out rate, low female enrolment, poor resources (including library resources), inexperienced administrators, and the low overall quality of graduates. Numerous radical recommendations are suggested to strengthen the university and improve the performance of its graduates and teachers.

853 **The establishment of the British Council in the Yemen Arab Republic, 1973-1978.**

Clive Smith. *New Arabian Studies,* vol. 3 (1996), p. 192-207.

An informal autobiographical account of the role played by the British Council in the development of cultural relations between North Yemen and Great Britain. The author discusses the use made of the library, the English-language teaching programme, the sponsoring of Yemenis to study in Britain, the distinguished British academics who lectured on behalf of the Council, and even the appointment of a full-time football development officer for a year.

854 **The world of learning.**

London: Europa Publications, 1948- . annual.

The 1997 edition of this leading reference work gives brief information on the Universities of Ṣanʿāʾ and Aden, including the names of deans and heads of department. The coverage of libraries, museums and other cultural and educational establishments is, on the other hand, very poor.

Science and Technology

855 **Mathematical astronomy in medieval Yemen: a biobibliographical survey.**

David A. King. Malibu, California: Undena Publications, 1983. 98p. (Catalogs of the American Research Center in Egypt, vol. 4).

A work of immense scholarship, which highlights the significance of the Yemeni scientific heritage. The author surveys the history of Yemeni astronomy, classifies its various sub-divisions, and then describes over 100 Yemeni astronomical and arithmetical manuscripts preserved in the libraries of Europe and the Near East, giving brief details of their authors. He suggests that the high point of Yemeni scientific writing was the 13th and 14th centuries, and points up the manuscripts' significance which lies in the fact that 'some of these preserve earlier Iraqi and Egyptian astronomical sources which are no longer extant in their original form and to the historian of Islamic institutions they are of interest because they cast new light on the astronomical orientation of the Kaʿba and on the early history of the institution of prayer in Islam'.

856 **The medieval Yemeni astrolabe in the Metropolitan Museum of Art in New York.**

David A. King. *Zeitschrift für Geschichte der Arabisch-Islamischen Wissenschaften,* vol. 2 (1985), p. 99-122.

The astrolabe under discussion was made in 1291 by al-Ashraf ʿUmar (d. 1297), son of the Rasūlid Sultan al-Muẓaffar Yūsuf (d. 1295) and 'is unique of its genre in that it contains tables for constructing astrolabe plates for specific latitudes in the Yemen and the Hejaz'. The author describes the astrolabe and the manuscript notes which accompany it and discusses the Arabic treatise which al-Ashraf composed regarding the construction of the astrolabe in general. The article is reprinted in a collection of the author's scientific papers entitled *Islamic astronomical instruments* (Aldershot, England: Variorum, 1987. unpaged).

857 **Energy and the environment into the 1990s: proceedings of the First World Renewable Energy Congress, Reading, U.K., 23-28 September, 1990.**

Edited by A. A. M. Sayigh. Oxford, England: Pergamon Press, 1990. 5 vols.

A collection of several hundred scientific papers dealing with various aspects of renewable energy such as solar power, thermal technology, wind energy conversion, photovoltaic technology, low-energy architecture, biomass technology and other renewable forms of energy such as wave power. Three papers deal with Yemeni topics: 'Strategy for sizing solar energy collecting systems in Yemen' (M. K. Al-Motawakel, S. M. Bin Gadhi, p. 386-90); 'The biogas program in Democratic Yemen' (Abdulla Hussain Algifri, p. 1882-6); and 'Renewable energy for People's Democratic Republic of Yemen (PDRY): why and how?' (S. M. Bin Gadhi, B. T. Nijaguna, p. 3015-19).

Literature

858 **Ṣanʿāʾ . . . ville ouverte: journal d'un Yéménite dans les années 50.**
(Ṣanʿāʾ . . . open city: diary of a Yemeni in the 1950s.)
Muḥammad ʿAbd al-Walī, translated from the Arabic by Luc Baldit.
Paris; Beirut: Edifra, 1989. 160p.

A French translation of a novel by one of the best-known North Yemeni prose writers who died prematurely in a plane accident in 1973. The author excelled in depictions of loneliness, alienation and vulnerability, using a simple, but highly direct style, and this book, one of only two novels he wrote, is an excellent example of his work.

859 **Tribulations and aspirations in Yemenite Hebrew literature.**
Reuben Ahroni. *Hebrew Union College Annual,* vol. 49 (1978), p. 267-94.

The author looks at the Hebrew poetry produced in North Yemen between the 16th and 19th centuries, and he finds it was characterized mainly by serious and religious themes. The influence of the Spanish Hebrew school of poetry can be sensed in the kinds of metre and rhythm employed by Yemeni poets, but the Spanish love of ornamental devices and secular themes finds few echoes, apart from the 16th-century author Zakhariyya al-Dahrī. This is a scholarly and informative article marred only by the author's strong anti-Arab bias which appears in comments such as 'Yemen which was and still is in the throes of abject savagery and barbarism'.

860 **Nashwān ibn Saʿīd al-Ḥimyarī and the spiritual, religious and political conflicts of his era.**
Ismāʿīl ibn ʿAlī al-Akwaʿ. In: *Yemen: 3000 years of art and civilisation.* Edited by Werner Daum. Innsbruck, Austria: Pinguin-Verlag; Frankfurt am Main, Germany: Umschau-Verlag, 1988, p. 212-31.

Nashwān ibn Saʿīd (d. 1117) was one of the most important poets of medieval Yemen and this brief article gives the reader not only an insight into his style by translating passages from his epic work on the Himyarite tradition in Yemen (and other poems as well), but also places him in his religious context, discussing, for example, his attitude to the Imamate and his views on the Qur'ān.

861 **Daughters of Yemen.**
Translated from the Arabic by Mishael Maswari Caspi. Berkeley, California: University of California Press, 1985. 264p. bibliog.

This anthology, collected by the author in Israel, contains the Yemeni Arabic text and English translation of poems which have been passed down orally from one generation to another by the Jewish women of North Yemen. The poems are arranged in the form of a life-cycle with the first poem dealing with a wedding and the last being a poem of death. Some written poetry by men is included to present a contrast 'as regards style, poetic imagery and metaphor and sophistication'. This is a valuable work both from the point of view of literature (many of the poems are poignant and moving) and of ethnography in that they chronicle poetically a way of life which no longer exists.

862 **Akhbār al-Yaman wa-ashʿāruhā wa-ansābuhā: the history, poetry, and genealogy of the Yemen of ʿAbīd b. Sharya al-Jurhumī.**
Elise Werner Crosby. PhD dissertation, Yale University, 1985. 377p. bibliog. (Available from University Microfilms International, Ann Arbor, Michigan, order no. 8601079).

ʿAbīd ibn Sharyah al-Jurhumī flourished under the Umayyads around 685-705, and his book is the first work of Yemeni literature to have survived from the Islamic period. His collection contains six 'saga cycles' dealing with legendary events set in pre-Islamic times, from the dispersion of the tribes from Babylon to the story of Solomon and the Queen of Sheba and the saga of the Himyarite kings. The author has translated the work in its entirety, including all the poetry, and has provided extensive notes and a good historical, literary and bibliographical introduction.

863 **The hostage.**
Zayd Muteeʿ Dammaj (Zayd Muṭīʿ Dammāj), translated from the Arabic by May Jayyusi, Christopher Tingley. New York: Interlink Books, 1994. 151p.

The only novel by North Yemen's most important living prose writer (he was born in Ibb in 1943), this tells the story of a young boy who was taken hostage by the Imam as a pledge for his father's political obedience. The author depicts vividly the boy's growing political and spiritual awareness and contrasts it savagely and satirically with the decadence and injustice of pre-revolutionary North Yemen.

864 **Modern poetry of Yemen.**
A. K. Julius Germanus. In: *Orientalia Hispanica, sive studia F. M. Pareja octogenario dicata.* (Spanish orientalia or studies dedicated to F. M. Pareja on his 80th birthday.) Edited by J. M. Barral. Leiden, The Netherlands: Brill, 1974, vol. 1, part 1, p. 305-19.

A study, written in slightly eccentric English, of several modern Yemeni poets from both North and South, including ʿAbd Allāh al-Baraddūnī (b. 1929), and ʿAlī Aḥmad Bākathīr (1910-69), who was born in Indonesia of Ḥaḍramī parents, but did most of his writing in Egypt. The author, who is not an expert on Yemen, offers examples of each poet's work in Arabic, accompanied by the English translation.

865 **Südarabien im Fihrist von Ibn an-Nadīm.** (South Arabia in the *Fihrist* of Ibn al-Nadīm.)
Pjotr Afanesjewitsch Grjaznewitsch. In: *Ibn an-Nadīm und die mittelalterliche arabische Literatur: Beiträge zum 1. Johann Wilhelm Fück-Kolloquium (Halle, 1987).* (Ibn al-Nadīm and medieval Arabic literature: contributions to the first Johann Wilhelm Fück Colloquium, Halle, 1987.) Wiesbaden, Germany: Harrassowitz, 1996, p. 7-20.

The author identifies various strands which deal with South Arabia in Ibn al-Nadīm's (d. 995) famous bibliographical compilation *al-Fihrist*, among them the history of the Arabic script and the origin of the Arabic language. Above and beyond this, the author considers that Ibn al-Nadīm's work 'provides the earliest information about literary production in Yemen and about authors and works which deal with its history and culture' from ʿAbīd ibn Sharyah al-Jurhumī (fl. 685-705) 'a half-legendary figure of early Muslim folklore', to the work of the earliest Zaydī Imam, al-Hādī ilā al-Ḥaqq (d. 911). This is a useful survey of a significant source for the culture of early Islamic Yemen.

866 **The literature of modern Arabia: an anthology.**
Edited by Salma Khadra Jayyusi. London: Kegan Paul International, 1988. 559p.

A representative selection of the poetry and fiction of ninety-five contemporary authors from the Arabian Peninsula, including translations from twenty-four Yemenis, divided almost equally between those from the North and those from the South (but, sadly, not including a single woman). None of the extracts are particularly long (about ten pages is the maximum, with one exception), but they do give the reader a flavour of the kinds of subjects and styles in current use in the Peninsula, in a form which is unequalled by any other anthology for variety and depth.

867 **al-Hamdānī.**
O. Löfgren. In: *The Encyclopedia of Islam,* new edition. Leiden, The Netherlands: Brill, 1971, vol. 3, p. 124-5.

A brief summary of the life and works of al-Ḥasan ibn Aḥmad al-Hamdānī (d. c. 945), who composed the important historico-literary work *al-Iklīl,* which is a major source for our understanding of the pre- and early Islamic culture.

868 **Contemporary poetry in Yemen: from the traditional style to modernism.**
ʿAbd al-ʿAzīz al-Maqāliḥ. In: *Yemen: 3000 years of art and civilisation.* Edited by Werner Daum. Innsbruck, Austria: Pinguin-Verlag; Frankfurt am Main, Germany: Umschau-Verlag, 1988, p. 330-5.

A brief look at the themes and styles used by poets from the last days of the Imamate to the 1970s. The author shows how contemporary poetry is adopting a 'more musical and realistic quality' and casting aside rules and conventions.

869 **Three contemporary Yemeni poets.**
Bahgat Riad Salib. Beirut: Dar Azal, 1989. 157p. bibliog.

The most substantial critical study in English dealing with any aspect of modern Yemeni literature, this work introduces Western readers to the poetry of ʿAbd Allāh al-Baraddūnī (b. 1929), ʿAbd al-ʿAzīz al-Maqāliḥ (b. 1939) and Muḥammad Ḥusayn al-Sharafī (b. 1940), all three of whom live in North Yemen. The work is descriptive rather than analytical, but the author does try to trace the influences on each poet, and he sets their work in the context of the political changes occurring in Yemen and the Arab World.

870 **South Arabian poetry and prose.** [Vol.] 1: **Prose and poetry from Ḥaḍramawt.**
Edited by R. B. Serjeant. London: Taylor's Foreign Press, 1951. 87p. (English text) and 184p. (Arabic text).

An anthology of colloquial poetry in Arabic script collected by the editor on a visit to Tarīm and surrounding areas in South Yemen and based on a vast collection made by ʿAbd Allāh Raḥayyim of the Bā Faḍl Mashā'ikh tribe. Many different kinds of verse are displayed and the material is enhanced by the editor's erudite introduction to the collection and his biographical notes on the poets. No more volumes of the series were ever published.

871 **Regional literature: the Yemen.**
A. El-Shami, R. B. Serjeant. In: *The Cambridge history of Arabic literature: ʿAbbāsid belles-lettres.* Edited by Julia Ashtiany (et al.). Cambridge, England: Cambridge University Press, 1990, p. 442-68.

Although very concise, this is still the most significant survey in English of the Arabic literature produced in Yemen between the 9th and 14th centuries. Brief details are given of poets and historians, as well as religious, scientific and philological authors, but the great wealth of literary talent which emerged in medieval Yemen still awaits a proper narrative study in a Western language.

872 **La littérature contemporaine en Arabie du Sud et ses aspects sociaux.** (Contemporary literature in South Arabia and its social aspects.)
Michel Tuchscherer. In: *L'Arabie du Sud: histoire et civilisation.* (South Arabia: history and civilization.) Vol. 3: *Culture et institutions du Yémen.* (Culture and institutions of Yemen.) Joseph Chelhod (et al.). Paris: Maisonneuve et Larose, 1985, p. 329-55.

A useful narrative survey of the novel and the short story in both North and South Yemen (with a brief excursus on the theatre) set against the development of culture and the press in the latter half of the 20th century. The author picks out what he considers to be the main figures, and describes their major works and the styles and techniques they employ.

Visual Arts

873 **L'art du bois à Sanaa: architecture domestique.** (The art of wood-carving in Ṣanʿāʾ: domestic architecture.)
Guillemette Bonnenfant, Paul Bonnenfant. Aix-en-Provence, France: Edisud, 1987. 192p. bibliog.

The most important work on wood-working in North Yemen, this serious study looks at the tools and techniques of wood-carving, before moving on to a detailed examination of the patterns, motifs and symbols found in the doors, shutters, windows and grilles of both the domestic and, to a lesser extent, the public architecture of Ṣanʿāʾ. The authors also offer significant new information on the Islamic inscriptions recorded in wood within the city.

874 **Les vitraux de Sanaa: premières recherches sur leurs décors, leur symbolique et leur histoire.** (The stained glass of Ṣanʿāʾ: preliminary research on their patterns, their symbolism and their history.)
Guillemette Bonnenfant, Paul Bonnenfant. Paris: Éditions du CNRS, 1981. 97p.

A study of all the decorative motifs in plaster and glass found among buildings in Ṣanʿāʾ. The authors look at the variety of themes found on doors, windows, façades and internal walls, dividing them into abstract designs (circles, hearts, etc.), symbolic designs (birds, coffee-pots, horns, snakes, etc.) and into motifs incorporating the name of God. This is an important and original contribution to our knowledge of North Yemeni domestic architecture.

875 **Forerunners of Umayyad art: sculptural stone from the Ḥaḍramawt.**
E. J. Keall. *Muqarnas*, vol. 12 (1995), p. 11-23.

The author, prevented in 1991 from continuing his excavations at Zabīd (see items 221, 239, 240), travelled instead to the isolated fort of Ḥiṣn al-ʿUrr in the Wādī Masaylah of the Ḥaḍramawt to investigate the carvings of some of the stone capitals there. After a detailed description of the sculptural reliefs, and after having examined numerous hypotheses, the author suggests that 'the Husn al-ʿUrr artwork can best be explained by seeing the original artistic inspiration as lying somewhere between Tarsus and Tyre, around 500 A.D.'. The author pursued his investigations in 'A second attempt to understand the historical context of Husn al-ʿUrr in the Ḥaḍramawt' (*Proceedings of the Seminar for Arabian Studies*, vol. 25 [1995], p. 55-62), where he again looks at vine motifs and the scale of the carvings, before investigating the reasons for the creation of the fort in the first place.

876 **Tablet weaving by the Jews of Sanʿa (Yemen.)**

Aviva Klein-Franke. In: *The fabric of culture: the anthropology of clothing and adornment.* Edited by Justine M. Cordwell, Ronald A. Schwarz. The Hague: Mouton, 1979, p. 425-45.

An illustrated study of the belts and ribbons woven and embroidered with gold and silver by Jews in Yemen. Although the craft was once common throughout North Yemen, the emigration of the Jews to Israel in 1949-50 has meant that the techniques have now been almost completely forgotten. Fortunately, the author was able to find a Yemeni Jew in Israel who built her a loom and demonstrated the complex weaving skills required to operate it; these the author describes at length. She also examines the products and locates the craft in its historical, economic and social context. Klein-Franke first published her researches in German, 'Tesig-Bandweberei mit Gold- und Silberfaden in Ṣanʿāʾ' (Tablet weaving with gold and silver threads in Ṣanʿāʾ) (*Baessler-Archiv*, new series, vol. 22 [1974], p. 225-46).

877 **The art of the Rasūlids.**

Venetia Porter. In: *Yemen: 3000 years of art and civilisation.* Edited by Werner Daum. Innsbruck, Austria: Pinguin-Verlag; Frankfurt am Main: Umschau-Verlag, 1988, p. 232-53.

A succinct but interesting discussion of the various arts practised during the reign of the Rasūlids (1229-1454). The author discusses metalwork, the so-called Rasūlid rosette, glassware, textiles and ceramics, and shows that although Mamlūk craftsmen from Egypt and elsewhere were intermittently active in the Yemen 'so little Rasūlid art survives with the exception of ceramics and these only sherds, that it is not yet possible to make any firm judgement on the true extent of their influence'.

878 **Yemeni pottery: the Littlewood collection.**

Sarah Posey. London: British Museum Press, 1994. 63p. bibliog.

Mark Littlewood worked in Aden for twelve years in the 1960s and 1970s and made a substantial collection of 181 ceramic pieces, which he collected all over South Yemen. The collection was eventually donated to the Department of Ethnography of the British Museum (now the Museum of Mankind), and this work is not only a catalogue of the collection, but also a technical, artistic and social study of ceramic manufacture and use in both North and South Yemen as they existed before the great economic changes of the past twenty-five years.

879 **Some observations on pottery and weaving in the Yemen Arab Republic.**
Shelagh Weir. *Proceedings of the Seminar for Arabian Studies,* vol. 5 (1975), p. 65-76.

An illustrated description of some of the techniques the author observed in pottery and weaving during a six-week study tour of North Yemen. The author visited several towns in the Tihāmah such as Ḥays, Hodeida and Bayt al-Faqīh, but also travelled both into the southern highlands (Qaḥẓah near Ibb) and the northern mountains (al-Ṭulḥ near Ṣaʿdah).

A map of Southern Yemeni rock art . . .
See item no. 236.

Research on rock art in North Yemen.
See item no. 238.

A bibliography of the arts and crafts of Islam up to 1st January, 1960.
See item no. 925.

Music and Dance

880 **Jemen.** (Yemen.)
Gabriele Braune. In: *Die Musik in Geschichte und Gegenwart: eine allgemeine Enzyclopädie der Musik.* (Music past and present: a general encyclopaedia of music.) Kassel, Germany: Bärenreiter, 1996, 2nd enlarged ed., vol. 4, p. 1439-46. bibliog.

A useful summary of the basic facts about music in both North and South Yemen, based on written sources in Arabic and Western languages. The author describes the historical development of music in South Arabia, the various regional styles, the local musical instruments and Yemeni dances. Her article is informative, if not without some lacunae and it lacks the anthropological insights of Philip D. Schuyler (see items 882, 883). It does, however, conclude with a comprehensive bibliography and discography.

881 **Some Arab folk-tunes.**
W. Idris Jones. *Transactions of the Glasgow University Oriental Society,* vol. 7 (1936), p. 10-16.

The author gives details of the words and music of six songs of differing types (a working song, a war song, a patriotic song, a shepherd's song, a camel-driver's song and a dance melody), which he collected in South Arabia in the 1930s. An abbreviated form of this article was published in *The Moslem World,* vol. 27, no. 1 (1937), p. 136-8.

882 **Hearts and minds: three attitudes toward performance practice and music theory in the Yemen Arab Republic.**
Philip D. Schuyler. *Ethnomusicology,* vol. 34, no. 1 (1990), p. 1-18.

The author examines three groups of North Yemeni musicians – *nashshādīn* or unaccompanied chanters performing at funerals, *fannānīn* or solo singers and *ʿūd* (stringed instrument) players, who perform at weddings and private functions, and orchestral musicians attached to the Ministry of Information and Culture. He looks at the social stratum from which they come, at how and when they perform and at the texts they use. This is a sensitive and skilful study which gives us insights into the Yemeni tradition, both musically and ethnographically.

883 **Music and tradition in Yemen.**
Philip D. Schuyler. *Asian Music,* vol. 22, no. 1 (1991), p. 51-71.

Using the theories of Edward Shils, the author attempts to define 'tradition' as represented by *al-ghinā' al-ṣanʿānī* or Ṣanʿānī song. He shows how tradition is closely linked to written transmission or *turāth* (heritage) and how 'the orchestration of *al-turāth* [by the Government of North Yemen] clearly serves the political as well as the cultural goals of the Revolution'. Tradition is also a very personal matter, and the author explores the singing of particular songs as examples of individuals maintaining tradition 'in order to engage the intellect and the emotions of the listener'. In the end, however, the author sees text, melody and metre as being the most reliable indicators of tradition.

884 **Bridal songs and ceremonies from Sanʿa, Yemen.**
J. Spector. In: *Studies in biblical and Jewish folklore.* Edited by Raphael Patai, Francis Lee Utley, Dov Noy. New York: Haskell House, 1973, p. 253-84.

This work was originally published by Indiana University Press in Bloomington, Indiana, 1960. The author conducted ethnomusicological research from 1951 to 1953 amongst newly arrived Yemeni immigrants in Israel. Each of the twelve songs recorded in text and music in this article plays a part in the marriage ceremony of Yemeni Jewry, an elaborate event which can last up to two weeks. Among the author's findings is that the text is more important to the singer than the melody and that Ṣanʿānī Jews rarely play wind instruments and are never found playing stringed instruments.

885 **Correspondance entre la musique tribale et la musique citadine (Sanʿa) dans la région des hauts plateaux yéménites.** (The relationship between tribal music and urban music (Ṣanʿāʾ) in the highlands of Yemen.)
Habib Yamine. In: *Le chant arabo-andalou.* (Arab-Andalusian song.) Edited by Nadir Marouf. Paris; L'Harmattan, 1995, p. 119-28.

An ethnomusicological study of the status of performers and their repertoires at marriage ceremonies in North Yemen. The author contrasts rural musicians and dancers with their counterparts in the capital and shows that, although there are some common elements to their performances, significant differences persist.

Qabyala: the tribal concept in the Central Highlands of the Yemen Arab Republic.
See item no. 526.

Folklore

886 **Proverbs and lullabies from southern Arabia.**
Walter Cline. *American Journal of Semitic Languages and Literatures,* vol. 57, no. 3 (1940), p. 291-301.

The author collected eighty-one proverbs and fourteen lullabies (which he offers in transcription and translation) from two or three informants along the southern coast of Arabia in 1929. He compares Yemeni proverbs with those from Syria and finds that whereas many of the latter preach industry and efficiency, 'favourite subjects in the Yemen are personal honour and prestige, retribution, patience and self-restraint, and the folly of unnecessary labour'.

887 **Märchen aus dem Jemen: Mythen und Märchen aus dem Reich von Saba.** (Fairy tales from Yemen: legends and fairy tales from the Kingdom of Sheba.)
Edited and translated by Werner Daum. Munich, Germany: Diederichs, 1992. 2nd rev. ed. 283p. (Die Märchen der Weltliteratur).

The best collection of Yemeni folktales, all twenty-four of which were told to the compiler by various native informants. The tales cover a variety of subjects, including *jinn,* wonder-working saints, miraculous springs, and, above all, women. The author includes an afterword – putting the tales in context – and some useful notes.

888 **From the land of Sheba: tales of the Jews of Yemen.**
Edited and translated by S. D. Goitein. New York: Schocken Books, 1947. 122p.

Numerous short tales, some less than a page in length, illustrating the lives of the Jews of North Yemen. The stories deal with both the past and the present and many of them are taken from written accounts. The author has described his experiences researching among the Yemeni Jewish immigrants to Palestine/Israel in 'Research among Yemenites' (in: *Studies in Jewish folklore: proceedings of a regional conference of the Association for Jewish Studies, held at Spertus College of Judaica, Chicago, May*

1-3, 1977. Edited by Frank Talmage. Cambridge, Massachusetts: Association for Jewish Studies, 1980, p. 121-35).

889 **Jemenica: Sprichwörter und Redensarten aus Zentral-Jemen.**
(Yemenica: proverbs and sayings from Central Yemen.)
S. D. Goitein. Leiden, The Netherlands: Brill, 1970. 194p.

A reprint of the 1934 edition published in Leipzig, Germany, by Harrassowitz, this is the only substantial collection of Yemeni proverbs available in a Western language. It was collected by the author from Yemeni Jews who had migrated to Palestine, and was compiled as much for linguistic as for folkloric reasons (it contains an introduction on the phonetics of Ṣanʿānī Arabic); it cannot be said to be easy to use. All 1432 proverbs are listed in transcription and in the order of the Arabic alphabet, according to the first radical. A German translation is given and occasionally further explanations, but the only subject approach is through the rather restricted index.

890 **Folklore and folk literature in Oman and Socotra.**
T. M. Johnstone. *Arabian Studies,* vol. 1 (1974), p. 7-23.

As a result of his linguistic researches into the living South Arabian languages (see items 493, 494), the author collected numerous tales and was able to observe the social life and customs of the Dhofari and Socotran peoples. This article discusses to some extent the social organization of these peoples, and then goes on to explore their beliefs and superstitions, many of which centre around spirits, shape-changing and animals.

891 **Demonizing the Queen of Sheba: boundaries of gender and culture in postbiblical Judaism and medieval Islam.**
Jacob Lassner. Chicago, Illinois; London: University of Chicago Press, 1993. 281p. bibliog.

Although not of direct relevance to the Yemen, since the author has no interest in testing the historical evidence, this is, nevertheless, a significant study, which shows how a legendary figure can be used by religious scholars to reinforce their own views. The author shows 'how successive retellings of the biblical story reveal anxieties about gender' as the biblical version of the Queen's visit to Solomon's court is transformed by later authors into an exemplary tale of the humbling of a woman before men. The author also examines how Jewish lore penetrated the Islamic imagination, and presents translations from relevant passages in the Bible, the Midrash, the Targum, Yemeni folklore, the Qur'ān and two later Islamic writers in the prophetic tradition.

892 **Texts on Yemenite folklore.**
Wolf Leslau. *Proceedings of the American Academy for Jewish Research,* vol. 14 (1944), p. 221-51.

The author, who is best known for his linguistic researches (see iems 496, 497), collected these five tales from a North Yemeni Jew who had emigrated to New York. The tales are given in transcribed Ṣanʿānī Arabic and English translation, and are presented without historical introduction or socio-anthropological explanation. Peculiarities of the dialect are, however, explained in the notes.

893 **Little Aden folklore.**
Oliver H. Myers. *Bulletin de l'Institut Français d'Archéologie Orientale,* vol. 44 (1947), p. 177-233.

The author examines various aspects of folk beliefs and customs in the villages of Fuqum and Burayqah in Little Aden. He suggests that some practices 'belong to the matriarchal and totemistic period', in particular the frequency of *manṣūbāt* (translated by the author as priestesses) but also various legends. The author also turns his attention to folk history, dancing, saints' tombs, and rituals associated with marriage, illness, death and children. This is an interesting article, although it lacks the underpinning a professional anthropologist or Arabist might have brought to the data, and the author's orientalist mentality occasionally breaks through the text.

894 **The Queen of Sheba.**
H. St. J. Philby. London: Quartet Books, 1981. 141p. bibliog.

A posthumous publication by the famous explorer and adviser to King Saud of Saudi Arabia, this work traces the historical evidence for the Queen of Sheba in the Bible and the Qur'ān and examines the 'somewhat apocryphal lines' along which the legend was developed by Arab historians, including the Yemeni, al-Ḥasan ibn Aḥmad al-Hamdānī (d. c. 945). This is a serious work of scholarship, beautifully illustrated, but sadly lacking detailed references to the author's sources. The introduction consists of an anecdotal biography of Philby by Gerald de Gaury.

895 **Solomon and Sheba.**
Edited by James B. Pritchard. London: Phaidon, 1974. 160p. bibliog.

After two useful historical and archaeological articles by the editor and Gus W. Van Beek respectively, which set the Queen of Sheba in her Biblical and South Arabian context, four scholars discuss the diffusion of the legend in the Judaic, the Islamic, the Ethiopian and the Western Christian traditions. The authors look at poetry, at painting and other figurative art, at religious and mystical material, and at folklore. A similar, but more wide-ranging collection of articles in German (including the figure of the Queen of Sheba in the cinema and the effect of the legend on modern Arabic literature), was edited by Werner Daum as: *Die Königin von Saba: Kunst, Legend und Archäologie zwischen Morgenland und Abendland* (The Queen of Sheba: art, legend and archaeology between East and West) (Stuttgart, Germany; Zurich, Switzerland: Belser Verlag, 1988. 216p. maps). Both volumes are lavishly illustrated.

896 **Divination, magie, pouvoirs au Yémen.** (Divination, magic, and occult powers in Yemen.)
Edited by Anne Regourd. Rome: Herder, 1995. 248p. (Quaderni di Studi Arabi, no. 13).

A special issue of the annual produced by the Oriental School of the University of Venice, this contains twelve articles (four in English, five in French, two in Italian and one in German) dealing with various aspects of the occult sciences and the central place they occupy in Yemeni culture. Two major themes running through the volume are the belief in *jinn* (articles by G. R. Smith, André Gingrich, Sylvaine Camelin) and on saints and *ṣūfī* (mystical) ceremonies (articles by Esther Peskes, François de Keroualin and Ludovic Schwarz, and Francine Stone.). Other contributions discuss therapeutic incantations (Marie-Claude Siméone-Senelle), the *zār* (casting out of spirits by women) ceremony (Tiziana Battain), the evil eye (Jean Lambert), magic cups (Giovanni Canova), lunar stations (Daniel Martin Varisco) and education and the transmission of knowledge (Anne Regourd).

897 **Women in Arabic proverbs from Yemen.**

Avihai Shivtiel. *New Arabian Studies,* vol. 3 (1996), p. 164-75.

A topical discussion of around fifty Yemeni proverbs, both Arab and Jewish, referring to women either directly or indirectly. The author divides the proverbs into those dealing with the positive characteristics of women, the negative characteristics of women, the advantages of marriage, the disadvantages of marriage, and mixed topics. The proverbs are given in transcribed Arabic and English translation, and explained where necessary, but the whole collection is not put into any real sociological or anthropological context.

Libraries and Archives

898 **Libraries and scholarly resources in the Yemen Arab Republic.**
Barbara Eileen Croken, Lealan N. Swanson, Manfred W. Wenner. DeKalb, Illinois: American Institute for Yemeni Studies, [c. 1985]. 22p. (English text) and 24p. (Arabic text.) (Yemen Guide Series, no. 2).

A guide in English and Arabic to twenty-two libraries, ranging from Western and international institutions like the British Council, the American Institute for Yemeni Studies, and the Food and Agriculture Organization to government libraries (National Institute of Public Administration, Central Planning Organization) and the national academic sector (Ṣanʿāʾ University, Yemen Centre for Research and Studies). Each entry lists subjects covered, hours of opening and exact location. Although dated, this work is still useful, something which can no longer be said of the companion guide by Manfred W. Wenner and Lealan N. Swanson, *An introduction to Yemen for researchers and scholars* (DeKalb, Illinois: American Institue for Yemeni Studies, 1984. 20p. bibliog. [Yemen Guide Series, no. 1]) – that work is now an outdated compilation of basic information on North Yemen for intending travellers.

899 **Treatment of early Islamic manuscript fragments on parchment: a case history: the find of Sanaʿa, Yemen.**
Ursula Dreibholz. In: *The conservation and preservation of Islamic manuscripts: proceedings of the third Conference of Al-Furqān Islamic Heritage Foundation.* Edited by Yusuf Ibish, George N. Atiyeh. London: Al-Furqān Islamic Heritage Foundation, 1996, p. 131-9.

Between 1965 and 1972, thousands of Qur'ān fragments were found in the Great Mosque of Ṣanʿāʾ. None of the texts were complete (they were probably deposited in the mosque because they were of no further use), but many of the fragments are datable to an early period. This article deals with an attempt by a German team to preserve the parchment fragments and is most interesting on the technical difficulties they faced and how they overcame them. Less successful was their attempt to train Yemenis in conservation techniques. For a brief analysis of the Qur'āns themselves, see *Masāḥif Ṣanʿāʾ* (item no. 904) and, more briefly, the paper by Gerd R. Puin, 'Observations on early Qur'an manuscripts in Ṣanʿāʾ' (in: *The Qurʿan as text.* Edited by Stefan Wild. Leiden, The Netherlands: Brill, 1996, p. 107-11).

900 **Libraries and information in the Middle East.**
Simon Francis. Boston Spa, West Yorkshire, England: British Library Publications Sales Unit, 1993. 125p. bibliog. (British Library Research Review, no. 16).

A résumé of basic information on the library systems of thirteen Middle Eastern countries, including Yemen (dealt with on pages 93-6), followed by an analysis of trends, which deals with such disparate subjects as library management, information retrieval and document delivery, automation, buildings, conservation, and publishing and book supply. The section on Yemen, gathered from published sources rather than a personal visit, gives very brief details of national, public, academic and specialist libraries in unified Yemen.

901 **Directory of Near and Middle East and North Africa research institutions in Western Europe (except Federal Republic of Germany): institutions in research and teaching, libraries, documentation centres and museums.**
Roswitha Gost. Bielefeld, Germany: Sociology of Development Research Centre, University of Bielefeld; Hamburg, Germany: German Overseas Institute, 1993. 234p.

Gives information on most of the universities in Western Europe (except Germany) which teach Middle Eastern or Islamic studies, often with information about the teaching staff, the courses offered, and the library facilities. Countries covered include Austria, Belgium, France, Italy, The Netherlands, Portugal, Spain, Switzerland, the United Kingdom and the Vatican. For information on German institutes teaching modern Middle East studies, and details of their library holdings, one can still consult the very dated directory by Rainer Büren, *Gegenwartsbezogene Orientwissenschaft in der Bundesrepublik Deutschland* (Contemporary Oriental studies in the Federal Republic of Germany) (Göttingen: Vandenhoeck & Ruprecht, 1974. 210p.).

902 **Middle Eastern photographic collections in the United Kingdom.**
Gillian Grant. Durham, England: Middle East Libraries Committee, 1989. 222p. (Middle East Libraries Committee Research Guides, no. 3).

An extremely thorough and well laid out directory of major and minor photographic collections held in Britain which deal with the Middle East. Many of the collections are described in detail, and the index of places and tribal groups directs the reader to the relevant countries, towns or regions. There are very many references to Aden, often relating to photographs held in regimental museums, but also numerous entries for Yemen, and various individual towns such as Ṣanʿāʾ, Hodeida, Shibām and Tarīm. There is also a useful index of personal names covering photographers, collectors and persons photographed.

903 **RIMA: répertoire des bibliothèques et des organismes de documentation sur le monde arabe.** (RIMA: directory of libraries and documentation units on the Arab World.)
Institut du Monde Arabe. Paris: IMA, 1986. 2nd rev. ed. 474p.

Despite its age, this is still a useful guide to libraries all over the world with collections on the Middle East. Four libraries are listed in North Yemen and one in South Yemen and the information given for each entry consists of full address, name of librarian or director, coverage, size of collections, classification scheme and other retrieval tools, and conditions of access. Elsewhere, the coverage of French, Swiss and North African libraries is particularly good.

904 **Maṣāḥif Ṣanʿāʾ.** (The Qur'ān copies of Ṣanʿāʾ.)
Kuwait: Kuwait National Museum; Dar al-Āthār al-Islāmīyah, 1985. 61p. (English text) and 41p. (Arabic text).

The illustrated catalogue of an exhibition held in the Kuwait National Museum from March to May 1985. The exhibition deals with the Qur'ān fragments discovered in the Great Mosque of Ṣanʿāʾ between 1965 and 1972, which have been worked on for many years by a German team led by Gerd R. Puin. His article in this catalogue, 'Methods of research on Qur'anic manuscripts: a few ideas' surveys the methodology used to classify the huge number of fragments. Other contributions in English are by Marilyn Jenkins on the ornaments found on ten fragments, and a paper by Ursula Dreibholz (see item no. 899) on conservation.

905 **Yemen.**
ʿAbd al-Wahhāb ʿAlī al-Mu'ayyad. In: *World survey of Islamic manuscripts.* Edited by G. J. Roper. London: Al-Furqān Islamic Heritage Foundation, 1994, vol. 3, p. 643-79.

An impressive, if still incomplete, survey of resources for manuscript research in Yemen. The article lists, in the first instance, union catalogues and surveys of libraries and manuscript collections in both North and South Yemen, and then proceeds to list individual collections held in Aden, Ḍaḥyān, Dhamār, Ḥurayḍah, Jirāf, al-Rawḍah, Ṣa'dah, Ṣanʿāʾ, Shahārah, Tarīm and Zabīd. As many of the collections are private, this is the first time for many of them that their status, conditions of access and contents have been described, often in great detail (such as the library of the Great Mosque of Ṣanʿāʾ). On the other hand, data about the publicly held collections in the national libraries and in the universities of Aden and Ṣanʿāʾ are very scarce.

906 **Middle East materials in United Kingdom and Irish libraries: a directory.**
Ian Richard Netton. London: Library Association Publishing in association with the Centre for Arab Gulf Studies, University of Exeter, 1983. 136p.

A comprehensive survey of collections of Middle East interest in national, university, public, special and private libraries in the British Isles. The author, who compiled the directory on behalf of the Middle East Libraries Committee, left no stone unturned in his efforts to track down relevant libraries and to obtain accurate details regarding opening hours, conditions of access, full address and telephone number, and names of the librarian or staff responsible for the Middle East collection. Each entry also receives a description of the size and relevance of their holdings. The author has prepared a new edition with additional information such as e-mail address and state of catalogue automation to be published early in 1998 as: *Middle East sources: a MELCOM guide to Middle Eastern and Islamic books and materials in the United Kingdom and Irish libraries* (Richmond, Surrey, England: Curzon Press).

Mass Media, Publishing and the Press

907 **Broadcasting in the Arab world: a survey of the electronic media in the Middle East.**
Douglas A. Boyd. Ames, Iowa: Iowa State University Press, 1993. 2nd ed. 386p. bibliog.

The author presents a country-by-country survey of the broadcasting services of the Arab states of the Middle East and North Africa, dealing with Yemen (curiously divided into separate chapters for North and South, despite the book being published after unification in 1990) on pages 107-13. The information on both radio and television services in Yemen is poor on quality and very outdated, relying, it would seem on 1980 edition of the *World Radio TV Handbook* (Edited by John R. Frost. London; New York: Billboard Publications), although the 1989 would have been available to the author, and the 1980 edition of *The Middle East and North Africa* (London: Europa Publications) (see item no. 17). Other Middle Eastern countries fare much better, and the general survey of satellite broadcasting, clandestine radio, etc., is useful.

908 **Les islamistes yéménites à travers leur presse: débats, enjeux et thèmes mobilisateurs.** (Yemeni Islamists through their press: discussions, challenges and rallying calls.)
Bernard Lefresne. *Monde Arabe Maghreb Machrek,* no. 140 (May-June 1993), p. 113-20.

A very interesting survey of the Islam-oriented Yemeni press undertaken a few months before the elections of April 1993. The author looked not only at the efflorescence of publications since unification in 1990, but also investigated closely the subjects dealt with in the journals. In general, he found that the press considered the state to be legitimate, but its administration was seen as too secular, although here there were radical disagreements between the pro-Wahhābī and pro-Zaydī factions. One factor which united all Islamist journalists was the fate of Muslims abroad, with authors condemning the intervention of the army in Algeria and the massacre of Muslims in Bosnia, and championing the Palestinian struggle, which was seen more in religious than in nationalist terms.

909 **Mass media and development in the Yemen Arab Republic.**
Mahmoud Gamal Mohammed. PhD dissertation, Ohio State University, 1987. 263p. bibliog. (Available from University Microfilms International, Ann Arbor, Michigan, order no. 8717692).

The primary aim of this thesis was to discover how central national development issues were to the mass media in North Yemen. After an introduction outlining the theoretical issues in question, the author moves on to a history of the press, radio and television in North Yemen, all introduced relatively recently compared to other countries in the Arabian Peninsula. He found that the control of the media became concentrated in the hands of the government in the 1980s, and through interviews, group discussions and the use of a questionnaire, he was able to establish that, whereas the government saw political propaganda as their top priority, those working in the media placed the emphasis on cultural issues, followed by development and education. This is a well-structured and useful dissertation.

910 **Ṣanʿāʾ: eine amtliche osmanische Provinzzeitung im Jemen.**
(*Ṣanʿāʾ*: an official Ottoman provincial journal in Yemen.)
Michael Ursinus. *Die Welt des Islams*, new series, vol. 29 (1989), p. 101-24.

Produced as part of the author's wider research into 19th-century Ottoman provincial newspapers, this is a detailed study of the early years (1879-81) of the Arabic and Turkish-language newspaper *Ṣanʿāʾ*, many issues of which have been recently discovered in Munich, Germany, in the Babinger bequest. After an introduction outlining the rise of the Ottoman newspaper in general, the author describes the publishing history of *Ṣanʿāʾ*, and investigates its content, which he finds closely reflects the interests of its enlightened editor, Hāmid Vehbī Efendi, the principal Secretary of the 7th Ottoman Army, which was stationed in Ṣanʿāʾ. This is a useful article, bringing to light a hitherto unknown source on Yemen, and showing the Ottoman occupation in rather more positive colours than is often encountered.

911 **Le Yémen et ses moyens d'information, 1872-1974: étude historique, politique, juridique, sociale et critique.** (Yemen and its media, 1872-1974: a critical, social, legal, political and historical study.)
M. Abdallah Yahia El Zine. Algiers: Société Nationale d'Édition et de Diffusion, 1978. 385p.

Based on the author's doctoral dissertation at the University of Paris, this thorough and comprehensive study (sadly, not easy to obtain in Britain), looks at printing, publishing and the press mainly in North Yemen from the Ottoman era to after independence. The author examines the official press, the provincial press, the Islamist press and the opposition press, including that produced outside the country (in Indonesia, for example). The work is full of examples taken from various newspapers, as well as comparative statistics, and the final section offers, in addition, a brief chapter on the cinema in Yemen.

al-Īmān **and al-Imam . . .**
See item no. 403.

Periodicals

912 **Arabian Studies.**
London: Hurst; Totowa, New Jersey: Rowman and Littlefield (vol. 1); London: Hurst (vols. 2, 3 and 4); London: Hurst; Montreal, Canada: McGill-Queen's University Press (vol. 5); London: Scorpion Communications (vols. 6 and 7); Cambridge, England: Cambridge University Press (vol. 8), 1974-90. irregular annual.

Edited throughout its run by R. B. Serjeant and R. L. Bidwell, this was one of the foremost vehicles for scholarly debate on any topic dealing with the Arabian Peninsula, excluding controversial contemporary politics and pure science. Succeeded by *New Arabian Studies* (see item no. 916).

913 **Chroniques Yéménites.** (Yemeni chronicles.)
Ṣanʿāʾ: Centre Français d'Études Yéménites, 1993- . annual.

Having appeared as a newsletter for its first two issues, containing mainly details of current research on Yemen both in France and elsewhere, volume 3 (1995) changed the pattern of publication by carrying five substantial articles on a variety of historical and archaeological topics, as well as obituaries, and details of recent conferences.

914 **Dirasat Yamaniyyah = Dirāsāt Yamanīyah.** (Yemeni studies.)
Ṣanʿāʾ: Yemen Centre for Studies and Research, 1979- . irregular.

Each issue contains two parts, one in English with articles on Yemen by both Yemenis and Western scholars, and one in Arabic. Few libraries take this journal currently, so access is limited.

915 **Jemen-Report: Mitteilungen der Deutsch-Jemenitischen Gesellschaft.** (Yemen report: proceedings of the German-Yemeni Society.)
Stuttgart, Germany: Deutsch-Jemenitische Gesellschaft, 1969?- .
two issues per year.

A newsletter in German, with each issue offering five or six short articles on a variety of topics, a chronology of recent events, reviews and notifications of new books, and extracts from the Yemeni press.

916 **New Arabian Studies.**
Exeter, England: University of Exeter Press, 1993- . irregular annual.

The successor to *Arabian Studies* (see item no. 912), this follows the same editorial pattern of a wide variety of scholarly articles with the exception of papers on contemporary political issues and pure science.

917 **Proceedings of the Seminar for Arabian Studies.**
London: Seminar for Arabian Studies, 1971- . annual.

The annual gathering of the Seminar for Arabian Studies is a well-known event which attracts scholars from all over the world. While archaeology and ancient South Arabian studies have predominated, articles on medieval and modern themes can also be found. The periodical *Archaeology and Epigraphy* (Copenhagen: Munksgaard, 1990- . quarterly) has recently also begun to include important articles on South Arabian archaeology.

918 **Raydan: Journal of Ancient Yemeni Antiquities and Epigraphy = Raydan: Ḥawlīyāt al-Āthār wa-al-Nuqūsh al-Yamanīyah al-Qadīmah.**
Aden: Mu'assasat Raydan, 1989?- . annual.

Although mainly in Arabic, this contains important articles in Western languages mostly on the archaeology and epigraphy of South Arabia. Authors who have published in the journal include Jacqueline Pirenne, Christian Robin and Jacques Ryckmans, all of them describing the results of the French Archaeological Mission in South Yemen. It is not particularly easy to find copies of this journal.

919 **Yemen: studi archeologici, storici e filologici sull'Arabia meridionale.** (Yemen: archaeological, historical and philological studies on South Arabia.)
Rome: IsMEO (Istituto Italiano per il Medio ed Estremo Oriente), 1992- . annual.

The vehicle for Italian scholars working in the South Arabian field, this concentrates on archaeology, but includes articles on other topics dealing with South Arabia such as language and architecture.

920 **Yemen Update: Bulletin of the American Institute for Yemeni Studies.**
Westbury, New York: American Institute for Yemeni Studies, 1991- .
two issues per year.

Replaces the *AIYS Newsletter* (Chicago, Illinois: American Institute for Yemeni Studies, 1979-90 [vols. 1-27]). This is a very useful mix of general news, brief articles (these cover an enormous range of topics), scholarly book reviews, and information on new books and articles in Western languages on Yemen.

Bibliographies

921 **The contemporary Middle East, 1948-1973: a selective and annotated bibliography.**
George N. Atiyeh. Boston, Massachusetts: G. K. Hall, 1975. 664p.

A first-rate bibliography of Western-language books and articles on the social sciences, dealing with every country of the Middle East. Both Yemens are covered on pages 250-9, with scattered references elsewhere. This work is an important supplement to the compilation of Thomas B. Stevenson (see item no. 935), because of its helpful annotations and the fact that it extends coverage of material on Yemen back to 1945.

922 **Islamic book review index.**
Edited by W. H. Behn. Berlin: Adiyok (vols. 1-6); Millersville, Pennsylvania: Adiyok (vols. 7-11), 1982-92. annual.

The only specialist source for book reviews on all aspects of Middle Eastern culture until the inclusion of book reviews in *Index Islamicus* (see item no. 926). This was a well-organized and well-presented publication, whose only drawback was the lack of a subject index.

923 **The Middle Eastern city and Islamic urbanism: an annotated bibliography of Western literature.**
Edited by Michael E. Bonine (et al.). Bonn: Ferd. Dümmlers Verlag, 1994. 877p. (Bonner Geographische Abhandlungen, vol. 91).

A comprehensive survey by a team of academic geographers of books and articles on Middle Eastern urbanism in general, and on individual towns and cities in the region. Both Yemens are covered on pages 444-56, and the section lists material not only on town planning and urban studies, but also on architecture, social science and archaeology. Despite the title, the entries are not annotated, but there are indexes of authors, towns and sites, areas and countries, and a subject index based on key-words (the latter is so wide-ranging that it can only really be used in conjunction with the geographical section of the text).

924 **Bibliographie sélective du Yémen axée sur les sciences sociales.** (Selective bibliography on Yemen concentrating on the social sciences.)
Joseph Chelhod. In: *L'Arabie du Sud: histoire et civilisation.* (South Arabia: history and civilization.) Vol. 3: *Culture et institutions du Yémen.* (Culture and institutions of Yemen.) Paris: Maisonneuve et Larose, 1995, p. 357-422.

A significant bibliography dealing mainly with Western-language material on geography, exploration and travel, environmental studies and ecology, history and archaeology, anthropology, sociology and folklore, law, religion, agriculture, economics and trade, literature, art, and health and welfare. The criteria for inclusion are not clear, and some important works are omitted, but there are numerous references to older and more obscure articles. An author index to the bibliography is provided.

925 **A bibliography of the arts and crafts of Islam up to 1st January, 1960.**
K. A. C. Creswell. Cairo: American University in Cairo Press; Vaduz, Liechtenstein: Quarto Press, 1978. 2nd ed. 1330 columns.

A reprint of the first edition of 1961 (published only by the American University in Cairo Press), this is a magisterial compilation of all the material that the author could find dealing with the historical architecture of the Middle East, and a wide selection of arts and crafts, including costume, calligraphy, arms and armour, gardens and jewellery. Entries on Yemen can be found in the sections on Arabia. The bibliography was followed by two supplements, the first covering 1960 to 1972 (Cairo: American University in Cairo Press, 1973. 366 columns), and the second 1972 to 1980 (by J. D. Pearson, Michael Meinecke, George T. Scanlon. Cairo: American University in Cairo Press, 1984. 578 columns). In the second supplement, Yemen appears with a sub-section of its own for architecture (p. 23-6).

926 **Index Islamicus, 1906-1955: a catalogue of articles on Islamic subjects in periodicals and other collective publications.**
Cambridge, England: Heffer, 1958. 807p.

A work with a complex publishing history, this is the single most significant bibliography dealing with the Middle East (including both Yemens). Despite its title, it has never restricted itself to Islamic subjects, but has covered history from the rise of Islam, all the social sciences, and language and literature. Since the 1976-1980 supplement, it has been including books and since the 1993 cumulation, book reviews. Originally without a subject index, this first appeared in the 1981-1985 supplement, and despite a certain lack of refinement, is a useful additional retrieval tool. Supplements have been published for 1956-1960, 1961-1965, 1966-1970, 1971-1975, 1976-1980 and 1981-1985. In 1986, the bibliography began to appear quarterly under the title of *Quarterly Index Islamicus* (London: Mansell, 1971-91; Bowker-Saur, 1992-93), but in 1994 reverted to the title of *Index Islamicus* (London: Bowker-Saur, 1994-), still appearing quarterly but now with annual cumulations. Plans for issuing the whole sequence from 1906 to the present on CD-ROM are advanced and publication is expected in 1998. The early volumes were edited by J. D. Pearson, and the work is now compiled by G. J. Roper and C. H. Bleaney. W. H. Behn has published independently (but using the same format), *Index Islamicus, 1665-1905*

(Millersville, Pennsylvania: Adiyok, 1989. 869p.) and *Supplement to Index Islamicus, 1665-1980.* (Millersville, Pennsylvania: Adiyok, 1995-96. 2 vols).

927 **Muslim women throughout the world: a bibliography.**
Michelle R. Kimball, Barbara R. von Schlegell. Boulder, Colorado: London: Lynne Rienner, 1997. 307p.

The most recent of the many bibliographies on Middle Eastern women, this is a competent listing of just under 3,000 books and articles in Western languages and includes numerous references to Yemen in the subject index (although the distinction between the Republic of Yemen, the Yemen Arab Republic and the People's Democratic Republic of Yemen is not always well observed). The reader who wants to look at material on women produced outside the academic mainstream by international and non-governmental organizations should consult the compilation by Joke Buringa (see item no. 570), while the reader with an interest in Arabic and European-language material should look at *La mujer musulmana: bibliografía* (The Muslim woman: bibliography) by Caridad Ruiz-Almodóvar (Granada, Spain: Universidad de Granada, 1994. 2 vols).

928 **La République Arabe du Yémen.** (The Arab Republic of Yemen).
Patrick Labaune, with Christian Robin, Günther Schweizer. Vol. 2 of: **Bibliographie de la Péninsule Arabique: sciences de l'homme.** (Bibliography of the Arabian Peninsula: human sciences.) Edited by Paul Bonnenfant. Paris: Éditions du CNRS, 1985. 182p.

A substantial, in some areas almost comprehensive listing of Western books and articles on North Yemen (including the pre-Islamic period). Arranged by subject, the bibliography covers history, travel narratives, geography, economics, religion, society and social welfare, politics and international relations, law, military studies, culture, art and literature.

929 **A guide to manuscripts and documents in the British Isles relating to the Middle East and North Africa.**
Noel Matthews, M. Doreen Wainwright, edited by J. D. Pearson. Oxford, England: Oxford University Press, 1980. 482p.

An excellent catalogue of Western-language manuscripts and papers on the Middle East held in British libraries, archives and record offices, including national archives such as the Public Record Office and the India Office Records. In the index, there are dozens of entries on Aden, many on Arabia in general, and several on Yemen, Ṣanʿāʾ and the Ḥaḍramawt. A revised edition was being prepared by J. D. Pearson, until his recent death.

930 **Cahiers bibliographiques: Yémen: trente ans d'édition sur le Yémen contemporain.** (Bibliographical notebooks: Yemen: thirty years of publishing on contemporary Yemen.)
Edited by Franck Mermier. Cairo: CEDEJ, 1989/90. unpaged. (Livres Arabes, nos. 6/7).

Although references to material in Arabic have been excluded from this bibliography on principle, Mermier's work justifies its inclusion here, since every entry in the subject chapters is translated into French. The bibliography lists thousands of Arabic books and articles published on both Yemens over the past thirty years mainly in Cairo, Beirut and in the Yemens themselves. Subjects dealt with in individual chapters are: society (includes education, women's studies, demography and administration); history and geography (includes travel narratives); law and economics (includes agriculture); language, literature and the media (includes folklore and music) and other categories (astronomy and medicine). There is an index of titles (in Arabic with subject keywords in French) but no author index.

931 **Middle East: Abstracts and Index.**
Pittsburgh, Pennsylvania: Library Information and Reference Services (vol. 1, nos. 1-3); Northumberland Press (vol. 1, no. 4-vol. 8); Seattle, Washington: Northumberland Press (vols. 9-11); Aristarchus Knowledge Industries (vols. 12-), 1978- . originally quarterly, now annual.

Initially an important adjunct to *Index Islamicus* (see item no. 926), since it indexed many weeklies and current affairs journals not covered by the latter, as well as including abstracts of periodical articles, and listings of editorials, interviews, book reviews and dissertations. Latterly, however, it has become a major disappointment, the sections on Yemen consisting mainly of the full text of many irrelevant articles and official publications, and references to numerous articles from the North American provincial press. Abstracts of articles from mainstream Middle Eastern journals, and listings of dissertations appear to have been abandoned.

932 **American doctoral dissertations on the Arab world, 1883-1974.**
George Dmitiri Selim. Washington, DC: Library of Congress, 1976. 2nd ed. 173p.

An unannotated list of 1,825 theses on the Arab world and Islam accepted at universities in North America, with a competent subject index. A supplement for the years 1975-81 was published in 1983; and for 1981-87 in 1989. A useful feature for anyone wishing to purchase or borrow the dissertation is the inclusion of the order number for the copy available from University Microfilms International, Ann Arbor, Michigan. North American thesis information by subject is now easily obtainable on-line for those with access to the relevant subscription service *Dissertation Abstracts Online* (URL: http://www.oclc.org).

933 **Theses on Islam, the Middle East and North-West Africa, 1880-1978 accepted by universities in the United Kingdom and Ireland.**
Peter Sluglett. London: Mansell, 1983. 147p.

The list is divided up by country, with entries for Aden appearing on page 50, and for Yemen on pages 112-13. Disadvantages of using the bibliography are the inadequate subject index and the lack of reference to the British Library number (required for borrowing or purchasing the dissertation from the British Library). For more up-to-date information, it is necessary to consult the *Index of theses accepted for higher degrees by the universities of Great Britain and Ireland* (London: ASLIB, 1950- . annual), issued by the Association for Special Libraries and Information Bureaux (ASLIB), in hard-copy and, latterly, on CD-ROM.

934 **The Yemens: the Yemen Arab Republic and the People's Democratic Republic of Yemen.**
G. R. Smith. Oxford, England: Clio Press, 1984. 161p. (World Bibliographical Series, vol. 50).

The first edition of this bibliography contained 401 entries. This second revised edition has retained only about a third of the entries from the first edition, while adding both new material, and some older books and articles omitted from the original.

935 **Studies on Yemen, 1975-1990: a bibliography of European-language sources for social scientists.**
Thomas B. Stevenson. Westbury, New York: American Institute for Yemeni Studies, 1994. 197p. (Yemen Bibliography Series, no. 1).

This is a model of its kind and the single most useful bibliography concentrating on the Yemen. Stevenson lists 1,267 entries for books, articles and dissertations, in almost all fields excluding archaeology, ancient history, literature and pure science. A comprehensive system of keyword indexing provides easy-to-use subject access.

936 **Cultural anthropology of the Middle East: a bibliography.** Vol. 1: **1965-1987.**
Ruud Strijp. Leiden, The Netherlands: Brill, 1992. 565p. (Handbuch der Orientalistik, Section 1, vol. 10).

A bibliography of almost 4,000 books and articles in Western languages on all aspects of Middle Eastern anthropology and ethnography. The work is divided into entries for monographs, which are annotated and entries for articles, which are not, and is organized by countries, with over 100 entries for both Yemens. A comprehensive subject index completes the volume. A second volume, listing publications appearing between 1988 and 1992 and adding 340 references to books and articles published earlier, has been announced for publication in 1997.

937 **Bibliography of population literature in the Arab world.**
United Nations Economic and Social Commission for Western Asia. Amman: ESCWA, 1993. 317p.

A very useful publication listing 2,285 books, articles and reports on all aspects of demography in the Arab World. The work is divided into six subject chapters: size, growth and structure of national populations; morbidity and mortality; reproduction and family formation; distribution and internal migration; international migration; and multi-variable (which deals with population policy, population education, and child welfare and health). Unfortunately, although there is an index of authors, there is no index to countries and the reader must search the whole of each chapter to find relevant entries.

938 **A bibliography of Islamic law, 1980-1993.**
Laila al-Zwaini, Rudolph Peters. Leiden, The Netherlands: Brill, 1994. 239p. (Handbuch der Orientalistik, Section 1, vol. 19).

After surveying Western-language books and articles on various aspects of general Islamic law, the authors undertake a country-by-country survey, which yields twenty-six references for both Yemens, by no means a complete record, but a useful indication of the current directions of research.

Biology of the Arabian Peninsula: a bibliographic study from 1557-1978.
See item no. 194.

Corpus des inscriptions et antiquités sud-arabes. (Corpus of South Arabian inscriptions and antiquities.)
See item no. 246.

Historical dictionary of Yemen.
See item no. 263.

A revised bibliography of medieval Yemeni history . . .
See item no. 332.

Éléments de bibliographie sur le zaydisme. (Bibliographical references on Zaydism.)
See item no. 519.

Bibliography on women in Yemen.
See item no. 570.

Health problems of Yemen and its populations: a bibliographic review.
See item no. 607.

Medieval agricultural texts from Rasūlid Yemen.
See item no. 805.

Mathematical astronomy in medieval Yemen: a biobibliographical survey.
See item no. 855.

Indexes

There follow three separate indexes: authors and editors (personal and corporate); titles; and subjects. Title entries are italicized and refer either to the main titles, or to the other works cited in the annotations. The numbers refer to bibliographical entry rather than page numbers. Individual index entries are arranged in alphabetical sequence.

Index of Authors and Editors

A

ʿAbbās, Iḥsān 364, 683
ʿAbd al-Walī, Muḥammad 858
Abdelamir, C. 776
al-Abdin, T. Z. *see* Zein al-Abdin, T.
Abduldaim, D. 754
Abdullah Mansûr *see* Bury, G. W.
Abir, M. 729
Abraham, N. 443, 446
Abraham, S. Y. 443
Abrahamov, B. 518
Abu-Amr, Z. M. 620
Abu Dawood, A. R. S. 624
Abū Makhramah, al-Ṭayyib ibn ʿAbd Allāh 312
Abu Nasr, J. 586
Adams, M. 1
Addleton, J. 730
Aden Museum 246
Adra, N. 28, 526, 562
al-Afandi, M. A. 731
Aghabri, T. K. M. 780
Ahmed, L. 2
Ahroni, R. 420-1, 502, 859
Aidrous, A. Z. 770
al-Akwaʿ, Ismāʿīl ibn ʿAlī 860
al-Akwaʿa, K. M. 690
Albright, F. P. 218
Albuquerque, A. de 108
Algifri, A. H. 857
Ali, M. 578
Allfree, P. S. 147
Allman, J. 414, 580
Ambraseys, N. N. 62
Amer, A. K. A. 732
American Foundation for the Study of Man 218, 222, 235, 244, 250, 255, 257
American Institute for Yemeni Studies 920
Amin, S. H. 663
Amirahmadi, H. 820
Amirkhanov, K. 258
al-ʿAmrī, al-Ḥusayn ibn ʿAbd Allāh 2, 4, 266, 369
Arab Banking Corporation 733
Arab Bureau (Cairo) 71
Arabian American Oil Company 76, 79
ARAMCO *see* Arabian American Oil Company
Arberry, A. J. 426, 523
Arendonk, C. van 313
Arnaud, J. L. 50
Arnaud, T. J. 119
al-Asaly, S. M. 734
Ashtiany, J. 871
Ashuraey, N. M. 527
ASLIB *see* Association for Special Libraries and Information Bureaux
Association for Special Libraries and Information Bureaux 933
Ataur-Rahman, M. 194
Atiyeh, G. N. 899, 921
Aubin, J. 352
Austrian Imperial Academy of Sciences *see* Kaiserliche Akademie der Wissenschaften
Avanzini, A. 275, 303, 479, 489-90
Azzam, H. T. 586

B

Badawi, A. 552
Badeeb, S. M. 696
Badger, G. P. 118
Bāfaqīh, Muḥammad ʿAbd al-Qādir 276, 490
Bågelholm, G. 590
al-Bahkalī, ʿAbd al-Raḥmān ibn Aḥmad 314
al-Bahr, A. A. 747

Balay, F. 690
Baldit, L. 858
Baldry, J. 315, 370, 396, 761
Balfour-Paul, G. 697
Balfour-Paul, J. 762
Balsan, F. 148-9
Bannister, K.E. 195
Barakat, S. 45
Barer, S. 422
Barlow, V. 178
Barnes, C. 781
Barnes, H. E. 210
Barral, J. M. 864
Barthel, G. 621
Bashear, S. 316
Bâtâyiʿ, Ahmad 252
Bates, G. L. 196-7
Bates, M. L. 317
Beaumont, P. 33
Becker, H. 763
Beckingham, C. F. 2, 109-10, 112
Bédoucha, G. 528
Beeston, A. F. L. 2, 179, 254, 264, 277-86, 288, 309, 357, 480-1, 503-4
Behbehani, H. S. H. 698
Behn, W. H. 922, 926
Behnstedt, P. 459-60
Belhaj, M. 780
Belhaven, Master of 150-1
Bell, Sir Gawain 371, 674
Bent, Theodore 120
Bent, Mrs Theodore 120
Berg, L. W. C. van den 444, 457
Bettini, L. 461
Betzler, E. 782, 792
Bevens, W. B. 68
Beydoun, Z. R. 63-4
Bidwell, R. L. 1-2, 59, 101, 120, 285, 372-4, 380, 912
Biella, J. C. 482
Bikhazi, R. J. 344
Bin Gadhi, S. M. 857
Birch, W. de G. 108
Birgisson, K. Th. 699
Birks, J. S. 812
Bisch, J. 152
Bissell, R. E. 700
Bittner, M. 492, 496
Blackburn, J. R. 318-19, 346
Blake, G. H. 33, 69
Blakely, J. A. 250, 257
Blatter, E. 198
Bleackley, D. 66
Bleaney, C. H. 823, 926
Blois, F. de 307
Bloomfield, B. C. 685
Blukacz, F. 28
Bockow, K. H. 89
Bollinger, R. E. 375
Bonine, M. E. 923
Bonnenfant, G. 873-4
Bonnenfant, P. 3, 46, 828-9, 873-4, 928
Borel, C. 156
Börner, A. 621
Bosworth, C. E. 262
Botting, D. 153
Bouagga, J. 90
Boussac, M. F. 243
Bowen, R. L. 218
Bowen-Jones, H. 1
Bowersock, G. W. 287
Boxhall, P. C. 154, 764
Boyd, D. A. 907
Bozorgmehr, M. 446
Bradley, C. 91
Brauer, E. 423, 431
Braun, U. 636, 703
Braune, G. 880
Brent, P. 102
Breton, J. F. 219, 288
Brice, W. C. 70
Brinkmann, R. 257
Briquel-Chatonnet, F. 303
British Museum 52, 153, 184, 199, 202, 878
British Museum (Natural History) Expedition to South-West Arabia 184, 199
Brouwer, C. G. 320
Brown, K. 60
Bruck, G. vom 567-9
Brunner, U. 227
Brynen, R. 661
Buheiry, M. R. 403
Bujra, A. S. 622
Bulliet, R. W. 26
Burchardt, H. von 434
Büren, R. 901
Buringa, J. 92, 570, 927
Burrowes, R. D. 26, 263, 612-15, 623, 659
Bury, G. W. 121-2
Büttiker, W. 200, 216

C

Cahen, C. 321
Camelin, S. 783, 896
Cameron, A. 347
Campanini, M. 770
Campbell, C. 436
Canadian Archaeological Mission 239-40
Canova, G. 896
Cantori, L. J. 758
Carapico, S. 616, 637-9, 653, 735-7, 784
Caspi, M. M. 861
Casson, L. 254, 289, 299
Catholic Institute for International Relations 591, 596
Caton, S. C. 529-31
Caton Thompson, G. 220
Caubet, D. 472
Ceccherini, R. 830
Centre for Arab Gulf Studies, University of Exeter 22-3
Centre Français d'Études Yéménites 913
Champault, D. 571
Chapman, D. W. 846
Chatelus, M. 3
Chaudhry, K. A. 738
Chelhod, J. 264, 322, 351, 431, 532, 571, 665, 837, 872, 924
Chelkowski, P. J. 613, 635
Chwaszcza, J. 92
Cigar, N. 624-5, 702
Ciuk, C. 221
Clarke, M. A. 195
Cleveland, R. L. 222
Cline, W. 886
Cohen, H. J. 424
Cohen, J. M. 757
Colburn, M. 570
Collins, B. B. 376

D

E

F

Index of Titles

S

T

U

V

W

Y

Index of Subjects

A

Aban ibn Saʿīd (Governor of Ṣanʿāʾ) 339
ʿAbbās, Iḥsān 683
ʿAbbāsids 324
ʿAbd al-Kūrī (island) 5, 202, 230, 548
ʿAbīdah (tribe) 119
Abyan 241
Abyssinia *see* Ethiopia
ʿAdan *see* Aden
Aden
  administration 7, 377, 381, 387-8, 397, 412, 689, 693, 725
  agriculture 7, 800
  anthropology 7
  Arabic dialects 464-5
  archaeology 234, 241, 259
  archives 929
  borders 122, 386, 400, 721, 724
  children 590
  customs 893
  economic conditions 7
  emigration 422, 433, 443
  First World War 370, 373
  forts and fortifications 343
  geography 7
  Great Britain (general) 27, 372, 381, 386
  Great Britain (19th century) 7, 400, 412
  Great Britain (20th century) 29, 162, 383-4, 387, 390, 395, 397, 409-10, 697, 712, 720-1
  history 338, 350
  Ibn al-Mujāwir 105
  industry 582-3, 747, 768
  Islam 689
  Jews 420, 422, 433, 437-8
  labour relations 384
  maps 74
  missions 524
  museums 246
  navigation 113
  nutrition 590
  opposition movements 374, 383, 395, 410, 620, 630-1
  Ottomans 122, 373
  photography 182, 902
  police 693
  Political Residents 372, 392
  politics 384, 386, 395, 397
  port facilities 12, 27, 384, 398
  pottery 234, 241, 259
  rituals 893
  saints 893
  Second World War 187
  steamships 398
  textiles 761
  trade 7, 350, 352, 761
  trade unions 630-1
  transport 398
  travellers 105, 108, 112, 118, 129, 137, 144, 159, 162, 172, 187
  United Nations 410
  water supply 653
  women 689
  see also Aden Protectorates; Eastern Aden Protectorate; Federation of South Arabia; Western Aden Protectorate
Aden Levies 150
Aden Pact (1981) 704
Aden Police Force 693
Aden Protectorates 8
  archaeology 229, 233, 259
  armies 150, 383, 385
  borders 122
  foreign relations 150-1
  geology 66
  history 147, 150-1, 162, 377, 381-2, 392
  Ottomans 122
  pottery 229, 259
  tribal relations 385, 405, 407, 721, 724-5, 770
  see also Aden; Eastern Aden Protectorate; Federation of South Arabia; Western Aden Protectorate
Aden Troop 385
administration
  ʿAbbāsids 325
  Aden 7, 377, 381, 387-8, 397, 412, 689, 693, 725
  afforestation 560
  aid 740
  Ancient South Arabia 293
  Ayyūbids 317
  bureaucracy 266, 592
  civil servants 576, 588, 690, 771
  cooperatives 737, 754, 758
  development projects 560, 597, 735, 740, 804
  Hadramawt 175-7, 179, 188, 387-8, 533
  health care 560, 597
  local politics 622
  local development associations 690, 754, 758

B

D

F

food 136
Munabbih (tribe) 566
Ṣanʿāʾ 59
women 571, 579
food subsidies 610
food supply 780, 819
football 853
foreign relations 21-2, 386, 388, 399, 408, 701, 719
Aḥmad (Imam of Yemen) 150-1, 413
ʿAsīr 723-4
China 698, 713
Civil War (1994) 659
Dhofar 713
Egypt 705, 770
Eritrea 16, 705
Ethiopia 4, 334, 704-5
France 372, 391, 400, 705, 724, 744, 770
Germany 159, 400
Great Britain 150-1, 396, 400, 721, 724, 728
Gulf States 712-13
Italy 159, 370, 396, 400, 724
Libya 704
mediation 705
Netherlands 109, 175, 177, 320, 351
North Yemen 614, 709
oil exploration and production 407, 724, 728
Oman 704, 713
Ottomans 122, 373, 380, 389, 396, 400, 721, 724
Portugal 108, 312, 351
Saudi Arabia 638, 643, 659, 661, 706, 711, 723-4, 728, 733
South Yemen 27, 623, 629, 633, 698, 702, 704, 708, 713
Soviet Union 633, 700, 702, 704, 710, 713, 715-17, 726-7, 729
United States 695, 707, 715, 718
Yaḥyā (Imam of Yemen) 413
forests *see* afforestation
Forskål, P. 115, 205, 215
forts and fortifications
Aden 343
Ancient South Arabia 288
Ḥiṣn al-ʿUrr 875
Socotra 253
Zaydīs 329
Foucault, M. 693
France
coffee 776
foreign relations 372, 391, 400, 705, 724, 744, 770
Great Britain 372, 391
Red Sea 744
trade 776
travellers 103
frankincense *see* incense
Free Zones Law (1993) 664, 770
Free Yemeni Movement 378, 401, 403
Front for the Liberation of Occupied South Yemen 631
frontiers *see* borders

G

gall-ink *see* khiḍāb
games 59
gardens 830, 840
gazetteers 79
Ancient South Arabia 73, 86
North Yemen 71, 83, 85
South Yemen 82
see also place-names
geckoes 216
gender *see* families; marriage; women
General People's Congress 612
General Union of Yemeni Women 582
geographers
Classical 73, 168, 254, 261, 302, 311
medieval 68, 78, 85, 254, 267
modern 44
place-names 78
geography 6, 17, 34
Aden 7
economic conditions 33-4, 69
education 44
al-Hamdānī 68, 85, 304
North Yemen 13, 34, 93
Socotra 5, 548
South Yemen 12
training 44
Wādī Mawr 35
see also atlases; gazetteers; geographers; geology; maps; place-names
geology 64, 208
Aden Protectorates 66
archaeology 67, 227
Dhofar 63
Eastern Aden Protectorate 62
maps 76
oil exploration and production 64, 76
South Yemen 12, 139
Wādī al-Jubah 67
Western Aden Protectorate 66
see also earthquakes; volcanoes
Germany
aid 44, 690
foreign relations 159, 400
libraries 901
travellers 104
ghayl irrigation 790, 801, 810
Glaser, E. 84, 124, 126-7, 269, 460, 684
glass and glasswork
archaeology 241-2
art 874
trade 242
glossaries *see* dictionaries
gods and goddesses *see* religion
Goody, J. 680

irrigation
dams 125, 256, 296, 799
ghayl 790, 801, 810
Hadramawt 781, 798-9
Ḥarāz Mountains 43
Marib 125, 256, 296, 788
North Yemen 79, 799, 803, 810
pumps 786, 790, 796
run-off 43, 785, 792
sayl 788, 790, 799, 810
Shabwah 219
South Yemen 781, 799
Tihāmah 786
Timnaʿ 218
Wādī Markhah 790
Wādī Mawr 35
see also water supply
Irshādīs 270, 450
al-Iryānī, ʿAbd al-Raḥmān 613
al-Iṣlāḥ Party 638-9, 642, 651, 653, 655, 660, 718
Islam 264
Aden 689
banking 16
constitutions 674, 687
doctrines 508, 513, 518, 520, 523
ḥadīth 316, 525
Ḥanafīs 514, 520, 525
islamization 22, 271, 325
Ismāʿīlīs 317, 336, 367, 508-9, 514, 516, 520
Jews 429-30, 436, 441-2, 502
jihād 511
law 28, 577, 583, 589, 677, 679, 683-5, 938
madrasahs 514, 517
muʿtazilism 513, 515, 518
newspapers 908, 911
politics 3, 16, 624, 642, 660, 908, 911
Qur'ān 513, 518
Shāfiʿīs 507, 514, 520
sufism 181, 510, 514, 525
takfīr 511
welfare organizations 16
Zaydīs 26, 28, 180, 313, 317, 328, 331, 341-2, 366, 369, 512-15, 518-20, 523, 544, 568, 672-3
Islamic Jihād Party 660
islamization 22, 271, 325
Ismāʿīlīs
daʿwah 336, 508-9, 516
doctrines 508
history 317, 336, 367, 514, 520
Zaydīs 509, 511, 516
Israel
emigration 438, 447, 453, 455, 458
families 447, 458
health care 458
museums 434
photography 455
women 447
Yemeni Jews 438, 447, 453, 455, 458
see also Palestine
Italy
foreign relations 159, 370, 396, 400, 724

J

Jabal Buraʿ (Tihāmah) 214
Jabal ʿIyāl Yazīd 417
al-Jabīn 608
al-Jaʿdī, ʿUmar ibn ʿAlī 507
Jamme, A. 158, 237
Java *see* Indonesia
Jesuits 109-10
Jews 424
Aden 420, 422, 433, 437-8
Ancient South Arabia 297, 307, 310, 503
anthropology 423, 888
Arabic dialects 467, 889, 892
architecture 844
art 876
dress 434, 876
economic conditions 427, 431, 848
education 427, 431, 848
emigration 422, 425, 435, 437-8, 445, 447, 453, 455, 458, 540
exhibitions 433-4
First World War 445
folk tales 888, 892
Great Britain 433
Ḥabbān 420, 432, 685
history 59, 158, 264, 421-2, 430, 435-7, 441-2
houses 844
Islam 429-30, 436, 441-2, 502
Israel 438, 447, 453, 455, 458
law 429-30, 436, 440-1, 589, 664
literacy 427, 848
literature 428, 859
marriage 427
material culture 423, 434
messianism 425, 430
music 884
Nadhīr 163
North Yemen 421, 426
Ottomans 425, 435-7, 441-2
Palestine 425, 435, 445
poetry 418, 502, 521, 859, 861
photography 434, 455
proverbs 889, 897
Ṣaʿdah 163, 540
Ṣanʿāʾ 59, 163, 429, 440-1, 844
songs 884
taxation 429, 440
travellers 127-8, 163, 431
United States 445
weaving 876
women 447, 589, 861, 897
Yaḥyā (Imam of Yemen) 429, 589

O

P

Q

R

Y

Z

Map of Yemen

This map shows the more important towns and other features.

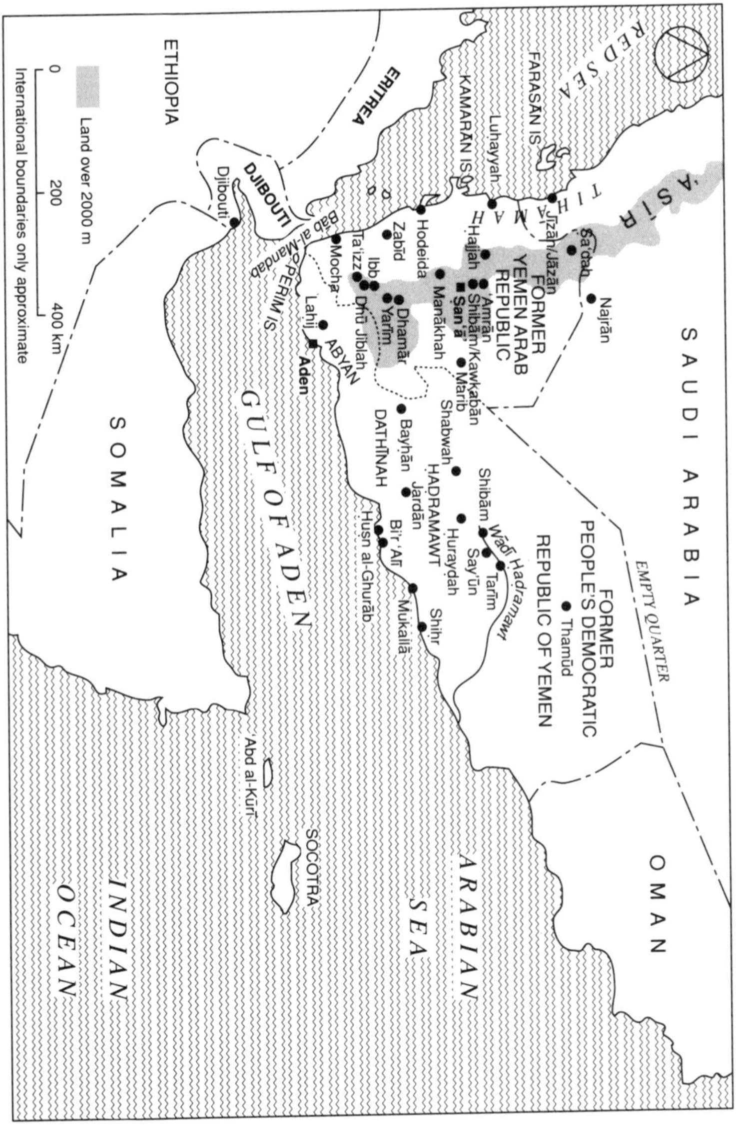

ALSO FROM CLIO PRESS

INTERNATIONAL ORGANIZATIONS SERIES

Each volume in the International Organizations Series is either devoted to one specific organization, or to a number of different organizations operating in a particular region, or engaged in a specific field of activity. The scope of the series is wide-ranging and includes intergovernmental organizations, international non-governmental organizations, and national bodies dealing with international issues. The series is aimed mainly at the English-speaker and each volume provides a selective, annotated, critical bibliography of the organization, or organizations, concerned. The bibliographies cover books, articles, pamphlets, directories, databases and theses and, wherever possible, attention is focused on material about the organizations rather than on the organizations' own publications. Notwithstanding this, the most important official publications, and guides to those publications, will be included. The views expressed in individual volumes, however, are not necessarily those of the publishers.

VOLUMES IN THE SERIES

1 *European Communities*, John Paxton
2 *Arab Regional Organizations*, Frank A. Clements
3 *Comecon: The Rise and Fall of an International Socialist Organization*, Jenny Brine
4 *International Monetary Fund*, Anne C. M. Salda
5 *The Commonwealth*, Patricia M. Larby and Harry Hannam
6 *The French Secret Services*, Martyn Cornick and Peter Morris
7 *Organization of African Unity*, Gordon Harris
8 *North Atlantic Treaty Organization*, Phil Williams
9 *World Bank*, Anne C. M. Salda
10 *United Nations System*, Joseph P. Baratta
11 *Organization of American States*, David Sheinin
12 *The British Secret Services*, Philip H. J. Davies
13 *The Israeli Secret Services*, Frank A. Clements